Cats For Dummies,® 2nd Edition

Cheat Sheet

Preventive-Health Checklist

Preventive care is more cost-effective than crisis care, and easier on both your pet and your bank account in the long run. The following are some preventive-care guidelines. Talk to your veterinarian to find out what is best for your pet.

Adult veterinary care

- ❑ Annual examination, which may include chemical profile and urinalysis, especially for older pets and prior to procedures requiring anesthesia.
- ❑ Combination vaccination, annually, as recommended by your veterinarian. Rabies vaccination as recommended by your veterinarian or as required by local law.
- ❑ Dental cleaning and scaling under anesthesia, as recommended by your veterinarian.

Adult home care

- ❑ Brush teeth, three times weekly.
- ❑ Trim nails, monthly.
- ❑ Regular grooming; bathing as required.
- ❑ Weekly home exam, including checking for lumps, bumps, injuries, and weight-loss.

Kitten veterinary care

- ❑ Initial exam and feline leukemia test within 48 hours of adoption and prior to introduction to other cats.
- ❑ Three combination vaccinations at three- to four-week intervals, starting at the age of six to nine weeks. Feline leukemia vaccination after initial testing, two vaccinations three to four weeks apart. Rabies vaccination at 16 weeks, or as required by law.
- ❑ Wormings as prescribed by your veterinarian, at two- to three-week intervals or until fecal test is clear.
- ❑ Spaying or neutering, as early as eight weeks as recommended by your veterinarian.

A start-up kit for kittens and adult cats

- ❑ Brush and comb
- ❑ Toys
- ❑ Dishwasher-safe bowls, one for water, one for food
- ❑ Enzyme cleaner for pet stains
- ❑ Soft cat collar (with elastic insert for safety) and an ID tag

- ❑ High-quality food, as recommended by breed or veterinarian
- ❑ Nail trimmer and Kwik Stop powder
- ❑ Litter box, litter, scoop
- ❑ Travel crate for car trips
- ❑ Scratching post or cat tree

For Dummies: Bestselling Book Series for Beginners

Cats For Dummies® 2nd Edition

Signs your cat needs immediate veterinary attention

Following is a list of some symptoms that require your cat to see a veterinarian. *Remember that when in doubt, day or night, don't wait: Call a veterinarian!*

- ❏ Seizure, fainting, or collapse.
- ❏ Eye injury, no matter how mild.
- ❏ Vomiting or diarrhea — anything more than two or three times within an hour or so.
- ❏ Allergic reactions, such as swelling around the face, or hives, most easily seen on the belly.
- ❏ Any suspected poisoning, including antifreeze, rodent or snail bait, or human medication. Cats are also especially sensitive to insecticides (such as flea-control medication for dogs) or any petroleum-based product.
- ❏ Snake or venomous spider bite.
- ❏ Thermal stress — from being either too cold or too hot — even if the cat seems to have recovered. (The internal story could be quite different.)
- ❏ Any wound or laceration that's open and bleeding or any animal bite.
- ❏ Trauma, such as being hit by a car, even if the cat seems fine.
- ❏ Any respiratory problem: chronic coughing, trouble breathing, or near drowning.
- ❏ Straining to urinate or defecate.

What to put in your feline medicine chest

Home care can be extremely difficult when a cat is frightened, leading to injuries for both owner and cat. We recommend in most cases coaxing the cat into a carrier and heading for the veterinarian. Here are some common first-aid supplies, though, that you may need if treating your cat's minor ailments at home:

- ❏ Adhesive tape
- ❏ Benadryl antihistamine
- ❏ Betadine antiseptic
- ❏ Cat restraint bag
- ❏ Cotton swabs, balls, and rolls
- ❏ Eye wash
- ❏ Forceps or tweezers
- ❏ Hydrogen peroxide
- ❏ Kwik Stop powder
- ❏ Scissors
- ❏ Sterile gauze, both rolls and pads
- ❏ Syringe with the needle removed, for giving liquid medication
- ❏ Syrup of Ipecac
- ❏ Thermometer
- ❏ Triple antibiotic cream or ointment
- ❏ Water-based lubricating jelly, such as K-Y

Copyright © 2000 Wiley Publishing, Inc. All rights reserved.

Item 5275-9.

For more information about Wiley Publishing, call 1-800-762-2974.

For Dummies: Bestselling Book Series for Beginners

Praise, Praise, Praise for Cats For Dummies!

"Cats For Dummies is wise, up-to-date, and written and presented in a form that is easy to understand and navigate."

— Vicki Croke, *Boston Globe*

"It's astounding how much helpful information the authors have accumulated and packed into a concise and easy-to-follow formula. Some of the information is, in fact, rarely found elsewhere.

— Steve Dale, Tribune Media

"Depending how far your relationship has progressed — or regressed — with your favorite feline, you can jump about in this handy guide."

— Ranny Green, *Seattle Times*

"If you own a cat or are considering cat ownership, *Cats For Dummies* is the one book you really must have. This educational, comprehensive, and entertaining book is probably the closest you'll get to a cat owner's manual."

— Amazon.com review

"Cats For Dummies is an excellent, engaging, encyclopedic primer and reference book for the person about to be adopted by a cat. This is a book that readers will undoubtedly pull off the shelf again and again."

— Margie Scherk-Nixon DVM, Diplomate, ABVP (Feline Practice)

"Cats For Dummies is catnip for the feline fanatic. It offers sound advice on cat care, behavior issues, products, services, and fascinating feline trivia, all served up with wry humor that entertains, even as it educates."

— Amy Shojai, Pet Author and President, Cat Writers' Association

"Cats For Dummies is terrific. It's an educational and fun read for all cat owners — new and experienced."

— Colleen Currigan, DVM, Veterinary Homecare For Cats

Praise for Gina's other books — Dogs For Dummies and Birds For Dummies!

"Written with intelligence, wit, and heart. If your dog had a credit card, he'd buy you this wonderful guide."

> — Carol Lea Benjamin, author of *Mother Knows Best: The Natural Way To Train Your Dog* and the Rachel Alexander and Dash mystery series.

"Gina Spadafori is one of the most knowledgeable dog writers I know. Her talents as a journalist combined with her passion for all things canine make her uniquely qualified to educate and motivate new dog owners."

> — Audrey Pavia, author of *Horses For Dummies,* former managing editor of *Dog Fancy* magazine, and former senior editor of the American Kennel Club's magazine, *American Kennel Gazette*

"I am really excited about Gina's book! This is a book I recommend to all my clients, and to anyone who has a dog. Gina's enthusiasm, knowledge, and compassion show on every page."

> — Linda Randall, DVM, Diplomate, ABVP

"An intriguing book filled with a wealth of practical information for dog owners that stands tails above the rest — two paws up!"

> — Darris O. Hercs, Executive Director, Humane Society of Sonoma County, Calif.

"Gina Spadafori and Dr. Brian Speer have done a remarkable job on *Birds For Dummies*. I found the book to be everything I hoped it would be. The information is first-rate and helpful to anyone with an interest or love for pet birds. . . . You will not be disappointed."

> — Walter J. Rosskopf, Jr., DVM, Diplomate, ABVP (Avian Practice)

" . . . *Birds For Dummies* is the most complete discussion of the pros and cons of pet bird ownership that I have ever seen. If more people read this book before they bought a bird, I would see fewer sick, maladjusted, and behavior-problem birds. If you own a bird, you should read this book; if you are thinking about owning a bird, you MUST read this book."

> — Michael J. Murray, DVM

 TM

BESTSELLING BOOK SERIES

References for the Rest of Us!®

Do you find that traditional reference books are overloaded with technical details and advice you'll never use? Do you postpone important life decisions because you just don't want to deal with them? Then our *For Dummies®* business and general reference book series is for you.

For Dummies business and general reference books are written for those frustrated and hard-working souls who know they aren't dumb, but find that the myriad of personal and business issues and the accompanying horror stories make them feel helpless. *For Dummies* books use a lighthearted approach, a down-to-earth style, and even cartoons and humorous icons to dispel fears and build confidence. Lighthearted but not lightweight, these books are perfect survival guides to solve your everyday personal and business problems.

> *"More than a publishing phenomenon, 'Dummies' is a sign of the times."*
>
> — The New York Times

> *"A world of detailed and authoritative information is packed into them…"*
>
> — U.S. News and World Report

> *"…you won't go wrong buying them."*
>
> — Walter Mossberg, Wall Street Journal, on For Dummies books

Already, millions of satisfied readers agree. They have made For Dummies the #1 introductory level computer book series and a best-selling business book series. They have written asking for more. So, if you're looking for the best and easiest way to learn about business and other general reference topics, look to For Dummies to give you a helping hand.

Wiley Publishing, Inc.

5/09

Cats

FOR

DUMMIES®

2ND EDITION

**by Gina Spadafori and
Paul D. Pion, DVM, DACVIM**

WILEY

Wiley Publishing, Inc.

Cats For Dummies®, 2nd Edition

Published by
Wiley Publishing, Inc.
111 River St.
Hoboken, NJ 07030-5774
www.wiley.com

Copyright © 2000 by Wiley Publishing, Inc., Indianapolis, Indiana

Published simultaneously in Canada

For general information on our other products and services or to obtain technical support, please contact our Customer Care Department within the U.S. at 800-762-2974, outside the U.S. at 317-572-3993, or fax 317-572-4002.

Wiley also publishes its books in a variety of electronic formats. Some content that appears in print may not be available in electronic books.

Library of Congress Cataloging-in-Publication Data:

Library of Congress Control Number: 00-104211

ISBN: 0-7645-5275-9

Manufactured in the United States of America

20 19 18 17 16 15 14 13 12

2B/RQ/RR/QT/IN

About the Authors

Gina Spadafori: Gina is the author of the best-selling *Dogs For Dummies,* which was given the President's Award for the best writing on dogs and the Maxwell Medallion for the best general reference work, both by the Dog Writers Association of America. With top avian specialist Dr. Brian L. Speer, she has also written *Birds For Dummies.*

Along with Dr. Paul D. Pion, she was given the CWA's awards for the best work on feline nutrition, best work on feline behavior, and best work on responsible cat care for the first edition of *Cats For Dummies.* She and her pets divide their time between Northern California and South Georgia/North Florida.

Paul D. Pion, DVM, Diplomate, ACVIM (Cardiology): Paul is co-founder, president, and CEO of the Veterinary Information Network, Inc., and a board-certified veterinary cardiologist. Paul has been awarded a Physician's Science Award by the National Institutes of Health, a Small Animal Research Award by Purina, the National Phi Zeta Award for one of the two most outstanding manuscripts in 1989, and a Special Recognition Award by the American Animal Hospital Association for innovations in the field of veterinary medicine.

Paul graduated from the veterinary college at Cornell University and has taught in the veterinary school at the University of California, Davis. While at UCD, he made an important research discovery that has touched the lives of every cat in the world: He proved that deficiency of a single amino acid, taurine, was causing heart disease in cats. His discovery was published as a cover article in *SCIENCE,* one of the most competitive and respected research journals and, more important, led to the reformulation of the world's cat foods and the virtual eradication of a heart disease that afflicted tens of thousands of cats annually in the late '80s.

Paul lives in Davis, California, with his wife, veterinarian Dr. Carla Weinberg, sons Luca and Joel, and a house full of pets.

Dedication

Gina: For my family and friends, two-legged and four-legged, especially my parents, Louise and Nino, and my brothers, Pete and Joe. And to my first cat, Calico, who was really a tabby, and to the two geniuses, Bruce and Paul.

Paul: To my parents, Howard and Libby, who shaped my soul; my sister, Jodi, who nurtured my soul; my brothers Danny and Michael, who are always there; my wife, Carla, who makes it all so wonderful. And to my sons, Luca and Joel, who I thank for teaching me to love and to look for more in life than work.

To my mentors, especially Bill Hornbuckle, Art Hurvitz, Quinton Rogers, Ryan Huxtable, and Margarethe Britton, who let me learn; to my colleagues, especially Mark Kittleson, Alice Wolf, David Bruyette, Roy Brenton Smith, Nicky Mastin, and Steve Moore, who let me grow; to my students, who taught me more than I ever hoped to teach them; to my staff and colleagues at the Veterinary Information Network and Pet Care Forum, who live my dream daily; and to Gina, who truly wrote this book.

Authors' Acknowledgments

Our first thanks must be to the many experts who read over our shoulders and made suggestions that helped us realize our dream of making *Cats For Dummies* a complete, cutting-edge reference that will improve the lives of cats and those who love them. William G. Porte, MBA, DVM, of Sacramento Veterinary Surgical Services, repeated his role from *Dogs For Dummies* and *Birds For Dummies* as our lead technical reviewer and again brought his keen observations to bear on the text.

To date only a few dozen board-certified feline practitioners are in the United States and Canada, and we are thankful to have had two of them review parts of this book: Margaret A. Scherk-Nixon, DVM, Diplomate, ABVP, of Cats Only in Vancouver, British Columbia, Canada's Veterinarian of the Year for 1997; and Alice M. Wolf, DVM, Diplomate, ACVIM, Diplomate, ABVP, of the Texas A&M University's College of Veterinary Medicine and one of two lead consultants for the Veterinary Information Network (VIN). Two other colleagues contributed greatly to this book: Monica M. Mastin, DVM, head of VIN database services, and Stuart W. Turner, DVM, an emergency-care practitioner at the Solano Pet Emergency Clinic in Cordelia, California.

Other veterinarians who helped us include David Bruyette, DVM, Diplomate, ACVIM, chief of staff of the VCA West Los Angeles Animal Hospital and the other lead consultant for VIN; James H. Sokolowski, DVM, Ph.D., Professional Services Manager, Waltham USA, Inc.; Duncan Ferguson, VMD, PhD, Diplomate, ACVIM, Diplomate, ACVCP, Professor, Department of Veterinary

Pharmacology and Physiology, the University of Georgia College of Veterinary Medicine; Roger Gfeller, DVM, Diplomate, ACVECC, chief of staff of the Veterinary Emergency Service, Inc., Fresno, California; Gary Landsberg, DVM, Doncaster Animal Clinic, Thornhill, Ontario; Ilana Reisner, DVM, Ph.D, Diplomate, ACVB of Ithaca, New York; and David Aucoin, DVM, Diplomate, ACVCP, Director, Veterinary Services, for Innovative Veterinary Diets.

We also wish to thank feline behaviorist Steve Aiken, Melinie diLuck of the Happy Tails Cat Sanctuary in Sacramento, California, Dusty Rainbolt and Michael Brim of the Cat Fanciers' Association, as well as researchers Janine Adams and Audrey Pavia. Kirsten Baitis was invaluable in helping us with the final stages of the manuscript.

The contributions of illustrator Jay Gavron are always eye-catching, and we're still smiling at Rich Tennant's "The 5th Wave" cartoons. We still can't believe our good fortune at having Lilian Jackson Braun write our foreword, and we can't thank her enough for her generosity.

The staff at Hungry Minds has to have one of the biggest concentrations of cat lovers at any company in the world. Thanks to Publisher Dominique Devito and the rest of the acquisitions staff — Tracy Boggier, Scott Prentzas, Nikki Moustaki. Thanks to Pam Mourouzis, Keith Peterson, and Tina Sims in Editorial for their work on this edition, and to Jennifer Ehrlich and William Barton, who shepherded through the original manuscript. Others who deserve mention are Angie Hunckler, Patricia Pan, and Regina Snyder.

Publisher's Acknowledgments

We're proud of this book; please register your comments through our Online Registration Form located at www.dummies.com.

Some of the people who helped bring this book to market include the following:

Acquisitions, Editorial, and Media Development

Project Editor: Keith Peterson

Acquisitions Editors: Nikki Moustaki, Scott Prentzas

Copy Editor: Tina Sims

Technical Editor: Dr. Bill Porte

Permissions Editor: Carmen Krikorian

Editorial Manager: Pamela Mourouzis

Editorial Assistant: Carol Stickland

Cover Photo Credit: Corbis © Scott T. Smith

Production

Senior Project Coordinator: Regina Snyder

Layout and Graphics: Barry Offringa, Tracy K. Oliver, Jacque Schneider, Julie Trippetti, Brandon Yarwood, Erin Zeltner

Proofreaders: Laura Albert, Corey Bowen, John Greenough, Betty Kish, Susan Moritz, Toni Settle, Charles Spencer

Indexer: Sharon Hilgenberg

Special Help
Amanda Foxworth, E. Neil Johnson, Ben Nussbaum, Nancee Reeves

---

Publishing and Editorial for Consumer Dummies

Diane Graves Steele, Vice President and Publisher, Consumer Dummies

Joyce Pepple, Acquisitions Director, Consumer Dummies

Kristin A. Cocks, Product Development Director, Consumer Dummies

Michael Spring, Vice President and Publisher, Travel

Brice Gosnell, Associate Publisher, Travel

Suzanne Jannetta, Editorial Director, Travel

Publishing for Technology Dummies

Richard Swadley, Vice President and Executive Group Publisher

Andy Cummings, Vice President and Publisher

Composition Services

Gerry Fahey, Vice President of Production Services

Debbie Stailey, Director of Composition Services

Contents at a Glance

Cartoons at a Glance

By Rich Tennant

The 5th Wave — By Rich Tennant

"Stuart—wake up! The cat's been grooming your eyebrows again."

page 11

The 5th Wave — By Rich Tennant

"It's 'Feathers', I think she's taking steroids."

page 135

The 5th Wave — By Rich Tennant

"Oh, he loves his string and ball, but once in a while he'll take out his little pottery wheel and spin bud vases out of modeling clay all afternoon."

page 71

The 5th Wave — By Rich Tennant

18 MONTHS OFF THE AFRICAN COAST

"'Let me bring him on board', you said. 'He's so cute and cuddly, he'll make a nice mascot for the trip home'. Well, bloody nice mascot he's turned out to be!!"

page 225

The 5th Wave — By Rich Tennant

"Well, she now claims she's a descendant of the royal Egyptian line of cats, but I'm not buying that just yet."

page 303

Fax: 978-546-7747
E-mail: richtennant@the5thwave.com
World Wide Web: www.the5thwave.com

Table of Contents

Foreword

I, too, was once a dummy when it came to cats, believe it or not. How did I ever get to be 35 years old without ever having had a pet? It happens.

True, I liked cats. Friends' cats sat on my lap at cocktail parties. Strays followed me on the street. And in my apartment I had a Goldscheider porcelain figurine of a Siamese, almost life size. But no cat!

Then I received a Siamese kitten for a gift. I panicked! How does one take care of a cat? What do they . . . *do?* What am I supposed to . . . *do?* The first night with that tiny furry bundle under my roof . . . well . . . I slept not a wink.

I looked for cat-care books, but they all assumed I knew more than I did. Which end of the cat is the front? (Not really. I exaggerate, but not much.)

Somehow we muddled through, Koko and I. He was my first Koko. I adored him, and — if I may say so — he adored me. Since then, I have had a dynasty of Siamese, and I write mystery novels that fool readers into thinking I'm an expert on felines. I love them, that's all. I empathize with them: I know what they're thinking . . . they know what I'm thinking.

If only I had had a nice, easy-to-read, easy-to-understand book "way back then" when I was a dummy.

— Lilian Jackson Braun, Author of *The Cat Who...* Mystery Novels

Introduction

Welcome to the second edition of *Cats For Dummies,* the most easy-to-use, up-to-date reference available on one of the world's most remarkable animal companions, the cat. We wrote it out of love for our cats, and respect and admiration for all cats. And we also wrote it to make a difference for cats and cat lovers everywhere.

We started the discussion about the first edition of this book at Paul's office, the heart of the Veterinary Information Network, the world's largest online service for veterinary professionals. Then his office was in a converted bedroom at his house; now the company has moved for the third time in its decade-long history to keep up with its growth. Paul hopes this new office building — with more than twice the space of the previous one — will last the company a while. But then again, he sort of hopes it won't!

On the day of that initial discussion, however, we knew nothing of the future. We didn't know how well that first edition of *Cats For Dummies* would be received, and we hadn't even considered that one day we'd be honored with a trio of top honors for its content. We just wanted to write a book that would put the power of knowledge in the hands of cat lovers so that they and their cats would be better for our efforts. We knew we wanted to pour our hearts and our souls into it, for the love of cats.

As we talked, though, we were interrupted by a furry presence. Paul's cat, PC, wanted us to know something.

With a cat's uncanny ability to know when something concerns her — or should — she was demanding our attention as we discussed the project and scribbled notes. She rubbed against our legs, purring and meowing, and then sat up on her haunches and waved her front paws at us. After that body language didn't work well enough for her purposes, she gathered herself and threw her sleek tabby body upward, landing in the middle of our paper. Her point finally made, she flopped down on the desktop and started to purr.

"Don't forget who's in charge here," she said, as clearly as if she could talk, her green eyes glimmering through half-closed lids.

We never have forgotten. And with this second edition, we welcome the opportunity to bring even more knowledge on cats and their care — and to update the cutting-edge information we put into the first edition.

PC, then as now the boss, approves of our ongoing efforts, we're certain.

Paul's cat,
PC (for
Prayer Cat),
has an
interesting
way of
getting the
attention
she
deserves.

What Cats Know . . . and What We Want You to Know

We wrote *Cats For Dummies,* 2nd Edition for your cat, true, but in an odd and certainly unfair twist of fate, your cat can't buy the book for himself. (Or maybe that's not so odd; after all, members of royalty never buy anything for themselves — that's what servants are for!)

Don't tell him this, but no cat can buy a book, much less read a book. Nor can a kitty make wise decisions regarding veterinary care, show you how to keep his claws in fine shape, or choose safe toys and equipment. He can't even tell you what you've done wrong with the litter box so it's just not the place to go when a cat has to . . . er, *go.*

He can't, but we can.

Understanding litter box problems is just the tip of the iceberg of things many of us don't know about our cats. Until very recently, cats have been sadly neglected concerning research into what keeps them healthy and what makes them tick, especially compared to the amount of attention given to other domesticated animals, such as the dog or the horse.

Reasons for this neglect are understandable, perhaps. Although cats, in their role as vermin killers, have been every bit as important to humankind over the centuries as any other of our animal partners, they've gone about their job in their own way and in their own style, as cats always do. Horses were developed and trained to run fast, cut cattle, and pull heavy wagons, while the cat caught rats and mice. Dogs were developed and trained to fill a hundred jobs, from herding to hunting to guarding — plus a few modern adaptations, such as serving people with disabilities — while the cat caught rats and mice.

They seemed to do fine on their own, these cats, slipping back and forth across the line between wild and domesticated for hundreds of years. Cats have always had those among us who loved and admired their beauty, but others have also been uneasy with the cat's independence — to the point of hating them, in some cases. Others simply found the cat worthless and had no use for the animal.

In the study of health and behavior, unfortunately, this latter group was largely in control — until recently.

Welcome to the Age of the Cat!

Although you still hear about those who dislike cats, their voices aren't the dominant ones today. More people love cats than ever before and are working to make the cat's life better than ever before, in areas ranging from important health studies, to increased understanding of behavior, to new equipment designed to make living with a cat easier for both of you.

The cat is now the top pet in the United States. More than 60 million in number, the cat eclipsed the dog in popularity in the 1980s and now holds a margin of popularity of more than 5 million. Cats hold their own as pets in other developed countries as well.

Cat lovers old and new have one thing in common besides their love for their cats: They spend money. Pets are a $20 billion industry annually, and goods and services for cats make up a significant part of that figure. That kind of clout is fueling research into feline health and has manufacturers scrambling to get out products to serve this market.

As the pet industry has changed, so has the veterinary one. Fifty years ago, veterinary students were primarily men from rural backgrounds; now, the nation's veterinary schools are sending out graduates who come from primarily urban and suburban roots, and more of these graduates are women. This change mirrors the one in the larger population that's driving the interest in cats and changing the future of feline medicine, both in the research field and in practice. A growing number of veterinary practices are cats-only, and there is an association of veterinarians who specialize in feline care.

Taken as a whole, these changes suggest that the cat is going to reign supreme for a good long time, finally getting the attention so long deserved. All we can say is . . . it's about time. And we're sure PC agrees.

Approaching Cat Ownership as an Informed Consumer

"Curiosity killed the cat" is a saying that has been around for years, but it's not curiosity that does in the vast majority of the millions of loving felines who die every year, some because they're homeless, others because of preventable health or behavior problems. Misinformation and unrealistic expectations are far bigger threats. A lot of myths are out there regarding cats — we dispel a few of them in Chapter 19 — and more are added every day, it seems.

You need to do your homework to avoid any surprises, and we've written *Cats For Dummies* to help you with exactly that task.

If, for example, you go into cat ownership with the sadly all-too-common belief that a cat is as easy to keep and almost as inexpensive as a houseplant, you're not going to be prepared for the costs of keeping a cat healthy — even though these costs can be quite reasonable. You're going to be surprised that your cat needs your love and attention on a regular basis. And you're going to be shocked to find out that you need to put some effort into training your cat to avoid clawing your furniture and to use the litter box. All these surprises can easily be avoided, for the good of both you and your pet, if you educate yourself.

We want you to become a savvy consumer of feline-related goods, services, and information; to avoid falling in love with the kitten some children are peddling from a box at the flea market unless you can be sure the little scrap of fluff isn't ill; to avoid choosing *any* kitten or cat until you decide on some of the basic questions, such as longhaired or short, pedigreed or not, or active or relaxed in temperament.

We want you to know even more. The new focus on things feline is wonderful, to be sure, but it also means that a lot of products are suddenly out there that may be nothing more than a waste of your money — and you need to know how to weed them out. You need to know the basics of nutrition to provide your pet with a healthy, well-balanced diet. And you need to understand the basics of litter box behavior so you can choose the products that work with your *cat's* sense of what's right (because a product that works for you but not for your pet is one that leaves you with both messes and resentment).

We want you to know it's worthwhile to take the time to learn about your cat, and about caring for your cat properly. You'll see why if you consider that a well-cared-for cat can be your loving companion for more than 15 years and that many cats live happily and healthily even beyond that milestone. These years are a gift; make them count!

Although cats offer years of love and companionship, many people put more research and effort into selecting a frozen dinner than they do into choosing the right cat and then caring for that animal properly. Your cat's love and companionship outlast not only tonight's dinner but probably also your home computer and your car, both of which you probably researched thoroughly before buying.

Your cat may also be with you longer than a spouse, and that's truly a sobering thought. We can't help you with your marriage, but we can help you with your cat by telling you everything you need to know to make the relationship work for you both — and for many, many years. A happy, healthy cat and a happy cat owner: We ask for no greater legacy for our work.

How This Book Is Organized

Cats For Dummies, 2nd Edition, is divided into five parts. If you're looking for a cat, you may want to start at the beginning. If you already have a cat, you can skip around, checking out the chapters that address your needs at any given time. Are you moving? Check out the chapter on cats and traveling. Have you taken a homeless and pregnant cat into your home? You want to review the parts not only on care of the mama cat and her new babies but also on how to raise those babies to be good pets, as well as how to find the right homes your angels deserve when the time comes for them to leave the nest.

We pack so much information into this book, we're guessing that, in time, you're probably going to want to read it all. How else are you going to find out just what about catnip makes some kitties crazy, how and why cats purr, and what you need to be careful about if you're pregnant and your cat uses a litter box? All this information — and more — is in *Cats For Dummies,* 2nd Edition!

No matter in what order you choose to read it, here are the basics of how this book is organized.

Part I: Starting to Think Cat

Although every cat is special and certainly unique, some are a little more distinctive than others. Many pedigreed cats fall into this category, such as the short-legged Munchkin, the hairless Sphinx, or the Scottish Fold (the cat with creased ears). Although the overwhelming majority of pet cats don't come with papers, we want to give you enough information about those who do so that you know what you may be missing.

Beyond these truly distinctive — some would call them strange — breeds, however, is plenty else to consider. Some cats are more active than others, some more talkative, some more relaxed. When considering a cat's coat, you need to think about hundreds of beautiful colors and combinations, not only in terms of longhaired and short. (Don't forget to think, too, how that beautiful fur may look on your carpet or favorite sweater!) You also need to know a little about where you're going to be looking for a cat — from breeders, shelters, pet stores, or friends and neighbors — so that you have your best chance at getting the right pet, one who's healthy and well socialized. This part also offers ideas on how to take care of wild cats — help that goes beyond feeding a cat colony and offers real hope to the animals.

Part II: Bringing a Cat or Kitten into Your Life

After you know "what" you're looking for — for example, an adult, a spayed female, a shorthaired cat from a reputable shelter — you're going to need help finding the "who" — that one special cat who's going to be your pet for the rest of her life. In this part, you find the information you need to make that choice. We include tests to help you pick out the best prospects — healthy, active, and outgoing kittens and cats. From such a pool, you can truly let your heart be your guide. Pick one — or maybe two!

We also include information on how to get your new relationship started right by covering these topics: how to manage introductions between your new pet and the other residents of your home, two-legged and four-legged; how to ensure that your house isn't full of health hazards for an inquisitive kitten; and how to show your pet in a positive and loving way where scratching and relieving himself are acceptable. You can also find out about feline body language so you can understand what your new cat is trying to tell you.

In this section, too, we offer advice on the best cat gear available. Shop until you drop? You bet! Your cat is sure to thank you for choosing the right products.

Part III: Maintaining a Happy, Healthy Cat

Taking care of your cat involves more than leaving out a bowl of food. In this part, we offer the latest information on good nutrition and preventive care, as well as what you need to know to spot and understand the most common cat health problems and to select and work with the veterinarian who's right for both you and your pet.

Even as we tell you how to care for your kitten's special health needs, we give you the information you need to make your cat's senior years comfortable and happy. Helping you — and your children — through the difficult process of saying good-bye is part of this section, too.

Part IV: Living Happily with Your Cat

In this part, you find guidelines to help you cope with behavior problems that drive pet lovers crazy — and, unfortunately, send many cats on a one-way trip to the shelter. Save your carpets, your upholstery, your houseplants, and your sanity with our guide to solving feline behavior problems. And because training needn't all be about *problems,* we offer some tips on getting your cat to perform a couple basic tricks. Who knows? Your cat may even enjoy it!

We cover the basics of breeding, too, including why letting your cat "litter" is a bad idea in most cases.

More people than you realize travel with their cats — and not just when they move (although we cover that, too). If you prefer to leave your pet at home while you're away, we give you tips on ensuring that he's well cared for in your absence. We even offer you a little information about showing your cat, enough to help you figure out if this activity is one you and your cat will enjoy.

Part V: The Part of Tens

From disaster preparedness to common household dangers to the best things ever said about cats, we save some of the very best for last. This information's all good reading — and even better with a purring cat in your lap!

Icons Used in This Book

Every ...*For Dummies* book has little pictures in the margins — we call them *icons* — to help you navigate through the book, and *Cats For Dummies,* 2nd Edition is no exception. We are different in that most of *our* icons are unique to this *For Dummies* book, and more adorable than you may find in others (except maybe *Dogs For Dummies* or *Birds For Dummies,* both also published by IDG Books Worldwide). Here's a rundown on what each icon means:

You don't *have* to read the information next to the *For Dummies* guy, but we really think you should anyway. You see a lot of him in the health sections especially, where we want to give you in-depth information but also offer you the chance to skip over it and still get a pretty-good basic understanding of whatever topic you're looking to find. If you're in a hurry, give him a pass. But come back, please, for that little bit of extra information. We think you're going to find it worthwhile.

This icon flags things that are especially useful for making life with your cat easier or making your pet happier and healthier. It highlights time- and money-savers, too!

Your cat wants you to read very carefully every word next to this icon. That's because this icon marks some of the best products and services available for cats — and for those who love them.

For related information or a more detailed discussion of the topic, you want to follow these paw prints to another spot in the book.

We put information that's especially amusing or intriguing in a lot of places, and we use this little symbol, the catnip of our icon family, to point out those cool cat facts for you so you're sure not to miss them.

If we think something's so important that it deserves restating or summarizing, this icon goes in to make sure you don't jump over that information. If you see this little flag, know that it marks information we think is worth reading more than once.

This icon denotes some of the most common mistakes cat owners make, along with tips for avoiding them.

Some Final Words

We don't like the use of "it" to describe our animal companions — and what's more, we refuse to use it! A chair is an "it." A cat tree is an "it." A car is an "it," although we can think of at least one that's named after a beautiful big cat — the Jaguar. (And don't forget the Cougar or the Lynx!) Animals, however, are living, thinking, loving beings: "hims" and "hers." And so are they alternately described in this book.

The use of "him" or "her" in any given reference applies to both genders, unless specifically noted otherwise.

How to Reach Us

We invite you to tell us about *your* cat and your tales of living with a feline companion. You can read the exploits of Gina's animals — as well as up-to-date information on animal health and behavior — as part of her weekly column, "Pet Connection," which is provided to newspapers by the Universal Press Syndicate and also appears every week in the Pet Care Forum (www.vin.com/petcare), part of the Veterinary Information Network (www.vin.com). You can e-mail us at writetogina@spadafori.com, but "snail mail" is just as nice to get at the following address:

Gina Spadafori/Dr. Paul D. Pion PMB 211
5714 Folsom Blvd.
Sacramento, CA 95819

Part I
Starting to
Think Cat

The 5th Wave   By Rich Tennant

" Stuart — wake up! The cat's been
grooming your eyebrows again."

In this part . . .

This part explains everything you need to know about selecting the perfect cat or kitten for your family. Thinking of a pedigreed cat? We tell you everything you need so you can start looking into not only the most popular breeds but also the more unusual, from evaluating personalities to finding the right breeder. The majority of people won't be getting a pedigreed pet, however, and we've got plenty of information for you if you're among them, including how to evaluate the various sources for cats and kittens.

Chapter 1

A New Appreciation of the Cat

*F*orget ancient Egypt, where the cat was honored as a god. The Golden Age of the Cat is now. More is written about cats and said about cats (and in a modern twist, posted on the Web about cats!) today than in all the generations before. Cats are the subject of musicals, of research into their diseases, of business reports that tally the billions of dollars spent to keep them healthy, clean, and amused. In the technology-heavy and time-short societies of developed countries, more people are discovering what poets, artists, and cat worshippers have known all along: Cats aren't just "dog lite" but are affectionate, beautiful companions in their own right.

The cat is civilized — but never fully. As the velvety paws of a cat hide her razor-sharp claws, the sleek body, purring in contentment, conceals the wild spirit that lives in every cat ever born. The cat gave her companionship to us so that we may caress the tiger, as the saying goes, and on some level, that must surely be part of the charm. Our lives today are so far from what we were once — a people involved in the daily struggle for survival, hunters and seekers, both predator and prey. If we're haunted by our primeval memories still, our cats are not. They live theirs every day. And we share those memories a little whenever we welcome cats into our homes.

The idea is both exhilarating and reassuring.

The feline body is a perfect package of grace and symmetry, of function creating a form that has inspired humankind for generations. For a look at the feline body — and how to tell whether things aren't as they should be — see Chapter 11.

Although dogs and horses, cattle, pigs, and poultry — and even tomato plants and roses — have changed enormously in our hands, the cat has not. The cat has recently expanded in physical variety — different coat colors and types, different ear shapes and body types — but all such variations are still quite definitely *cats,* more alike than different. Look at the tabby-striped African Wild Cat — thought to be the ancestor of our domestic cats — and you see an animal much like the one purring in your lap.

The cat chose domestication on her own terms and chose our companionship the same way. We're only now starting to understand fully what a wonderful gift we've been offered.

From Humble Beginnings: How Cats Became So Popular

As with the cats of ancient Egypt, changes in the way we live have prompted the cat's boom in popularity. Early humans found the pack instincts of dogs useful from the beginning — both for hunting and, later, for tending flocks — but the cat was of little use to humankind until our ancestors started cultivating and storing grain. The earliest evidence of domesticated cats dates from about 6,000 years ago — as opposed to 12,000 for dogs — but the most telling indications of the presence of domestic cats are about 4,000 years old.

Figure 1-1:
The cat chose to be domesticated, but the hint of the wild always remains.

Emmy/Photograph by Stacy Hindt

The cat then became honored — even worshipped — for a skill we sometimes wish today had been lost along the way: hunting. Before the cat stepped in, rodents had a fine, fat time in the grain storage bins. The cat's hunting prowess evened the score a great deal and opened the door for small cats from Africa to take over the entire world, carried as useful workers on grain-laden ships throughout the ancient world. Farmers everywhere were grateful for their aid.

Although you still find cats plying their trade as rodent-killers on farms all around the world, the cat's greater role today is strictly as a companion. And in this, too, the cat excels.

As important as the cat's hunting skills were to our ancestors, today the sight of a half-eaten mouse brought in as a gift is appreciated by few. In Chapter 19, we set the record straight regarding a popular myth about cats and hunting.

Two things have changed in developed countries to make the cat's rise in popularity inevitable.

First, more of us are living in smaller quarters — in apartments, in condominiums, in houses on smaller lots — than ever before. Although such conditions aren't conducive to the keeping of dogs — even though many people make it work anyway — such living conditions are in no way a deterrent to keeping a cat, especially an indoors-only one. Cats quite happily share the same environments people choose, living in city apartments and on farms, in cold climates and in warm ones, in small houses and in mansions. Marvelously adaptable, cats handle being alone much better than dogs do.

Second, many of us have little time or money for a pet — but a greater need for companionship than ever before. As children, we need someone to listen to us. As young adults, we delay starting a family — or choose never to start one at all. In our middle years, we're nearly pulled apart by the demands of job and family. Our older years may be more active than ever before but can also be lonely, spent far from our children.

Nonjudgmental listener and ever-affectionate companion, the cat makes a difference in many lives — and with relatively little investment of time and money. Truly, the cat has found a niche again — this time, to stay.

Frances and Richard Lockridge knew how important cats can be to children when they observed in *The Quotable Cat* (Contemporary Books): "No cat has ever said, 'I love you,' except to the sensitive ears of children." We think many cats have expressed their love — but sometimes adults aren't listening well enough to hear them. For more wonderful cat quotes, see Chapter 24.

COOL CAT FACTS

Thank you, Edward Lowe

One other thing made the transition of the cat from pest control to pet possible — or, rather, one person: Edward Lowe, the inventor of Kitty Litter.

Prior to Lowe's brainstorm, cats either went outside to relieve themselves — as many still do — or went in boxes filled with sand, soil, or sawdust, none of them a very practical solution for easy clean-up and smell control.

In 1947, cat lover Kaye Draper of Cassopolis, Michigan, sought sawdust for her cat's box from a local business. The firm also sold kiln-dried, granulated clay for cleaning up grease spills. Edward Lowe, son of the shop's owner, suggested that the woman take home some of the absorbent clay instead, and an industry was born.

After she came back for more, Lowe decided he was on to something. He put the clay in five-pound bags, wrote "Kitty Litter" on the front, and suggested to a local store owner that he sell the bags of clay for 65 cents — at a time when sand went for a penny a pound. The owner laughed, so Lowe then changed strategies: "Give it away," he said, "and see how it does."

Kitty Litter made Lowe, who died in 1995, a millionaire many times over. The sales of cat-box fillers run between $600 and $700 million a year, according to *The New York Times,* with about a third of that going for the brands Lowe founded.

(For more on cat-box fillers — how to choose them and how to use them — see Chapters 8 and 15.)

By the way, the name of Kaye Draper's cat somehow escaped being recorded for posterity. We think a little credit is due to him (or her), too.

Some Common Misconceptions about Cats — and the Facts

Even as cats reign supreme at the top of the popularity charts, a lot of people still harbor misconceptions about them. Many of these people would probably enjoy having a cat in their lives if they'd only open their minds and their hearts.

Most of the ideas about what cat's *aren't* come from comparisons to what dogs *are,* and, of course, that's not the right way to look at things. Other ideas about cats apply to those who're mostly outdoor, or semi-wild. A cat who is well-socialized from birth and closely bonded with his human companions is another animal entirely.

Remember, too, that what's a fault in the eyes of some is a virtue in the eyes of others. The overexuberant affection of a bouncy big dog isn't for everyone, believe us.

For more cat myths — and the truth — see Chapter 19.

And now, let us happily set matters straight.

"All cats are cold fish"

No doubt about it — cats pick their moments. As they have from the first, cats choose the companionship of humans on their own terms.

Although some cat critics claim that the animals are in it only for the food, any cat lover knows otherwise. Cats are "in it" for the warmth, too. Laps, beds, and even the tops of TVs and computer monitors offer many opportunities for taking nice long naps, which cats spend most of their time doing.

Oh, but it's more than that. Cats consider the people in their life as family and show it in many ways. If they bring you prey, they're providing for you. If they gently knead you with their paws while purring, they're treating you as they did their mothers. If they play with you, they're treating you as littermates or other cat pals. If they kiss you, don't kid yourself — it's legit!

Cats need their contemplative moments, of course, as do we all. A cat needs time to think — about how much she loves you . . . or how tasty that little mousy would be. But anyone who has lived with a cat will vouch for the sincerity and constancy of a cat's affection.

Figure 1-2:
A clean-smelling pile of warm laundry is heaven to many cats.

Lightning/Photograph by Lisa Wolff

Grayheart/photograph by Randy Anderson

Figure 1-3:
Although cats can seem distant at times, they crave companionship.

COOL CAT FACTS

People who don't like cats often complain that a cat chooses a cat hater's lap out of a whole room full of cat lovers who'd love to offer theirs. This behavior is often given as an example of the independent — or even malicious — nature of the cat. The truth is that something else is at work: Cats feel threatened by direct stares and avoid strangers who take such liberties. In a room full of cat lovers and one cat hater, probably only one person *isn't* looking invitingly at the cat — and that's the one who gets the cat's vote.

"Cats love places, not people"

Well-documented stories abound of cats traveling hundreds — even thousands — of miles to return to an old home after moving. This amazing behavior leads many people to believe that cats prefer places to people. Sadly, the same belief prompts some to leave their cats behind if they move, figuring that the animals are happier at the old house and hoping the new residents take them in.

Most of these abandoned cats join the sorry ranks of the ferals (undomesticated or wild) — or are taken to the shelter to be euthanized.

That cats are very territorial and mark their own property certainly is true — they even mark *you* with their scent, as they rub against your legs, hands, or face. Their territorial behaviors don't mean they prefer places to people, but they do suggest that cats have a hard time relating to the humans they love in the context of a new home — and may try to find you in your old house.

Your cat loves you just as much in your new home as in your old one — but he needs time to adapt.

Moving a cat to a new home requires planning, patience, and care. For information on how to make the move work for you both, see Chapter 18.

"Cats can take care of themselves"

Unquestionably, cats are easy-keepers. But anyone who adopts a cat thinking that cats are like houseplants, just more furry, is in for a big surprise. Kittens and cats seek and need attention and affection. They also need both preventive and routine care for any number of common ailments. Behavior problems such as litter-box avoidance are more common than most people think. To care for your cat well, you need a few basic supplies, a high-quality diet, and a veterinarian you know well enough to ask the questions you need answers to if problems arise.

Although cats do need care, they are still low maintenance compared to a lot of other pets. Cats are wonderful pets for people who work, people who travel, and people who just want the easygoing companionship a cat can provide. Your cat always keeps up his end of the bargain — make sure that you keep up yours.

Cats are among the most easy-going, adaptable, and inexpensive pets you can choose, but they do have their own special needs. Your responsibility is to protect your cat and provide him with the care and love he needs. In return, you have a beautiful, loving companion for many, many years.

Can You Have a Cat If You Have Allergies?

Even as more people than ever before have come to appreciate cats, one group of cat lovers keeps its distance — and wishes they didn't have to. That's because one of the biggest barriers to keeping a cat is allergies. More people are allergic to cats than to dogs, and cat allergies are oftentimes more severe as well. For people — and especially children — with asthma, cat allergies can be life-threatening.

The first thing you need to know about allergies is that the *fur* isn't what causes the problem; it's an element called *Fel D1* found in cat saliva and deposited on skin and fur when a cat grooms. This allergen becomes part of the *dander* — flakes of skin and secretions and saliva that a cat spreads wherever he wanders and that become airborne as he's petted or when he jumps or shakes.

The second thing you need to know relates to the first: Because the allergen-laden skin flakes are what cause the problems, a hypoallergenic cat is not possible. Cats with little or no fur can't help you, allergists say — even though some breeders of cats such as the hairless Sphinx or the lightly furred Cornish and Devon Rexes insist otherwise.

Still, some people live with both cats and allergies, and if you're considering doing so — or struggling with the situation already — find an allergist who doesn't greet you with, "First, find new homes for your pets." In some cases, for some people, that unfortunately becomes the ultimate — and only — resolution of the problem. But giving up your cat needn't be the starting point for attacking animal allergies. It's your life, after all.

Here are some other tips for living with cats and allergies:

- ✔ **Don't neglect your other allergies.** Working with an allergist to get them under control may give you enough "breathing room" to make life with a cat bearable. Remember always that allergies and asthma are serious health problems, not to be taken lightly.

- ✔ **Establish your bedroom as an "allergy-free zone."** More than one-third of our lives is spent sleeping, and so making that time less stressful for the body is very important. Close off your bedroom and reduce dust-collecting surfaces by removing carpets and rugs, wall hangings, stuffed animals, and collectibles from the room. Invest in an air cleaner and keep air ducts and ceiling fans clean. Banish feather pillows and down comforters. Use zippered, dustproof covers on the mattress and pillows. Combat dust mites by washing bedding frequently in hot water.

  Make the bedroom completely off-limits to pets at all times. Although there's not a pet lover alive who doesn't enjoy a purring cat on the bed, keeping the bedroom "allergy-free" is probably a necessary compromise for allergy sufferers.

- ✔ **Try to limit exposure to other allergens.** Avoid cleaning solutions, aerosol products, cigarette smoke, and strong perfumes and consider using a mask while doing yard work and housework, especially at the height of the pollen season. Better yet: Get someone else to mow the lawn, do the vacuuming, and clean the litter box. Again, keeping *all* allergies under control can help your body handle your cat more easily.

- ✔ **Keep your pets clean and well groomed.** The best situation is for a member of the family who doesn't suffer from allergies to take over these pet-care chores. Weekly bathing of your cat in clear water is a must — it keeps down the dander levels. Add soap if your cat needs a real bath, but it's not necessary for allergen control — clear water is fine. Some commercial preparations claim to keep the dander levels down, and more than a few people swear by them, which makes them worth experimenting with to see whether they can help you.

Give your cat a bath? Are we crazy to suggest it? Check out Chapter 9 for tips on how to get kitty clean — without getting clawed.

The Indoor versus Outdoor Controversy

With the evolution of the cat from semiwild hunter to loving companion animal has come a change not only in how cats are loved but also where cats are kept. Increasingly, more cats are living indoors.

Still, even though litter boxes can be easy to care for and odor-free, some people refuse to deal with them. Add to these folks the ones who can't believe a cat can be happy unless he runs free, and you've got half of one of the hottest controversies among cat owners: Should cats be kept exclusively indoors, or should cats be permitted outside?

The subject is so hot that almost all reputable breeders and an increasing number of shelters and rescue groups refuse to place a cat with someone who does *not* promise — in writing — to keep the animal exclusively indoors. With some breeds, this restriction is imperative: Imagine the tiny, nearly furless Devon Rex or the naked Sphynx trying to survive in the outdoors!

The truth, however, is that all cats are living dangerously if you allow them to go in and out at will. With correct diet and preventive care, an indoor cat can easily live for 15 to 20 years — or more. A cat with outdoor privileges is lucky to live a fraction as long, although many exceptions do exist, of course. Here's a list of the things that can "do in" the outdoor kitty:

✔ **Cars:** Cats can be hit, of course, but cars also present a danger even when parked. Heat-loving kitties crawl up into the warm engine and can be seriously injured — or killed — if someone starts the car again while the cat is still there.

✔ **Dogs:** Some dogs are gleeful cat killers, and woe to the cat who wanders into the territory of one of them. Some mean-spirited people even encourage their dogs to attack cats — and let the animals off the leash to do it!

✔ **Coyotes:** A well-fed cat is a tasty temptation to wild predators such as coyotes. And you don't need to live in a rural area: Coyotes have been found even in Brooklyn and are common in many other urban areas.

✔ **Poisons:** From antifreeze puddles to garden chemicals to rat poison (in baits or the stomach of dead vermin) to plants, an outdoor cat can easily get a lethal dose of something he wouldn't be as easily exposed to indoors. (Risks exist for indoor cats, too. Chapters 6 and 22 tell you how to avoid them.)

✔ **Disease:** Feline leukemia, feline immunodeficiency virus, and feline infectious peritonitis are three of the contagious and often lethal diseases your cat can pick up from other cats — through fighting or mating, primarily. And speaking of fighting, outdoor cats spend a lot of their time defending their turf — and you spend a lot of your time and money taking them to the veterinarian to patch up their bite wounds and abscesses. (More about infectious diseases is in Chapter 12.)

✔ **People:** Some people hate cats and go out of their way to hurt them. Others — such as gardeners — feel justified taking action against cats who foul flower beds and vegetable gardens. Also a threat are those who steal cats to sell for biomedical research. These people all pose a grave danger to your pet.

Enough accidental and deliberate threats are out there to make keeping your cat inside seem like a very good idea. But consider things, too, from the angle of *your* responsibility. Are you really being fair to your neighbors if you let your cat relieve himself in their yards because you don't want to deal with a litter box? If your cat carries a disease such as feline leukemia, is letting him out to infect other pets the right thing for you to do? And if you haven't spayed or neutered your pet, doesn't allowing her (or him) out to breed make you partially responsible for the surplus kittens and cats killed by the millions each year?

We leave the answers up to you and to your conscience.

As for the other question of whether cats can be happy living an indoors-only life, the answer is a resounding "Yes!" Kittens raised indoors become cats who don't miss the outdoors, and with patience, you can convert even grown cats. Toys, scratching posts, indoor gardens, and screened patios or balconies all make the indoor cat's life special — as may the addition of a second cat (or even a dog) for companionship.

For more on what you need to keep a cat happy indoors, see Chapters 8 and 23.

Figure 1-4:
You must decide whether your cat will live indoors or out — or have access to both!

Kelsey and Tim/Photograph by Linda Stark

Chapter 2

Narrowing the Choices

In This Chapter

- Deciding between a kitten and a cat
- Debating the male or female issue
- Choosing between longhaired and shorthaired
- Understanding the pedigreed cat
- Exploring characteristics by breed
- Considering the not-so-ordinary everyday cat

You've taken everything into account: Your home. Your time. Your finances. A cat is in your future, beyond a doubt, but what *kind* of cat? As you picture your living room, do you see a docile Persian on the couch, lush coat gleaming as the sunlight hits it? Do you picture an active Abyssinian, giving you a brief but imperious look from a perch high atop a bookshelf a split-second before executing a perfect leap to the top of the hutch? Or perhaps you see a nonpedigreed — a calico, perhaps — with a temperament somewhere in between, her tail held high in the universal cat greeting: "Hi there. Adore me."

But wait! You have more to consider. Before you get to imagine Your Perfect Cat, you must determine whether a grown cat would work better for the life you lead than would a kitten, no matter how adorable. Before you consider whether a random-bred or pedigreed cat will suit you best, you must consider the issue of fur: long or short? And what about gender? Do females make better pets, or do males?

CAUTION

The decisions you make must keep for a very long time. The cats themselves pay the price for wrong spur-of-the-moment decisions — just check out any shelter for proof.

As serious as that thought is, remember that choosing a feline companion is also a great deal of fun. You get to see oodles of beautiful cats, play with adorable kittens, and consider the incredible variety of the world's most easy-going, adaptable, and ever-more-popular companion.

Random-bred or pedigreed, grown cat or kitten, whatever gender, fur length, color, markings, or variety you choose, we want you to be in love with your cat for years to come. So read on.

After you decide what kind of cat or kitten you're looking for, you want to be just as deliberate about choosing a place to get your new pet and in picking out the very animal who's right for the life you're leading. We discuss breeders, shelters, rescue groups, and other sources in Chapter 3, and hints for picking out the right kitten or cat — including temperament tests and health checks — you find in Chapter 5. You may even wish to give a feral cat or kitten a chance. Find out more about these special animals in Chapter 4.

Kitten or Cat: Which Is a Better Choice for You?

When people think about adding a cat to their lives, they seem to automatically think "kitten." And why not? A kitten seems to make perfect sense, a little fluffball who'll grow into your household and your heart. For some people, though, an adult cat is a better option. And even if you're perfectly set up for a kitten, you ought to consider an adult as well, for you'll find many wonderful pets among the ranks of grown cats, and most will never get a second chance to show how perfect they can be.

Don't rule out either before you consider each fairly.

Everyone loves kittens!

Even people who profess to dislike cats can't look at a kitten without saying "awwwwwww." Baby animals are all adorable, but kittens seem to have something special going for them. Maybe it's those large eyes, following every movement intently. The oversized ears, twitching to and fro. The playfulness, chasing and pouncing on everything that moves, be it your fingertip or a piece of kibble batted across the linoleum. The tousled fur a kitten can't quite seem to groom into the sleekness every adult cat considers her duty to maintain. A kitten is all these things — and more.

What many people don't think about as they're falling in love is that a kitten can be a lot of work and aggravation. They can mean a lot of expense, too, because many a kitten seems to use nearly all a cat's nine lives, which means you may end up seeing the nice people at the emergency veterinary clinic a time or two in the first year. With a kitten, you also need to put more effort into training, from making sure the tiny baby understands what's expected regarding the litter box to helping your kitten learn to stay off the counters. You also need to kitten-proof your home — or keep your baby confined in a safe part of the house whenever you're not watching him — and then spend months during which, every day, you're picking your little tiger off the drapes, off the kids, off the back of the couch, or off your slippers every time you walk down the hall.

For tips on "kitten-proofing" your home and basic early training, see Chapter 6.

A kitten may be a poor choice for families with very young children or for someone who's handicapped by advanced age or illness. For all their spunk, kittens are fragile and may accidentally be hurt by young children who don't understand the concept of "gentle." Similarly, a kitten isn't the best choice for anyone who's a little unsteady on his feet or isn't able to chase or otherwise keep up with an energetic feline baby.

On the other hand, a kitten can be a dream come true to a family with older, more-responsible children, or a source of delightful amusement to an active older adult. You just need to look carefully at your living situation and consider the problems and pleasures a kitten will bring.

Finally, consider the matter of time. An adult cat does quite well on her own alone in the house while you work — most of the time she's sleeping anyway. A kitten needs your time, for raising her and for watching over her to keep her out of trouble.

Adult cat considerations

Adult cats offer some compelling advantages and few disadvantages — the most serious disadvantage being simply that they aren't as "baby cute" as kittens!

Kittens get away with all their endearing goofiness because they measure way off the adorability scale, but if you suspect you're going to get tired of having your feet attacked, if you worry about your children not being gentle enough, or if you don't want to be figuring out what your little baby is into every second of the day and night, an adult cat is a better option for you.

If you adopt an adult cat, you know exactly what you're getting. Body type, coat, and eye color are set. Laid-back or active, quiet or vocal, cuddly or demanding, an adult cat has already settled into his own persona. These considerations may not be as important in a pedigreed cat, because you know, based on your kitten's background and the breeder's knowledge and reputation, what your kitten is likely to grow into in terms of body type and temperament. But in a nonpedigreed kitten, these qualities are really anybody's guess. If you want to make sure that you're getting, say, a mellow pet, choose a cat beyond the ants-in-his-pants kitten stage. (More on pedigreed cats later in this chapter.)

The easy care and generous affection of adult cats make them perfect pets for people for whom walking dogs would be difficult or impossible. And study after study confirms the importance of a cat in the lives of those who feel isolated by age or disabilities.

One of the most compelling reasons to adopt a mature cat is that many of these adults have little hope of getting a second chance after they hit the shelter, no matter how healthy, beautiful, and well mannered they are. Kittens are so adorable they're hard to pass up, and so many people never even look at the cages of adult cats when they're at the shelter.

The possible disadvantage of adopting an adult cat is that you may be choosing a pet with behavioral problems — not using a litter box, for example. A good shelter, rescue group, or breeder practices full disclosure of any known health or behavior problems with the animals up for adoption. Remember, however, that many animals are given up for behavior problems that can be resolved or aren't their fault — such as the cat who's looking at a filthy litter box every day and decides to do his business elsewhere.

Litter box problems are one of the top reasons adult cats are taken to a shelter. Although keeping a cat who refuses to use a litter box is certainly frustrating, the problem isn't incurable. To understand why a cat avoids the litter box and to set up a retraining program to correct the problem, see Chapter 15.

An adult cat's personality may be set, but his affections aren't — a grown cat bonds with you just as tightly as a kitten does. We think that adult cats are even more likely to appreciate you for taking them in.

Most people — maybe even you — will still choose a kitten over a cat; such is the power of packaging. But we want to make sure that you aren't automatically excluding some wonderful pets. Look at kittens, sure, but check out the cats, too. Strike a blow against ageism! We think you get brownie points for adopting an animal who has everything going for her — except kittenhood. Adopting an adult cat is also a great time- and money-saver.

She-Kitty, He-Kitty: Which One's Better?

You're not going to get a definitive answer out of us on this one, even if we had one, which we don't. Males and females make equally good pets, under one very important condition: *altering*.

Male or female, a cat who is what the experts call *whole* or *intact* — in other words, fully equipped to reproduce — is a royal pain to live with. When females are "in season" — which happens several times a year, for a couple weeks at a time — they're yowly escape artists who attract noisy suitors from miles around. Some people think males are even worse. By the time they're sexually mature, they begin *spraying* — marking territory with a special pheromone-spiked urine with a smell that's not only foul but also nearly impossible to eradicate. They're also roamers and fighters.

Altering goes a long way toward eliminating spraying, but more is involved in curing this disagreeable behavior. For the lowdown on this smelly problem, see Chapter 15. What's involved in altering — commonly known as *spaying* or *neutering* — a cat? The answer's in Chapter 16.

The experts — even reputable breeders who keep intact cats for their breeding programs — all agree that neutering is the key to a cat's being a good pet, no matter the gender. An important contribution that those involved in the sport of showing cats have made is to ensure that animals who can no longer breed can still compete — in classes for *alters*. This aspect of showing is wonderfully progressive and supportive of those who like to show their lovely cats but not breed them.

After cats are altered, is one gender then a better pet than the other? The answer depends on whom you ask. Some people believe males are a little more outgoing; others suggest that females are smarter. (We got into an argument over that one after one of us — not Paul — snorted "of course!" And then we each came up with examples of smart males and outgoing females, the latter group including Paul's cat, PC.)

Despite Paul's interest in computers, "PC" doesn't stand for "Personal Computer" or even "Politically Correct." It's short for "Prayer Cat," and it comes from the tabby's endearing habit of sitting up on her haunches and "praying" for what she wants, holding her front paws together before her. (Check out PC's photo in this book's introduction.)

Perhaps the biggest reason some people prefer one gender over another we can sum up by using the word *always* — they have *always* had males (or females), have *always* been happy with their choices, and see no reason to change.

If you're thinking about adopting a pedigreed kitten, you may not have a choice about the gender: Males may be all that the breeder is offering for sale, especially if the breed is rare or in development. That's because the females are held back to remain part of the breeding stock or shared only with those the breeder believes are willing to show and breed the kitten as she recommends.

Both male and female cats make good pets, and we can't really steer you in one way or another. If you have a personal preference, go with it. If not, make all your other decisions and then go with the kitten that best fits your criteria, male or female.

Let the Fur Fly

We need to get one thing straight up front: Almost all cats shed. The "almost" is there to apply to those cats who haven't any fur — such as those of the Sphynx breed, who still manages to carry a little down that rubs off on your clothes.

Cats can have three kinds of hair in their coats — down, awn, and guard. The *down* is the shortest, finest, and softest hair. The *awn* is the coarsest, and the *guard* (sometimes called the *primary hairs*) is the longest. Not all cats have all three varieties. The Sphynx, as just noted, has only down hairs, and few of these. The Cornish Rex has only awn and down. The awn hairs are usually shorter than the guard hairs (and longer than the down), but when awn and guard hairs are the same length, as in the Russian Blue, the cat is called *double coated.*

Some cats, such as the kinky-furred Rexes, shed very little. Some longhaired cats shed a lot — or seem to, because the hair they drop is longer. Even the ordinary garden-variety domestic shorthair is going to lose enough fur to drive the overly fastidious person nuts. If you really can't stand the thought of cat fur on your sofa, your sweater, or even in your food from time to time, give this cat thing some serious thought.

Are you allergic to cat fur? The chances are good that you're really allergic to something else. For what that may be, and for strategies on coping with cats and allergies, see Chapter 1.

In considering a cat's coat, think about three things:

- ✔ **Aesthetics:** Some people like the sleek look and feel of a shorthaired cat; others adore the flowing softness of the longhairs. The shorthairs have about them the air of a tiger: You can see their muscles move as they walk, see the coiled promise of power while they sleep. In longhairs, the power is even more subtle, hidden by lush thickets of lovely long fur. Do you prefer to rub your hand down a sleek pelt or bury your fingers in a longhaired one? This preference is the first of your decisions.

- ✔ **Fur levels:** Here is where the trade-offs start to come in. Although nearly all cats shed, the difference in shedding levels between short- and long-haired cats can be dramatic, especially in cats that are prized for the volume of coat, such as with Persians. Are you prepared to live with a lint roller in your bathroom, your glove box, and your desk drawer at work? Would you be appalled to have a friend pick one of those glorious 4-inch pieces of fur off the back of your sweater? If you're on the low end of fur tolerance, you'd better stick with shorthaired cats. (If you have no tolerance for fur, maybe you'd be better off with a tank of fish.)

- ✔ **Time and money:** Longhaired cats require extra care. They mat easily and need to be combed out every other day or so and brushed thoroughly on a weekly basis. *Hairballs,* or clumps of fur caught in the cat's digestive system, can be a constant problem with longhaired cats, requiring medical attention. If your cat's mats get out of control, you need to have her professionally groomed — most likely shaved — and that costs money.

Longhaired cats are more challenging to live with in other ways, too. Their urine and feces can get caught in their coats (which is why many owners generally prefer to keep those areas of their cats clipped short), and litter may catch on the tufts of fur in their paws and get tracked all over the house.

For more information about good grooming, see Chapter 9. For guidelines on choosing litter, litter boxes, and accessories, see Chapter 8.

Your cat's coat also has a bearing on whether you can consider letting him be an indoor-outdoor cat. The sparse coats of some of the Sphynxes and the Rexes offer no protection against sun or cold; on the other end of the scale, although the hearty coats of the Maine Coons and Norwegian Forest Cats stand up to the elements, the silkier coats of the Persians may need to be protected from the elements.

Although coat length, type, and color are truly a matter of personal preference in terms of picking out a cat, you do need to watch out for one thing that's related to coat color: White cats with blue eyes have a high probability for deafness. Some of these cats have eyes of different colors and are deaf only on the side with the blue eye. (You can check for deafness by snapping your fingers or clapping your hands behind a cat or kitten's head.) Though a deaf cat can still be a good pet — indoors only, for her own protection — you'll still want to know what you're getting into before you adopt.

Should You Consider a Pedigreed Cat?

You should consider everything! Although pedigreed cats make up a very small percentage of the overall cat population — less than 5 percent, according to some sources — some people would never consider having anything but a pedigreed cat of their particular favorite breed.

One fan of pedigreed cats is Lilian Jackson Braun, whose best-selling *The Cat Who . . .* mysteries have charmed cat lovers for years. Braun's breed of choice is the Siamese, and so, too, is her detective's. In fact, if not for that very first Siamese cat, a gift from her husband, there would probably be no such mystery series at all.

Although the development of dog breeds has been going on for as long as dogs have been around, the interest in purebred cats is a relatively recent phenomenon, starting in the last century. Probably the most compelling reason for the difference is that people needed dog breeds to perform various tasks — herding, hunting, and guarding — whereas the cat walked in perfectly suited to the needs of humankind: Then, as now, no more efficient hunter of rodents could be found. Why mess with perfection?

Some people have always appreciated cats as much for their beauty and companionship as for their hunting skills, and some of these folks have worked to preserve and develop cat breeds and to nurture the development of new — and ofttimes controversial — varieties.

Beautiful colors, beautiful cats

Considering how little they had to begin with, modern breeders have developed an incredible variety of colors and patterns in today's pedigreed cats. The Cat Fanciers' Association lists more than 60 color patterns for the Persian alone.

Not that what they started with wasn't beautiful — and isn't beautiful still.

By far, the most common cat color/pattern is the "tiger-striped," or *tabby,* markings that you can still see in the wild ancestors of the domestic cat. The name *tabby* comes from *Atabi,* a silk imported to England long ago that had a striped pattern similar to that of the domestic tiger cat.

Tabbies comes in many colors, such as red (more commonly called "orange," "ginger," or "marmalade"), cream, brown, or gray. The tabby pattern is so dominant that, even in solid-colored cats, you can often discern faint tabby markings, especially on the head, legs, and tail.

Smoked, shaded, and *shell* describe the varying amounts of tipping that appear on each individual hair, with *shell* being a dash of color at the very tip, *shaded* a little more tipping, and *smoke,* at the other extreme, being a coat so heavily tipped that it may look solid, except as the cat moves and the lighter color becomes visible underneath. Fur can also be *ticked* — that is, banded with color, as in the *agouti* pattern seen in the Abyssinian, where dark-colored bands alternate with lighter ones on each hair shaft.

Pointed cats are those such as the Siamese, with lighter-colored bodies shading to darker, complementary colors at the *points* — the face, the ears, the legs, and the tail.

Bicolors are any other color (or pattern, such as tabby) paired with white, and *particolors* have three or more colors, as is true of calicoes (commonly with patches of white, red, and black) or tortoiseshells (with swirled red, cream, and black).

Mixing these color types can have some unpredictable results. The spotted Ocicat, for example, was created as the result of mating a Siamese and an Abyssinian!

What are the benefits of owning a pedigreed cat? Predictability is probably the main one: If you buy a pedigreed kitten from a reputable breeder, you know in large part what you're getting. Size, body type, coat color, and levels of activity and vocality are imprinted on each kitten at the time of conception. Although each cat is still an individual, you can rest assured that your individual Siamese is going to have more in common with other Siamese in terms of looks and personalities than it does with any Persian ever born. The Siamese is active and talkative; the Persian is calm and quiet. If your tastes in a feline companion run to either of these extremes, choosing an appropriate pedigreed cat is the most likely way to have your wish.

Pedigreed cats also offer a little more variety than the everyday cat does. If you like a long, sleek cat, certain breeds fit that profile. The same, too, is true for a thicker-set body type, called *cobby* by fanciers. Color choices, too, are broader. The slate gray of the Korat and Russian Blue, really a dilution of the gene that produces black, is almost unheard-of outside the world of pedigreed cats, as is the glossy warm tone of the Havana Brown.

And what about the novelty factor? Only in the pedigreed ranks can you find cats with ears that fold forward or back, cats with kinky fur — or none at all — and cats with little or no tails or short legs. Some of these breeds are controversial — to say the least! — but they certainly do expand the choices when the time comes to "think cat."

Concerning pedigreed cats, cat lovers like them big, and they like them furry. Or at least that's the picture you get from the Cat Fanciers' Association, which lists the Persian at number one on the popularity parade, followed by the Maine Coon, another hefty longhair. Rounding out the top five are the Siamese, the Abyssinian, and the Exotic (the shorthaired Persian). Worldwide, there are close to 50 cat breeds, many so rare that only a few hundred representatives exist in each.

The overwhelming majority of cat seekers do *not* choose a pedigreed cat. For some, the choice may be a matter of price and convenience. Pedigreed cats can be expensive — a couple of hundred dollars, at least, and climbing into the thousands of dollars for kittens of rare breeds and colors. They can be hard to find, too, if you journey past the most-popular breeds. Upkeep on the coats of some breeds may also limit many cat lovers to admiring them from afar.

Although most pedigreed cats are as healthy as their nonpedigreed relatives, you do need to be aware of some health concerns. The Persian, for example, is prone to respiratory problems, blocked tear ducts, and runny eyes because of the short face that some breeders prize. Other problems are associated with the very attributes that make some breeds special: Skeletal defects can pop up in Scottish Fold and Manx litters, for example. Reputable breeders are aware of the genetic problems in their breed and work to keep them at bay. Anyone you're considering buying a pedigreed kitten or cat from should honestly discuss any problems in their breed and what is being done to reduce their frequency.

Characteristics by Breed

Pedigreed cats are roughly divided by experts into two groups that are distinguished by body type and activity level.

The breeds in the first group, the *Oriental,* are notable for their long, sleek bodies and active participation in the world around them. They're not happy unless they're supervising dinner, climbing to the top of the bookshelf, teasing that dopey dog, or seeing what every member of the household is up to. The way these cats see the world, you're not capable of running your own life without their help. Cats in this group, such as the Siamese, Burmese, and Abyssinian, are often touted as being more intelligent and trainable.

Do you want a chatty cat?

One trait that is highly predictable by breed is noisiness. Some breeds are so quiet you hardly know they're around, and others tell you every thought that crosses their minds, every minute they're awake, with all manner of meows.

Siamese are probably best known for being chatty, but other breeds keep up their end of the conversation, too. The Balinese, a longhaired version of the Siamese, is, not surprisingly, very vocal, as are the Oriental Shorthair and Colorpoint Shorthair, also versions of the Siamese, and the Tonkinese, another breed developed from the Siamese. Other feline conversationalists include the Bombay, the Burmese, the Rexes, and the Ocicat.

The quietest cat breeds are generally those with heavier builds and more mellow dispositions: the Persian, the British Shorthair, and the Maine Coon.

The *non-Orientals* see things a little bit differently. If you're big and beautiful, the world comes to you with all your needs. Why interrupt a good nap to see what's on top of that bookshelf? Cats in this group, such as the Persian, Ragdoll, and British Shorthair, are generally happy to sleep in your lap while you read — and not bat at the pages as you turn them!

At first, the differences between these breeds may also seem to relate to their coats, with the sleek shorthairs falling in the Oriental group and thicker-set longhairs in the other. That assumption would be true except for the work of those who want to offer you even more options in a cat, such as longhaired versions of the Siamese (the Balinese) and Abyssinian (the Somali) and a breed that's pretty close to a shorthaired version of the Persian (the Exotic).

The history and legends behind the various breeds of pedigreed cats are almost as interesting and colorful as the cats themselves. Two books that are good jumping-off points for more in-depth research into cat breeds are *The Cat Fanciers' Association Cat Encyclopedia* (Simon & Schuster) and *Cat Breeds of the World: An Illustrated Encyclopedia,* by Desmond Morris (Viking). You can also check out the breed profiles on the Cat Fanciers Web site at www.fanciers.com/breed.html.

Unlike purebred dogs — who are divided roughly by purpose: sporting, herding, and so on — pedigreed cats aren't quite so easy to categorize. Not surprisingly, really, if you consider that each cat himself is unique — and if you don't believe it, just ask him!

Not happy with the two divisions the experts offer, we break down the various breeds into categories, a task almost as difficult as herding cats themselves. The breakdown's not perfect — some longhaired cats are also among the largest, for example, and some of the more active breeds are also distinctive in other ways. (In such cases, we list the breeds twice, once in each category.) But we figure that breaking the almost 50 breeds down into categories would make thinking about what sort of breed you may want a little easier.

The go-go group

Consider the Siamese the prototype of this group. Always into everything, always looking to see what you're up to, and always loudly suggesting ways you can do it better — these characteristics are the essence of this cat, one of the world's most easily recognizable breeds with his distinctive "pointed" markings. The Siamese is such an important breed that its genes went into the development of many others, such as the Himalayan (a pointed version of the Persian); the Balinese (essentially a longer-haired Siamese); and the Birman, Burmese, Havana Brown, Ocicat, Oriental Shorthair (a Siamese in solid colors and total-body patterns), Colorpoint Shorthair (a Siamese with more options in point colors), and Tonkinese. Not surprisingly, many of these breeds — the Himalayan alone not among them — are also high on the activity scale.

A cat doesn't need to be Siamese — or related somehow to the Siamese — to be above-average in terms of being on the go. Not as talkative generally, but just as busy, is the Abyssinian, with markings that suggest a mountain lion and a reputation for being one of the most intelligent and trainable of all breeds. Other breeds with energy to burn are the Bombay, the kinky-coated Cornish and Devon Rexes, the Egyptian Mau, the Somali (a longhaired Abyssinian), and the hairless Sphynx.

REMEMBER

Although these breeds can be a constant source of amusement with their energy and fearless ways, they can also be a handful. You should be prepared to endure cats on the drapes — the better to get up, up, up! — and kittenish behavior that endures for a lifetime. These cats never stop and are as likely to want to play at 2 a.m. as at 2 p.m. They surely want to be *with* you all the time, but *on* you? That's another matter. Lap-sitter kitties these are generally not — they've got things to do!

Figure 2-1:
You couldn't get these cats to sit still for a photograph! Active breeds include the Abyssinian, Burmese, Cornish Rex, and Siamese.

The people who choose these breeds do so for a reason: They're fun! If one of these cats is in your future, get a good cat tree — see Chapter 8 — and lay in a huge supply of toys, because you're going to need them.

A touch of the wild

One of the many things we humans find appealing about cats is that, even in the most tame and loving of our household companions, a touch of the tiger remains. Indeed, the tiger's stripes remain on many of our pets, reminding us always of the connection — a reminder strengthened whenever you watch a cat walk, run, or leap. The grace and power are the same for big cats and for small.

Our cats may have chosen domestication, but on their own terms. And always, always, with a little bit of wildness held in reserve.

That we love this essential wildness is apparent in our long-standing interest in cat breeds that retain the look of the wild about them — not with the "ordinary" tiger stripes of the tabby but with spotted coat patterns evocative of another great wild cat, the leopard.

One of the most controversial of these breeds is the California Spangled, because of the decidedly unique way its creator sought to market the kittens — in the Neiman Marcus Christmas catalog. Priced at $1,400 each, the kittens were the topic of much heated debate from people who thought selling cats by catalog sent the wrong message — that cats were little more than living toys or decorator accessories.

As is true of the California Spangled, most cats with a spotted "wild look" haven't any wild blood in them at all — they're the results of breeders trying to develop coat patterns that resemble the domestic cat's wild cousins. You can put into this category the Ocicat, derived from breedings of the Siamese and Abyssinian and named for the Ocelot, which it resembles. The Egyptian Mau (*Mau* means *cat* in Egyptian) is another spotted wonder, a lovely cat bred to resemble the cats seen in ancient Egyptian artwork.

A cat of a different variety altogether is the Bengal, a cat developed through breedings of domestic cats with wild Asian Leopard Cats. Fanciers say the wild temperament has been removed by generations of breeding only the most sociable and friendly Bengals, although the look of the wild cat it came from remains.

The temperament of these "wilder" breeds generally lies somewhere in the middle between the go-gos and the more easygoing breeds, which we discuss next. They're not placid layabouts, but neither are they as active as some breeds. For those who love the look of a leopard in a manageable, loving package, these cats are perfect.

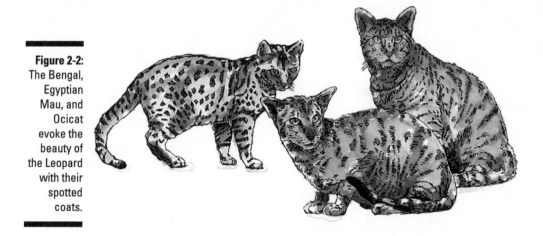

Figure 2-2:
The Bengal,
Egyptian
Mau, and
Ocicat
evoke the
beauty of
the Leopard
with their
spotted
coats.

Longhaired beauties

The Persian is the other cat besides the Siamese that nearly anyone, cat lover or not, can recognize in a crowd. The incredible coat of this breed has enchanted cat lovers for centuries. Whenever companies look for a breed that says "glamour" to use in their advertising, that they usually settle on a Persian is no accident. This cat is a glamour-puss, no doubt about it.

Perhaps no cat besides the Persian comes in as many varieties, each cat resplendent in that incredible coat: tabbies of every color, torties, calicoes, every imaginable solid color, and tipped coats, too. The markings of the Siamese can be found in the Himalayan, which in cat shows is considered a pointed Persian.

If you're looking for a more natural longhair, you have plenty of options. The Turkish Angora and Turkish Van are two ancient longhaired cats. The Norwegian Forest, Maine Coon, and Siberian cats are longhairs that still have the rough-and-tumble look of farm cats about them. And don't forget the Birman, the sacred cat of Burma, a breed that looks somewhat like a Himalayan, with color darker at the points, except for the perfectly white-mitted paws.

The Ragdoll is another pointed longhair with white mittens of more-modern origins — it was "invented" in the 1960s — and is another choice for those seeking a longhaired cat, especially one designed to have an extremely laid-back temperament. Another lovely longhair with a relatively short history is the Chantilly/Tiffany, a cat with silky hair, commonly chocolate colored.

In the longhaired ranks, too, are a few breeds you can distinguish from their better-known relatives only by the length of their coat. Put in this class the Cymric, a longhaired version of the tailless Manx, as well as the Somali (a longer-haired Abyssinian), Balinese (a longer-haired Siamese), and Javanese (a longer-haired Colorpoint Shorthair).

The biggest challenge facing those who own longhaired cats is coat care. The long, silky coat of the Persian mats easily and requires daily attention to keep it in good form. Other longhaired coats aren't quite as demanding, but they all require more attention than the coats of shorthaired cats. And they all shed rather remarkably! Ingested hair, commonly called *hairballs,* is a bigger problem in longhaired cats, too.

For everything you need to know about grooming these longhaired beauties — including choosing a groomer for your cat — see Chapter 9. In the same chapter, you find more information on hairballs.

The temperament of longhaired cats depends on what's underneath that lovely coat. If an Oriental body is underneath — such as in the Balinese — you've got an active cat. The larger, more thickset body types, such as those of the Persian and Norwegian Forest Cat, tend more toward the laid-back end of the spectrum.

Figure 2-3:
The Birman, Himalyan and Persian are all cherished for their luxurious, long coats.

The big cats

Although you'll never see a pet cat as big as a St. Bernard — or at least, we certainly hope not — a few breeds definitely warrant the heavyweight category where cats are concerned. Although most healthy cats — pedigreed or not — weigh between 8 and 12 pounds, some of the big cat breeds range between 15 and 20 pounds, especially the males. Now *that's* a cat who can keep your lap warm on a winter night!

The biggest domestic cat is thought to be the Siberian cat, with some males topping 20 pounds. This breed is pretty rare, however, so if you're looking for maximum cat, you may want to consider the Maine Coon, number two on the Cat Fanciers' Association's list of most-popular cats, or maybe the Norwegian Forest, another longhaired chunk of a cat. Other longhaired cats with an above-average size include the Ragdoll, Turkish Van, and American Bobtail.

For a lot of cat without the fur, consider the British Shorthair, the American Shorthair, and the Chartreux.

The large cats are generally fairly easygoing in temperament and more laid-back than many other breeds. If you're looking for a more active and involved pet, these breeds are not the ones for you.

The Maine Coon has long been popular both as a pet and a show cat. In fact, a brown tabby Maine Coon named Cosey won the first major cat show in North America, held May 8, 1895, in New York City's Madison Square Garden. The engraved silver collar and medal presented there is now the most important piece in the Cat Fanciers' Association's collection of cat memorabilia and art.

Figure 2-4:
The Turkish Van, Maine Coon and British Shorthair are perfect breeds for those who like their cats large.

Something different

New cat breeds are created all the time, some by accident, some by design. Many cat breeds start after someone notices a kitten with something "different" — ears, legs, or other characteristics that set him or her apart from other cats. These cats are some of the rarest around and among the most controversial. They're also among the most expensive to acquire — if you can find one at all.

Coat — or lack of it — sets some breeds apart. Primary among these breeds is the Sphynx, a cat who's nearly hairless — nothing more than a little fuzz on his face, feet, and tail. The Rex breeds — Cornish, Devon, German, and Selkirk — all sport kinky hair, as does the LaPerm and the American Wirehair.

Some breeders of Rexes claim an additional distinction for their breeds: They claim that the cats are hypoallergenic. Some people with allergies may be able to tolerate certain breeds more than others, true, but unfortunately, no such thing as an allergy-proof cat exists. For tips on making living with a cat easier on your allergies, see Chapter 1.

Tails — or lack thereof — are the talk in other breeds. The Manx is undoubtedly the best-known tailless or short-tailed cat, but others are on this list, too. The Cymric is a longhaired Manx; the Japanese Bobtail, American Bobtail, and Pixie-Bob round out the ranks of the tail-challenged.

And what about ears? Two breeds are based on an ear mutation: the Scottish Fold, with ears that fold forward, and the American Curl, with ears that arch backward.

Undoubtedly the most talked-about new breed has been the Munchkin, a cat with short legs. Although some people say that the breed is a mutation that shouldn't be developed into an actual breed, others see little difference between having a short-legged cat breed and a short-legged dog breed, of which several exist. One thing is certain: The controversy over breeds developed from mutations isn't about to abate anytime soon.

Should you consider any of these breeds? Of course. If you're looking for something that's sure to start a conversation whenever company comes over, these cats are just the ticket. But be prepared, too, to hear from those who think it's a bad idea to perpetuate such genetic surprises.

Figure 2-5:
The short-legged Munchkin, short-tailed Japanese bobtail, ear-altered Scottish fold, and nearly hairless Sphynx are all certain to start a conversation.

The unCATegorizables

What did we tell you earlier? Herding cats is hard work, and some breeds refuse any efforts at being categorized. One, the Singapura, a Southeast Asian breed that resembles an Abyssinian, is noteworthy for being exceptionally small, which practically puts the breed in a category of its own.

And where do you put the Snowshoe, a cat with many breeds in its background who resembles a white-mitted Siamese but isn't as active? We couldn't decide.

Three other breeds are of medium size and temperament but are notable for their coats. Count among these the Korat and Russian Blue, from Thailand and Russia, respectively, both remarkable for their stunning blue-gray coats — as is the Nebelung.

The Not-So-Ordinary Everyday Cat

Most people couldn't care less if a cat has a pedigree or a fancy breed name — they just like cats and are content to adopt one that strikes their fancy or wanders into their lives. Calling a nonpedigreed cat a "mixed breed" isn't exactly right, however, because most breeders are so careful with their pedigreed cats that the possibility of an unplanned breeding is almost nil. The everyday cat really is completely random-bred, produced as a matter of complete serendipity with no rhyme or reason at all — at least not where humans are concerned! We like the British name for these cats — moggies.

Still, randomness being what it is — random — you can find some nonpedigreed cats that look very close to their show-going cousins. A big, brown, longhaired tabby that has more than a passing resemblance to a Maine Coon, for example. In the very real terms of love and affection, such cats are neither more nor less valuable than their pedigreed counterparts.

Even without human meddling, cats display a remarkable range of traits and appearances. Some of the more popular are the tuxedo-marked cats. Calicoes and tortoiseshells are fabled, too, and more than one cat lover has a soft spot in her heart for a ginger tabby.

Are all calicoes and tortoiseshell cats female? The surprising truth is in Chapter 19.

The point here is that *all* cats have the potential to be a special pet to someone, no matter where they come from, no matter what they look like. And cats are really more alike than they are different in terms of health, general size, and behavior.

The differences count only in relation to what you want in a pet. You need to know your own heart before you choose to let any cat into it.

Figure 2-6:
The tuxedo, calico, and the most common pattern — the tabby — reflect the variety found among random-bred cats.

Chapter 3

Considering Sources

• •

In This Chapter

▶ Looking into shelters and rescue groups

▶ Telling the good breeders from the not-so-good

▶ Recognizing the potential problems of pet-shop cats

▶ Adopting kittens from your neighbor

• •

*Y*ou know what you want: random-bred or pedigreed, longhaired or short, kitten or cat, male or female. You've done your homework, and you're getting closer to sharing your home with a cat. (And if you haven't narrowed your choices down yet, you may want to take a look at Chapters 1 and 2.)

Where do you find that special cat or kitten?

One thing is certain: You find no shortage of cats. During the warm months that mean "kitten season," you can find people with kittens to give away nearly everywhere — at your workplace, in front of your grocery store, at flea markets, shelters, and pet stores. Adult cats are plentiful, too, yours for the adopting. As for pedigreed cats, they're a little harder to find, but even then it's possible to find one pretty easily.

Why should you make choosing your new pet more trouble than you need to? Why not pick out that adorable little calico kitten from the neighbor cat's third litter? As for pedigreeds, does it really matter whether you seek out a reputable breeder or buy from a pet store or someone who's breeding for fun and maybe a little profit? If the cat's registered, aren't the sources for pedigreeds all the same?

Buyer beware! And we mean that most adamantly, even if you aren't buying at all, but adopting a free cat or kitten. Stop, and do your homework.

All sources are not the same, which is why you should take your time in getting your kitten or cat and not just fall in love with the first fuzzy face you see.

How much should you spend?

Prices for cats and kittens vary widely: You can pay from nothing at all to the (generally) less than $50 that shelters charge (which may include start-up veterinary care and altering — such a deal), to $300 to $1,000 for an "ordinary" but well-bred pedigreed cat from a reputable breeder or a pet store, to more than a couple thousand dollars for a well-bred "show-quality" kitten or one of a rare or red-hot breed. In general, however, a pedigreed "pet-quality" kitten of a common breed from a reputable breeder costs between $300 and $800.

Even if you pay nothing for your cat or kitten, you need to put some money into a few basics — a supply of food and cat-box filler, dishes, cat box, scratching post or cat tree, and a couple toys. Figure on spending from $100 to $200. If your pet isn't already vaccinated, wormed, and spayed or neutered, figure another $100, give or take, at the vet's.

The true cost of a cat is in the upkeep, but at least you get to make payments on that. You can keep the cost of the most basic, proper care — food, litter, basic gear, preventive veterinary care, boarding or pet-sitting while you're on vacation, and perhaps grooming for longhaired cats — to a reasonable minimum of $300 a year or so. Add in occasional veterinary emergencies and the strictly optional, but enjoyable, addition of tempting feline merchandise — lavish toys, high-end, high-tech litter boxes, books and magazines, and cat-themed goodies for you — and a cat can be a pretty pricey pet.

The important thing is not the cost but the health and temperament of your new pal. Better you should get a friendly kitten glowing with good health from your local shelter than a sickly or shy "bargain" pedigreed from a poor-quality breeder. Pedigreed or random-bred, go to the source that offers healthy, happy pets, and you'll save money in the long run.

You can get a good pet from any source, and many people out there can prove it. One friend of Gina's, for example, has a wonderful cat she found as a half-dead kitten in a dumpster. But your chances of getting a healthy, well-socialized kitten are best if you work with reputable shelters and rescue groups or reputable breeders. Nothing is more heartbreaking than falling in love with a kitten only to have your veterinarian tell you that your new companion tested positive for feline leukemia, a topic we cover in Chapter 12.

What does a feather have to do with picking out a kitten? Check out Chapter 5 for information on how to choose that one special companion from a litter of adorable babies or a shelter full of gorgeous homeless cats.

What You Need to Know about Shelters

A few years ago, Gina went to a conference for shelter workers and sat in on a seminar on making cats comfortable and keeping them healthy in the high-stress environment of a shelter. One of the presenters was a woman who'd made great changes in how her facility handled cats, and she had the pictures to prove it.

Previously, the cat facilities at her shelters had been a converted dog run with a lid on it to prevent escapes. All the cats were thrown into that run — and "thrown" is exactly how they got there. The only way a cat left that run was for adoption or death, and either way, the escape was the same: He was lassoed by a noose on the end of a pole and lifted out by the neck, hissing in anger and crying in terror. Imagine what a horrible impression a cat who'd been treated that way would make on a prospective adopter! (Not that the impression mattered much, however, because nearly all the cats were put to death at that horrid place.)

That shelter has changed so much today, and so have many others (sadly, though, not all). Cats and kittens are treated with more respect and caring, even at the end of their lives, and are housed in ways that make them feel more comfortable and keep them healthier, even in the challenging environment of a shelter. Many shelters today offer clean cages in a quiet area away from dogs, or multicat "colony" housing, making the surroundings as pleasant as possible for the cats. The shelter's door opens only one way for too many animals — the numbers of kittens and cats are greater than those of adoptive homes — but the best groups do everything they can to find new homes for their animals.

Creative outreach programs working in partnership with the media and with businesses such as pet-supply superstores take pets where the people are to increase the volume of adoptions. And shelters themselves are changing — after years of listening to people talk about avoiding the gloomy surroundings, progressive organizations are giving their buildings a face-lift to make them light, bright, and inviting. The best shelters have well-trained, caring staffs and a healthy core of volunteers to keep cats socialized and counsel potential adopters about their responsibilities to their new companion.

Today's shelter cats are more adoptable than ever before, thanks to programs that evaluate pets and perform basic health services — and some extraordinary ones — before animals are made available to the public. Forget your old ideas about shelters as nothing more than gloomy places for pets to die — *bright, clean, airy,* and *upbeat* are the words to describe many shelters today.

Making a decision about a shelter cat or kitten is difficult. You want to take them all, and the realization that some of these animals aren't going to find a new home softens even the hardest heart. But you aren't doing anyone any favors if you let your heart make all the decisions here. Take a friend to help keep you from settling — and make sure that your friend isn't a bigger mush than you are, or you may both end up with the wrong pet! Play it cool.

Be aware of some potential problems with shelter pets. Shelter kittens and cats are stressed, which puts them at higher risk for contracting upper respiratory infections, which are generally treatable. They can also come into contact with sick animals and contract feline leukemia (FeLV), feline infectious peritonitis (FIP), and feline immunodeficiency virus (FIV), which aren't curable. (For more information on these diseases, see Chapter 12.) To be fair, FIP can turn up in a cat from any source, and a kitten from any source that's not testing can turn up positive for FIV or FeLV.

Although most shelter cats — like most cats in general — are shorthaired and of no particular breed, purebred cats do show up in shelters, although not with the frequency of purebred dogs. You may never see a rare breed of cat — such as the Devon Rex or Havana Brown — show up at your local shelter, but if you're looking for a more common Persian or Siamese, keep shelters in mind. You could get the breed of your dreams at a very reasonable price. And because purebred cats get no special considerations in shelters, you're saving a life to boot.

All shelters are not the same. Some are run by municipal animal-control facilities, some by nonprofit humane organizations — and decent shelters exist in both categories. Good kittens and cats are in any shelter, no matter how run-down the facilities and demoralized the staff. After all, a cat can't help where he's dumped. But just as you can improve your odds of buying a healthy, happy kitten by choosing a reputable breeder, you can better the chance of a successful adoption by choosing a *progressive shelter,* one that visibly cares about the animals, the adopters, and its staff.

You probably aren't offered the choice of not spaying or neutering your shelter cat, because most shelters either do it for you or require that you do it as a condition of adoption. For more on spaying and neutering, see Chapter 16.

Animal-control shelters

Municipal animal-control facilities are perhaps the easiest to figure out. Finding homes for pets was not the reason these facilities were founded and is not their primary purpose to this day — although many of them do a good job of it, nonetheless.

Animal-control departments were formed to protect people from animal-borne menaces — primarily rabies. They remove dead animals and enforce regulations, such as those regarding the licensing of animals — a rabies-control measure even cats fall under in some areas — and the number and kind of animals people can keep. They respond to calls about vicious animals, as well as calls involving animals that disturb a neighborhood because of noise or odor. These departments also serve as a "convenience" to people who no longer want their pets, disposing of the animals through adoption, euthanasia, or, in some locales, sales to biomedical research.

Animal-control shelters have never been well-funded operations, and this situation hasn't improved in recent years. With so much required of them by law and so few resources, readying animals for adoption and counseling prospective adopters can't be at the top of the animal-control director's list of priorities. And yet, because of caring people in many of these departments and in the communities they serve, volunteers fill the gap at some shelters, offering adoption counseling and assisting with animal care.

Because of these programs, municipal animal-control shelters can be good places to adopt. But many of the private nonprofit shelters have the potential to be better, because their mandate has always put helping animals at the top of their lists.

Private nonprofit shelters

Private, nonprofit shelters come in all varieties. Some are squalid outfits that serve as little more than a fund-raising gimmick for the people in charge. Others are organizations with well-funded endowments and programs that not only help homeless animals but also work to improve conditions for all animals — and animal lovers — in their communities.

Most shelters fall somewhere in the middle: Their buildings could use some work, their budgets are always tight, and they do the best they can with what they have to provide for the animals in their community. Many good, loving pets are available at these shelters.

Don't forget the locals!

"Humane Society" and "Society for the Prevention of Cruelty to Animals" (SPCA) are generic terms freely used in the United States and Canada by animal organizations that have no connection to one another or to national organizations such as the Humane Society of the United States (HSUS), based in Washington, D.C., or the American Society for the Prevention of Cruelty to Animals, in New York City. And yet, local shelters are often stymied in their fund-raising efforts by people who have "given to the national organization" and consider their charitable efforts complete — even though money given to the HSUS and ASPCA is used to fund their own programs, not those of the local shelters.

Don't forget your local animal shelter or rescue groups when giving. These groups do the most for the animals in your community.

Some national animal organizations do a great deal for animals, but others seem to exist mostly to raise money. (The same can be said, of course, of smaller, local groups.) The newspaper *Animal People* does a great job reporting on the operations of animal groups large and small, publicizing good programs and wasteful ones alike. Each year, the nonprofit newspaper prints an overview of how the largest animal groups spend their money. For more information, contact Animal People, P.O. Box 960, Clinton, WA 98236. Or visit its Web site, at `www.animalpepl.org/`. Animal People is itself a nonprofit organization. To support the no-holds-barred reporting of animal issues, consider a contribution to these hard-working folks as well.

New buildings don't necessarily a good shelter make, but you certainly want to work with a shelter that clearly cares enough for its charges to make sure they're kept in areas that are clean and don't facilitate the spread of disease.

Shelter work is difficult and stressful, and employees and volunteers can suffer burnout quickly. A well-run shelter is as compassionate to its staff as it is to the animals, because one has a lot to bear on the treatment of the other. Look for a shelter where employees are helpful and knowledgeable and clearly interested in helping the shelter's animals find responsible new homes.

The best shelters have a good handle on a cat's history, health, and temperament before putting her up for adoption. They've also done what they can to enhance her chances of success in a new home through socialization and screening for the right home. They not only provide preadoption counseling but also offer behavioral advice after the adoption. Some even offer reduced-cost veterinary services for former shelter animals.

Look for ways to help the shelters that don't measure up. Usually, it's a question of money and volunteers, and you can do a lot to contribute in these categories. Contact your local shelter to find out how.

Figure 3-1:
Shelters offer plenty of adoptable animals to choose from — kittens and cats both.

Photograph by Richard D. Schmidt

Volunteer Rescue-and-Placement Groups

Thousands of small groups do what they can for cats without the benefit of a shelter building, and many of these organizations are excellent sources for pets. Made up of dedicated volunteers, these groups rescue and tame feral cats, hand-raise motherless kittens, find homes for cats and kittens who need them, and raise money to help spay and neuter the pets of people who can't afford the cost themselves, such as seniors on fixed incomes.

These groups fill a vital need. Some specialize in hard-to-place animals that a shelter may not even allow to be put up for adoption. By fostering cats in their homes, these grass-roots volunteers give hope to animals who are considered by some organizations to be too old, too young, too wild, or too disabled to be adoptable. With love and patience, many of these animals can turn around and become fine pets for people who understand their special needs.

Many of these community-based groups are involved with helping out colonies of feral cats, maintaining the adults in place and taming the babies to find them new homes. Because of the sea change in how wild cats are handled, we've pulled together the latest information into a brand-new Chapter 4.

The scoop on "no-kill" shelters

Those organizations that call themselves "no-kill" shelters are the subject of controversy in the animal-welfare community. Most shelters have far more pets than they can place, which sets up a grim game of "musical homes" that results in the death of millions of animals every year. No-kill shelters often get their name by refusing to accept animals that aren't adoptable or by refusing all animals if they're full. The turn-aways often end up at another shelter, one where the staff often very much resents having to be the bad guys that have to do the killing.

Some no-kill shelters have a fairly broad definition of "adoptable" that includes those animals who can be made adoptable through medical care or behavioral modification. These outfits also realize that the number of surplus animals will never fall unless the problem is resolved at the source. For that reason, they're aggressive about spaying and neutering, as well as helping people who are considering giving up their pets work through the problems. As the no-kill movement continues to develop, you'll see a lot more of these programs. And we think that's wonderful.

That said, we must say that as someone who's looking to adopt an animal, you shouldn't get distracted by policy debates. Look for a shelter offering healthy, well-socialized animals and adoption counseling to help you pick out the right one for you. The type of shelter with a well-trained staff and a solid volunteer corps is your best bet for a successful adoption, no matter what its policy on euthanasia.

Adopting a cat or kitten from a grass-roots community group is a wonderful way to reward these hard-working volunteers for selfless efforts on behalf of cats. It's worth the effort to seek out one of these groups when it's time to adopt a cat or kitten. Who knows? You may even decide to volunteer yourself!

Breeders: The Reputable, the Ill-Informed, and the Avoid-at-All-Costs

The Cat Fanciers' Association (CFA) estimates that a very small number of cats (less than 5 percent) are *pedigreed* — that is, registered with the CFA or another organization, such as The International Cat Association (TICA). Although around 50 individual breeds of cat are recognized by various groups around the world, most of these breeds are pretty rare. Many of the rarer breeds hardly show up in "ordinary" pet homes at all, because their breeders are dedicated to preserving and improving the lines and either keep most of their kittens or place them with other dedicated breeders.

The more-popular breeds, such as the Persian and Siamese, have many fanciers, including those folks who aren't the least bit interested in showing — they just want a good pet with a certain "look." A breeding industry has sprung up to service the market created by people who want "just a pet." Although this supply-and-demand plan may make sense, read on. Breeders who produce animals just for the pet market aren't usually your best choice.

A lot of people don't seem to realize that a cat is not like a piece of electronics. Finding a cat isn't a matter of searching for the right product like you were shopping for a multidisc CD player. Finding a cat isn't a matter of deciding on the right brand and then shopping aggressively for the best price and most convenient location.

Registration means nothing concerning a cat, and the breeder's knowledge and reputation mean everything. Think of a registry as being like the department of motor vehicles — you fill out the paperwork and send in the money, and the DMV sends back something that says, in effect, "Yep, it's a car." That slip of paper doesn't say a thing about the reliability of that car or whether the vehicle has a manufacturer's defect that can cause you trouble down the road. The department of motor vehicles didn't manufacture the car, and it's not guaranteeing quality.

The same is true of a feline registry, except most require even less in the way of proof that what they're registering even exists. Everything is done on the honor system. We surely don't need to tell you that where the possibility of making money exists, some people aren't very honorable. Others are well-meaning but just not knowledgeable enough about genetic problems and socialization to be breeding cats. You want to avoid both kinds of people if you're looking for a pedigreed cat.

Thinking of breeding your cat? In Chapter 16, we show you why breeding cats is both less profitable and more of an effort than you realize, how breeding puts your own pet at risk and makes him harder to live with, and how breeding contributes to the problems of surplus pets — even if you're thinking of breeding purebreds.

If you still want to breed cats, that same chapter includes a basic primer on matchmaking, kitten raising, and placement — the "good breeder" way.

Finding the elusive "good breeder"

A reputable breeder can be very hard to find and may not have a kitten available just when you want one — such as right now. Those facts alone send many buyers to other, less-than-ideal sources.

If everything goes well, you're going to have your cat for as many as 20 years. Doesn't taking a little time to find the right breeder seem reasonable? To make a few phone calls, read a book or two, search the Internet, and take a few field trips? To ask questions of a person who's lived for years with the breed you want so that you can get more answers than a book provides?

Figure 3-2: To find a healthy pedigreed cat such as this Persian, it's important to find a reputable breeder.

Photograph courtesy of Michael Brim, Cat Fanciers' Association

So what to look for? In most cases, you want someone who puts her best up against others in competition. A good breeder is almost certainly showing her cats — because how can she know she's creating excellent examples of her breed if she doesn't have them judged?

That's just the beginning. You want *expertise*. A pet store with a selection of kittens often can't provide you with information on the breed you want, because the staff, no matter how well-meaning, can usually offer only cursory information about the breeds the store stocks. A backyard breeder with one "let the kids watch" litter can tell you what living with her Siamese is like but hasn't the expertise to talk about the breed as a whole. And neither source, of course, is offering cats bred expressly for the top-quality health and temperament you should demand.

A serious, reputable breeder can tell you more than you could possibly imagine about the breed. The breeder's commitment to the kitten you buy doesn't end after the sale is final. You get a healthy, well-socialized kitten and technical support that would be the envy of any software company.

Shopping at the cat show

A cat show is the ultimate in window shopping for a cat lover and prospective kitten buyer. You want to find good breeders? Go where they turn up to show off their pride-and-joys. A cat show is the place.

Wander along the aisles with a smile on your face, and ask all the questions you want. Unless they're just getting ready to have their cat judged, most exhibitors are happy to talk — you're asking about one of their favorite subjects, after all: their cats!

You probably can't get all your questions answered, however, and you're likely to want to talk to the breeders later. So ask for business cards or write down phone numbers — along with notes about the conversation you had with each one so that you remember later what you discussed. Ask about kitten availability and planned breedings, but don't get too deep into it at the show — the breeder is pretty busy. Enjoy the day and all the gorgeous cats and plan your more serious discussions for later, by phone and in person.

We've put together a basic primer on how to find and enjoy a cat show in Chapter 2.

Check out the free educational materials that may be available at the show site. You can often find flyers for upcoming shows, along with informational material on the breeds, cat care, and cat charities. The people staffing the table are happy to answer your questions and are usually quite knowledgeable.

Perusing publications

Attending a show is probably the most enjoyable way to start tracking down a breeder, but you have other options, too.

Feline magazines offer breeder advertisements, as do a couple notable annuals, *Cats USA* (put out by the *Cat Fancy* folks) and the *Dogs In Canada* annual, which has a cats section. The registries also put out publications that carry breeder advertising, such as the *Cat Fanciers' Almanac*, the *CFA Yearbook*, the *TICA Trend*, or *TICA Yearbook*. Listings for these registries are in the Additional Resources appendix of this book, or you can check them out via the Cat Fanciers site at www.fanciers.com.

What do you mean I can't have a cat?

Some people are absolutely astonished — and more than a few are positively irate — if they're turned down while trying to adopt a cat, especially from a shelter or rescue group. After all, aren't they doing the shelter a favor by taking an animal off their hands?

That may not be how a shelter or rescue group sees it.

Reputable breeders of pedigreed cats have always put conditions on the sale of their animals. They want to ensure animals that aren't of breeding quality don't reproduce, and they want their kittens to go to homes where they can receive the kind of care the breeder feels is necessary. Reputable breeders can lay down the rules because they're dealing with only a litter at a time — and they're prepared to keep all their cats rather than place them in a home they may feel is unsuitable.

For shelter cats, however, the alternative to adoption is too often euthanasia. Isn't any home better than that?

"No," say some shelters. Spay-neuter requirements are common — and necessary, given the overpopulation of cats — but some groups require far more. They may turn down people who work all day or who travel "too much" or have young children in the home. They may require that the cat be kept indoors and not be declawed. Written approval by a landlord may be required before an animal is adopted out to someone who rents.

Our feeling is that these restrictions, although well-meaning, are sometimes too inflexible. And, in fact, many of these regulations are created not for the benefit of the animals but to appease and appeal to donors who fund the organizations. We feel that these are honorable and good people and organizations, but we suggest to many of the larger fund-raising organizations that it is time to reevaluate their policies and to look at what has driven policies to be what they are today.

These organizations need to be more flexible when it comes to adoptions. Although some children can be dangerous to a tiny kitten, for example, others are gentle and respectful. Some owners who travel take far better care of their pets than do those who're home all the time. Each person should be evaluated on a case-by-case basis.

What if you're turned down? Take a little time to consider again whether you're really ready for a cat — these rules, after all, are based on the shelter's experiences with people who generally don't make good cat owners. If you're still convinced that you're qualified, ask to discuss the matter with the shelter director — or go to another source.

Some questions for the breeder

Reputable breeders are not only happy to answer questions but also welcome them as the sign of the caring buyer they want to share their cats and kittens with. You can find out a lot about the breeder by asking a few questions. Try these and listen carefully for the right answer:

✔ **How long have you been breeding cats? How many breeds do you have? Do you show? Why or why not?** You're looking for someone who has been breeding cats long enough to know what she's doing. Someone who concentrates on one breed, or maybe two or three related ones. Showing? It's a sign of someone who's not just into breeding to make a buck.

✔ **What congenital defects are in this breed? How are you breeding to avoid those defects?** You want someone who's up-front and knowledgeable about problems in the breed, and someone who's actively working to minimize them.

✔ **How large is your breeding operation? Where do your cats spend most of their time?** You're looking for someone who isn't overwhelmed with cats, so each kitten can get the care and socialization that are so important. Make sure you get a look "behind the scenes" to ensure the cats are kept in healthy conditions — don't just take the breeder's word for it.

✔ **Are your cats tested for infectious diseases? May I have the kitten checked out by my veterinarian before I adopt?** A reputable breeder keeps his cattery clear of preventable illness by making sure infectious diseases don't exist among his cats in the first place and by never allowing cats who haven't tested negative for these diseases to interact with his cats. As for a vet check . . . it's always important to get a professional opinion.

✔ **What sort of health guarantees do you offer? What happens if the kitten gets sick?** Not even the most reputable of breeders can offer a 100 percent guarantee that your kitten is going to stay healthy. Your pet may become ill within days of your bringing her home, or she may manifest congenital health defects months or even years later. A reputable breeder, shelter, or rescue group is going to want to play fair and is prepared to compensate you for some of the financial loss — although sadly, not the personal one — should your new kitten become ill or die.

✔ **What makes this kitten or cat "pet quality" or "show quality"?** Most people looking for a pedigreed cat end up with "pet quality" because of the large expense associated with acquiring "show quality" cats and because breeders prefer to place their "best" cats with people whom they know intend to show them. A knowledgeable, reputable breeder can honestly assess a kitten's show potential and explain what "defect" classifies the animal as pet quality.

A pet-quality cat is in no way a lesser companion. Very few cats are born with the traits they need to be truly competitive in the show world. Their markings may be wrong, or their coats may not be lush enough. Their ears may not fold forward or curl back as their show standards dictate, or their "expression" may not match the ideal for their breed. These missing traits don't mean those kittens aren't beautiful or loving. As long as their faults aren't health- or temperament-related, such cats are wonderful prospects for purchase or adoption.

These publications do not screen breeders, however, so proceed with caution. If you can't find anyone locally for the breed you want, call the nearest advertised breeder. If he's a reputable breeder, he likely belongs to a national or regional breed club and can give you a referral to a breeder nearer to you — if one is around.

Spotting the less-than-ideal breeders

A very few breeders are downright evil and fail to provide for even the basics of their animals' needs. A few more are mentally ill, living in filthy homes packed to the rafters with freely mating cats. These people are fairly easy to spot and avoid — unless their kittens are cleaned up and sold elsewhere.

The majority of "bad" breeders — "backyard breeders," as they're commonly known — are not uncaring. They're just uninformed. They don't know that many of the cats they produce can end up in shelters or spend their lives in pain from a congenital illness. They just want a litter "so the kids can see" or because "kittens are fun" or because they heard that breeding cats is an easy way to make a little money. They aren't bad people, but they're still not good breeders.

Following are a few things that should give you pause in dealing with a breeder:

- ✔ **Lack of knowledge about the breed:** Someone who doesn't know much about the breed, its history, or its standard isn't someone who's too concerned about producing kittens that are fine examples of the breed.

- ✔ **Ignorance or denial of genetic defects:** Many breeds have some problems, some of which can be avoided by careful breeding. A person who isn't aware of congenital defects certainly isn't planning her breedings to avoid them.

- ✔ **No involvement showing cats:** You improve the odds of getting a high-quality purebred if you buy from someone involved in showing or otherwise involving their cats in competition. Such involvement suggests a level of commitment that's likely also to be present in the care of the cats.

- ✔ **Not letting you observe the litter, meet the mother or other cats, or see where the kittens were raised:** Healthy, well-mannered adults and a clean, well-run cattery are a breeder's best testimonial. If a person doesn't want you to see anything except the kitten she's trying to sell, you ought to be wondering why.

- ✔ **No documentation:** If the kitten's represented as "CFA registered," the registration papers should be available. (The same goes for other registries, too.) So, too, should the papers backing up health claims. A sales contract spelling out the rights and responsibilities of both parties is highly desirable. Such a document provides you with recourse should the kitten not turn out as promised — if it has congenital health problems, for example, or isn't suitable for showing, if that was part of your intent in buying him.

✔ **Doesn't seem to understand the importance of socialization:** Kittens need to be nurtured, loved, and handled to make good pets. Someone who can't explain what they've done in this area or who tries to sell a kitten less than 12 weeks old probably doesn't understand enough to be breeding cats.

Such caution is all about increasing the odds of success. Can you find a pedigreed kitten who's going to be a good pet from a backyard breeder advertising in your local newspaper? Without a doubt. But you're more likely to find one if you take the time to find a reputable, knowledgeable breeder.

Pet Stores: What about Those Kittens in the Window?

You don't need to put much effort into buying a pedigreed kitten at a pet store. Pet stores usually stock kittens of the most popular breeds by the handful — and maybe some mixes, too. If you go to a pet store, you don't need to talk to breeders, do your homework, or wait, either. Pet stores may offer some health guarantees. And they take credit cards. What could be better or more convenient?

A growing number of U.S. pet supply stores refuse to sell kittens (or puppies) because of concerns over commercial breeders and pet overpopulation. Instead, they offer space in their stores to local shelters or rescue groups to reach out to prospective adopters. Above all, know your source. Realize that obtaining a kitten or cat is best accomplished by being an informed consumer. Some people have ended up with a pet they truly love from a retail pet store.

Your Neighbor's (Or Coworker's) Kittens

So what about that litter of kittens a coworker or neighbor is offering up for free? You have no real reason not to consider them if they meet your requirements and they're healthy and well socialized.

Those are pretty big "ifs," however. Take a kitten from a "free-to-a-good-home" source and you may end up with more problems than you imagined. If the kitten turns up positive for feline leukemia or a treatable health problem, do you have any recourse against the person from whom you got the kitten? Hardly. The chances are high the mother was never tested for disease and the father was unknown.

Consider such a litter if you want; many people have done just fine by adopting from such a source. But make sure that your kitten is healthy and socialized and try as best as you can to suggest that your pet and her littermates be the very last that the mother cat produces.

Adult cats are a slightly different matter. They're offered up for a lot of different reasons, some as frivolous as a change of decor, some as unavoidable as the death of an owner or the development of a child's serious allergy to cats. Many of these displaced kitties are wonderful pets, and you have no reason not to adopt one, as long as you make sure that the cat is healthy and isn't being placed for behavior problems, such as avoiding the litter box. If everything checks out, give one of these guys a chance!

Chapter 4

Ferals: Special Cats, Special Considerations

*I*f you've ever put a saucer of milk out for a hard-luck kitty, or if you're spending your lunch hour sharing sandwiches with the ferals near your office, this is the chapter for you. We added this new information to this edition in hopes of helping the estimated 60 million cats in the United States who live wild and need our help to survive.

Perhaps because the cat of all our animal companions chose their own path to domestication, it's only natural that many cats should live still in the shadowed zone between tame and wild. In the alleyways of our largest cities, the parks of our ubiquitous suburbs, and the rural spaces in between, millions of cats spend their lives living just out of our reach.

The feral life is not an easy one, to be sure. Feral cats — domestic cats living a wild life — breed constantly, with each young mother producing as many as three litters a year. Of those kittens, few live to maturity. Those cats who do live to see their first or second birthdays struggle to live much beyond them. Starvation, disease, predators, and traffic take a heavy toll.

Cats become feral when people don't care for them, or don't care about what happens to them. For example, people move and leave their cats behind. Or people let their cats breed and don't pay attention to the fate of the kittens. Or people figure that their cat can do just fine on his own, and they drop the hapless kitty along a country road or in a city park because they don't want the responsibility of caring for him anymore.

On top of everything else, feral cats must contend with people who believe them to be pests and who therefore decide that the best way to deal with them is to exterminate them. Until recently, these beliefs were nearly universal. Communities dealt with the problems caused by feral cats — real or imagined — by trapping and killing them.

More than a few cat lovers knew there just had to be a better way to deal with these homeless cats. These cat lovers were determined to find a better way and they did. In a little more than a decade, the future for ferals has brightened considerably, with programs designed both to lessen the numbers of cats on the street and to help the cats who remain live more comfortably.

One person can make a difference. Progressive thinking — and action, in an increasing number of communities — is decreasing the population of feral cats and helping those who remain to live healthier lives while minimizing the potential for conflict and controversy.

Help for the Wild Ones

It's only fair that feral cats have human help to make their way in life easier, because humans were largely responsible for the problem in the first place. Because cats are so adaptable to their environment, and because they can manage pretty well on both sides of the line dividing "wild" from "tame," many people let their pet cats cross that line — or throw them across it by abandoning them. And when cats go wild, they . . . well, go wild. They pick up the natural wariness of all wild creatures. And they breed, and breed, and breed.

Feral cats have always been around and will always be around. But we can do something about their numbers and their suffering. And we should.

Finding the solution that isn't

We're going to go out on a limb here and say that any plan for dealing with feral cats that includes rounding them up and killing them is based on an idea that needs updating. These catch-and-kill plans don't work (at least not for long) because they ignore the fact that as long as people keep allowing their cats to breed, and keep dumping their unwanted cats, feral cat colonies will keep re-establishing themselves, year after year after year. A couple of cats, then a couple dozen, then more — and it's time for the great round-up again.

Because we're faced with a never-ending supply of cats, the old idea of mass killings cries out for an alternative, one that lessens the impact of ferals while dealing with them in the most humane way possible. How can we, as cat lovers, settle for anything less?

Offering a new way of thinking: Trap, Neuter, Release

If you accept the idea that feral cats will always be around, then wouldn't it be better to make dealing with them easier on the environment, the animal-control budget, and the cats themselves? Enter the idea of managed care for feral cats — Trap, Neuter, and Release.

Trap, neuter, and release is a proven method of humanely dealing with wild cats. Millions of people feed feral cats — from the person who sets out some tuna for the cat who hangs around the back door, to those dedicated souls you can find at any pet-supply store, stocking up on large bags of whatever food's on sale. What if these caretakers went one step further and slowed down the rate of feral reproduction? Could a cat colony be managed in place? Some tried it, and the answer soon became obvious: Yes, there was a better way.

The people who hauled 20-pound bags of cat food to the cats they wouldn't let starve, who named the adults, and who tried to find homes for the kittens decided to try an extraordinary idea: Alter the cats and let them go again. (We talk about how to manage feral cats with this humane strategy later in this chapter.)

Spaying or neutering a feral cat never seemed to be worth the effort, at least as far as officials in many communities were concerned. If you trapped a wild cat, the reasoning went, killing him seemed to make more sense than altering him. With so many more docile cats and kittens around, a feral is a poor prospect as a pet. So why not just do him in?

Perhaps they were just trying to end the heartbreak of seeing litter after litter of kittens born into a very hard life. But before too long, some feral cat caretakers started realizing that their efforts to control the feral cat population were working out better than they had imagined possible. They discovered that a policy of "trap, neuter, and release" goes a long way toward taming the problems of cats gone wild.

If you're one of those people with a soft spot for ferals, you're certainly in good company. One animal group has estimated that 17 million people feed feral cats.

But aren't these cats pests?

People hate and fear feral cats for any number of reasons, and those who care for feral cat colonies have to argue their way past a whole mountain of objections in their efforts to have cat colonies managed rather than destroyed. But it turns out that the needs of the cats, and the concerns of both those who love them and those who hate them, can be solved through the management of feral colonies.

Programs in the United States are modeled after those in the United Kingdom and other European countries, as well as parts of Africa. Successful programs in the United States include those assisted by shelters such as the San Francisco SPCA, as well as small grassroots groups dedicated to managing cat colonies.

If you work on behalf of feral cats, you need some help to counter those who think your efforts don't make much sense. The following list covers the most common objections and explains how a trapping, neutering, and releasing program helps:

- ✔ **So long as cats remain, so will the problem.** Well, maybe, but you aren't going to get rid of feral cats. Studies have shown that as long as a source of food exists, feral cats will move in. Institutions such as college campuses, military bases, and hospitals are tailor-made environments for feral cats. Where there is food, there will be cats. It makes sense to try something that has been shown to work elsewhere.

- ✔ **Feral cats fight and are noisy.** *Unaltered* feral cats fight and are noisy. Cats are breeding machines: Females are in heat virtually all the time they're not pregnant, and males spend their time fighting and yowling for mates and territory. Neutering removes a lot of this behavior.

- ✔ **Feral cats can trip people, or even attack people, causing liability for the property owner.** As much as possible, feral cat colonies are fed away from areas where people are numerous. Ferals are by nature afraid of people. If they don't have to go near them to find food, they usually won't.

- ✔ **Feral cats have more kittens than can possibly survive, and dead animals are a health hazard.** In a managed cat colony, neutering keeps animals from reproducing. Instead of dozens of sick or dying kittens, a managed colony produces a few babies who can be caught, altered, tamed, and placed.

- ✔ **Feral cats cause traffic accidents, as drivers swerve to avoid hitting a loose cat.** Altered cats don't need to roam in search of mates, and well-fed cats don't need to roam in search of food. The chance of a feral cat turning up under the wheel of a car is lessened when the animal is content to stay in territory where he feels safe and knows he'll be fed.

- ✔ **Feral cats are carriers of disease.** In a managed colony, cats are vaccinated for rabies (which can be transmitted to humans) and tested for feline leukemia and other diseases that can be transmitted cat to cat. Cats infected with feline leukemia are not released; they're either put in a single-cat home with an understanding owner or humanely killed.

A special concern is *toxoplasmosis,* a disease that can cause birth defects, and that can be transmitted through contact with the feces of an infected cat. Actually, you put yourself at a higher risk for toxoplasmosis by handling improperly cooked meat than by handling a cat. Keeping cats away from areas of heavy human traffic keep whatever risks there are minimal.

For the birds

Don't feral cats eat birds? Cats aren't native to a wild environment, and birds are. Shouldn't we be worried about protecting endangered birds?

Of course we should. But feral cats aren't the biggest threat to wild birds — people are. Consider: Feral cats have always been around, and so have birds. But now bird numbers are declining. Are cats to blame? Nope. The bigger threat to birds is loss of habitat, not cats.

Besides, when cats hunt, they're better at catching rodents. You could argue that feral cats do us a favor by keeping the rodent population down — and those critters really do spread some nasty diseases.

Cats aren't a fraction of the threat to birds that humankind represents. And a feral cat colony that's well maintained is even less of a threat than one that's not. A managed colony doesn't grow, and isn't as hungry. Fewer cats, and fuller cats, are both good news for birds.

Toxoplasmosis is a legitimate worry for pregnant women, but you can reduce the risks significantly by taking a few basic precautions. Please see Chapter 19 for tips on how to handle your cat safely while you're expecting. As for diseases that put your pet at risk, the best way to protect your cat is to keep him inside, and work with your veterinarian to decide which vaccinations are right. Check out Chapter 11 for more on vaccinations and information on rabies.

Getting Your Feet Wet: How to Help

You don't have to care for every homeless cat in your community to start making a big difference in the lives of ferals. Everyone can help, in many small ways that all add up. You just have to care enough to make the effort.

First, do no harm

Feral cats are there because people put them there, or let them go wild. You can help be a part of the solution by making sure no cat you know adds to the problem. We offer a few ideas to get you started:

- ✔ Consider keeping your own pet cat indoors. A cat can lead a perfectly healthy, happy life without ever setting a paw outdoors. You'll always know where your cat is and who she's hanging out with if you keep your pet inside — and you also know for sure that your cat won't end up a feral. (We offer tips on changing a free-roaming cat to an indoor one in Chapter 6, as well as tips to keep indoor cats happy in Chapter 23.)

✔ Alter your cat. Cats who are spayed or neutered make better pets. Spayed females aren't always crying for mates, and neutered males are less likely to spray urine. And if your cat doesn't reproduce, you don't need to worry about finding responsible homes for the kittens. One unspayed female, if allowed to breed freely, can be responsible for thousands of kittens, as her kittens breed, and their kittens breed and so on. A simple fix is all it takes, and it can be done as early as 8 weeks. (For more on neutering, see Chapter 16.)

Helping the helpers

You don't have to actually do the hands-on work of caring for cats to help the feral cat population. You can get involved by simply supporting those people and groups who do. Here are a couple of suggestions:

✔ Support feral cat management with your voice, your vote, and your donations. Let your community government know that you oppose any program that has a goal of eradicating ferals. Write letters, go to hearings, and let your voice be heard on this issue. Support nonprofit groups in your community that put trap, neuter, and release programs in place. The support doesn't always have to be monetary. You can contribute items for a group's garage sale fund-raisers, or you can donate materials — everything from old towels to cars — that the groups use in their work.

✔ You may be able to find other cat rescuers by asking at your local shelter or by checking with pet-supply stores that offer adoption space to community groups.

✔ Considering adopting a formerly feral cat or kitten. Even in areas where cats are trapped, neutered, and released, a few kittens always manage to be born. And no matter how hard animal activists work to educate, some people always figure that dumping a cat is easier than finding him a home. Kittens and domesticated cats are often available for adoption from feral cat groups, and are something to consider when you're thinking of getting a cat. (For help in selecting a cat or kitten, see Chapter 5.)

Feeding feral cats: Help or harm?

Feeding feral cats without caring for them otherwise isn't very helpful. Some people do this on a grand scale, and we have no doubt their hearts are in the right place. But feeding feral cats who haven't been neutered leads to a population explosion, with all the problems that entails. In the end, your cats may be fruitful and multiply to the point where they become a real nuisance, and when that happens, someone will call for their removal.

If you feed feral cats, we're not suggesting you should stop. Your cats have come to rely on you, after all, and to stop feeding will hurt them. Instead, get educated on how to keep population levels down and cats healthy, and see whether you can find help in your community to get your colony under control.

Not ready to take that big a step? Then maybe you'd better think twice before offering your tuna sandwich for the very first time to a feral cat. If you *are* ready to take that step, the information you need to get started is in this chapter.

Learning to Care for Feral Cats

Caring for feral cats is not a responsibility to be taken lightly, nor is it a short-term project. The animals will come to rely on you. If you don't believe you can handle the long-term commitment of caring for cats, it's really best not to start.

But if you are ready to really help the wild ones, you don't have to re-invent the wheel. By following the lead of other cat-lovers, you can make learning how to manage a cat colony — including trapping cats to be altered and released — as easy as possible.

Strength really is in numbers! Working with an established group, or at the very least with another person as committed as you are, makes caring for feral cats much easier. Having someone to share the good days and the bad can mean the difference between burning out and continuing to help the cats who need it most.

You can find excellent information about caring for feral cats on the Internet. We include a couple such Web sites in Chapter 21.

Setting up a routine

If you already feed feral cats, you're ahead of the game. If not, you need to get your ferals on a routine, which makes it easier to trap them later. Seeing your cats every day also allows you to monitor any changes in the group and to be aware of newcomers, pregnancies, or new kittens.

Cats are creatures of habit. If they know that food appears in a certain place, at a certain time, you can be sure they'll be there. Pick a time that's convenient for you and a spot that's away from high-traffic areas.

Critter quandry

Gina has a former coworker who called her one day about the feral cats on the property she'd just bought. The woman was a lifelong dog owner who'd never paid that much attention to cats, but suddenly she was dealing with a dozen of them every day. The cats expected her to pick up the feeding duties that the previous property owner had taken on.

The woman didn't know what to do. "Can you tell me who to call?" she said. "I need someone to pick up these cats and find them good homes. I'll be home this weekend, if that's convenient."

Gina let her know as gently as possible that she was pretty much on her own with her new cats, and told her about the choices she would have to make on their behalf. She guessed the advice would fall on deaf ears, and she'd never hear about the cats again.

Gina guessed wrong. The woman did her research and decided to trap, neuter, and release the cats. A year later, their numbers had stabilized, and the cats were doing well. And the woman came to enjoy their presence!

Feeding your cats and then taking the leftover food away makes them more interested in turning up on time for dinner. Removing food after your cats are done also prevents wildlife from getting into it and helps keep rodent populations in check.

Once you start feeding them, they're your responsibility — every day. And that's why you'll find the role of caretaker much easier if you find someone with whom to share the job. That way, illness and vacations won't mean hungry cats, and you can reduce your chance of burnout.

Lining up help

Because the heart of a compassionate program of caring for cats gone wild involves trapping and neutering, you need some help from the beginning to understand how to use these tools.

Tracking down traps

If the word *trap* is conjuring up some ghastly leg-hold bit of cruelty, please stop worrying. The traps used to capture cats are designed to catch and hold them safely. Made of sturdy wire, these boxlike cages have a door that snaps shut when a cat enters — holding the animal until help can arrive.

Perhaps the most convenient source of traps and advice on how to use them is your local animal-control department. Many lend out traps for free to citizens who put down a deposit to ensure the equipment will be returned.

Figure 4-1:
Box traps are designed to lure cats inside and then hold them safely until help arrives.

If you're trying to work with cats on a university campus, hospital, or military base, check with the maintenance department to see whether they have traps — most do, although you may need to go through some paperwork to use them.

Although borrowing traps is probably the best way to get started, you can also buy them directly from the same companies that sell to animal-control departments. One such source is Tomahawk Live Trap, P.O. Box 323, Tomahawk, WI 54487; www.livetrap.com.

Setting up veterinary care

After you trap a cat, you need a place to take him. In other words, you need a veterinarian.

Talk to your own veterinarian first. She may well be interested in your project and willing to help, and even if she's not, she's likely a good source of referral to other veterinarians who are more actively involved in the care of feral cats.

What you're asking your veterinarian to do is make a charitable contribution, of her time and her staff's time, and of her equipment and supplies. Spaying, in particular, is major surgery, and veterinarians routinely do it at a loss, as their contribution to helping combat animal overpopulation.

Don't forget to check with your local humane society in your search for veterinarians who are interested in helping out. Some shelters have veterinarians on staff to provide low- or no-cost neutering, or they can refer to those in the community who donate a certain amount of surgeries each month.

Be sure that the veterinarian is aware that you'll be bringing in feral cats. These animals are more difficult to handle, and the staff needs a heads-up before you bring any trapped cat in. Good communication is the key to working with your veterinarian under any circumstances, and that's doubly true when you're dealing with these special needs cats.

Veterinarians make a notch in the ear of a feral cat after neutering. That way, if the cat is ever trapped again, cat caretakers and veterinarians will know that the surgery has already been performed.

Trapping cats

After you have your trap and your veterinarian is on standby, you're ready to get down to the business of catching cats. Make sure that the trap is clean to start with. Scrub with hot, soapy water and follow with a spray of diluted bleach (a half cup of bleach to a gallon of water will do). If you can manage it, prepare several traps at once. Cats quickly become wary of the traps after seeing others caught, and your best chance may well be a mass trapping.

Stop feeding your cats for a couple days before you put traps out. You want them hungry!

Set the trap in a protected area, such as under a bush, or in the shade of a fence or building. Cover the trap with an old towel or blanket to make the cat feel more secure after he has been captured.

If you set out more than one trap, position them so that they're out of sight of one another. Set the trap according to the instructions that came with it, and choose something irresistible as bait. A common recommendation is canned cat food, with a big spoonful of tuna canned in oil on top. Another hit with ferals — canned mackerel, which is relatively inexpensive and very smelly!

Check your traps every three hours or so — and more frequently in cold or hot weather. Traps offer no protection against the elements. A trapped cat is also vulnerable to attack by dogs or by people intent on mayhem.

After you have a cat trapped, don't attempt to remove him from the cage — you'll be bitten. Keep the cage covered and use the handle to transport the cat, cage and all. Your veterinarian and her staff are trained and experienced at handling less-than-cooperative cats. Don't risk a bite!

Neutering cats

Discuss with your veterinarian what medical care the cat needs in addition to altering. You'll likely want the animals tested for infectious disease, treated for parasites, and vaccinated. Any cat who turns up positive for feline leukemia (FeLV) or feline immunodeficiency virus (FIV) should be placed in a single-cat home, if possible, or humanely killed. A tough call, to be sure, but part of the deal when you care for feral cats.

Remind your veterinarian to use absorbable material for closing the wound made by altering. Once you've turned a neutered feral loose again, you won't be able to catch the animal again to have stitches removed.

If the cat or kitten you've brought in is destined to be tamed for a future as a pet, ask the veterinarian to trim the animal's claws. Taking the sharp tips off the claws will make the cat much easier for you to handle.

Releasing cats

Bring a carrier to the veterinarian so the animal doesn't have to be returned to the trap — you'll need that for more trapping after all. Your veterinarian will put the cat in your carrier while he's still unconscious. Take him home and leave him in the carrier, in a quiet place. Have food and water available, but leave him alone otherwise. When the cat is fully conscious, he can be released to his old stomping grounds.

Line the carrier with newspapers, and with an old towel. The cat will likely relieve himself when he wakes up, so you want something absorbent in the carrier to keep him as comfortable as possible.

Figure 4-2: Cats should be spayed as soon as kittens are weaned, to prevent "more littering."

Miss Parker/Photograph by Susan R. Scheide

Taming the ones you can

Because of the sheer numbers of cats available for adoption, you'll be doing what's best for feral cats by making sure as few as possible are born. But what do you do with the kittens? And what about the cats themselves? Are there homes out there for them?

Adult cats are a hard sell, and not enough homes are out there for friendly, tamed cats, much less wild ones. For the most part, any feral adults you trap will be neutered and released back into the colony. The same is true of any kitten past the "adorable" stage. Once they get leggy and lose that kittenish appeal, you'll find it nearly impossible to place them, so you probably ought to neuter and release even these youngsters.

If a cat suddenly turns up and seems well fed and in good health, chances are that he is a stray or has been dumped. Many of these cats are friendly — they were pets, after all — and may be the exception to the rule. Even if a little skittish when trapped, these strays will likely settle down quickly and relish a second chance to be a loving pet. By all means try to find an owner through flyers, newspaper ads, and so on, but don't be disappointed if no one responds.

Young kittens have the best chance of being tamed and placed. If you catch them young enough and take your time, many will tame quite nicely.

Patience is the key

Feral kittens have been taught by their mothers to be wary of humans, and it takes some time to counter that training. The younger the kitten when she's removed from the wild, the better — an ideal age is from 5 to 8 weeks old.

You may end up with a kitten who's younger than 5 weeks, sometimes because the mother has been killed, other times because that's when you were able to trap the baby. Your veterinarian can help you determine the age of your kitten. If the kitten is too young for solid foods, your veterinarian can provide you with formula and show you how and how often to bottle-feed.

A feral kitten is not going to react in the same way a kitten who has been born to a pet cat will. You have to know that up front. Your kitten will hiss and spit in fear, and she may well try to bite you if you come close. You must be willing to take your time and help the kitten adjust gradually. Kittens born wild are rarely sociable with large groups of people, but many form a tight and loving bond with the one person they trust.

While you're gently getting a feral kitten used to the idea of human contact, he's thinking of contact of a different variety. Even the littlest cats have formidable teeth and claws and will use them when they think they're in danger. Cat bites and scratches are not to be taken lightly. Wear long sleeves and protective gloves around feral cats and never try to grab a cat who's wriggling free. Let him go. (This applies to fully domesticated cats as well.)

Gentle handling over time

Before you start taming your kitten or cat, make a trip to your veterinarian. You want to make sure the animal isn't deathly ill, and you need to have him treated for any problems and vaccinated as your veterinarian recommends. Discuss neutering as well — the procedure is now done on pets as young as 8 weeks of age.

When you get your kitten home, set her up in a cage or carrier with food, water, and a cat box, preferably located in a quiet, lightly trafficked room with an easy-to-clean floor and a door you can keep closed. And then let her be. She'll need to chill for a while.

At this stage, visit the kitten frequently, but resist the urge to handle her. Talk to her and leave a radio playing when you're gone, but stay strictly *hands off* for the first two days. After a couple of days, an easy way to socialize a wild one is to bring the animal's carrier into a corner of the busiest part of the house — like the kitchen. Cover the entire carrier except the front grill to make the cat feel more secure while she gets used to the sights, sounds, and smells of a human household.

When the kitten seems to have settled down some, use a towel to gently catch and hold the animal, getting her used to being handled. Watch those teeth and claws: A scratch behind the ear probably won't be too objectionable to the youngster, but one beneath the chin will likely get you bitten.

Keep petting sessions very short. Better to build on a small amount of trust than to scare a kitten and have to go back to the beginning.

After the youngster seems more comfortable around you, let her graduate from the carrier or cage to a small room. Leave a carrier with the door propped open as a "safe haven" that can provide security and a warm place to sleep. Let her come to you. Don't try to pull her from the carrier or from behind a favorite hiding place. Make use of her natural playfulness to help forge a bond: Use a toy-on-a-string to lure the kitten into a chase game. Treats are another way to convince a kitten that you're a friend.

Your kitten will do best if placed fairly soon into her new home. We include tips on how to find a good home for a cat or kitten in Chapter 16, and the same strategies work for the formerly feral. Just be honest about the animal's past and shortcomings. Some people relish the opportunity to take on the challenge of a cat with special needs!

Part II

Bringing a Cat or Kitten into Your Life

The 5th Wave   By Rich Tennant

"Oh, he loves his string and ball, but once in a while he'll take out his little pottery wheel and spin bud vases out of modeling clay all afternoon."

In this part . . .

This part explains how to test the personality of a cat or kitten to help choose the right individual for you. Should you consider two kittens at once? How about taming a wild kitten or cat. We offer both the pros and the cons. You also find out how to introduce your new pet to the current residents of your home, not only your children but also other cats, dogs, and pets of all sorts. Finally, we tell you exactly what you need in the way of supplies to keep your cat happy and healthy.

Chapter 5

Choosing Your Feline Companion

・・・

In This Chapter

▶ Considering a cat's background and environment

▶ Determining which kitten is right for you

▶ Evaluating the adult cat

▶ Looking for signs of good health in kittens and adult cats

・・・

*I*s the old saying about cats true, that you choose a dog, but a cat chooses you? Not really. Although sometimes a cat just walks into your life and sets up housekeeping in your heart, the days are gone for most of us when all you had to do to get a cat was set a saucer of milk on the back-porch step.

So where can you find an "ordinary" cat? (We use that term guardedly, because every cat is a unique work of art and love.) They're everywhere! In the warmer months that mean "kitten season," you can hardly turn around without someone trying to give you an adorable ball of baby cat fluff. A litter of tabbies is advertised on the bulletin board at work. Your neighbor waited too long to spay her kitten, and wants you to look at a tuxedo-marked kitten, so handsome. You pause outside the grocery store to look at the kittens some children are giving away out of a cardboard box. And you know that in your local shelter the number of choices is multiplied many times over and tinged with the sense of urgency for the kittens and cats for whom time is rather quickly running out.

Choose with your head, looking for the animal most likely to fit in with your life and your expectations. Choose with your heart, for the love between you is a bond that will sustain both of you for years.

No matter your choice, however, always remember how lucky you are to be able to bring a cat into your life. Living with a cat's companionship is truly one of life's sweetest pleasures — one that is soon to be yours for many years to come, if you take your time at this stage of the game.

Figure 5-1:
A cat is a lifetime of love and commitment. Take your time when choosing one.

Natasha/photograph by Elizabeth Cárdenas-Nelson

If you haven't so much as thought about the gender of the cat you want — much less the breeding or age — take a look at Chapter 2. If you're still not sure whether you're cat material, Chapter 1 can help you decide. And finally, Chapter 3 helps you evaluate the places to get a kitten or adult cat — from your coworker to a pet store to a breeder to a shelter — in hopes of avoiding the biggest mistakes people make when adopting an adult cat or kitten.

Evaluating the Environment

The first step in choosing a kitten or adult cat is not looking at the animal herself, or her littermates, but the environment in which she has been raised. After all, you're looking to adopt an animal companion, well socialized and healthy.

Domestication is a product of heredity and upbringing, and few of our closest animal companions are as able to step back and forth across the line between wild and tame as nimbly as the cat. The cat is able to fend for herself on the edges of human society, hunting and scavenging and carving out a life with little human intervention, and even less human contact — at least for a while, for the lives of these feral cats are often very short.

The difference between cats who live on the streets and the ones purring contentedly in the lap of human luxury can be summed up in two words: luck and socialization.

For an animal to be comfortable around humans, he must know that humans aren't his enemy. For an animal to love human companionship, he must be *socialized,* carefully and frequently, usually from an early age. Behaviorists working with all kinds of animals have known this fact for decades; more recent research applies it specifically to the cat.

Before their eyes even open, kittens begin learning and becoming comfortable with their world. If humans (or other animals, such as dogs) are part of this world, cats become better pets as a result, more loving and attentive. Without the human touch when young, all the subsequent kindness and socialization in the world doesn't count for as much: Your cat will probably always be a little tentative and shy.

Although socialization is probably the most important factor to consider when evaluating a kitten, there are others. The quality of care that the mother cat gives her kittens, for example, depends upon the quality of care she herself receives. Cats are resourceful, courageous, and dedicated mothers, doing their best to provide for their young under the most challenging conditions. No matter how hard a mother cat tries to care for her babies, however, the stresses of a life of deprivation can have a negative effect on her kittens. Studies have shown that when a mother cat isn't adequately fed, her kittens develop slowly physically and may never catch up mentally or emotionally.

Proper care of the mother and frequent handling of the kittens are essential to the creation of a loving, outgoing, and relaxed feline companion. That said, we must admit to knowing more than a few former ferals who've done okay as pets. They take more time and patience, though, so you need to be aware.

We evaluate pet stores and shelters, breeders good and not-so-good, and all the other sources for kittens in Chapter 3. In this chapter, we assume that you've weighed your choices and chosen the right source, and now it's time to choose the right pet from that source. If you don't know the pros and cons — including some rather disturbing ones — of various sources, it pays to review them in Chapter 3. As for feral cats, we talk about these special cats in our brand-new Chapter 4, including a section on taming them.

Getting a read on a kitty's history

So what do you do in order to find out about a kitten's or adult cat's history? Sit down with him and say: "Tell me about your kittenhood"? Unfortunately, it's not that easy. Some cats are talkative to the extreme, but actual words tend to fail them. To find out about a cat's past, you have to be a little more observant — look and listen for the clues that suggest you have a cat with whom you can live.

In some cases, especially with kittens, finding out about the mother cat and that all-important socialization is easy: All you have to do is ask the owner. This is certainly true if you're buying a pedigreed cat and dealing with a reputable breeder who knows the importance of good nutrition for the mother and handling and exposure to new things for the kittens. This breeder is happy to tell you everything that went into the development of your kitten, from how she considered the mating, matching pedigree to pedigree, to what she fed the expectant mother, to how and how often she handled the kittens.

If the breeder shows her cats, she's just as interested in well-handled kittens as you are — if not more so. The kittens she picks for competition need to be able to deal with frequent baths and grooming, car and airplane rides, noisy exhibition halls with lots of gawkers, and judges handling them thoroughly to assess their *conformation,* or physical closeness to the written blueprint for the breed, called a *standard*.

We discuss the world of cat shows — and whether you can find a place in it for you and your cat — in Chapter 18. But what about the kittens your coworker wants you to see? Her family, too, may have provided a perfect environment out of common sense and the kindness of their hearts. The mother may be a beloved family pet or a cat in trouble they took in to help out. Again, ask about the mother's health and consider the environment the kitten was raised in. A litter raised indoors, in the heart of a family, with children to handle them and dogs to get used to (if you have dogs), with pans rattling and people talking — and even yelling — is full of superb pet prospects.

Making special considerations

If we seem to be suggesting choosing only kittens whose backgrounds you can verify and whose mothers you can meet, let us assure you that's not the case. Millions of wonderful kittens and adult cats are available for adoption from shelters, from dedicated foster-and-placement volunteers, and even from adoption outreach programs that take kittens and adult cats where the people are, whether it's in the adoption center of a pet superstore or the streets around an office area.

In these cases, you have to rely on your observations and on trust with the (one hopes) reputable animal organization that brought the animals out (ideally after getting a read on their temperaments and health first).

You have to give these animals a little leeway, especially the adult cats. Although healthy, well-socialized kittens can play in nearly any surroundings, even the best cats may be miserable and disoriented in the cages of a shelter. We discuss more on evaluating kittens and cats individually a little later in this chapter, but for now we just want you to remember: Don't make environment count for everything. Many a kitten or adult cat has risen from unfortunate beginnings to make a great pet. You just need to spend more time observing the adult as an individual, that's all. And maybe listen to your heart and take a chance.

Choosing a Kitten

Although you shouldn't automatically consider a kitten — there's a lot of good to be said about an adult cat — most people are thinking "kitten" when the time comes to bring a cat into their lives. And you certainly can't deny the charm of a kitten.

Many times people make their choices based on aesthetic reasons — although personally we think *all* cats are beautiful! Some people are drawn to gray tabbies, others to calicoes and tortoiseshells. That is no problem, of course, for the beauty of a cat is one of the pleasures of sharing a life with one, and beauty *is* in the eyes of the beholder.

But make sure your kitten is more than just a glamour-puss. Make sure he has a temperament you can live with, and make sure, above all, that he's healthy. Evaluating both of these criteria takes a little time.

Should you bring your children along to look at kittens and cats? How could you not? That said, the youngest children — below the age of 3 or so — may indeed be best left behind, for they have yet to learn how to be gentle in their handling of animals and could scare or even hurt a delicate kitten. (After you adopt a new family pet, you need to work on teaching your child how to handle her.)

School-aged children can help with the personality testing, which is, after all, really about playing with the kittens (see the upcoming section, "Personality testing your kitten"). From the age of 9 or 10 or so, children can be fully involved in the process, right down to choosing the kitten and caring for her at home — both under adult guidance. Kids and cats are good together!

Adopting at the ideal age

Many breeders don't let their kittens go to a new home before the age of 14 or even 16 weeks, when the baby's immune system is fully working (more on that in the vaccinations section in Chapter 11). By then, the kitten has enjoyed a wonderful start in the company of her littermates and mother — as well as children, dogs, and other realities of life among the two-legged.

Kittens benefit from the extra time with their littermates for the first 12 to 14 weeks of their lives, which is why most experts suggest that kittens adopted at this age have the best prospects for becoming healthy, well-adjusted pets. We'd draw the line at 10 weeks of age (at least), which is about the time when a kitten has developed the skills he needs to use as an adult, and we consider prime adoption time to be from 12 to 14 weeks of age.

At what age do kittens open their eyes? When can they walk, and hear, and leap? You can find information on kitten development from birth on — and how you can influence it in a positive way — in Chapter 16.

Remember that you're trying to find the best feline companion you can, trying to be an *informed consumer* and make your decision as much — if not more — with your head as with your heart. A person who is trying to sell or give you a kitten who's too young — especially one freshly weaned at six to seven weeks of age — is probably more interested in "getting rid of" the kittens than in finding them good homes. You have to wonder what other shortcuts were taken with the litter, especially regarding how the mother was handled and how the litter was socialized.

Looking at a litter

You want to consider the litter as a whole, from the moment you first see them and vice versa. If the first thing you see is the tails of a half-dozen terrified kittens diving for cover, perhaps these babies aren't socialized enough for you.

What should you hope to see? Playful, confident kittens, friendly and inquisitive. Glossy coats that beg to be stroked. Bright eyes looking in your direction.

Wear comfortable clothes to look at a litter, and be prepared to get down to their level to check things out. Sit on the floor with them, and encourage them with chirps and wiggling fingers to interact with you.

After you get a sense of the group as a whole, start to sort out the personalities of each individual kitten. Take your time — which should be easy, for few things are more pleasurable than playing with a litter of healthy kittens.

Observe which kittens are the most active or the most tentative. The kitten who never stops may not be the best choice for you, especially if you're looking for a companion to purr contentedly in your lap while you read or watch TV. The shy one may be a poor choice, too, especially if yours is an active household, with lots of comings and goings and a constant parade of children and guests.

If the litter's a good one, though, you should have two or three kittens that are kind of "medium" — friendly and playful, but not too crazy. These are the ones you should observe most closely; one of these is likely your best choice.

You may find the entire litter a little sluggish and slow afoot. Ask the owner whether the kittens just ate, or have spent the better part of the last two hours chasing each other through the house. If that's the case, ask to visit another time so you can better evaluate the true personalities of the kittens when they're fully awake.

Sometimes you may not be able to evaluate a kitten in the company of her littermates. This situation is especially true in shelters, where litters are commonly split when they come in. The practice — which is a sad necessity at the peak of kitten season — involves taking one or two kittens from each litter to place for adoption and sending the rest back for euthanasia. The lucky ones may just be more handsomely marked or more playful than their littermates, but they, too, may eventually meet the same fate. It's not the shelter's fault: They're just coping with pet overpopulation as best they can.

If you can't see the whole litter, you can still pick a wonderful pet. Kittens from different litters are often placed together for companionship and space considerations, so you can still observe how well each kitten interacts with others. And the most important part of choosing — personality testing — is still available to you.

Personality testing your kitten

Talk about fun! Checking out kittens is really about playing with them, and that's something you can never have enough of. Following are some ways to find out whether a kitten is for you:

- ✔ **Evaluate her interest level.** To do so, take the kitten away from her littermates so her focus is on you.

- ✔ **Concentrate on her as an individual.** All kittens are adorable, so try to look beyond that and such things as color or that cute little Groucho mustache. Sure, you ought to like the looks of your cat, but the personality is more important in the long run.

✔ **Don't hurry.** If you rush things and take the first kitten you see, the kitten who would have been a better match for you may never find a home.

✔ **Come with kitten-testing tools.** Bring a feather, a Ping-Pong ball, or a cloth mouse. A piece of string or yarn is fine, too, as long as you remember that none of these should ever be left with a kitten or adult cat as a permanent plaything, because they are too often eaten and can cause havoc in the feline intestine.

You may have to improvise some, depending on the surroundings. A shelter may not have the facilities for you to observe a litter at play or test a kitten individually. That doesn't make them a bad place to get a kitten! Instead of evaluating a kitten who has some room to roam, you may need to do your play-testing through the bars of a cage.

The feather test

We like to use a feather, but in truth it can be any of your testing toys. You're looking for a kitten bursting with good health and playfulness, one who isn't afraid of people and, better yet, considers them the source of all good things.

At this stage, you should already noticed the overly shy kittens, and you especially should have sadly removed from consideration the kitten who spits and hisses in terror at your approach. If you're working with a shelter, they've probably already removed these poor babies, leaving only the most adoptable out. Pick up one of the friendly kittens carefully, with a reassuring but gentle grip under her belly, and set her down in your observation area.

Figure 5-2:
Use a feather or other attention-getter to ensure that your prospective pet is as inquisitive as a normal kitten should be.

Let her explore her new environment a little while you settle onto the floor, and then, when she's satisfied with her surroundings, chirp at her and tease her with the feather (or string, or other toy). She should pursue it eagerly, batting at it and pouncing as she goes, and sitting up on her haunches to swat at it as you tease with it overhead.

This is all normal behavior for a healthy, outgoing kitten, and if yours shows it, she's passed the feather test.

A moment of calm

The kitten you want should be neither too shy nor too assertive and active. The kitten should be comfortable being held, enjoying your stroking and soothing voice. One who constantly struggles to wriggle free and keep playing — even if not doing so out of fear — may grow up into a cat who is too active for you.

So spend a few moments of quiet time with each of your contenders and see how they react to you as an individual. Let your heart weigh in a little here, and be receptive to the idea that one of these little fluffballs may be the one who's meant for you.

The perfect match when it comes to cats is the animal who is friendly and well socialized, who has an activity level you can live with, and who appeals to your aesthetic sense of what feline beauty is all about. There are millions of kittens from which to choose, and many of them meet all your requirements.

Should you buy a kitten you've never seen?

If you have your heart set on one of the rarer breeds of cats, you may well have to resign yourself to letting a breeder pick out a suitable kitten and ship it to you by air.

Understandably, this sort of deal involves a lot of trust on both sides, and you want to be sure you're dealing with the most reputable and experienced of breeders. (You can find information on how to find such a person in Chapter 3.) But if you are confident you're working with such a person, then you should be fine — and so should your kitten.

May we make another suggestion, though? A rare-breed kitten can set you back several hundred — or even thousands — of dollars. What's a little travel expense on top of that, when you're talking about a companion who'll be with you for the better part of two decades?

Go see the litter. Go see your kitten. And fly home with him in your care. An unaccompanied kitten must travel as baggage in the pressurized cargo hold. If you're with your new pet, he can go with you in the cabin as carry-on luggage in an airline approved carrier.

It's a much better deal for the kitten, and for the nerves of the caring people at both ends. Oh, and for more on traveling with a cat, see Chapter 18.

Never get a kitten on impulse. The pet you choose will bring pleasure into your life for many years, so take your time and select the kitten who's right for your family.

Considering the Second-Chance Kitty

Perhaps because kittens are so very appealing, adult cats have the lowest adoption rate at many shelters. While prospective adopters head straight for the kitten section, hundreds of thousands of adult cats purr hopefully in their cages, and thrust their soft paws beseechingly through the bars as if they understand the importance of catching someone's attention.

Too many never get a second chance, and that's a real shame.

It's a tragedy for the cats, of course, but it's also unfortunate for many people who don't realize that an adult cat may, in many cases, be a better choice. You know pretty well what you're getting with a grown cat — activity level, sociability, and health. Given time in a loving environment, a grown cat forms just as tight a bond with his new people as any kitten can, and we believe that in some cases recycled pets are more appreciative, somehow, of a chance at a happy life.

With adult cats, as with kittens, knowing a little of the animal's background is important, especially if your family has children or dogs. You can ask your questions about background directly if adopting from the cat's original owner, but most shelters also try to provide some basic information, which they ask of the people giving up their pets.

Figure 5-3:
Shelters are stressful and disorienting to a cat, so try to spend a little quiet time when evaluating a cat for adoption.

What if the information isn't flattering to the cat? For example, suppose that he has become available for adoption because of his failure to use a litter box? This is a tough situation, because you don't know the contributing factors — maybe the litter box was never cleaned or was left in a spot that was convenient for the owner but disconcerting for the cat. (More on litter box problems — and solutions — in Chapter 15.) With so many cats available, the commonsense answer is to count this kitty out. But if the cat checks out otherwise, it's really a judgment call, another factor for you to weigh before making a decision — but only if you have the time and patience to work on solving the problem.

If at all possible, take each adult cat you're considering away from the caging area of the adoption center or influence of her previous family. Sit down with her in your lap, alone, in a quiet place and try to get a feel for her as an individual. Shelters are stressful places, so she may need a few quiet minutes to collect herself, but the most calm, confident, and outgoing of cats respond pretty readily to your attention, relaxing in your lap, pushing for strokes, and purring. This is the kind of cat you're looking for.

Recognizing Good Health in Kittens and Cats

Don't fall in love with a sick cat. With so many kittens and cats available for adoption, it just doesn't make sense to take a chance on one who may cost you a great deal of money in veterinary costs — and may not be with you long, anyway.

Feral cat considerations

In every community, dedicated volunteers trap, tame, and find homes for *feral* cats — those gone wild. Although these efforts are commendable and more than a few end in success stories, a formerly feral cat or kitten can be a poor adoption prospect. A feral cat or kitten isn't usually going to be as friendly and relaxed as an animal who has spent his whole life in the presence of humans. It's always hard to say "no" to an animal in need, but with the sheer numbers of cats and kittens so desperate for a home like yours, you may want to think twice before you choose a pet with built-in problems.

On the other hand, you may want to take a chance. Some former ferals will be fine in time, especially in a small, quiet household. (Typically such cats bond to one person only, and are shy with others.) Or maybe you like taking on the challenge such a cat represents, or feel good for having helped a hard-luck kitty.

If you do choose such a cat or kitten, go into the situation with your eyes open. And if you want more ways to help the wild ones, Chapter 4 helps get you started.

Some signs of health are obvious to anyone; others require a veterinarian's help to pinpoint. Before you settle on a promising kitten or cat, perform your own health check, and be sure to follow up with your veterinarian within a day or so.

The outer cat

General impressions are important. You should get a sense of good health and vitality from the animal you're considering adopting. He should feel good in your arms: neither too thin nor too fat, well put-together, sleek, and solid. If ribs are showing or the animal is potbellied, he may be suffering from malnutrition or worms — both fixable, but signs of neglect that may indicate deeper problems with socialization or general health.

With soothing words and gentle caresses, go over the animal from nose to tail, paying special attention to the following areas:

- **Fur and skin:** Skin should be clean and unbroken, covered thickly with a glossy coat of hair. Bald patches may mean *ringworm,* not a parasite but a fungal infection that you can catch, too. Part the hairs and look for signs of fleas: The parasites themselves may be too small and fast for you to spot, but their droppings remain behind. If you're not sure, put the cat on a clean surface, such as a stainless-steel counter or white towel and run your fingers against the grain. Then look on the surface: If fleas are present, you see the droppings as little bits that look like pepper. If you add water to them, they turn reddish in color — because they're made up of dried blood. You shouldn't count a cat out because of a few fleas, but a severe infestation could be a sign of a health problem, especially for kittens. (Some kittens become anemic from having so much of their blood sucked by the pests.)

- **Ears:** These should be clean inside or, perhaps, have a little bit of wax. Filthy ears and head-shaking are signs of ear mites, which can require a prolonged period of consistent medication to eradicate.

- **Eyes:** Eyes should look clear and bright. Runny eyes or other discharge may be a sign of illness. The third eyelid, a semitransparent protective sheath that folds away into the corners of the eyes nearest the nose (also called a *haw*), should not be visible.

- **Nose:** Again, the cat should have no discharge. The nose should be clean and slightly moist. A kitten or cat who is breathing with difficulty, coughing, or sneezing may be seriously ill.

- **Mouth:** Gums should be rosy pink, not pale, and with no signs of inflammation at the base of the teeth. The teeth should be white and clean of tartar buildup.

- **Tail area:** Clean and dry. Dampness or the presence of fecal matter may suggest illness.

Figure 5-4:
All kittens are adorable, but look beyond the pretty face for signs of good health and temperament.

Abigail/photograph by Linda M. Seals

Even though we believe you're best off finding the healthiest, best-socialized cat or kitten you can, we do applaud those who take on the challenges of the neediest. Gina's friend, Jan, for example, lives happily with a houseful of some of the weirdest cats imaginable. One of the newest additions to her home is Mimi (short for Screaming Mimi, to give you an idea of this cat's worst trait). Jan found Mimi trapped in a drain pipe, a half-starved, seriously dehydrated kitten with ear mites, fleas, and worms. The veterinarian told Jan she didn't think the kitten would make it, but Mimi pulled through and grew to be a sleek and glossy adult. Not that anyone would know, for Mimi hides from company. But she's an affectionate companion to the woman who saved her life.

The inner cat

In the best circumstances, your kitten or adult cat will come with a clean bill of health certified by the shelter or other placement service, or vouched for by the cat's own health records kept by the person trying to place him. If that's not the case, you need to have any adoption prospect checked out by a veterinarian for serious problems you can't see. Following are some problems you should have your pet checked for:

✔ **Infectious diseases:** Feline leukemia is the biggest concern. Though many cats live with the virus well enough for years, you may want to consider carefully the added worry and health-care expense of owning such a cat. Then, too, if you already have cats, you may want to safeguard their health by not exposing them to the contagious virus. Your veterinarian can determine the presence of infectious disease with a simple test, and explain to you the results — and your options. (For more on this nasty disease and others, see Chapter 12.)

✔ **Parasites:** Worms are the biggest problem. Your veterinarian needs to verify their presence and prescribe an appropriate course of treatment.

Don't put the cats you already have at risk by introducing a sick animal into your home. Have your new cat cleared by your veterinarian before you bring him home.

If your prospective pet clears the health check, he should start a regimen of preventive care right away to ensure continued good health. You can find information on preventive care and choosing a veterinarian in Chapter 11.

Taking a Leap of Faith with Your Eyes Open!

At the beginning of this chapter, we state that the old saying "you choose a dog, but a cat chooses you" doesn't hold true for most people these days, but it still happens enough for you to keep your heart open to all the possibilities. For every "rule" we include in this chapter — don't adopt a sick cat, don't adopt a shy cat, don't adopt a cat with a behavioral problem, don't adopt a feral cat — we know of a handful of smashing success stories that prove the exception.

But these stories of love over adversity all have in common cat owners who went into the situation with open eyes and a willingness to spend the time (and in many cases, the money) to make a healthy, happy pet out of an animal with a problem.

If you want to take a chance on a kitten or adult cat with a problem, more power to you. But be honest about what you're getting yourself into. A kitty with a problem is harder (and often more expensive) to live with than one who has everything going for him. And remember, too, that if you later decide you made the wrong decision with a problem cat, you'll probably be unable to find him another home.

Many things are possible, if you try. But if you're not able to put in the extra effort, be *sure* you choose a healthy, well-socialized cat who has a better chance of working out in your life, one with whom you can more easily form a relationship that will better both your lives for many years.

Chapter 6

Getting the Relationship Started Right

• •

In This Chapter

▶ Making your house safe for your cat

▶ Bringing your cat home

▶ Introducing a new cat to your other pets

▶ Choosing a purrfect name

▶ Capturing your kitty on film

• •

*B*ringing home a new pet is one of life's most exciting experiences, no matter whether you're an 8-year-old girl whose parents have finally given in to your begging for a kitten or an 80-year-old man looking forward to enjoying the quiet companionship of an older cat. The moment that cat or kitten comes home is the time when you and your cat are perfectly poised between two worlds: one of promise and one of reality.

For the reality to be the happy one you dreamed of when you first selected your cat or kitten, you need to work to make sure that your new pet gets off on the right paw in your household. You need to ensure your house is safe for your new cat or kitten. Your children need to be aware of how fragile a pet can be and know how to handle their new companion appropriately. If you have other pets in the household, no matter the species, you need to set up introductions so all your pets feel comfortable and are kept safe as they settle into their routines and learn to enjoy — or at least tolerate — each other's company.

Just as important, you're going to be spending the first few weeks — months, in the case of kittens — working to lay the groundwork for a lifetime of good behavior. If you want your new pet to use the litter box, choose the scratching post over your sofa, and never consider your hand a biteable plaything, you need to set the rules from the beginning and stick to them, gently but firmly. Cats love routine, and after you settle yours into one that's good for both of you, you'll both be much happier.

If you've adopted an adult cat with behavior problems, don't give up! Instead, turn to Chapter 14 for help with coping with the most common problems, such as scratching furniture, or to Chapter 15 for working with cats who avoid the litter box or spray urine.

Please don't be too put off by the prospect of *work* in learning to live with your new pet. All worthwhile relationships require patience and good humor to succeed. Although the first few weeks with a new kitten or cat can sometimes be a trial for all involved, the same period can also be a very special time for you and your pet. You're learning to appreciate the unique beauty and personality of your cat, and your cat is learning to trust and to love you.

Before you know it, you're looking back fondly on those first few crazy weeks when love was new.

If you're bringing home your first kitten, consider going back for a littermate or another kitten. If you want two cats, the easiest method is to adopt two kittens at the same time, preferably from the same litter. Kittens don't have the sense of territory that grown cats have, so they settle down together into a new home nicely. If you have a cat already, don't worry: We give you tips for managing the introductions later in this chapter, in "Hello, Kitty!" As for more help with managing a multicat household, you'll find everything you need in Chapter 17.

Pre-Cat Preparations

"Curiosity killed the cat" is a saying that has been around nearly as long as cats themselves. And the fact that cats, even indoor ones, can get in some real jams is quite true. Kittens, small, active, and endlessly curious, are even more at risk.

If trouble's to be found, a kitten's sure to find it. For that reason, you need to look at your home closely and make some adjustments before bringing your new pet home — not only for safety, but to make the transition easier for everyone.

Eliminating household hazards

Four words apply when preparing your house for a feline invasion: *Think like a cat.* Look at your home in a new way: as a big place full of exciting new things for a kitten or cat. Look low at nooks and crannies your new pet can get into. Look high at objects or furnishings your pet can get on top of. Look at household belongings that a cat can knock over, because if he can, he will. And mostly, look at things your cat can get into that can hurt him — those are the ones you really need to change.

Plaything problems

If you like to sew, knit, or do any kind of needlework, invest in a container to keep your materials completely hidden whenever you're not working on your projects. That's because cats and kittens love any kind of string, yarn, thread, or ribbon, without regard to the grave dangers such playthings pose if swallowed. And if the idea of your kitten swallowing thread doesn't give you the shivers, think about that needle going down the same pipe.

Likewise, find a secure storage place for ribbon, balled twine, or anything similar. Don't forget the string on your blinds! Wad the cord up into a short bundle and tuck it behind the blinds, out of your kitten's view. It doesn't have to stay there forever, but it's best hidden for now.

Covered wastebaskets are a must in dealing with curious kittens and cats. The kind with lids that pop up after you step on them and close after you remove your foot are great for keeping your cat out of what he shouldn't be into — such as food waste in the kitchen and tissues and dental floss in the bathroom. Sure, you can try to teach your pet to stay out of wastebaskets, but sometimes the path of least resistance is the way to go. Covered wastebaskets aren't that expensive, and they pay for themselves in cleanup time and aggravation. Another alternative: Put wastebaskets out of reach under the sink or in a cabinet or broom closet.

Figure 6-1:
Kittens and cats love to play with yarn, thread, and ribbon, but these items can pose a serious danger to your pet. Don't let him play with them unsupervised.

Raffy/Photo courtesty of Megan Boese

Speaking of the bathroom, make sure you hang your toilet paper in a way that makes it less entertaining — read, "nearly impossible" — to unwind. Stop this delightful sport by putting the paper on the spool so that it unwinds from *underneath.* That way your pet's efforts to bat from the top get him nowhere. If the folks in your family can't remember this advice when changing rolls — or your cat's more into shredding than unrolling — check out a pet-supply store, catalog or Website for plastic shields that fit over the roll.

Another bathroom hazard is the toilet. Cats are fascinated by fresh water, and unless you want your kitten to take a bath — or worse, drown — remember to keep the lid down. If your home has a sump pump, make sure that's covered, too.

For plenty of ideas for cat-safe playthings — including many that don't cost you a dime — see Chapter 8.

Hiding places

Cats like to find dark, quiet places, especially if they're stressed. As long as those places are safe ones, you shouldn't discourage your cat from seeking them out. But kittens don't have as much common sense as cats and can get themselves into places they can't figure their way out of — and you may have a hard time getting them out of some of those places, too. Which is why, where kittens are concerned, you need to decide which places they should stay out of and work to discourage them from exploring those areas.

If you've already been through the get-into-everything stage with a human baby, you probably already have those nifty little devices on your cupboard that prevent anyone but human adults from opening them. If not, take a look at your cupboards. Do they close securely, or do they fit together so poorly that a little paw can tease them open? If the latter's the case, think about kitten-proof latches — magnets, hooks and eyes, or other types. Check your local hardware store for a selection.

Your new pet may also find the area behind your refrigerator, sofa, or bookcase appealing. You may be able to block off access with cardboard while your kitten is small or put down two-sided tape at the entrance — cats hate to walk across sticky surfaces!

Another place to look out for — chests of drawers. Although your kitten or cat may find your sweater drawer perfect for naptime, he won't like being trapped if you accidentally close the drawer with him in it. Even more dangerous: the kitten who likes to explore behind an open drawer who may get slammed against the back of the chest as you close the drawer. Remember to close your drawers immediately after you open them, and you can avoid both problems (although double-checking for your kitten whenever you close a drawer anyway certainly couldn't hurt). Be careful, too, about other areas your cat or kitten can get locked into, including closets and basements. More than a few cats have died of dehydration after being trapped, and others have died from heat after being caught in small areas and exposed to the sun.

Know where your cat or kitten is: If he's not in a safe room when you leave and he's not looking at you as if to ask "Where are *you* going, pal?" find out where he is *before* you leave.

Higher and higher

Although the more relaxed breeds, such as Persians, may eventually prefer a more leisurely life on the ground, active breeds such as Abyssinians and Siamese — as well as every kitten ever born — are going to do their share of climbing. It's natural behavior, which means the best you can do is to direct it in an acceptable way — praise your cat for climbing a cat tree instead of your expensive drapes.

After your kitten first comes home, move your drapes out of harm's way while he's growing up: Tie your drapes up out of reach or fold them over their rods to get them off the floor. Encourage him to use the cat tree by staging games there and by offering praise and treats.

For tips on how to pick out a cat tree, see Chapter 8. For help with scratching problems, see Chapter 14.

Don't forget the trouble your kitten can cause while up high on shelves or tables. Put your most delicate knickknacks in the closet until the kitten-crazy days are past. Plants do better not on shelves but hanging from the ceiling. Don't expect miracles: If you live with cats (or any pets or children), things are going to get broken.

Figure 6-2: Cats and kittens love to curl up in small, dark places, but not all of them are as safe as this cat-tree cubbyhole.

Scotty/Photo by Gay Currier

Bob Walker and Frances Mooney have completely remodeled their house to keep their cats happy. Bob's wonderful books, *The Cat's House* and *Cats Into Everything* (Andrews and McMeel), show how. But living with cats hasn't kept the couple from displaying their collection of artwork. They bolt down larger objects, such as lamps and sculptures, and use a product called Quake Hold to keep smaller things secure. Quake Hold is a putty that seals objects to their display surface. It may be hard to find outside of earthquake-prone California (where Walker and Mooney live); if so, try double-sided tape or Velcro, or ask at your hardware store whether Quake Hold can be ordered for you. Check out the Mooney's house on the Web, too, at www.thecatshouse.com.

Other things to look out for

Never question the ingenuity of kittens to get into trouble — and never forget to take precautions to keep them out of it. Here are a few more potential dangers to be aware of:

- ✔ **Electric and phone cords:** Bundle up the extra cord and tuck it out of sight — and spray anything that remains within reach of your kitten with something that tastes nasty, such as the commercial chew-stopper Bitter Apple, available at most pet-supply stores. Be especially careful if using small appliances such as irons — one good tug on the cord and your cat could get smashed. For the tangle of cords connecting your home computer to its printer, monitor, modem, or what-have-you, check at your hardware or computer store for cord containers. Gina uses one that looks like the exhaust hose from a clothes dryer, only narrower, with a slit along its length in which you tuck the cords.

- ✔ **Windows:** Make sure your windows have screens that fit and are securely attached, especially on upper-story windows. Screens keep your indoor cat from becoming an outdoor cat and protect any cat from a nasty fall.

Before you decide your house is as close to cat-safe as possible, double-check it against our list of ten common household dangers in Chapter 22.

Organizing a "safe room"

With so many tempting troubles, you probably aren't surprised at our recommendation that you prepare a small place for your new kitten or cat to hang out whenever you're not around to watch her. An adult cat needs such a room, too, but for the adult cat, the idea's more about easing her into your home than protecting her from hazards.

Buy the equipment your cat needs before you bring him home. For information on how to pick out appropriate bowls, litter boxes, and toys, see Chapter 8.

The other reason for a safe room is *training*. Keeping your cat or kitten in a small area in the early stages of your relationship limits his options. He learns to scratch on a scratching post or cat tree and comes to understand that his litter box is the best place to relieve himself.

For more on preventing and curing behavior problems, see Chapters 14 and 15.

Figure 6-3: Kittens and irons don't mix. A playful kitten can pull an iron over by chewing on a dangling cord.

Milkdud/Photo by Beth Jenkins

A kitten's place

A bathroom is the ideal place to keep your kitten whenever you're away — it's easily kitten-proofed and just as easily cleaned. Pick up bathmats and toilet covers and put them away. Take the towels off the rack and make sure everything else, including soap, razors, shampoo bottles, and medications — *especially* medications — is safely put away. Someday you may be able to leave toilet paper on the spool by placing it so that the paper unrolls from below — as described in the section "Plaything problems," earlier in this chapter. But for now, you may want to take the paper out completely if your kitten's little, especially if the room's a spare bath, or just put the whole thing in a cabinet or under the sink to keep the roll from getting shredded. And don't forget to close the toilet lid — a curious little kitten could drown in the bowl.

Earlier in this chapter, in the section "Higher and higher," we suggest you raise your drapes out of the way. Do the same for your shower curtain, too, tying it up, flipping it over the rod, or — better yet — removing it entirely in the beginning. If you have a shower enclosure, keep the door to it shut.

After you're done, you have a pretty sterile place, which is surely no fun for your kitten. But don't worry: We're going to tell you how to liven it up again.

Indoor kitty: The conversion

If your new cat or kitten has had access to the outdoors, the best time to convert him to an indoors-only kitty is the moment you bring him home. The change requires resolve on your part and a determination to provide your new companion with everything he needs to be happy indoors — good food and fresh water, a clean litter box, a scratching post, toys, and, most important, your companionship.

What if you've had your pet for a while and are thinking of making such a change? It's still possible to do so. Pick a day — and that's that. Does such a change come easily? Not immediately, we must admit.

Cats are highly territorial, and the day you reduce your cat's territory by cutting him off from the outdoor part that he has been enjoying is the day you're going to start hearing about it — lots. Your cat is amazed at your stupidity at first: "Hey, you! I can't believe you're so dumb that you forgot how to open the door!" Later, he's positively astonished at your failure to respond: "The door! Pay attention! I want something."

Don't give in. If you allow the insistent meows and pointed stares to wear you down to the point of opening the door, you've taught your cat a lesson you'd rather he didn't know: "All I need to do is put up a fuss, and I get what I want." If you try to keep him inside again, he's going to be even more obnoxious.

Be patient but firm. Dissuade him from the door with a shot from a spray bottle and keep him occupied with games and attention. If he likes catnip, get a fresh supply to rub on his toys and scratching post.

Within a couple weeks, your cat starts to settle in to his new routines, and you'll no longer need to worry about the dangers he faces outdoors.

Set up the room for your kitten by putting her litter box in one corner and her food and water dishes in another spot. (Put the dishes too close to the box, and your cat may be offended and may choose not to eat — or may decide to "go" elsewhere.) You also need to add a sturdy, nontippable scratching post, a bed, and some toys.

You can easily understand how a safe room can keep your kitten out of trouble, but in fact, it's doing a little more than that. By keeping your kitten's options to a minimum, you teach her how to direct her natural behaviors in ways you can approve. If she has a scratching post but no couch, for example, she learns where scratching is acceptable.

So how does your cat or kitten learn where scratching *isn't* acceptable? See Chapter 14.

A cat's room

Although you can use the exact same setup for a newly adopted adult cat that you use for a kitten, you may choose a spare bedroom instead. The number-one reason for confining a kitten is to keep her out of trouble; the number-one reason for confining an adult cat, however, is to give her a place where she can feel secure while adjusting to her new home. She isn't going to get into as much mischief as a little one — although you still need to look at the room with an eye to eliminating the most obvious hazards.

Look at the traffic patterns of your house and choose the quietest, least-trafficked room for your new adult cat. If it's a little-used spare bathroom, choose that. A spare bedroom? A den? The decision you make depends on your own home.

No matter which room you choose, you still need the same accoutrements: bowls for food and water, a litter box, a place to sleep, a scratching post, and some toys.

Kitten or cat, the first few days go more smoothly and safely if you prepare for your new pet in advance — and if your new pet eases into the household by spending quiet time alone.

Bringing Your New Pet Home

The day your pet comes home is a big step for both of you. If she's a kitten, she's leaving her littermates and her mom and throwing her lot in with you, an incredibly large and, to her mind, ungainly and unpredictable creature. If she's a grown cat, she's dealing with the uncertainties of her recent life and is unsure of what the future may hold. As you would for a child visiting your home, be there for your cat but don't force yourself upon her.

For four days after joining Paul's family, his cat, PC, lived in a tiled sunroom, refusing to partake in any social behavior. In fact, she would jump four feet in the air every time Paul tried to coax her to interact during his cleaning and feeding time in *her* room. But slowly and surely, she acclimated to his presence and her new surroundings, and her need for social interaction drew her out — on her own terms. She's now the friendliest cat you would ever hope to meet.

Try to arrange some time off work after your cat first comes home, or at the very least, pick her up the first morning of a weekend. You want to spend some extra time with her, and a little extra attention here helps with the bonding.

You want the transition to be as smooth as possible, and a safe trip home is an important step. The first rule of transporting a cat: Use a carrier! The second rule: Use a carrier! You may also want to bring towels, both the paper and old bathroom variety, and a bottle of pet-mess cleanup solution in case of an accident — although don't try to clean up any mess *inside* the carrier until you and your new pet are safely home.

The name game

Naming a cat is great fun, because you have no limits whatsoever to the name you can choose. Most cats probably end up with a couple of names — a longer, more formal name such as Evangeline, and a shorter, come-to-dinner name such as Evie, or Kitty-Butt, or Baby-Evie-Face.

Because your cat doesn't pay all that much attention to what you call him anyway — unless you happen to be talking about something he wants, such as dinner — you can really let your imagination go wild.

Look in atlases for interesting place names and turn to literary references for great character names or the names of authors. Or think of names that are related to your profession or great loves, such as in the case of the friend of Gina's, an amateur hockey player, who named his cats Slapshot and Puck. Although plenty of name-your-pet books are out there — and they're all fun reading — we find that a name-your-baby book is just as useful.

Make naming your cat a family project and use this opportunity to interest your children in a trip to the library. You don't have that many opportunities in your life to name a family member, so make the most of it!

Did we mention that you should use a carrier to bring your pet home? Although you should never transport any cat without this important safety device, you're really engaging in risky behavior whenever you try it with a cat you don't know. We don't care how much your children want to hold their new pet — it takes only one scratch or bite for a frightened cat to get loose in your car if he's not in a carrier. After that, he could go out the window, so please keep the windows up if you insist on not using one. But really, you should use one! A loose cat could also crawl under your feet while you're driving. Even if all he does is get up under the seats, you're going to have a heck of a time removing him from your car after you get home. Dragging him out by any piece of him you can reach, by the way, won't convince him that you're a swell person. But, even worse, you could end up with some nasty scratches. A simple carrier will avoid all these problems. So get one!

If you have another cat in your home, the first place you should take your new cat or kitten is the veterinary hospital. You could risk your resident cat's life if you don't. Your new cat or kitten needs to be checked for infectious viruses such as feline leukemia and other contagious health hazards such as ear mites and upper respiratory infections. *Don't risk your resident cat's health in your enthusiasm over your new pet.* Make sure your new pet is vet-checked before attempting any introductions. If that's not possible — you save a stray on a Sunday, for example — make sure you keep the new cat completely isolated until you can get him to your veterinarian. See Chapter 11 for important preventive-care information, and Chapter 17 on living with more than one cat.

Watch the birdie, kitty!

Don't forget to have the camera ready to record the special day your new pet comes home. If you're adopting a kitten, keep the camera close by with fresh batteries because over the next couple months, you're going to kick yourself for missing some great shots if you don't — and hate yourself later for not having pictures of your wonderful cat as a baby. They grow up awfully fast!

Here are a few tips for taking great cat pictures:

✔ **Get your children involved.** Your children can help you with your pictures by teasing your new pet with a toy on a string. Or try zooming in close to get pictures of kids and cat together. On the day your new pet comes home, let the kids make some memories, too. Get them each one of those throwaway cameras. You're sure to be delighted at some of the shots you get back — and they're going to be doubly so!

✔ **Head (safely) outdoors.** Natural light — early morning is best — avoids the dreaded red-eye shot, where the flash makes your beautiful kitten come out as a monster. Taking pictures outside gives your new pet a more natural, healthy look. If your cat is a solid, dark color, use your flash even outdoors (if your camera enables you to do so): The flash brings out the detail in your pet's face.

Make sure that your kitten or cat is out of harm's reach when taking photos in natural light. Use a screened porch or sunroom if you have one available. An alternative is photographing your pet as she naps lazily in a sunny spot.

✔ **Get close.** If you want a good picture, go where your pet is. Shoot at just below your kitten's eye level and zoom in as closely as you can for good detail.

✔ **Watch your backgrounds.** Think neutral — a plain wall, not a cluttered cabinet. Think contrast — light for a dark cat, dark for a light one. If your tabby cat loves to sleep on the busy fabric of your sofa, consider throwing a solid blanket down first. (Or, better yet, always protect your sofa with a covering — it keeps the cat hair off your upholstery!)

✔ **Be creative.** If you want your kitten to kiss your children, do as the pros do: Put a little butter on your children, and let the kitten kiss it off.

✔ **Make the most of modern technology.** Digital cameras and scanners make it easy to salvage a picture you wish had turned out better. It's easier than ever before to scan an image into your computer and then use software to improve it — adjust the lighting, eliminate those funny flash eyes, and so on. And when you're done, you'll have a wonderful photo to e-mail to a friend or post on the Internet.

The place where you adopt your cat, such as a shelter, may provide you with a cardboard carrier for the ride home. And that's fine for this first trip, but you want something sturdier for the long haul. Carriers made of high-impact plastic are not expensive; they last a lifetime, and they give your cat a feeling of security whenever he travels. For tips on picking out a good carrier, see Chapter 8.

Hello, Kitty!

To say that cats don't like change is an understatement — and being introduced to a new home is big change. Some cats hide under the bed. Some stop using the litter box. Efforts to soothe others may be greeted with a hiss or a growl — or even a swipe with claws bared.

Although these are all normal feline reactions to stress, the bad habits that cats may develop while coming to terms with something new could become a permanent part of their routine. Which is why, for your new cat's sake and your own, you need to remember one word when introducing a new pet to your household: *slowly.*

Although a healthy, curious, and outgoing kitten may handle changes a little better, don't press your luck with a baby cat either. Be patient as your new pet learns to be comfortable in his surroundings and settles into the routine of your household.

The trick to introductions is the "safe room" you've (we hope) already set up, as described in the section "Organizing a 'safe room,'" earlier in this chapter. Kitten or cat, this room is a place where your new pet can feel safe — and be safe — while adjusting to his new home. How you use this room depends on the circumstances of your household, as we explain in the following sections — a frightened cat or kitten needs it more, and often longer, than does a well-socialized and correctly trained older cat.

Children

Children and cats are natural together, but you need to lay some ground rules for the safety of both from the moment your new pet comes home. Kittens can be injured by the loving attention of children, especially young ones who haven't learned how delicate a young pet can be. And with more than 600,000 cat bites reported every year in the United States, you can clearly see that some cats give as good as they get.

Does the number of cat bites surprise you? Compared to dogs — 3 million reported bites a year in the United States (and often more severe ones to boot!) — cats are a distant second in the bite department. But you must still take precautions for your human family members. Make sure your pet is vaccinated for rabies — more on that in Chapter 11— and make sure you treat any bite seriously. If *your* cat's the biter, wash the wound thoroughly with soap and water and contact your doctor immediately if the skin is broken. Cats harbor some pretty nasty bacteria in their mouths, and a disease called *cat scratch fever* can even be deadly for people with suppressed immune systems. Don't take any hint of infection associated with a cat bite lightly. If you don't know the biter, contact your local animal control and public health officials — the cat could be rabid!

The key to keeping children and cats together safely is to make sure their interactions are supervised and to teach children how to handle and respect cats. Here are some tips, by age group:

- **Infants:** Under no circumstances should a cat (or any pet) be left unsupervised with an infant. Although the idea that your cat poses a risk to your baby has been debunked — see Chapter 19 for more information, as well as precautions for pregnant women — keeping your cat away from your baby while you're not present is just common sense. Some people have even gone so far as to put a screen door on the room to the nursery, and to be honest, this precaution isn't a bad idea.

- **Toddlers:** Children at this age can really try a cat's patience, even though they aren't being anything but normal toddlers. Young children can't understand that poking, squeezing, or patting roughly aren't appreciated. Although most cats figure out quickly that children this age are best avoided, your child could be bitten or scratched if your cat is cornered or startled. Keep an eye on all interactions and consider putting a baby gate across the entry to your cat's safe room so that he can have a place where he isn't pestered.

- **Young children:** From the time a child's in school, he can start learning to care for a pet and take an increasing amount of responsibility — under supervision, of course. One way to teach younger school-aged children to play carefully is to play the "copycat game." If your child pets the cat gently, stroke his arm gently to show how nice it feels. If he pokes the cat, poke him — gently! — to help him make the connection.

Teach all children to hold a cat correctly, with support under his chest and his legs not dangling. A cat who feels secure is less likely to wriggle free with a claw or a bite.

Anyone who lives with a cat should know that a cat's tummy is the place most likely to draw an angry response if you touch it. Even cats who at first seem to like being petted there can get revved up and grab on with claws and teeth. Teach your children to avoid this sensitive area and to pet in a spot most cats enjoy, such as behind the ears. For more on cat body language, see Chapter 7.

Other cats

Introducing a second cat to the household is one time when patience is never more important. Despite your resident pet's initial misgivings, adding a companion can be a wonderful idea, especially for an indoor cat who spends a lot of time alone.

For more on the advantages of living with more than one cat — and tips on how to cope — see Chapter 17.

A kitten is usually an easier introduction, because most older cats accept a baby more readily than they do another adult. But even with a kitten, keep a close watch on the situation and be prepared to separate the two as described in the following paragraphs.

Territorial conflicts are greatly reduced if both cats are altered. Unneutered males, especially, don't take intruders lightly and will probably start spraying urine to mark their territory. For more information on altering, see Chapter 16.

Prepare your safe room for the new cat or kitten with a second set of bowls for food and water, a litter box, a scratching post or cat tree, and some toys. (Separate gear may be a temporary arrangement, or it may be lifelong, depending on the cats involved.) This separate room is your new pet's home turf while the two cats get used to each other's existence.

Don't forget to take your new cat or kitten to your veterinarian first. After you're sure your new pet is healthy, the introductions can begin.

Figure 6-4:
Children should learn how to hold a cat correctly, with support for the cat's legs and a reassuring hand over his body.

Figure 6-5: Bring a second cat home in a carrier and let your first cat discover the newcomer. The cats need to be kept apart during the early stages of introduction.

Bring the cat home in a carrier, and set the carrier in the room you've prepared. Let your resident cat discover the caged animal and don't be discouraged by initial hisses. Let your resident cat explore, and after the new cat is alone in the room, close the door and let him out of the carrier. If he doesn't want to leave the carrier at first, let him be. Just leave the carrier door open and the cat alone. He'll come out when he's ready.

Maintain each cat separately for a week or so — with lots of love and play for both — and then on a day when you're around to observe, leave the door to the new cat's room open. Don't force them together. Territory negotiations between cats can be drawn out and delicate, and you must let them work it out on their own, ignoring the hisses and glares.

Eventually, you can encourage them both to play with you, using a cat "fishing pole" or a toy on a string. And slowly — that word again — feed them in ever-closer proximity.

Most cats — but not all — eventually learn to live together happily. After you see your two sleeping together, playing, or grooming each other tenderly, you'll know the effort was worth it.

Dogs

Before you bring home a cat or kitten, make sure your dog knows two basic commands: "Leave It" and "Stay." You're going to be saying those words a lot in the first couple weeks, so the time to practice making sure your dog knows them is *before* you bring home your cat or kitten. Here's how to teach your dog these useful commands:

- ✔ **Stay.** Start with the "Sit," with the dog at your side, holding the leash in a straight line up from his head with all the slack out. Flash an open palm in front of your dog's nose and then say, "Stay." Step out in front of your dog so that you can block his forward motion. If he moves, snap the leash to correct him, flash your hand, and repeat the "Stay" command. If he stays, return to your position alongside him after a second or two, tell him "Okay," and praise him. From there, it's a matter of building up time and distances in slow increments. If you're working at the end of the 6-foot leash and your dog is staying reliably, tug on the leash a little without making a sound. If he moves, go back and correct him with the leash, repeat the command sequence, and try again. If he resists the tug, return to your position alongside him and release him with an "Okay" and praise.

- ✔ **Leave It.** With your dog in a Sit-Stay and your hand in a fist, flat surface up, offer your dog a biscuit with the other. As she reaches for it, say "Leave It" and bop her under the chin, enough to close her jaw but not lift her off her feet. Offer the biscuit again, repeating the "Leave It" command, and if she hesitates or turns away, praise her. Few dogs need this demonstrated more than twice.

For more on dog training or anything else concerning living with a dog, you ought to buy the companion book to this one, *Dogs For Dummies*. The book was named the best general reference book by the Dog Writers Association of America as well as the best entry in the DWAA writing contest — topping more than 1,000 entries in 50 categories. We are a little proud of it, especially Gina, since *Dogs For Dummies* was her very first book.

Bring your new cat or kitten home in his carrier, and as with the cat-to-cat introductions, put the carrier in the safe room. Bring your dog in on a leash, with the cat still safely housed, and let the two get a look at each other. Let your dog sniff, but if he's getting a little overly excited, use the "Leave It" command and praise him for minding.

Then take your dog out, close the door to the safe room, and let the cat come out of the carrier when he's ready. Allow the animals to get used to each other's scent for a couple weeks and then put a baby gate across the door to the safe room to keep the dog out. Let the cat choose the level of interaction.

Never tolerate aggressive behavior from your dog. Keep a leash on him until everyone's settled and use the "Stay" and "Leave It" commands to keep him under control.

Although some cats and dogs maintain an armed truce, at best, others become the best of companions. These things take time, however, so be patient.

New dog, old cat

Of course, sometimes a cat's not the new kid on the block — a dog is! If you're planning to add a dog to your cat's world, take some time beforehand to prepare her.

Take a look at your cat's food and water dishes. Are they in a location where a dog could get to them? Because cat food is higher in protein than dog food, many dogs think it's a wonderful treat. But cat food isn't good for your dog, and your cat isn't going to be interested in sharing. So move the dishes up to a place where your cat can eat without being pestered.

How about your cat's litter box? Again, make sure that it's in a "dog-free" zone, both for your cat's peace of mind and to keep your dog from indulging in a dreadful canine vice: eating cat feces. A hooded litter box may do the trick, but a better idea is to set up the area so that the dog can't get near the box. The method you use depends on the size of your dog. Putting a cat door in the door to a spare room keeps a big dog out; putting the litter box in the unused guest bathtub keeps most little dogs at bay. (For instructions on how to teach your cat to use a cat door, see Chapter 8; Chapter 15 offers more tips on keeping dogs out of the litter box.)

Make these changes a couple weeks before bringing home a puppy or dog so your cat can get used to them.

Don't allow your new dog to chase your cat — keep a leash on him so that you can correct him in the early stages. Don't force your cat to interact — let him deal with the interloper in his own way and in his own time.

Although doing so may not seem fair, because your cat was there first, if your cat reacts badly to the stress — not using the litter box, for example — you may need to resort to the introduction methods for a new cat we discuss in this chapter and keep him sequestered in a room with his food and water, litter box, scratching post, and toys during the acclimation process.

Other pets

If you have birds, reptiles, fish, rabbits, or rodents, no introductions are necessary. *Keep your cat away!* Never forget that, although your cat may be a loving companion to you, he's still hard-wired with the instincts of a hunter, and your smaller pets are his natural prey.

Don't take chances. Make sure that, whenever you're not around to look out for them, your other pets are kept safe from your cat. Close the door to the room where they stay, and correct your cat with a squirt bottle if you see him expressing an interest.

Many people live in homes with all kinds of pets coexisting quite peaceably. But don't ever take for granted the natural instincts of your animals. Some are predators, and some are prey. (Cats are actually both, depending on the circumstances.) Be vigilant and never give one pet the opportunity to hurt another.

Bonker/Photo by Aaron Springer

Figure 6-6:
Keep your cat away from those pets that are her natural prey, such as fish, rodents, and birds.

Chapter 7

Learning Feline Body Language

Communication is at the heart of any good relationship, and that's just as true when the bond is between a person and a cat as it is when it's between two people. Finding out more about the way your cat communicates can only strengthen the connection between you, making your life together more pleasurable for you both.

Understanding a cat is as remarkable as understanding a person from another planet, in a way, because the worlds you and your cat inhabit are vastly different. Ours is a world of words, of machines, of complex lives; our cat's is a world of nature, of body talk and sound, of simple pleasures. By understanding our cats, we can spend a little time in their world, so simple and relaxing. Perhaps that's one of the reasons spending time with a cat can lower your blood pressure — that easygoing attitude is contagious.

Learning to "speak cat" isn't just for our benefit. If we work to understand the way our cats communicate, we can care for them better, understand what they want, avoid unnecessary conflict, and catch the first signs that they're sick.

Picking up on your cat's body language is one way to spot illness, but an at-home exam is just as important. Check out our preventive-care tips in Chapter 11.

Making Sense of Cat Senses

Like most predators, cats have keen senses; they wouldn't have survived long enough to be domesticated if they didn't. Even today, when many cats have their food served to them in their own bowls, many felines don't have things so lucky. For them, a wonderful collection of natural talents is all that stands between them and starvation. That any of the wild ones survive at all, for any length of time, is a tribute to the senses of the cat.

Figure 7-1:
The body language of cats speaks volumes, as with this cat who's telegraphing a message of content-ment and relaxation.

Charlie/photo courtesy of Jennifer Ehrlich

Smell

People and cats are living in completely different worlds in terms of the sense of smell. The cat's sense of smell is many times more powerful than a human's (and a dog's is more powerful still). Are you surprised now that the litter box you think is "tolerable" is offensive to your cat?

Of course, the litter box is a modern problem, and the cat's sense of smell is good for much more than deciding when it's not clean enough. Smell plays a role in the establishment of territory (see the sidebar "Scent-marking" later in this chapter), in the finding of prey, and in the determination of whether "found" food is safe enough to eat. Dogs are scavengers who eat just about anything; cats are true predators: Fresh food, please, and freshly killed is even better. Ever wonder why your cat turns up her nose at canned food that's been out a while? Simple: It doesn't *smell* right.

If your cat is so finicky that no delicacy you serve suits her — or you're nursing a sick cat — warm the food up to just above room temperature before serving: about 85 degrees (or what we humans would call "lukewarm"). Doing so makes food smell better to a cat, and therefore that food becomes more enticing. For more on feeding and nutrition, see Chapter 10.

In addition to their noses, cats use a body part called the *vomeronasal organ,* at the front of the roof of the mouth, to help them process smells, especially those of a sexual variety, such as the smell of a female cat in season. Whenever cats use this organ, they open their mouths a crack and "taste" the smell, a facial expression called *Flehmen.*

Scent-marking

The correct "smell environment" is so important to your cat that he engages in various marking behaviors to make everything in his world smell like him — even you! Here are a few of your pet's scent-marking behaviors:

- **Rubbing:** Your cat has structures called *sebaceous glands* at the base of his hair follicles that produce *sebum*, a substance that serves two purposes: coating the fur for protection and depositing scent on objects in the cat's environment. These glands are most numerous around your cat's mouth; on the chin, lips, upper eyelids, and the top of the tail base; and near the anus and sex organs. If a cat rubs with his head (a behavior known as *bunting*), or any of these parts of his body, he's depositing sebum — and scent — on everything he touches. Our pitiful noses can't detect these deposits — and it's probably just as well.

- **Urine-spraying:** Although few humans mind being marked with sebum as our cats rub against us lovingly, we don't at all approve of another of the cat's territorial behaviors: urine-spraying. Although any cat may spray, the behavior is most common in unneutered males. These cats feel especially driven to mark their territory with their pungent urine by backing up to objects (or even people) and letting fly with a spray. (For information on how to deal with spraying problems, see Chapter 15.)

- **Clawing:** If your pet digs his claws into his cat tree (or your couch!), he's not intending to be destructive. Scratching keeps claws in shape by removing the outer layer of material and keeping the tips sharp; scratching also provides your cat with the opportunity for a good, healthy stretch. Perhaps not many cat lovers realize that scratching is also important for scent-marking. As a cat claws, the pads of his feet come in contact with what he's digging into, and that motion leaves behind scent from the sweat glands in his feet (which is why even declawed cats "press the flesh" against objects in their territory). No matter how useful clawing is to a cat, it's a problem for many cat lovers, one we offer tips to help you live with in Chapter 14.

- **Grooming:** Your cat's attention to having "every hair in its place" has many reasons, but one of them is scent-marking. Your cat's tongue covers every inch of his body with his own saliva, which contains his favorite perfume: *Eau de Moi*.

For a couple final thoughts on how important "smelling right" is to a cat, consider this: Cats often groom themselves right after being petted — to cover your scent with theirs! Your cat may also pay extra attention to your scent after you've stepped out of the shower, remarking you with sweet rubbing to make sure everyone knows you're "his."

Hearing

Unlike our unmovable ears, cats can use their external ears like satellite dishes, "tuning" them independently toward any sound that catches their attention. The ears of cats can catch sounds two octaves higher than humans can hear, a range of hearing higher than the dog's. The ability to hear high-pitched sounds is necessary, of course, when you're listening for the squeaking of your rodent dinner!

Your cat can learn to understand many of the words you use in speaking to her, such as, "Would you like to eat now?" The fact that a cat ignores most of them doesn't mean she isn't listening — she's just being a cat!

Vision

The common belief is that cats are color-blind. Not so. Researchers believe that cats can distinguish between colors but don't see much of a reason to try.

The marvels of feline vision pertain more to the cat's ability to see in exceptionally dim light conditions — important for animals who hunt at night — and their keen edge in detecting motion and distance, important traits for a predator who needs not only to find dinner but also to pounce on prey with great accuracy.

The "night vision" of cats is made possible by a special layer of cells behind the light-gathering retina that enables the cat to "double" the ability to discern objects in darkened conditions. Whereas humans reflect back red (from blood vessels) in the dark if a light (such as a headlight) hits the back of their eyes, cats reflect back a golden or green flash because of these layers, called the *tapetum lucidum.*

Taste

Because cats prefer to consume fresh animal tissues for their nutritional needs, you shouldn't be all that surprised to find out that they haven't much of the appreciation for sweets that humans do. As can humans, cats can discern whether dishes are bitter, salty, sweet, or sour, although their interpretation of the desirability of these tastes no doubt varies from ours. Because cats have fewer taste buds than humans do, the feline sense of smell probably plays a large role in determining the desirability of food.

The rough feline tongue is an extraordinary tool, perfectly adapted for grooming (including removing fleas) and cleaning the meat off the bones of their prey.

Touch

The hairs of a cat's coat and the whiskers of his face are extremely sensitive, and complement the night vision that cats enjoy when moving about after dark. Cats love to touch and be touched (the latter within certain personal cat limits), in part because touching — especially with the tongue or the head — is a way of spreading around a cat's all-important personal scent.

Figure 7-2:
Cats love to touch and be touched — although they're sometimes too "cool" to show their appreciation.

Photo by Linda Stark

Speaking "Cat"

No kitten ever needed a book to understand feline body language — or human body language, for that matter. Although cats are not as adept at understanding us as are dogs — whose wolf ancestors developed an intricate body language to keep the peace in the family structure, or *pack* — felines can communicate reasonably well with cats and other animals, too. (If you doubt the power of trans-species communication, consider how perfectly most dogs understand the "back off" sign of a cat with an arched back.)

Dogs can read cats, and cats can read dogs, and both do a better job at interpreting nonverbal cues than do the overwhelming majority of humans, who must seem stupid to animals. Throw in the verbal language of cats — meows and caterwauls, hisses and purrs — and you may need to reconsider your view that cats "can't talk." On the contrary, your cat could well argue that *you* don't listen.

Eyes

Your cat's eyes react automatically to light conditions, the pupils narrowing to vertical slits in bright sunlight and growing to large, black pools in darkness. Beyond those reactions, however, your cat telegraphs his emotional state in his eyes. Eyes that are opened wide but not so wide as to look "startled" suggest the polite interest of a relaxed cat. Wide eyes and large pupils suggest fear. A stalking cat (whether on the hunt for a mouse or a toy) has eyes that are open, "hard," and intensely focused. A cat who's ready to lash out narrows his eyes and focuses his pupils — beware!

Although cats don't appreciate being stared at — didn't your parents ever tell you that's rude? — they do appreciate "sharing a blink." Kiss the way cats do: Catch your cat's eyes with yours and then slowly blink. Your cat may even blink back!

Ears

A stalking cat turns both his satellite-dish ears straight forward, the better to catch the slightest peep from a hidden mouse. The ears of a relaxed cat are up and usually to the side, moving around to focus more keenly on sounds that may mean the temporary end of his comfortable period. If frightened, the cat's ears take a more sideways cast. The position you should never ignore, however, is the completely backward and flattened ears of a cat who's ready to lash out with a bite or a slash, whether in defense or aggression.

Tail

Tail up and flipped forward over the back is the cat's way of saying, "Hi, how are you; nice to see you; isn't it time to get my dinner?" — a relaxed and friendly greeting of affection and trust. A cat who's uncertain puffs out his tail, holds it low — perhaps even tucked under — and moves it from side to side. If stalking, the cat's tail is held low and stiff, except for twitching at the end as if the force required to hold one's body still is too much for a cat, who must release nervous energy from the end of his tail. (This "hunting twitch" may also be seen in play.)

The tail is one of the best physical indications of a cat's impending aggression. (See the sidebar "Prelude to a hiss," later in this chapter.) A cat who's becoming agitated whips his tail from side to side; often the tail is puffed out as well. A tail wag is *not* the friendly gesture in cats that it is in dogs, for sure!

Voice

Each cat, like each person, develops a voice uniquely her own, similar to others of her kind but never quite a match. Cats have a wide range of sounds available to them to express their emotional state; here's the collection:

- ✔ **Meows:** From the short chirping sound a mother cat makes to her kittens to the longer "I want it now" noises of a hungry pet, cats manage to get a lot of variety from a couple basic sounds. They vary them in endless ways, holding their vowel sounds sometimes and other times clipping them short. Cats even have a meow we humans can't hear, because the noise is outside our range of hearing. Live with a cat for a while, and you come to understand the specific meanings of your pet's various meows, which in broader terms usually mean, "Hi ya. I want something."

- ✔ **Caterwauling:** Even people who don't have cats know this sound, a multi-octave yowl usually performed as a duet between two cats who're getting ready to rumble. The message: "Get out of here or you'll be sorry." These concerts can happen anytime two cats contest territory but are especially frequent during the mating season, starting in spring.

- ✔ **Chattering:** If a cat is excited by the prospect of a kill or the possibility (for a male) of mating, you sometimes observe a rapid clacking of teeth.

- ✔ **Growling:** Really more of a softer, sustained low yowl, without the up-and-down variation of the caterwaul. Growling is the sign of a frightened or angry cat and is often punctuated by hissing and spitting — the latter two sounds being particularly useful for convincing dogs to back off!

- ✔ **Purring:** The feline equivalent of a smile. Like a smile, a purr turns up in some situations that aren't so happy, sort of an "I'm nice, so don't hurt me" message. Content cats purr, but so do injured or frightened ones, as well as cats giving birth or nursing kittens.

- ✔ **Screaming:** A cry of intense pain. We hope you never hear it, especially from your cat.

COOL CAT FACTS

Do cats have more than five senses?

Two phenomena that have been well documented over the years suggest that cats have a few more things going for them than we mere humans can understand.

One of these is the ability to "predict" seismic events, such as earthquakes. Cats (and other animals) appear to be sensitive to signs of increasing tension below, a theory promoted by those who claim that before an earthquake, the number of lost cats and dogs increases — presumably because the animals are attempting to escape from danger.

Another interesting skill is the cat's ability to return to what he recognizes as "home" from hundreds of miles away — after his family moves, for example. Although some of these cases are surely mistaken identity on the parts of the people and cats involved, others are well documented, and experiments have shown that cats have a particular sensitivity to the earth's magnetic field and so are masters of direction — no road maps needed.

We may never understand exactly what's behind these "extra senses," but that's probably fine with our cats: They'd prefer we admire their special air of mystery!

"Biscuits" of love

Cat lovers all know the special paw motions of a happy cat in the lap, although no one seems to agree on what to call this pleasurable bit of body language. Call it "making biscuits" or "kneading," the message is the same: affection and trust.

Making biscuits is a holdover from kittenhood. When cats are babies, they move their paws against their mother's side when nursing. When your cat does this to you, she's telling you that she considers you her mother, purring and kneading in a demonstration of feline love.

Hair and whiskers

Scared or angry cats hold their hair erect in an effort to look bigger; in the early stages of fear or aggression, some cats just puff out their tail. Whiskers have a broader repertoire in expressing emotion. If a cat is curious or angry, he holds his whiskers forward (cats also do this in the dark to help them "feel" their way around). Cats pull their whiskers backward when frightened.

Most cats have 24 whiskers, divided on either side of the nose and arranged in four horizontal rows. The top rows and bottom rows can move independently of each other, and each whisker — they're technically called *vibrissae* — is imbedded deeper than normal hairs to enhance its sensory input. Another odd whisker fact: The kinky-coated Cornish Rex and Devon Rex have curly whiskers as well!

Even though whiskers are important to cats — your pet may become disoriented if they're removed, which is why you never should cut them — there is no correlation between the length of whiskers and the width of a cat. If your cat gets fat, his whiskers don't grow to match. A portly cat who comes to count on his whiskers to gauge the width of a hole may well find himself stuck.

Posture

The way a cat holds her body must be placed in context to be understood, observed along with signs from the tail, ears, eyes, voice, and fur (including whiskers) to correctly interpret your cat's emotional state. A cat who's enjoying being petted from head to toe, for example, often arches her back to maximize contact with the stroking hand. In another situation, an arched cat is one you shouldn't be touching under any circumstances, or you may get injured. The difference is the context!

Study the overall cat to make sure, but the following list gives you a first impression of what different positions mean:

✔ **Inquisitive:** The friendly, curious, or inquisitive cat is relaxed, moving forward comfortably with tail up. Ears are up, too, and pointed slightly to the sides.

✔ **Defensive:** A cat who's just defensive, angry, or scared arches and puffs out her fur in the classic "Halloween cat" pose. From this pose, a defensive cat makes a run for it if he can; a truly furious cat attacks. A cat who's really in trouble rolls over onto his back to bring into play his formidable defensive weapons — claws and teeth.

✔ **Aggressive:** A cat who's going to attack crouches low, his back a little higher than his front, ready to put his powerful hind legs to use in a leap forward. Fur on the *hackles* (over his shoulders) is up, as is the fur on his tail. This cat is one who means business; back away and let him be!

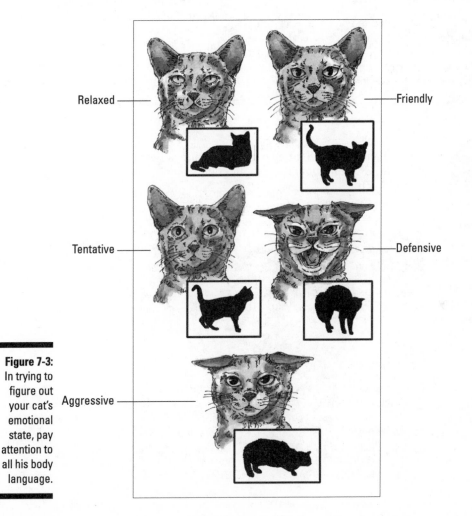

Figure 7-3:
In trying to figure out your cat's emotional state, pay attention to all his body language.

Prelude to a hiss

Human stupidity (from the cat's point of view, that is) in misreading or ignoring body language earns more than a few cat lovers a scratch or bite from time to time — the result of misinterpreting a cat's "I've had enough" signs.

The classic example of this phenomenon is the cat who, while being petted, "suddenly" grabs the hand that pets him with teeth and claws — to the shock and sometimes anger of the human doing the petting.

In fact, these "out of the blue" attacks rarely are. Before the biting or clawing, a cat gives out subtle (to us, anyway) signs of diminished tolerance. Primary among them: an increase in the stiffness and twitching of the tail.

Often, the problem starts with petting your cat's tummy, a very vulnerable area for any animal. Your cat may even offer his belly out of love, but after you start to pet, he may become increasingly uncomfortable with the attention. Most cats just don't like tummy rubs, although exceptions to this rule certainly do exist.

Watch your cat's body signs: If he's tensing or that tail starts twitching, stop petting *immediately.* Not only does doing so save you claw and teeth marks, but stopping before your cat strikes also slowly builds up his trust in you and his tolerance for physical attention. (For more information on feline aggression, see Chapter 14.)

A cat in any defensive or aggressive posture is best left alone, even if he's your cat. Give him time to chill out completely before you even attempt to approach.

Figure 7-4:
Judging from his very recognizable body language, this cat clearly has had more than enough of the photographer who'd been trying to take his picture.

Photo by Richard D. Schmidt

Chapter 8

All the Right Stuff

· ·

In This Chapter

▶ Looking at litter boxes and fillers

▶ Making sure your cat has ID

▶ Choosing scratching posts, cat trees, beds, and bowls

▶ Selecting traveling gear

▶ Buying all the best toys

▶ Getting the buzz about catnip

· ·

No barn cat ever imagined the way some of our cherished pets live today. Although cats have for uncounted generations relied on their own wits and skills to find food and water, a place to relieve themselves, a place to sleep, and things to amuse themselves, our increasingly indoors-only cat population looks to us to provide them with their basic needs, and to do so, you need cat gear.

But what choices you have! Forget about the old adage of making a better mousetrap: Make a better cat toy, and the world is sure to beat a path to your door today. Even more compelling: Make a perfect litter box, and you're certain to retire rich, as the inventor of Kitty Litter, the late Edward Lowe, did a generation ago.

At the basic level, cat gear takes care of your pet's needs in an inexpensive, no-nonsense way. But sometimes spending a little more can make your life easier and your cat's life more full, the latter an important consideration for the indoor cat who stays alone while you're at work. Besides, shopping for cat supplies can be great fun!

Although we cover the kinds of dishes you need for your pet in this chapter, we tell you what to put in them in our section on nutrition in Chapter 10. Information on the best grooming supplies for your cat — and how to use them — is in Chapter 9.

Finding the Best for Your Cat

Never before have people had so many choices in shopping for pets. In recent years, pet superstores have popped up everywhere, with a bigger selection of supplies than were carried by a half-dozen of the mom-and-pop pet stores of a generation ago. In the shadow of the retailing behemoths, small businesses have had to focus on finding a new niche, providing services such as free delivery, a higher level of pet-care advice than the superstores can offer, or niche products such as jeweled collars, wind chimes, and high-end toys and treats.

At supermarkets, where the emphasis is on age-old brand names and generic store brands, the appeal is convenience. Pet supplies are one of the top categories in any grocery store in terms of shelf space, and grocery retailers and their suppliers have done a great deal in recent years to improve the quality of their offerings. Of course, much of the reason for this increased interest in pet supplies is the supermarkets' desire to keep their share of the multibillion-dollar sales volume intact from the onslaught of their new competitors. Those competitors include the pet superstores, general retailers such as Wal-Mart, and warehouse stores such as Sam's Club.

And what about catalogs and the Internet? The boom in mail-order business hasn't missed the cat-supplies industry, with available catalog selections as varied as those of the pet superstores and as focused as those of high-end cat boutiques. The biggest explosion is online, where well-funded Web sites have been launched in hopes of cutting out a big piece of the pie. Huge Web sites with large advertising budgets suggest some form of online shopping for pet supplies is definitely here to stay.

Finally, don't forget the little guys! Many of the most creative and attractive merchandise for cats are handmade in small quantities. Craft fairs, cat shows, and farmers' markets are good places to look for these items.

Although experimenting with brand names and generic products is fine, remember always that the final determination of suitability on any product comes down to two things: First, is it safe for your pet, and second, does your pet like it?

You don't always need to think "new" when you need cat supplies. Many a top-quality cat tree or carrier has turned up at yard sales at a fraction of the cost for new, so keeping your eyes open at such sales often pays off for you and your cat. (Remember to clean secondhand gear thoroughly before use.)

A Place to Go

No product is more important to a harmonious relationship between you and your cat than a litter box. What behaviorists call *inappropriate elimination* — a cat who goes where he's not supposed to — is the top complaint cat lovers make about their pets and one of the primary reasons why adult cats end up in shelters.

The litter box you choose and what you put in it are two of the most critical purchases you'll ever make, and you need to be aware that you may not get the formula right the very first time. Be aware of all the possibilities and be prepared to experiment to find just the right combination of box and filler that's right for your cat's temperament and health.

Every bit as important as choosing the right litter box and filler is making it inviting and comfortable for your pet to use. If you have a cat who's refusing to use the litter box, you want to read Chapter 15, which contains the information you need on the causes of and cures for litter-box avoidance.

Getting the poop on litter-box choices

More choices in litter boxes exist than ever before and range from the recycling of old baking pans and dishpans to the inexpensive options of cardboard throwaways, to higher-priced models that make cleaning easier — or even automatic. The following list describes just some of your choices:

- ✔ **Disposable pans:** Small cardboard litter boxes are popular with shelters, rescuers, pet stores, and some breeders but probably aren't too practical for long-term use for your pet cat. Still, you may consider keeping a few of these on hand in case a stray walks into your life, for young kittens, or for cats who need nursing back to health. They're good for travel, or for use in time of disasters, too. Gina once cared for a cat with a broken leg, and the smaller size of disposable litter boxes worked well with the large carrier the cat stayed in while recuperating.

- ✔ **Household items:** A 9-x-13-inch metal baking dish, too worn for cooking, can be a good first litter box for a kitten — its low sides making it easy for babies to hop in and out of. Plastic dishpans, with their high sides, can be a good choice for cats who like to kick their litter everywhere.

A truly novel idea in the do-it-yourself litter box category comes from feline behaviorist Kate Gamble, whose cat-behavior videos are just about the best around. (See the Additional Resources appendix in the back of this book for ordering information.) Gamble, who is associated with the San Francisco SPCA, uses a plastic box sold for storing blankets, cutting one side down to make an easier opening and covering the cut edges with duct tape to prevent fur snags. She says the high sides of this design are another way to combat litter-kickers; to combat tracking, she puts the box lid underneath to collect litter from her cats' paws.

- ✓ **Simple plastic pans:** Millions of cats have done just fine with this design, and yours may be among them. Relatively inexpensive and widely available, these pans come in a variety of shapes, sizes, and colors. Some have special rims to keep more filler in the box. Make sure the one you choose is easy to scrub clean.

- ✓ **Covered pans:** Manufacturers say covered pans keep odors down and prevent dogs and children from getting into the filler. Unfortunately, some owners take the approach that, if they can't smell the litter box, it doesn't need attention — and the cat who feels otherwise finds someplace else to go. If you choose this kind of pan, don't forget you must be as on top of its cleaning as you would with any other variety — and don't blame your cat for mistakes if you aren't.

Cats with asthma should not use a covered litter pan — they need the increased ventilation an open-air variety offers. For more on cat asthma and other common health problems, see Chapter 12.

- ✓ **Self-cleaning pans:** No one likes to clean the litter box, but some cats are so fussy that, if you let this important chore wait, your cat may turn her nose up and go elsewhere. In recent years, inventors have come up with new pans that make cleaning a nearly "hands-off" affair, thanks to the easy-clean properties of clumping cat-box filler. Some of these boxes have lift-and-sift inserts that collect used clumps as you lift them, while you roll others over, running litter through a collector that catches and holds the clumps. Although generally a little more expensive than ordinary hoodless pans, these systems may be a good option if you're so squeamish about litter-box cleaning that, as a result, you don't do it frequently enough.

The electric self-cleaning litter box must be considered the top-of-the-line; indeed, its manufacturers promote it not as a litter box but as a household appliance. The system uses clumping litter and removes waste automatically after each use, thanks to an electronic eye that notices when a cat steps in and a ten-minute timer that ensures that he's long out of sight before the cycle begins. The machine runs a rake through the litter, catching clumps and depositing them in a sealed bin for later disposal. On the way back, the rake smoothes the litter for the cat's next visit. Ingenious!

Although no one's exactly fond of dealing with soiled litter, some people should avoid it entirely — pregnant women and people with immune systems suppressed by disease or medical regimens. That's because some cats harbor a parasite that can be dangerous to fetuses and to people with impaired immune systems. The danger should be kept in perspective, however, and does not require anyone to get rid of a cat. For the facts on the parasite and on the disease it causes (called *toxoplasmosis*), see Chapter 19.

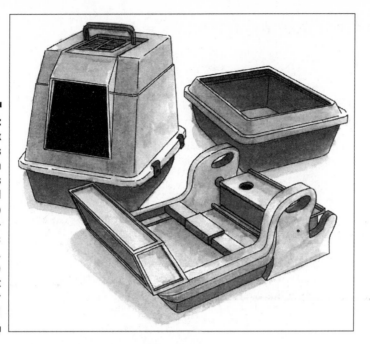

Figure 8-1:
Litter-box
choices
range from
simple pans
to hooded
models to
self-clean-
ing electric
appliances.
The choice
is yours, but
only if your
cat agrees!

Litter-box accessories

No matter what kind of litter box you choose, you have some additional
options to choose from — items intended to keep things neater or make
cleanup easier. Here's the rundown:

- **Scoops:** These utensils range from flimsy plastic to last-forever high-
  quality plastic and metal. You probably need one even for self-cleaning
  litter boxes — scooping one mess is often easier than sifting the whole
  box. Skip the flimsy scoop and get something that's going to last you a
  while.

- **Liners:** Intended to make changing the entire contents of the pan easier,
  liners work fine . . . if your cat likes them. If your cat digs deep with
  claws extended, he may not like catching himself on them. Experiment
  and see what works best for you both.

- **Mats:** You'll put up with less tracking of filler if you put a mat of some
  sort under your cat box. You can find mats made just for this purpose in
  any pet-supply store or catalog, or you can use an ordinary door mat or
  carpet remnant.

The scoop on litter

Some experts have credited the invention and improvement of litter as the driving force behind the cat's rise to the position of top companion animal, and certainly such a case can be made. Before absorbent filler became widely used and accepted, the alternative — sawdust and sand — left so much to be desired in the way of smell and ease of use that cats were often banished to the outside to eliminate their waste. After modern litter took off, however, cats became an integral part of the lives of an ever-increasing number of people, leading to the high popularity of felines today.

Many choices are out there when it comes to cat-box fillers, but you must always remain aware that the decision of which one's the "right" one rests solely with your cat. A litter you like won't be of much use if your cat hates it and goes elsewhere.

Even the best cats have accidents, and you want to keep cleaners at hand for any eventuality. The most important thing to remember: *Never* clean up a pet mess with an ammonia-based product: It makes the area smell even *more* like urine — ammonia being a component of urine — and attracts the pet back to the site for more messing.

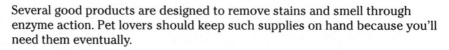

Several good products are designed to remove stains and smell through enzyme action. Pet lovers should keep such supplies on hand because you'll need them eventually.

Clay litter

A half-century old and still a significant part of the market, *clay litter* is the product that started the cat revolution. Clay litter is the least-expensive option in terms of price per pound, but you need to use more of it because clay litter needs to be completely replaced weekly to combat odors — although some brands do have deodorizers built in.

Some believe that clay tracks less and is safer for the tiniest kittens. (See the sidebar "Litter health risks, real and not-so-real," later in this chapter.)

Clay is easy to use with disposable boxes and so is popular with shelters and rescuers. Liners may make replacement of the entire contents of a cat box easier.

Clumping litter

Call *clumping litter* the second revolution, if you will. And even if you won't, have no doubt about the increasing popularity of this product among cat lovers.

Does an indoor-outdoor cat need a litter box?

Are you intending to be one of those people who never deals with a litter box at all? Unless you're living on ten acres of your own private property, we think you should reconsider your decision and get your cat a litter box.

We're guessing that your neighbors are going to agree.

Letting your cat use the great outdoors as he chooses is unfair to your neighbors and unhealthy to the people who come in contact with cat waste in their own flower beds — including members of your own family.

We're not going to rehash the arguments against letting cats roam freely — they're listed in Chapter 1 already — but we do stress that, if your cat wanders the neighborhood, you need to do what you can to get him to do his business at home. Keep a litter box clean and accessible to him at all times.

Clumping, or *scoopable,* litters dissolve around the moisture in urine or feces, reforming as a lump encasing the mess, which can then be easily scooped, raked, or sifted out. Because the entire mess is scooped out each time — assuming the clump doesn't break — odor problems are minimized. As with clay brands, some clumping litters have deodorizers in them.

Although clumping litters are more expensive per pound, they require you to use less because all you need do is replace the litter you've removed with the waste. Although clumping litter does need to be replaced eventually, that chore can wait for a month or more, depending on the quality of the litter (some brands clump better than others) and the number of cats using the box.

According to *CatWatch,* a monthly newsletter put out by the Cornell Feline Health Center (subscription information is listed in the Additional Resources appendix at the back of this book), preference polls indicate that cats prefer clumping litter to other varieties. This means that cats who may avoid the litter box if it's filled with other litters may use a clumping variety without problems.

Drawbacks to clumping litter include tracking problems, because the material that sticks to moisture on cat mess clings just as easily to moisture on cat paws. A mat will help to catch the mess.

Even worse than clumping litter's tendency to stick to a cat's paws is the mess than can develop around the genital area and back thighs of a cat with long silky hair, such as a Persian. Moisture in this area collects litter and can cause these cats problems with grooming and even defecating if the problem is left unattended. To avoid these problems, keep your cat's fur cut close on his inner thighs and other areas where urine may catch, and make sure that you've set up a frequent grooming regimen to catch any granules. For more information on grooming, see Chapter 9.

Litter health risks, real and not-so-real

As we mention elsewhere in this chapter, hooded boxes aren't recommended for cats with asthma. The same goes for dusty litters (as opposed to low-dust varieties) and litters with deodorizers, both of which may irritate these sensitive cats.

One health risk that seems to have no basis in anything but rumor and anecdote is the purported problem with clumping litter causing intestinal blockage — and death — in kittens.

The idea traces to anecdotal reports in cat lovers' magazines, later picked up and spread on the Internet. To date, no scientific study has confirmed that such a problem exists.

To err on the safe side, some veterinarians suggest avoiding clumping litter until the kitten is out of the taste-testing-everything curiosity stage. But even that advice is just a precaution for kittens only, and you don't need to fear any harm if you use clumping litter with adult cats.

Alternative litters

Coming up third in consumer preferences are various alternative fillers, including those made from wood fiber, corn cobs, pelleted newsprint, and other recycled materials. Some cats and cat owners love these alternatives; others can't stand them. Feel free to experiment until you find something that you, your cat, and your pocketbook can all be happy with.

Some litters call themselves "flushable," meaning that you can put waste and filler together into your toilet for easy disposal. Whether this approach is a good idea for your household depends on your home, the age of your plumbing, and whether you're on a sewer system or a septic tank. Gina likes to offer the advice of her favorite plumber: "Don't put anything in the toilet unless you've eaten it first." If you want to experiment, consult your favorite plumber first or, at the very least, keep his number handy!

You're better off sealing waste in plastic bags and putting the bags in your trash can for pickup. One more disposal alert: Public-health officials warn emphatically that you should *never* put the waste of a cat — or any carnivorous animal, such as a dog or ferret — in your garden compost pile. (The waste of plant-eating pets such as rabbits is fine, however.)

Kitty Come Home: Collars, Tags, and Microchips

Cat lovers are notoriously resistant to putting collars on their cats. Some just get tired of replacing the ones their cats keep slipping out of; other people are convinced that their roaming darlings may get caught on a tree branch by their collars and hang themselves.

Both groups are taking incredible chances with their pets' lives. Cat collars are an inexpensive insurance against loss, and as for the danger of being collared, your cat is many times more at risk for being lost than caught by his collar.

If you let your cat roam, give him a ticket home with some form of ID.

Traditional ID

Cat collars are made of lightweight material and designed to "give" enough to enable your cat to wriggle free should the collar ever catch on something. Don't get a puppy collar by mistake — dog collars are meant to prevent escapes, and cat collars are made to enable them. A wide choice of colors should keep any fashion sense happy, except your cat's, who'd just as soon do without. The fit should be snug but not uncomfortably so — you should be able to slide your little finger underneath.

After you've got the right collar, order a tag. ID tags come in high-impact plastic in a variety of colors and shapes or in metal, also in many varieties, including circles, cat's heads, reflectors, and so on. Because cat's tags are small, don't bother with putting your cat's name on it — she's not going to answer anyway. Instead, use the space to put your address and a couple extra phone numbers so that someone who finds your cat can locate you or a friend, neighbor, or relative of yours, day or night. If you're concerned about dangling tags, look for those that attach flat to the collar.

We've been really happy with a service called 1-800-Help4Pets and feel better with that company's tags on our pets' collars. 1-800-Help4Pets is a round-the-clock hotline to help your pet get home. The service also provides for boarding or emergency veterinary care if you can't be immediately located. (Information on the service can be found in the Additional Resources appendix.)

What about a bell to slow down a feline hunter? It couldn't hurt, but some cats learn pretty quickly how to move without setting off the bird-warning device. The only sure way to keep your cat from hunting is to keep him inside. For tips on turning a free-roaming cat into an indoor one, see Chapter 6.

If your cat's constantly coming home with nothing around his neck and you're handy with a sewing machine, try Gina's quick and easy way to keep IDs on your pet. Buy ⅜-inch elastic from a fabric store and order fabric name tags such as you'd put in children's clothes when they go to camp. Measure the elastic for a close fit, attach the label with thread or glue, and then sew or glue the ends of the elastic together to make a collar. If you like, you can dress up the creation with rickrack or other accessories from the fabric store — just avoid anything your cat could chew off and swallow, such as sequins. Make these easy ID loops a dozen or so at a time, and your cat will never lack for a comfortable collar!

Figure 8-2:
An ID tag is one piece of gear that can save your cat's life, by getting him safely home if he ever becomes lost.

Some communities require free-roaming cats to be licensed as a way to offset the costs of handling strays and to ensure compliance with local rabies-vaccination requirements. To find out whether your community is one of these with licensing requirements for cats, call your local animal-control agency. In response to concern about dangling tags, some agencies issue tags that slip over collars, and a few offer the option of tiny ear tags.

Microchips

The microchip is permanent identification no bigger than a grain of rice, which your veterinarian imbeds under the skin over your pet's shoulder blades by using a large needle. (But don't worry: One yowl is about all you hear at most, and then the job's done!)

COOL CAT FACTS

Walking the cat?

Indoor cats can be trained to enjoy an outing outdoors on leash, and for this treat, you need a harness. (Because cat collars are made to enable cats to slip out of them, don't use a collar with a leash.)

Choose a harness designed for cats, not for dogs, in a figure-8 design. Harnesses, like collars, come in many colors, with lightweight leashes to match.

Don't expect your cat to heel like a dog, however. Walking a cat consists of encouraging your pet to explore, with you following, offering plenty of praise and maybe a treat or two.

Never leave your cat tethered and unattended, which leaves him vulnerable to attack or to a terrifying time of hanging suspended from his harness should he try to get over a fence.

Microchips have been of dubious value for returning lost pets in the past, however, because one company's chips couldn't be read by another company's scanner, and shelters couldn't and wouldn't cope with competing systems. That's changed, with moves by manufacturers toward one industry standard and with the entry of the American Kennel Club as a registry of microchipped animals in the United States and Canada — any animals, not just AKC-registered purebred dogs. The cost ranges from $20 to $50 to have your pet chipped by your veterinarian, but it's a good investment in his safety.

Check with local pet-supply stores, cat and dog clubs, shelters, and veterinarians in your area for reduced-cost microchip clinics.

You should register your pet with AKC Companion Animal Recovery — 800-252-7894 — which offers 24-hour matchup service, 365 days a year. If someone calls to report finding your pet, the service releases your number so that you can be reunited with your baby quickly.

Most lost pets are found not by shelters but by neighbors, and neighbors don't have microchip scanners in their collection of home appliances. Which is why, although we highly recommend a microchip for permanent ID of your cat, we also advise you to make sure that your cat wears a collar and ID tag — whether it's one you ordered, a community-issued license tag, or one from a tracking service like 1-800-HELP4PETS — at all times, too. If someone hits your cat — sadly, a common occurrence with a free roaming pet — a tag at least ensures that you don't keep wondering whether your pet is ever coming home. It's a small consolation, but believe us, knowing the fate of your pet beats spending months wondering.

A Place to Scratch

The most important thing to remember about scratching is that it's as natural a part of your cat's life as breathing. Your cat needs to scratch, and you need to provide him with a place to dig in his claws and pull.

What you need, in other words, is a scratching post, cat tree, or other scratching toy such as those that affix to corners or hang from doorknobs.

If you're going to have any success in getting your cat to scratch where you want — instead of somewhere you don't, such as the corner of your couch — you're going to need to choose a scratching place that's not only sturdy but also made of a material your pet can enjoy digging into.

Stability is important, because the first time a scratching post comes crashing down on your pet is the last time he ever uses it, rest assured. As far as material, *sisal,* a natural ropelike covering, is popular with cats, as is a carpet with loops that aren't too shaggy.

Scratching posts are usually small, less than 3 feet in length, and either vertical on a wide base or horizontal, like a log — mimicking what cats like in the outdoors, some scratching posts *are* logs. (Or you can bring in a log on your own.)

The best investment you can make for your pet's enjoyment is a tall cat tree with a top perch. Cats love to look down on people because doing so reinforces their belief in their own superiority! A cat tree also offers a nook for those moments when a cat simply can't stand to be bothered with anyone. Some cat trees come with dangly toys attached, or you can add your own. Just make sure that anything attached or added is cat-safe — nothing that can be swallowed, such as strings or sequins.

If you're even a little bit handy, you can make your own cat tree by using scrap lumber and carpet remnants. Check out do-it-yourself plans at your local library or home-improvement retailer.

You can make a scratching place even more appealing by adding catnip. More about catnip — why it makes some cats crazy — comes later in this chapter, in the sidebar "Catnip and other leafy delights."

A scratching post, cat tree, or other scratching toy is an important part of training your cat to leave your furniture alone. See Chapter 14 for tips on solving scratching problems. Clipping helps keep your cat's claws in shape; see Chapter 9 for directions on how to clip your pet's nails without injuring either one of you.

Figure 8-3:
A good cat tree is stable and offers lots of options for playing, napping, or hiding.

Sweet Dreams: Beds

Have you ever heard the old joke about the 800-pound gorilla? No? Let us enlighten you:

Question: Where does an 800-pound gorilla sleep? _Answer:_ Anywhere he wants.

Now apply that to your 8-pound cat, because honestly, the answer is pretty close to the same. Within the limits of your tolerance (keeping your cat off your kitchen counters, for example) and his safety (keeping him out of clothes dryers), your cat is going to sleep pretty much anywhere he wants: Your couch. Your bed. Your clean clothes. Your dirty clothes, should you be sloppy enough to leave them where your cat can find them. Not to mention your lap, the top of your computer monitor, your chest, the top of your TV, your face, your bathroom sink, your feet, and the top of the book you're reading, especially if you're trying to turn the page.

That doesn't mean that you can't — or shouldn't — get your cat a bed of his own. After all, consider the matter from the infallible vantage point of cat logic: As your cat sees things, what's his is his and what's yours is his. Got a problem with it?

One of the best beds you can offer your cat is actually on top of a cat tree, a perch perfect for snoozing high above the humans and even lesser beings, such as dogs. Cat perches that affix to window sills also provide your cat a place to nap while the world goes by, as well as offering an indoor cat the opportunity to sun himself.

Comfortable places to sleep are important to cats, who manage to spend nearly two-thirds of their lives with their eyes closed.

Soft, round "cup" or "cuddler" beds are popular with some cats, and cushions are a hit with others. Hammocks are just the ticket for some as well. You just need to experiment to see which your cat prefers.

Fabric beds can harbor flea eggs and larvae, so make sure any bed you buy has a removable cover for frequent washing. For more tips on controlling fleas, see Chapter 9.

Bowls and Waterers

As with everything else concerning your cat, her food and water bowls must be acceptable to her, or you've wasted your money. In addition, they also must be made of a material that doesn't scratch — food particles and bacteria can collect in tiny gashes — and that can be completely cleaned, preferably in the dishwasher.

For the most part, that's going to mean stainless steel or high-impact plastic crock-style dishes. Fortunately, the latter come in colors and patterns to fit any decor, and some specialty catalogs and boutiques also allow you to order personalized dishes.

Plastic dishes are suspected in causing some skin lesions on the face of cats. If a cat develops frontal face, chin, or lip lesions, changing from plastic bowls to another type is a good idea.

Some cats share food dishes readily, but many don't. Some share a supply of dry food from a single dish but require their own individual servings of canned food — at room temperature, puh-lease! If your cats are hissy about sharing, keep food dishes for each cat and feed your babies with some distance between them.

The most important advice about dishes is to keep them clean. Cats are fastidious, especially about their water, and many turn up their nose at any sign of old food or stale water.

Figure 8-4:
No water bowl will satisfy some cats, such as this one who drinks straight from the tap.

Innovations abound in the pet-dish area. Some feeders allow you to leave enough food for a weekend, releasing each meal to your cat at preset intervals. Another product is designed for multicat households where one cat eats more than his share and the other one's finicky. The greedy cat wears a collar that triggers a discouraging tone if he gets near the other cat's dish!

Water dishes haven't been neglected by cat-loving inventors either. Although dishes with a reservoir of water have been available for a long time, some new water dishes play to the cat's love of water by providing water that's so fresh it's still *running*. These products constantly recycle water through the unit.

The biggest problem with water dishes with reservoirs attached is that you can too easily forget to keep them clean. These units need to be broken down daily and given a good scrubbing, because cats prefer their water fresh.

All you need to know about what to put in that fancy cat dish is in Chapter 10.

Home Away from Home: The Carrier

Every cat needs his own carrier. A sturdy carrier makes going to the veterinarian's, traveling, or moving safer and easier for your pet and offers you some options in times of disasters.

The right cat carrier can make introductions to other cats and pets easier, too. For more information, see Chapter 6.

Even the best carriers are a bargain at less than $25 or so if you shop around, and the chances are good that you can pick up one for next to nothing from yard or estate sales. Look for a carrier that provides your cat with a feeling of security and the ability to look out at the world. The ones we like are made of two pieces of high-impact plastic with small vents along the top, the top and bottom held together by bolts, and with a grid door of stainless steel.

Don't choose the following types of carriers:

- **One that's all wire:** Your cat is made even more nervous by being exposed on all sides.

- **One made of wicker:** Although they may look attractive, you need something you can clean thoroughly if accidents happen. (And they always do!)

- **One made of cardboard:** The cardboard carrier you may have gotten at the time you adopted your cat or kitten is fine for taking him home, but it isn't durable enough to rely on in the long run.

A high-quality cat carrier is an inexpensive investment in your cat's safety. Don't neglect the purchase.

Carriers figure into many parts of your cat's life. For tips on making your cat's trip to the veterinarian easier, see Chapter 11. For information on traveling or moving with your cat, see Chapter 18. And finally, for everything you need to know to protect your cat in a disaster, see Chapter 20.

The Ins and Outs of Cat Doors

So exactly why does the cat who just came in suddenly want to go out — and vice versa? Is he just trying to drive you crazy? Well . . . not exactly.

Cats like to keep an eye on their territory, and if their territory includes a piece of the outdoors, they're going to want to check on it frequently. And after they're out, who's looking after the indoor turf? The cat needs to come inside to check.

Installing a cat door can end your days as door opener, giving your cat the opportunity to come and go as he pleases. But that's not all cat doors do. Some cat lovers have installed cat doors in interior doors as a way to keep dogs (dogs larger than a cat, that is) out of the room with the litter box. A cat door doesn't need to lead to the outdoors either: Putting one in as a gateway to a screened porch is a great way to give your indoor cat access to the smells and sounds of the world at large.

Teaching your cat to use a cat door

After you install your cat door, just leave it be for a week or so until your cat takes its presence for granted. (Remember always that cats aren't keen on change.)

To teach him to use the door, tape the flap up securely for a few days so that he comes to appreciate the fact that he can conveniently come and go on his own schedule through this magic portal. (And we do mean securely. If your cat gets clobbered by the flap, it takes a long time to coax him near it again.)

Then put the flap down and put a little butter or margarine on the bottom edge of the flap and encourage him with tasty treats and praise from the other side. You can also drag toys on a string through, encouraging him to chase them.

Repeat these lessons in very short intervals over the course of several days, and your cat gets the hang of it, sure enough. If you have a cat who already uses the cat door, you usually don't need to do anything. Your new cat or kitten learns from the other cat. (Or even from your dog, if the pet door is shared.)

The basic cat door has a flexible plastic flap that opens as your cat pushes on it and seals shut again with magnets to keep the heat, cold, or wind out after he's passed through. Although these flaps are plenty weatherproof in sunnier climes such as California, where Gina and Paul live — with pet doors in both their houses — they may be a little drafty in areas with more-severe winters.

Gina has known people who've built sort of an airlock onto their houses: a tunnel with pet doors at both ends to minimize drafts. (Although she admires such ingenuity, on the whole, such cold-climate necessities make her happy to live in California.)

You have a couple options in installing cat doors. If you have a sliding glass door, you can buy panels with a pet door built in that fit on the end of the slider. If you have problems with neighbor cats coming in, you can find cat doors that work electronically, opening only for those cats wearing a collar with a special, battery-operated transmitter.

Other cats aren't the only animals who can learn to use your cat's door. Raccoons and opossums can, too, and so can skunks. One of Gina's friends learned this the hard way after she walked into her laundry porch and surprised a skunk dining eagerly on dry cat food. We're not sure whether the smell ever completely disappeared from her house. (For information on how to get skunk smell off your cat, see Chapter 9.)

The other problem with cat doors is the things your cat can bring through them. Gina's neighbors have a black-and-white tomcat who once brought a full-grown blue jay through the cat door — and released the terrified bird in the living room!

Cool Toys for Your Cat

At last, the fun part! For an indoors-only cat, toys aren't a luxury: They're an important way to keep your pet exercised, and they fight boredom and help to form a strong bond of companionship between you and your pet. As with everything else regarding cats, the choices in cat toys are many and getting even more varied by the day, as cat-loving entrepreneurs try to create a cat toy that sells millions.

One of the earliest cat toys was invented by Dr. A. C. Daniels, who patented his Catnip Ball in 1907. The wooden ball was hollow for putting catnip in — his own special brand, preferably. The ball was followed by other catnip toys, and the company, founded in Boston in 1878, is still making cat toys today.

The best you can buy

You can spend a lot of money on cat toys, including some pretty nifty battery-operated gadgets that whirl mice around on tracks or pull pieces of fluff around the room. Remote-control mice are available, too, complete with a wireless control — batteries not included, of course.

Your cat can have some fun with all of these to be sure, but we've found that some of the best cat toys don't cost much at all. At the top of the list are "cat fishing poles" that have bangles, feathers, or a stuffed toy at the end of a sturdy string tied to a flexible pole. These toys allow you to play with your cat (a good thing) without letting your pet learn that pouncing on your fingers or hands is okay (a bad thing).

Little fur mice are fun, too, as are balls with little jingle bells inside. Save the squeaky toys for your dog, however, because you cat probably isn't going to like them. Other hits include toys stuffed with catnip, as well as Ping-Pong or foam balls, pipe cleaners twisted into fun shapes, or even rabbits' feet.

Knock yourself out experimenting! We guarantee that your cat's not going to mind. Just make sure that you check out every toy for safety, eliminating anything your cat can swallow.

Freebies cats love

Speaking of cat toys, some of the best things in life are free — or nearly so. When Gina ran a cat-toy poll in her Pet Connection column, the top toys all were freebies, and number one on the list were the plastic rings that hold down the lids on plastic milk jugs.

Figure 8-5:
Cat toys
come in all
shapes and
sizes, with
the single
aim of keep-
ing your cat
entertained.

Tiffany/Photo by Sherry Mazzara

Plastic rings aren't the only popular freebie. Many cats like empty cardboard boxes and empty *paper* grocery bags. (Put away the plastics ones, however, because they can suffocate your cat.) Some other favorite playthings include folded empty cigarette packs (or the wrappers off them), drinking straws, the clear plastic safety rings around cottage cheese or sour cream lids, and the centers of toilet-paper, tape, and calculator rolls.

For the cat who loves to retrieve, try wadded-up tissues or paper, or the corks from wine or champagne bottles. Empty plastic film containers are great to bat around, as are nuts in their shells and even small vegetables such as Brussels sprouts or baby carrots.

Freebies that can turn dangerous are string, floss, ribbon, twine, rubber bands, or anything that your cat can swallow. You're best advised not to use these things at all in play, but if you do, make doubly sure that you put them completely away after the game is over.

More Fun Stuff

You don't find too much in the way of dress-up for your cat, mostly because your cat has too much dignity to put up with some of the really silly things dogs do. But if you want to go nuts with cat-related items for yourself, plenty of possibilities are around.

Figure 8-6:
The best toys are often free — including bubbles!

Millie/Photo by Ron Bell

We could write a whole separate chapter on cat-themed stuff you can buy for *you:* bumper stickers and T-shirts; plates and cups; calendars and stationery; wind chimes, mailboxes, and tote bags; and jewelry, both kitchy and fine. You're going to find all this stuff on your own, and you're probably going to buy a lot of it. And we're not going to stop you, because we've got plenty of these things, too.

Cat shows, craft fairs, online auctions, and high-end pet boutiques are great places to look for these items — and you can have a lot of fun doing it. And no, you can't have Gina's hand-painted Siamese tile. Don't even ask.

Catnip and other leafy delights

Not all cats like catnip — the ability to appreciate the herb is genetically programmed, with slightly more cats in the fan club than not.

Catnip — *Nepeta cataria* for you botanists — produces bouts of ecstasy for those cats who like the stuff. A substance called *nepetalactone* that's present in the leaves and stems causes the behavior, which lasts for just a few minutes and can include rolling, rubbing, leaping, purring, and general uninhibited happiness. Kittens under the age of 3 months do not react to catnip, and even in those cats who truly adore the "high," the plant is nonaddictive and harmless.

Valerian is another herb that makes cats happy, and the two can be grown as part of a cat garden. For more on cat-safe plants, for nibbling or for fun, see Chapter 10.

Part III
Maintaining a Happy, Healthy Cat

The 5th Wave   By Rich Tennant

"It's 'Feathers', I think she's taking steroids."

In this part . . .

This part focuses on your pet's health, with everything from grooming to nutrition, preventive medicine to the most common diseases cat lovers face in their pets. You'll find information on how to choose a veterinarian in this part too, as well as how to determine if your cat needs the help of a professional groomer. Does your cat need to see a veterinarian immediately? Our urgent-care guidelines help you decide. Special care for older cats is the focus of the final chapter, along with the facts you need about euthanasia, and pet-loss resources to help you through a difficult time.

Chapter 9

Good Grooming

• •

In This Chapter

▶ Understanding why cats groom themselves

▶ Appreciating the benefits of a groomed cat

▶ Choosing and using grooming tools

▶ Brushing and bathing your kitty

▶ Getting out what your cat gets into

▶ Controlling parasites

▶ Trimming your cat's claws

• •

You can lose yourself in a cat's fur. Warm under your fingers, glossy-sleek to your eyes, a cat's fur can relax you, make you smile, and ease the strain of a hard day before your feline companion even starts to purr. In so many lovely combinations of color and pattern, of texture and length, the coats of our cats are an inspiration to those who appreciate the gifts of nature: a supple pelt covering a body that is itself a perfect picture of symmetry, power, and consummate grace.

For a cat, a coat may seem a source of pride — so much does she preen it — but it's really much more. A healthy coat of fur can protect her from the elements and hide her from both predator and prey. Instinctively, she knows the importance of each hair and spends a great deal of her time cleaning her fur in a ritual as old as cats themselves, pulling dead hair free along with the dust from her rambles, restoring order and shine with her marvelously adapted tongue, as rough as sandpaper and handier than any comb.

Considering how much time your cat spends grooming, do you really even need to be involved in the process? Yes! Taking care of your cat's coat — as well as her claws — keeps her healthier, makes her easier to live with, and strengthens the bond between you. With some cats, human help is a must, for they have coats they can't handle alone. Pushed to beautiful extremes by selective breeding, the long silky coats of cats such as Persians need constant human attention to stay mat-free, comfortable, and oh-so beautiful.

Although many pedigreed cats *must* have help with their grooming, *all* cats benefit from human intervention. After you get the hang of grooming, you both feel better for it.

Some cats need a lot more grooming than others. For information on coat types as you're selecting a pet, see Chapter 2. Your cat's teeth need regular at-home attention as much as his coat and claws do, and we cover preventive dental care in Chapter 11. Good nutrition is important to maintaining a healthy coat, too, and for information on feeding your cat, turn to Chapter 10.

Fur, the Purrfect Complement

Your cat's coat is more than beautiful. Long or short, it provides him with protection against the elements, insulating against both cold weather and hot. The original coat pattern of cats is the tabby, still very common and much beloved, and perfect for hiding a cat in the shadows of meadow or woodland.

The protective properties of coat color are relative, of course, to the kind of life a cat leads. A dark color or pattern may be an advantage for hunting or hiding in the night, but it's a distinct disadvantage to the cat who roams the streets of city and suburb — black isn't as visible to drivers in the dark.

Most cats have three kinds of hair in their coat: short, fluffy, insulating *down;* wiry, mid-length *awn;* and longer, straighter, protective *guard.* (The specialized hairs we call "whiskers" make up a special fourth category, the *vibrissae.*)

Not all cats have all three kinds of hair, and even those who do may have them in different proportions or lengths. The kinky-coated Cornish Rex, for example, has no guard hairs at all, and its down and awn hairs are crimped — as are its whiskers! The Persian, by contrast, has a straight coat in which even the down hairs are long by comparison to most cats, making the tendency to mat very pronounced.

Why Cats Groom

Cats do their best to keep every hair in order — and not just for the sake of appearance. Grooming has a number of advantages to your cat, including the following:

✔ **Weatherproofing:** Separating and smoothing each hair help to improve the fur's insulating abilities, keeping both heat and cold at bay. As a cat grooms, he also distributes the oils from his skin throughout his coat, giving it a measure of waterproofing.

Grooming on autopilot

Kittens are groomed by their mothers for the first few weeks of their lives, but by the third week, they start grooming themselves as all cats do, in a very particular order, licking carefully and nibbling free any mats or dirt along the way.

Whenever cats sit down to groom, they start by licking their lips and then wetting the side of their paw, rubbing the damp paw over the side of their face; then they repeat the same sequence of motions on the other side.

After their faces are clean, they lick their front legs, shoulder and side, and then they hike first one hind leg straight up and then the other in the position cat lovers know so well, cleaning their privates and then the legs themselves. They finish the process by licking their tail clean, starting at the base and working to the end.

What a system! The end result is a beautiful cat, ready for anything the elements have to offer.

Feona Rose/Photo by Elizabeth Cardenas-Nelson

✔ **Scent-marking:** Grooming helps to distribute a cat's scent across his whole body, a phenomenon very reassuring to this scent-oriented animal. Scent is so important that a cat often licks himself right after being petted, both to re-establish his own scent and to drink in yours. And that's not the only grooming act that puts a cat's scent where he wants it: The act of digging his claws into a fence post (outside) or sofa or cat tree (inside) not only keeps his nails sharp, but also leaves secretions from glands in his paws on the object he fancies.

✔ **Parasite control:** Although your cat can't keep up with a major flea and tick infestation, he does his best by nibbling the pests off his body. (For more on your role in controlling fleas and ticks, see "Keeping external parasites under control," later in this chapter.)

✔ **Sociality:** In a multicat household, especially one with littermates, you often see cats grooming each other. This behavior — which is also performed on beloved humans — is a way of reinforcing a cat's connection to his family.

Grooming has so many benefits that you can easily see why, next to sleeping, it's one of the most important tasks on any cat's list!

Changes in the condition of your cat's coat or grooming behavior may be a sign of illness. See Chapter 11 for more information.

What's in It for You?

Many cats live their whole lives without anyone laying a brush on them, much less a set of nail clippers. And a bath? We must be nuts to even suggest it! But even if your cat isn't a high-maintenance type with silky, long hair, helping your cat with his grooming offers some benefits to you, as well:

✔ **Shedding:** The fur you catch on a comb or brush doesn't end up on your sofa cushions, sweater, or the cream cheese on your bagel in the morning. Please note, though, that a certain amount of cat hair just goes with sharing your life with a cat. There's even a clever saying floating around, author unknown: "No outfit is complete without cat hair." Funny, but true!

✔ **Smell:** Most cats are fairly fastidious, but some cats, especially unneutered males, can be a little offensive from time to time. Longhairs can get urine and feces in their fur, which can be uncomfortable — and unhealthy — for you both.

✔ **Hairballs:** More of a problem in longhaired cats than short, but still, no one likes listening to a gagging cat, and stepping on a coughed-up mass in bare feet is even less appealing! Regular grooming by you keeps the volume of fur swallowed by your cat as he grooms himself to the utmost minimum, and that means fewer hairballs on your lovely Oriental rug. (More about hairballs later in this chapter, in the sidebar "Help for hairballs.")

✔ **Bonding:** Although your cat may not like your getting involved in his grooming at first, if you're persistent, especially with the praise, your cat eventually comes to enjoy the time you spend together at this important task.

✔ **Destructiveness:** Keeping your cat's claws trimmed reduces his need to scratch, because one of the reasons cats claw is to remove the worn outer casings of the nails. (For more on scratching, however, make sure you read Chapter 14.)

✔ **Money:** Good grooming saves you money in more ways than one. By reducing your cat's need to scratch by keeping his claws in good shape, you save money on replacing things he may destroy. Grooming is also part of a preventive-care regimen: Paying attention to your pet's body not only helps him avoid some health problems but also helps you detect signs of illness early, which is better for both your wallet and your pet. Just the contact is good — many owners don't realize until then that their pet is losing weight or has new lumps and bumps or even open sores. The laying on of hands is a great preventive-care and bonding routine — aim to systematically touch all parts of your cat at least once per week. Getting your cat used to being touched and having his ears and mouth looked in will make the trip to the veterinarian much easier and more pleasant for all — you, your cat, and your veterinarian, too.

✔ **Allergies:** Studies have shown that good grooming, including regular baths, can help allergy sufferers cope with their pets. Some cats have allergies, too, such as to flea bites, and your attention to his grooming makes your cat's life more comfortable.

If you're allergic to your cat, check out Chapter 1 for our strategies for coping with your sneezing and wheezing.

Keeping your cat well groomed cuts down on shedding, but if you think you're going to be living in a cat-hair-free house, you're seriously deluding yourself. If you're going to live with a cat, you're going to need something to get the fur off your clothes. You can use masking tape, wrapped around your hand with the sticky side out, but we like the lint rollers that you can always keep sticky by peeling off another layer. Some pet-supply catalogs sell these in bulk, and you can also find them at warehouse stores. Because you need to keep one in your home, your car, and your desk at work for your cat's entire life, shopping around for a good price pays!

Tools of the Trade

A little money is involved in the collection of the right tools to help you with your cat's grooming. Buy high-quality tools from a reputable pet supply outlet and keep them together so that you know where to find them.

Gina keeps her pet-grooming supplies in a plastic container with a snap-tight lid, safe on a shelf in the hall closet. She keeps an extra comb in a drawer in the TV-room coffee table, so she can take advantage of a pet's good mood while everyone's watching TV.

Coat-care tools

You need a few things to keep your cat's fur clean and neat. Exactly what you purchase depends on your cat's coat type.

Grooming some cats for the show ring takes a great deal of work and years of learning to get it right. If you're really going to be competitive, work with your breeder or another mentor to learn what you need to, including show grooming. Our guidelines in this chapter are for keeping a pet cat in fine form and aren't meant to prepare your cat for showing.

Here's what you need for your cat:

- **Short- and medium-coated cats:** Start with a couple stainless-steel combs — one with very narrowly spaced teeth, called a *flea comb,* and one with slightly wider teeth for clearing dead hair, small mats, and debris (the package will describe it as *fine*). A *slicker brush,* with its slender, bent wires, is good for applying the finishing touches to a mat-free coat; alternatively, you can buy a grooming glove — sometimes called a *hound glove* — that fits over your hand, with coat-massaging nubs on the palm so that you can pet and brush at the same time.

- **Wire-coated breeds:** Your supplies depend on the amount of coat your pet has. Some wire-hairs have crimped hair of all three varieties (down, awn, and guard) and hence a coat that's "normal" except for being wiry. Other cats have very little coat at all, and what they do have is primarily down and awn hairs. If your cat has a thick hair coat, you need the same equipment as for a short- or medium-haired cat. If your cat's fur is very sparse, you need a flea comb and a soft-bristled baby brush.

- **Long-coated cats:** Use a *pin brush* — so named because it looks like a pin cushion — instead of a slicker brush and add a medium- or coarse-toothed comb to the mix, as well as the same fine-toothed comb you need for most other cats. (Depending on the thickness of your pet's hair, a flea comb may be of little use, because it's almost impossible to pull through your cat's coat.) You also need a detangling spray and cornstarch or talcum powder for mats. (More on how to use the cornstarch and talcum powder later in this chapter, in the "Getting the gunk out" sidebar.)

Some combs don't have handles, but the kind that do are probably more comfortable to use. It's a matter of personal preference, though.

For all cats, you need shampoo. Choose one made especially for cats, or use human baby shampoo. For long, silky coats, add a cream rinse. Cotton balls keep ears dry while bathing, and cotton balls and swabs help with post-bath ear care.

Do not use dog shampoos with flea-controlling chemicals on your cat — they're toxic. Although you can use flea-control shampoo designed especially for cats, you really don't need to: An ordinary shampoo sends fleas down the drain just as surely as one with pesticides. Not all the fleas will be rinsed away, though, so it's a good idea to follow up with a flea comb.

Flea-control tips can be found in their own section later in this chapter, "Keeping external parasites under control."

Nail-trim aids

Your cat keeps his claws in shape by removing the worn outer coverings — called *sheaths* — and exposing the new claw below, either by chewing the sheaths off or leaving them in whatever he claws. (If you look closely at your cat's scratching post, you'll probably find old sheaths stuck in the fabric.)

Keeping your cat's claws trimmed is a good practice for two reasons: First, doing so cuts down on destructiveness by removing some — but not all — of your cat's desire to dig his claws into objects. Second, it makes things a little more comfortable for us thin-skinned humans to live with cats — as anyone with a cat who likes to "knead" with claws going in and out while napping on a lap can testify!

You have at least two choices in terms of nail trimmers: *guillotine* or *scissors-type*. Guillotine trimmers have a little oval guide into which you slip your pet's nail and a blade that extends into that guide after you squeeze the trimmer. The scissors-type works like scissors, not surprisingly, with the nail going between two small, crescent-shaped cutting blades. Either kind works perfectly well and is a matter of personal preference. Paul also uses human fingernail or toenail trimmers on his cat, so you can experiment with those, too.

You also need to pick up something to stop the bleeding should you nick the vein in your pet's nail. Kwik-Stop powder is available in most pet-supply stores or catalogs.

Don't be put off by packaging suggesting that either kind of clipper is for use on dogs — they work just fine on your cat, too. Some scissors clippers are made just for cats, but you may find these a little too small to use easily and prefer the regular "dog" clippers.

The Importance of Patience

Over the long haul, you're going to have very little success doing anything your cat doesn't want you to do, so keep this in mind when contemplating any grooming procedure.

Although some restraints on the market are designed to make dealing with a completely uncooperative cat possible — and we cover them elsewhere in the section "Cat + water + soap = Oh, my!" — neither one of you is going to enjoy using them. And if you need to fight your cat to care for him, you aren't going to bother struggling for very long — it's just human nature.

Still, you'd be surprised at what some cats are willing to tolerate. Show cats, for example, are conditioned to tolerate a great deal of grooming, traveling, and handling by strangers — and with very little fuss. That's what they're used to, after all, and the show life is the only one they've known. Although your cat may never display the confidence and outgoing temperament of a seasoned show cat, you can do a lot to help him put up with some of the same grooming routines — and maybe even learn to enjoy them. Here are some tips:

- ✔ **Start young.** Get your kitten used to being handled, brushed, combed, and bathed, and prepare him for nail trimming by gently handling his paws, pushing a claw out, releasing, and praising.

- ✔ **Go slowly.** Introduce new routines a little bit at a time and build up your cat's tolerance over time.

- ✔ **Give yourself a fresh start.** If you adopt a longhaired cat or kitten who's matted, arrange to have him shaved down by a groomer (or maybe the shelter or adoption group) so you don't start out your relationship by jerking on your cat's fur. Sure, the cat looks funny, but the coat grows back quickly, and by the time it does, your cat is more used to you and to grooming.

- ✔ **Reward your cat.** Use treats, praise, and gentle petting to let your pet know that you approve of his behavior. You can't make a cat do anything he doesn't want to, so praise is the only way to go.

- ✔ **Know when to call it a day.** You'll do better if you stop before your cat becomes impatient, annoyed, or afraid, but if you miss the signs — or feel yourself becoming cross — stop what you're doing and end the session on a note of praise and petting. If you've really blown it, just let go and chalk it up to experience — and try again another time.

Never, never, never hold onto a cat who is becoming irritated. Most dogs will respond more like a child and not physically respond to an authority figure, but most cats will respond explosively if feeling cornered. The best thing to do is to let an annoyed cat get her way and to try again later. Failure to respect a cat's temper can result in serious use of claws and teeth that you do not expect from your loving pet.

Are you having trouble reading your cat's mind? The signs of a coming explosion of fear or anger are so subtle that some owners miss them. Read up on feline body language in Chapter 7.

Keeping Kitty Coats in Shape

The amount of time you spend grooming your cat's fur depends on a couple factors, primarily the kind of coat your cat has. With their long, silky coats, Persians and Himalayans need daily brushing, combing, and detangling, frequent baths, and even professional grooming on occasion (see the sidebar "Does your cat need professional grooming?" later in this chapter). Other longhairs, such as the Maine Coon, have coats that don't mat quite so easily, although they, too, need more attention than the easy-care coats of the pedigreed or nonpedigreed shorthairs or the fine fur of some of the lighter-coated pedigreeds, such as the Cornish Rex.

Cats with medium or short coats are fine with weekly grooming and a bath now and then — more frequently if you have allergy sufferers in the home or if you're especially sensitive to finding hair everywhere. For most cats, though, you just want to pitch in often enough to ensure that mats aren't forming and fannies are kept clear of debris. More frequent attention than that is never a bad thing though, please note.

Figure 9-1:
Sometimes it's easiest with a long-haired cat to cut the coat short rather than struggle to remove mats.

Mac/Photo by Kathie Schutte

Combing and brushing

Short-, medium-, and wire-haired cats are a breeze to groom after you get your cat used to the idea of being touched by grooming tools. Run the comb through your cat's fur, follow with the slicker brush or grooming glove, and then step back and admire the shine!

One benefit of shorthaired cats: You can use a flea comb on them. Flea combs have narrowly spaced teeth that catch the little bloodsuckers where they eat: on your cat. To use one, comb with the fine comb first and then flea comb from the skin out, a tiny bit at a time, flicking the pests into a bowl of warm, sudsy water as you go. After you're done, flush the fleas away — most of them are drowned by then anyway.

You need to realize, however, that combing fleas from your pet does *not* solve a flea problem. See "Keeping external parasites under control," later in this chapter, for a total flea-control program.

For longhaired cats, a flea comb is hard to use, and grooming is a little more involved. Here are the steps to follow:

1. **Divide your cat's coat into sections with the "medium" or "coarse" comb and work through the fur slowly and gently.**

2. **Repeat Step 1, but this time use the fine-toothed comb.**

3. **Follow with a brushing, and again work with a small section at a time, using the pin brush.**

   Work against the grain and then with it to put the coat back in its correct place.

4. **Don't forget lots of praise!**

Pay special attention to the areas where the legs meet the body, behind the ears, and under the tails — all places that are mat magnets for longhaired cats. (For more on mats and other coat problems, see the sidebar "Getting the gunk out," later in this chapter.)

Lightly mist the part of the fur you're brushing with a little water from a spray bottle. Doing so makes working the brush through the coat easier and helps keep the long outer coat from breaking. You can also try a commercial detangler — you'll probably have more luck if you choose a product in a spray bottle, not an aerosol, because the hissing sound from a pressurized can isn't going to be a hit with your cat.

If your cat's an unneutered male, you may notice his tail on top and near the base is greasy, with a brown secretion near the skin. This phenomenon is called *stud tail* and is a result of the excessive production of oil from a gland

Figure 9-2:
Good grooming not only keeps your cat's fur in shape, but it also keeps her looking beautiful.

J.C./Photo by Phyllis Mathias

on the tail. (All cats have this gland, but usually only tomcats have problems with it.) Neutering usually solves the problem for good, but otherwise you need to control the mess by bathing.

Do you really need another reason to get your cat neutered? Unneutered toms can be really difficult to live with, for more reasons than their tail. Read up on neutering in Chapter 16.

Be aware of changes in your cat's coat, especially patches where hair is sparse or even missing. These patches could be signs of parasites, allergies, fungal infections, or even hormonal problems — all of which need to be checked out by your veterinarian.

Cat + water + soap = Oh, my!

No matter what your cat thinks, bathing can't kill him — or you either, for that matter. Cats with long, silky hair need bathing as frequently as once or twice a month; most shorthaired cats can benefit from a sudsing every few months.

Your cat should be combed out before bathing, because mats and tangles, once wet, can never be removed — you must cut them out. If your cat will tolerate it, tuck a little piece of cotton in both ears to keep them dry (but don't forget to fish them out later!).

Getting the gunk out

Many things your cat gets into — or that get onto him — must be clipped out. Before hauling out the scissors, try some of these techniques to fix the following problems:

✔ **Burrs or foxtails:** Your cat gets most of these out himself, but if you find one that he can't, try putting a little nonstick cooking oil spray on the area and then gently use your fingers to work the burr free. (If your cat freaks at the hissing of a spray can, go straight for the scissors.)

✔ **Mats and tangles:** Work cornstarch or talcum powder into the affected area and then grab the mat at the base to make sure you don't cut your pet or pull on his fur. Then use a sharp pair of scissors to oh-so-carefully slice through the center of the mat a couple times from the skin outward. If you're patient — and gentle — you should be able to tease the rest of the fur free with your fingers and your comb. To finish the job, comb through the area and then brush to remove the dirt and dead hair that caused the problem in the first place. (If your cat's extremely matted, however, the kindest thing to do is have him shaved down.)

✔ **Paint, oil, or tar:** Cats are extremely sensitive to petroleum-based products. If your cat gets into more than a small patch of any of these substances, call your veterinarian for advice. A spot or two you can probably deal with on your own. *Never* use solvents to remove paint, oil, or tar: They irritate your cat's skin and are toxic if ingested, and they're flammable! Instead, wash your cat in Joy or Dove dishwashing liquid to remove petroleum-based products (which is what wildlife rescuers use to clean animals caught in oil spills). Tar may soften in mineral or vegetable oil but still likely needs to be clipped out.

✔ **Gum or other sticky substances:** You can try a little peanut butter to lubricate the fur enough to slide the gum out. You may have to resort to clipping, though.

✔ **Skunk:** The best cure for skunk odor is a mixture of one quart hydrogen peroxide, one-fourth cup baking soda, and two tablespoons dish soap. Wet your cat thoroughly with the mixture, let sit a few minutes, and then rinse well. **Caution:** Do not attempt to keep this mixture on hand — it'll explode any closed container you put it in, which is why such a surefire cure isn't commercially available.

Used as directed — mixed fresh, rinsed off, and discarded afterward — this homemade solution is safe. If you'd rather deal with something that you can safely store, however, buy a commercial deskunking product from your veterinarian or pet-supply outlet.

A final cautionary note: Cats have a lot more sense than dogs do in avoiding skunks, so if your cat comes home sprayed, the first thing you should do is check his rabies vaccination status — rabid skunks can behave belligerently. If your cat is current on his shots, go ahead with the bath. If you see any new bite wounds, however, stop and call your veterinarian immediately, for your cat's sake and your own. Rabies is not something to take any chances with!

Wash your cat in the sink (which is easier on your back and gives you better leverage) and use warm water. Here's what you need before you even think about wetting down your cat:

- **Towels:** You need them to dry your cat off afterward, of course, but also put one in the bottom of the sink to give your cat some firm footing. Alternatively, you can place a small window screen in the sink to give your cat something to dig into with his claws — besides you, of course!

- **Spray nozzle:** Don't make your cat stand in water: Use a gentle spray nozzle at close range to get him wet and rinse him off afterward. If your sink doesn't have a spray attachment, buy the kind that slips over the end of the faucet. You can find them inexpensively in any home-improvement or hardware store.

- **Shampoo:** Use cat or human baby shampoo, never a flea soap for dogs.

To bathe your cat, follow these steps:

1. **Take a firm hold of your cat at the scruff of the neck and ease him into the sink.**

2. **Wet him gently and thoroughly with the spray nozzle.**

3. **Start shampooing by working a complete ring of lather around the neck and then working back from there.**

4. **Rinse completely.**

5. **Repeat the process if he's really dirty.**

6. **Follow with a cream rinse if your cat has a silky coat and then rinse again.**

7. **Did we mention rinsing? Rinse, and rinse again. You don't want to leave soap or conditioner residue. At best it'll flake off and make your cat's coat look unsightly. At worst, prolonged exposure to bathing products may irritate your cat's skin.**

8. **Towel dry and then let your cat stalk off haughtily — he's earned it.**

9. **Keep him inside your warm house until he's completely dry.**

   You can try to use a blow dryer on him, but doing so may prove more trouble than it's worth. He's already upset enough. Keep him where he's warm and let him be.

 Okay, we admit it: We make the process sound much easier than it is. Bathing your cat is never going to be the favorite activity for either one of you, but if you're tentative, your cat will know it. Keep your grip firm, because if he senses any slackening, he's going to make the most of the opportunity to get free. If you feel yourself losing control, just let go: Better to regroup than get slashed.

Help for hairballs

Veterinarians call them *trichobezoars,* but cat lovers call them "hairballs," or, more commonly, simply "gross." Whatever you call them, hairballs — hair ingested as a cat grooms himself and then vomited back up in clumps — are a normal part of living with a cat and are usually not indicative of a health problem. If coughing up a hairball is an intermittent event — a couple times a month or up to once a week or so — and your cat appears otherwise normal, it's likely not a concern.

Your veterinarian may suggest the use of a mild laxative (mineral oil) preparation or an increase in fiber in the diet to help the hairballs "pass" in most situations. Canned pumpkin is a great way to increase the fiber in the diet. One or two teaspoonfuls mixed daily with canned food or with the water from a can of tuna (for humans) will keeps things moving nicely. You can also ask your veterinarian about some new high-fiber foods that are designed to help keep a hairball problem to a minimum.

Don't let your cat become a laxative junkie, however, as daily use may tie up and decrease the absorption of important fat-soluble vitamins. These products should not be used more than twice weekly except on advice of your veterinarian. Instead of changing your cat's diet, consider combing him more frequently to remove excess hair.

If your cat's pattern of coughing up the occasional hairball changes, make an appointment with your veterinarian to find out why.

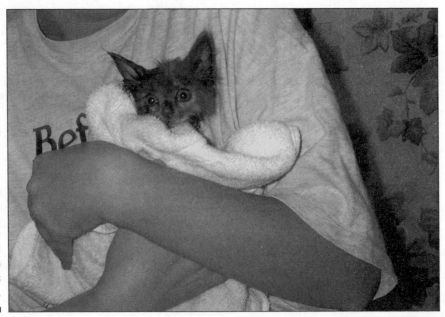

Figure 9-3: If you start bathing your cat when he's young, he'll always tolerate the procedure better than if he'd grown up before his first bath.

Mädchen/Photo by Kristin Cocks

Although most cats learn to tolerate bathing, especially if you start when your cat's still a kitten, you may find putting him in a mesh bag for bathing an easier way to go. You can use the jumbo-sized ones made for running delicates through the laundry or buy one especially made for bathing cats from a pet supply store, a catalog, or an online retailer. These bags keep your cat secure while you bathe him, but remember: If he's really opposed to the process, don't push it. Consider a groomer instead.

Keeping external parasites under control

Fleas, ticks, and ear mites are more than annoying — they can be a serious health risk, especially to cats who are very young, old, or feeble.

Persistence is the name of the game in controlling external parasites. The good news: Means of controlling some of these pests have improved in the last decade and especially in the last couple years.

Figure 9-4: Fleas and ticks never go away, but you can keep them under control with regular attention.

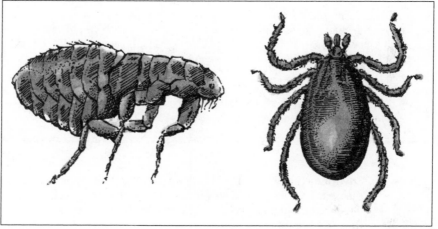

Flea control

If you have a massive flea infestation, you need to have a game plan. You need to treat your pet and his environment. You must treat to kill biting adult fleas, and you must treat to keep developing fleas from reaching adulthood. You need to do all you can to keep flea populations manageable with regular vacuuming of pet areas and regular washing of pet bedding.

Once you have fleas under control, you'll probably be able to keep them that way by using a topical medication (such as Frontline or Advantage) available from your veterinarian. These new products have proven to be very safe and reliable.

Are those . . . pimples?

If you're grooming your cat on a regular schedule, you'll find you're more observant of changes in his body, such as the subtle weight loss that can be a sign of illness. However, you don't need to be overly observant to notice *feline acne,* which is just what it sounds like: pimples or blackheads on the chin of your cat. Most classic acne cases occur in cats who are simply not good chin groomers. (Like people, some cats are just not as fastidious as others.) Be aware, though, that many things can contribute to the development and severity of feline acne and other conditions that mimic it.

The root of the problem can be as difficult to pin down as to treat. A few possibilities include the following:

- Tiny parasites called *demodex mites* that live in the hair follicles. (These are rare in cats, however.)

- Ringworm, which is not a worm but a fungus (and one that you can catch, too!).

- Contact dermatitis, a skin allergy. The culprit in these cases is often a plastic food dish.

- An abscess.

- A food allergy.

- An inhalant allergy (something your cat's breathing in that's causing an allergic reaction on his skin).

You need to take your cat to your veterinarian to work out the exact problem and the correct treatment. The area needs to be kept washed, at the very least — but don't squeeze the blemishes! You may also get prescription creams and pills. If you're following your veterinarian's directions and the problem shows no sign of improvement within a couple weeks, discuss a referral to a dermatology specialist.

The good news is that feline acne is more of an aesthetic dilemma than a serious health concern. As long as the area doesn't become infected, your cat won't be bothered by the blemishes. The other cats won't make fun of him — honest.

Environmental flea control is very difficult if your cat is free to roam where he pleases. Treating your own yard is worthless when you have an outdoor cat, because he's just as likely to pick up fleas from other yards or other cats. For these cats, a topical medication from the veterinarian is your first — and likely only — line of defense. If you're starting from . . . er . . . scratch with a houseful of fleas, here's a battle plan to help you get the infestation under control:

- **Treat your house.** Treat either with a spray or a fogger that contains both a quick-kill component, to kill adult fleas, and an insect growth regulator (IGR), which keeps immature fleas from developing. You'll need to repeat the treatment in two weeks. Alternatively, you can use a borate powder, which kills fleas by dehydrating them. Check with your veterinarian for product recommendations and follow directions carefully.

- **Treat your pet.** For indoor cats, the Program monthly liquid or pill can handle long-term flea-control once you have rid your home of the pest.

Because it doesn't kill adult fleas, though, you likely aren't going to be satisfied with its results on its own if you don't start with a flea-free environment. The product works by transmitting a chemical that prevents the eggs laid by the biting flea from developing. *Tip:* Add the liquid to a little tuna juice to encourage your pet to lap up all the medication. Two other products, Frontline and Advantage, work on killing adult fleas. The products are liquids that are applied externally between the shoulder blades. Depending on where you live — most humid places are a year-round flea paradise — Frontline or Advantage may be all you need for flea contol. You can also use a flea comb frequently (see the section "Combing and brushing," earlier in this chapter), but skip flea collars, sprays, and powders — they're not as effective as newer forms of flea control.

The things that haven't been shown to work — although a great deal of money is spent on them every year — include electronic flea collars and various nutritional supplements such as garlic, brewer's yeast, and vitamin B. Any evidence as to their efficacy is purely anecdotal and has not stood up to scientific scrutiny. The best "natural" flea control remedies on the market are already in your house: your washing machine and vacuum cleaner. Weekly washings of pet bedding and daily vacuuming of pet sleeping areas do a great deal to help reduce flea populations.

Flea-control efforts fail if pet owners put only minimal and sporadic effort into them. Such efforts always leave populations of either adult or developing fleas safe to reinfest treated areas. Work with your veterinarian to get the right product and right schedule for keeping fleas under control.

Flea control efforts can turn *dangerous* if you use too many products and in the wrong combinations. *Always* read directions carefully, making sure that the product is safe for the use you intend, as well as around other pets in your home. If in doubt, talk to your veterinarian about your entire flea-control program. Especially if your cat's a kitten, ill, or elderly, talk to your veterinarian first about which products and combinations are safe and effective.

Ear mites

A small amount of wax in your cat's ears is perfectly normal and can easily be cleaned out with mineral oil on a cotton ball or swab. But if your pet's ears appear filthy, he's probably got ear mites — highly infectious little pests that feed on the lining of the ear canals.

You need to see your veterinarian to be sure that it is indeed ear mites you are dealing with and, if so, to get effective therapy.

Because of their highly contagious nature, ear mites are especially common in shelter cats and kittens. One hard-luck kitty can infest a whole shelter.

Ear mites can be really difficult to shake, so be persistent. Use any medication your veterinarian gives you for as long as is recommended. Sometimes people stop when they no longer see signs of the mites. Developing mites are then free to grow up and reproduce. Mite medication needs to be given for a period long enough to break the reproductive cycle, so don't stop medicating your cat early.

Cats can also get dirty ears, or infections. Cleaning ears out every couple of weeks with a cotton ball and an ear-cleaning solution from your veterinarian — do not use rubbing alcohol — will keep your pet's ears in fine shape.

Ticks

Your cat picks up ticks in his rambles and usually dispenses with them himself while grooming, but occasionally you find one of the bloodsucking beasties in a place your cat can't get to easily, such as at the base of his ear. You probably feel the tick first as a bump while petting your cat and see it as a dark attachment. (The size varies depending on the species of tick and how much of your pet's blood it has sucked in.)

Don't touch a tick with your bare fingers. Ticks can infect you with Lyme disease if you're bitten and the tick attaches itself. Use a glove, tweezers, or a tick remover. Grasp the body firmly and pull with a steady motion. Wrap the tick in toilet tissues and flush, or if you see more than one, drop them into a small bowl of rubbing alcohol and then flush the lot after you're done. Don't worry if a piece of the imbedded head remains behind: It works its way out in time — just put a little antiseptic on the spot to prevent infection and keep an eye on the area until it's healed

If your cat has a chronic problem with ticks, make sure you're using a topical flea-control medication from your veterinarian that's also effective at controlling ticks.

Clipping Your Cat's Claws

The hardest part of clipping your cat's claws is getting your cat to cooperate — remember what we said elsewhere in this chapter about patience! If you get only one claw done a night, don't worry about it, because you can get through them all soon enough.

To clip your cat's nails, push gently on his pad to expose the nail. In the center is a pink area coming partway down: This area is a vein, called the *quick,* and you want to avoid it to prevent bleeding. Slide your clipper to a spot just beyond the pink and squeeze the tool with a smooth, strong motion. If you can't see the quick, just cut the "hook" off the nail, and you should be fine. Don't forget to praise your pet for being tolerant.

Does your cat need professional grooming?

If you have a longhaired cat, you may find that the mats get out of hand from time to time, and if this happens, we feel that your cat is better off being clipped down. You can try this yourself, but your relationship with your cat is probably better off if you have a professional do the dirty work. Cat skin is loose, and it's easy to nick if you don't know what you're doing.

You may also want to schedule regular professional grooming for longhaired beauties if you find that you just can't keep up. Same goes if you can't seem to keep areas that get dirty, such as the region under the tail, clipped down.

Ask your veterinarian or breeder for a recommendation to a professional groomer and check out the setup before dropping your cat off. You want to make sure that your pet is kept apart from dogs for his own peace of mind and separate from other cats for his health. A groomer who's used to working with cats — and enjoys working with cats — has a facility that makes their stay there as safe and comfortable as possible.

Also consider mobile groomers, who bathe and groom your pet in a van in front of your home or in your driveway with no other animals around.

Should your cat be sedated for grooming? Discuss this with your veterinarian. In general, cats should be sedated only when under a veterinarian's care.

Figure 9-5: A scissors-type trimmer is one of the tools you can use to keep your cat's claws clipped. Be patient and gentle, and reward your cat with treats and praise for cooperating.

If you do draw blood, apply a touch of Kwik-Stop powder to the tip to stop the bleeding, and call it a night before your cat returns the favor and draws blood from you.

In pet-supply outlets, you find full-body restraints designed to make nail-trimming and medicating easier. Some of these are quite clever, with openings that allow you to get at one paw at a time while keeping your pet gently immobilized. These devices are fine if you can't get the job done any other way, but we think your cat would prefer you to work with him slowly and gently to teach him to put up with claw-clipping instead.

Chapter 10

Feeding Your Cat

. . . .

In This Chapter

▶ Understanding the challenges of creating commercial pet food
▶ Discovering your cat's nutritional requirements
▶ Choosing the right food
▶ Feeding a fat or finicky cat

. . . .

*T*he very first thing you need to understand about feline nutrition is that cats are *obligate carnivores;* in other words, they developed with specialized nutritional needs that before the age of commercial cat foods could be met only by eating other animals. Human beings can do without animal-based protein, and many do so quite nicely. But a cat? No way. Everything about your cat says "hunter," from the claws on his feet to the fangs in his mouth to the way his body's put together for silent stalking on soft paws, a sudden spring, and a sharp bite to the neck of a bird or rodent.

Although some pet cats still hunt — to the detriment, some argue, of songbird populations — few must do so to survive. And that brings us to the second thing you need to understand about feline nutrition: The industry that's grown to supply your cat's needs is very, very big.

How big? Try billions of dollars spent for cat food just in the United States, from tiny pop-lid tins of the most delectable "gourmet" kitty paté to the biggest bags of least-expensive food that caretakers of feral-cat colonies spread in alleys, on riverbanks, and in vacant lots for the legions of the not-so-lucky.

If you doubt us when we tell you about the vastness of the pet-food industry, do a little research on your own. You won't have to go any farther away than your local supermarket or pet-supply warehouse. Pet food takes up as much space in your supermarket as any product line there, with the possible exception of cereals and candy — made, in many cases, by the same companies! And at the pet-supply warehouse . . . so much cat food is sold that it must be moved around by forklift.

And don't forget your veterinarian, who likely also sells food — so-called "premium" brands as well as therapeutic diets meant to help your cat deal with various health problems from obesity to kidney and heart disease to plaque buildup on his teeth.

So many manufacturers. So many places to buy. So many *choices!* Where do you begin to find the food that provides your cat with what he needs: the essential elements of nutrition found for generations in the bodies of billions of prey animals? Can you really find such nutrition in a can, box, or bag?

We guide you through all of it, of course: We tell you what's known and, more important, what isn't known about feline nutrition; what your cat needs and what's being marketed directly at *your* desires, not your cat's; how to keep your cat eating correctly after you choose the "right" foods — so that your cat doesn't get too fat or too thin.

Is all this information important? You bet, especially if you want a cat in good health with a shiny coat, bright eyes, and energy to burn. Good nutrition keeps your cat's body purring along through the years, and choosing good food is as important as anything else you do in the hope of providing your pet with a happy, long life.

Convenience . . . at a Price?

Like the cat box and litter, commercial pet foods are a modern addition to the lives of cats, created as much — if not more — for the convenience of people as for the needs of their pets. Which is not to say that cats haven't picked up something from the deal as well. Prepared pet foods have freed cats from worrying about their next meal so that they can enjoy being pampered, thus living longer, healthier lives than ever before.

A few false steps were taken along the way to developing cat foods, to be sure — some health problems were actually caused by nutritional deficiencies in manufactured pet food products. Two notable examples of nutrition-related health problems: *dilated cardiomyopathy* and *feline lower urinary tract disease,* or *FLUTD*. Another health problem, *hyperthyroidism* (that seemed to suddenly appear in cats around the world in the late 1970s and is still absent from some locales where commercial pet foods are not as popular), increasingly gets attention from researchers interested in feline nutrition.

What will they find? Perhaps they will discover that something in foods or some other manufactured agent is responsible for the rise of this disease or, quite the contrary, that improved nutrition, health care, and other factors leading to a greater proportion of the feline population living longer are unmasking this problem of aged cats.

Maintaining the "Perfect" Cat Diet

Part of the challenge of manufacturing a cat food is that whatever you come up with as a commercially viable product that people are willing to buy is usually a long way from what you start with, especially if you consider what cats eat if left to their own devices. If cats ran the pet-food industry, in fact, the recipe for a good, nutritious meal would probably read as follows:

Take one small mouse from the freezer. Thaw. Put in a blender and hit "frappé." Serve at feline body temperature on a clean plate.

Yuck, you say? That's probably why, instead of one fresh, frozen mouse, you're going to give your cat a dry food, where the label lists the first five ingredients as corn gluten meal, ground yellow corn, chicken, brewers rice, and wheat flour. Or you're going to feed him a canned food that lists wheat gluten and brewers rice just a notch or two below turkey.

Rice? Wheat? Corn? What gives? Are cats carnivores or aren't they?

Yes, but not all their needs must be met by animal-based food, as they would in the wild. The commercial pet-food industry has managed to provide what seems impossible: a diet with a high percentage of plant material that, nonetheless, keeps an obligate carnivore well fed.

As we said earlier, this balancing of convenience, nutrition, and aesthetics (appealing to both human *and* feline tastes) is a lot harder than it looks. All in all, commercial pet food has to be considered one of the great marvels of living in a modern age — and it keeps getting better, as our knowledge of nutrition increases.

Do cats need to drink cow's milk? Not at all, although in most cases, a little dose of the white stuff is much appreciated — unless they are lactose-intolerant. Check out the facts on these and other feline myths in Chapter 19.

Fulfilling Basic Nutritional Needs

A lot of different elements (about 60) go into keeping your pet healthy, all working together to keep his body working as it should be. These nutrients each play a role, and although some seem to have a bigger part than others, each is necessary to keep your cat's body functioning. We touch on each of the main feline nutrition needs in the following sections.

Protein

As part of their animal-consuming design, cats naturally have high *protein* requirements — more than double the amount per pound of body weight than dogs or humans do. Kittens need even more — about quarter again as much to support their rapid growth into adults.

Consumed protein provides the *amino acids,* which your cat reassembles into the protein parts of his body. All animals require these life-giving nutrients. Some amino acids, called *nonessential,* are synthesized in the cat's body; others, called *essential,* must be obtained from food. Variety is the important thing to remember when considering protein sources. A combination of meat, poultry, fish, dairy products, and other protein sources ensures that your cat is getting all the essential amino acids he needs in his diet.

Protein comes from both animal and plant material, and varies in *digestibility,* or the amount of protein that's available to your cat as his body makes use of the food he eats. Meat, poultry, dairy products, and eggs are highly digestible and, therefore, are high-quality sources of protein; some other parts of animals, such as feathers, beaks, and bones, are not as highly digestible. Grains are somewhere in the middle in terms of digestibility.

Carbohydrates

Carbohydrates — sugars and starches — are a source of energy, but not one that cats need in their diets to survive. Of all the ingredients in prepared cat foods, carbohydrates are farthest from what they would acquire naturally in our mouse cocktail formulation.

This is not to say that cats *can't* use the carbohydrates that commercial cat foods provide, and a good thing, too, because by weight these plant products are the largest component of most commercial cat foods. Enzymes in cats' bodies break down and convert the sugars and more-complex carbohydrates into products they can use.

Can a cat be a vegetarian?

Many people choose a diet devoid of animal-based proteins, and they want to extend their dietary choices to their cats.

No matter how opposed you may be to the idea of meat, your cat's body has a different opinion, and when your cat's health is at stake, you'd better listen.

Besides *taurine*, cats require more than a dozen nutrients including vitamins, fatty acids, and amino acids veterinary nutritionists call *essential*, because they can't be manufactured in a cat's body and must be obtained from an outside source — that is, from animal tissues.

The fiber in commercial foods serves another function: It aids in keeping waste products moving through the digestive system and helps prevent constipation and *obstipation* (total blockage), which is why canned pumpkin is a good thing to give a cat with hairballs. (For more on hairballs, see Chapter 9. Obstipation is a problem often seen in older cats, so it's covered in Chapter 13.)

Fats

In our society, we worry endlessly about the amount of fat in our diets, which experts say is too high. But again, we must realize that cats are not people, and their dietary needs are different concerning fats — commercial cat foods have a fairly high percentage of fat to increase a cat's desire to eat.

Fat from animal sources carries essential fatty acids that cats can't derive from vegetable sources. Fat also is essential for the absorption and movement around the body of certain vitamins, and it also provides food that appeals to the feline nose and palate.

A cat can't thrive on a diet of dog food, and fat is a major reason. Dogs can manufacture essential fatty acids from vegetable sources; cats can't. The protein levels in dog food are also too low for your cat's health. Most dog food also lacks enough taurine to meet the needs of your cat.

Not surprisingly, cat food isn't any better for your dog than dog food is for your cat. The higher levels of protein may be troublesome for older dogs with kidney problems, and the high fat content contributes to obesity and may cause diarrhea.

Vitamins

Vitamins are divided into two categories — *water-soluble* and *fat-soluble*. Both are important to your cat's health, and the lack of any of them in your cat's diet can have dire effects. Water-soluble vitamins include the B vitamins, niacin, panthothenic acid, folic acid, biotin, choline, and vitamin C. Cats require niacin, which is not present in high concentrations in nonanimal food sources in their diets. Fat-soluble vitamins are vitamins A, D, E, and K. Cats also need animal products to ensure they get vitamin A, because cats can't manufacture vitamin A from carotene. Don't expect to feed your cat carrots to ensure good eyesight — it won't happen!

Oil-based hairball remedies can tie up the absorption of fat-soluble vitamins, which is why you shouldn't be giving them on a regular basis without talking to your veterinarian. For more on hairball treatment and prevention, see Chapter 9.

Minerals

Mineral nutrients your cat needs include potassium, magnesium, zinc, calcium, iron, phosphorus, sodium, chloride, and others. Like vitamins, they make up a small part of your cat's diet, but in the correct amounts, they're essential for good health.

In the past many were concerned over excess ash (especially magnesium) in cat foods. This worry proved to be unfounded but continues to be a marketing gimmick many cat owners and veterinarians respond to by opening their wallets.

The important thing to know about vitamins and minerals is that your cat needs the correct amount — but not more. "If a little is good, a lot must be better" simply doesn't apply in the case of vitamins — and nearly all other nutrients. The oversupply of vitamins and minerals can prove dangerous, which is why you should not give your pet supplements unless you've discussed it with your veterinarian first. Although excess amounts of water-soluble vitamins are passed in the urine, fat-soluble vitamins can — and do — build up to toxic levels.

Water

Do you think about nutrition as being about what your cat eats? Don't forget that what your cat drinks is just as important to her well-being. Water — clean, fresh, and ever-present — is essential to nearly every process of your cat's body, which is 70 percent water.

Concerns over fat preservatives

In the last few years, a lot of controversy has been generated over the use of preservatives — primarily BHT, BHA, and ethoxyquin — to keep the necessary fats in pet foods from going rancid. These synthetic preservatives have been blamed for just about every pet health problem, not to mention the increase in violence on our streets and the perceived decline in traditional values. Those who hate these additives *really* hate them, believe us!

Many manufacturers have adopted the "if you can't beat 'em, join 'em" approach, which is why some products are now labled "ethoxyquin free" or "naturally preserved," usually with vitamins C and E. And some canned products boast of being completely free of preservatives of any kind.

But here's something we believe you must bear in mind: *No good scientific evidence exists to support the decision to avoid synthetic preservatives, either by manufacturers or consumers.* If the issue worries you, choose a food that doesn't have these preservatives. But be aware that you have likely fallen prey to marketing strategies and fear rather than scientific fact in that buying decision. In fact, more data exists supporting the *beneficial* effects of these products in foods (reduced cancer, reduced birth defects, and so on) than do allegations of negative effects.

This, of course, does nothing to end the controversy.

Figure 10-1: A cat who's fed a proper diet will be a happy, healthy companion.

Murphy/Photo by Vicki Halloran

The tiniest cells of living beings cannot survive without water. Nutrients are carried and wastes removed by water. A cat can go without eating for weeks if need be (please don't test this fact, though), but without water, death comes in days.

Always make sure to supply your cat with water and encourage her to drink by keeping the dish clean and the water fresh. Some cats prefer running water, and some owners oblige by opening taps to drip for their pets. Some manufacturers even sell pet fountains that constantly recycle water to make it seem fresh to a finicky feline. If your pet-products supplier doesn't carry these products, check out the ads in the back of any cat magazine. Feline fountains pop up pretty regularly there.

Choosing Foods

Pet food is more complexly regulated than human food is, and most passes the testing of the *Association of American Feed Control Officials* (AAFCO). This may sound impressive, but only one kind of verification passes Paul's muster.

Manufacturers have two ways to go when substantiating their claims. One is based on a chemical analysis of the food, and some say that motor oil plus a few vitamins and minerals could pass — not very impressive! The second is more sound and is based on feeding the food to cats. To pass these feeding tests, the pet-food manufacturers provide their products to cats and then ensure that the products are maintaining good cat health.

Before researching this chapter, it had been several years since Paul had reviewed the AAFCO feeding requirements. He was quite pleased to learn that they are more stringent and complete than he remembers from when he was a researcher in the area of feline nutrition in the 1980s. He was particularly proud to read the requirement for testing blood taurine concentration, since taurine deficiency was the focus of his study.

Still, if Paul were king — and his friends and family do have to remind him on a regular basis that he is not — he'd ask that all foods be required to support two generations of normal health: in other words, that a food would be fed for several months to adults who then successfully produced kittens who were subsequently raised on the food and matured normally and produced normal litters of kittens. This testing would provide pretty conclusive evidence that nothing major was wrong in the formulation.

The problem is that these tests would take almost two years, which would be quite expensive in terms of direct costs and more so in terms of the time it would take to bring a product or reformulation of a product to market. Fortunately, the competition in the industry has heated up to the point where the major companies have decided that they cannot afford a major mistake, and many pursue what in essence amounts to these types of studies.

For these reasons, we recommend you stay with the big-name manufacturers when choosing food for your cat. They are probably the only ones who can afford to do this type of extensive internal testing. For this reason, some say the most valuable information on the bag is the company's phone number. Call your cat's food manufacturer and ask what the company has done to ensure that you can rest assured that their food meets all your cat's needs despite the limitations of AAFCO testing.

You could perform hours of research on all the ingredients in cat food. Whole books are available on the subject; you could go to the library at your closest school or college of veterinary medicine and lose yourself in the stacks for days. We don't think you need to go to such lengths, however, to make sure your kitty's eating right. We think you can do just fine if you follow our simple guidelines:

- ✔ **Choose foods that are appropriate for your cat's age.** Although older cats can do just fine on regular adult cat food, kittens need more fat and protein and so should be fed products designed for them. Look for the words "Complete and Balanced Nutrition" on the label, as well as the AAFCO animal feeding tested statement "for all life stages" (for kittens). This does not mean you need to buy kitten food for your kitten. In fact, unless your veterinarian suggests a special food, we feel most comfortable with at least part of any cat's diet including a food with the "all life stages" statement on the label. That way, your cat gets the variety of food he needs to ensure that all his nutritional needs are met. If your cat is gaining weight because of the calorie-dense nature of a food designed for all life stages, try mixing the food with one meant exclusively for older cats to reduce his caloric intake.

- ✔ **Choose foods from major manufacturers.** The older, nonpremium pet-food brands were hurt by the growth of the "premium" pet food market, but their manufacturers have done a lot to improve their product in recent years, and we have no problem in recommending them. Whether you buy your cat's food from the supermarket, a pet-supply store, or your veterinarian, as long as you're dealing with a major manufacturer's food that carries the "AAFCO animal tested" statement, you should be fine.

Large, established pet-food companies have a huge investment in maintaining the quality of their products, and they test them constantly in feeding trials. Don't choose generic or store brands unless you know for certain which manufacturer made the food in the same way as its regular brand. Store brands are usually just major brands that have been relabeled and are less expensive — and if they are, who are we to suggest not saving a few pennies? Skip trendy brands from unknown manufacturers, though — the accountability is just not there.

Should you pop the extra dough for the more expensive "premium" foods from these manufacturers? That's up to you. Some owners like them because they often contain higher-quality, more digestible ingredients that are more easily absorbed, which means that the cat uses more of the food and ultimately deposits less in the litter box. But other than that, the fact is these diets offer no proven health advantage.

Choose a variety of foods to ensure nutritional balance. Feline nutrition is still as much defined by what we don't know as what we do. The best way to make sure your cat is getting all the nutrients he needs is to feed him a variety of food types — poultry, beef, and fish — from a variety of major manufacturers. Varying your cat's food also keeps him from becoming "addicted" to one kind — that may go off the market. Unless your cat is sensitive to changes in his diet (reacting by refusing to eat, having diarrhea, or vomiting), feed him a variety of food from a variety of manufacturers, mixed or on a rotating basis.

What type?

Even knowing what to look for in a cat food doesn't answer all your questions as you're gazing at all the choices in a pet-supply store. Cat foods come in different forms, with advantages and disadvantages to each. The following list describes the three main types of cat food from which you may choose:

- **Dry food:** Also called *kibble*, this variety comes in a box or bag, is less expensive than other kinds, and gives you the most options for feeding your cat. You can fill a dish with dry food and leave it out, and it doesn't go bad. Dry food enables you to make sure your pet has food if you must leave him alone for more than a few hours at a time. Dry food also helps reduce tartar buildup on your pet's teeth. Cats generally aren't as crazy about dry food, however, as they are about freshly opened canned food.

- **Canned food:** Cats love this stuff, but it's expensive to feed because you're paying for a lot of water. Canned food lasts almost forever . . . until you open it, and then it lasts about half an hour before your cat decides it's no longer fresh enough to suit him. You can refrigerate leftovers (although you need to bring them to room temperature before feeding again), or you can buy the tiniest cans, which are even more expensive. Canned food can be great for nursing ill or older cats, however, especially those whose teeth make dry food hard to handle. We recommend feeding a variety of flavors to keep your cat from getting hung up on any one brand and flavor — it could go off the market, after all, and then where would you be?

- **Semi-moist:** Sort of a midway point between dry and canned in terms of ease of use and cost, semi-moist foods are often criticized for appealing more to humans — with clever shapes and artificial colors — than to cats.

The distinctiveness of the "pointed" cats — such as this handsome blue-pointed Siamese — came about naturally but has been further developed by modern cat fanciers. (Photo courtesy of Katherine M. James, DVM)

The influence of genetics gives different colors and markings to these two feline friends sharing the high spot of a cat tree. (Photo by Ginger S. Buck)

The vast majority of cats are what fanciers would describe as "moderate" in type. They are a presence both sleek and solid, gravitating toward neither extreme. (Photo by Eric Ilasenko Photography)

The body type fanciers call "Oriental" is long and slender. Show cats such as this one become used to being handled in a way that shows off the sleekness of this body type. (Photo courtesy of Katherine M. James, DVM)

The Persian is perhaps the most easily recognized example of the shorter, more compact body type that cat fanciers refer to as "cobby." (Photo by Eric Ilasenko Photography)

The Manx is one of a handful of tailless breeds. Another tailless cat is the Japanese Bobtail. (Photo by Marj Baker)

These distinctive ears give the Scottish Fold its name. Both kinds of ears — folded and not — are typically found in Scottish Fold litters. Another breed with a different kind of ear is the American Curl, with ears that curl away from the face. (Photo by Bruce Russell)

A recent mutation produced the short-legged Munchkin cat — along with a storm of controversy. Fanciers of the breed say the cat is just the feline version of the Dachshund but a normal cat in all other respects. (Photo by C.W. Ware Photography)

"Domestic shorthair," or "DSH," is the notation veterinarians make when describing a cat like this one, but the words hardly do justice to the sleek beauty of the not-so-ordinary everyday cat. (Photo by Stacy Hindt)

Like their shorthaired relatives, longhaired cats come in all shapes, sizes, colors, and markings. Their fluffy coats can sometimes be harder to maintain. (Photo by Carolyn Wait)

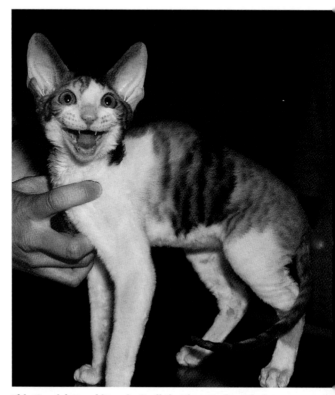

This Cornish Rex kitten isn't all that happy about being held, but it may be the best way to slow this active breed long enough to get a good look at its soft, wavy coat. (Photo courtesy of Katherine M. James, DVM)

In the classic tabby pattern, the stripes turn into swirls along the cat's sides. (Photo by Ginger S. Buck)

This Bengal shows off a variation of the tabby theme: His stripes have broken into spots, and so he is called a "spotted" tabby. (Photo by Lisa Wolff)

Stripes that run straight down a cat's sides give the appearance of the ribs of a fish; hence, the description of these cats as "mackerel" tabbies. (Photo courtesy of Katherine M. James, DVM)

Although they both share an Oriental body type (and a warm cat bed), these two cats have distinctly different markings: One is a solid ebony Oriental shorthair; the other is a blue-point Siamese. (Photo courtesy of Katherine M. James, DVM)

Just to complicate matters, another gene came into play to mute the effects of color. In the case of this Persian, the gene for black has been "diluted" to produce a cat that fanciers call "blue." (Photo by Eric Ilasenko Photography)

The variations of eye color are also quite interesting, especially in a cat like this one, who has ended up with eyes that are two different colors. (Photo by Ginger S. Buck)

Seemingly always ready for a formal occasion, the striking tuxedo cat is a particular favorite among cat lovers. (Photo by Eric Ilasenko Photography)

The amount of white can be very small, as on this cat. Just a kiss of white is enough to mark the beautiful face of this animal. (Photo by Eric Ilasenko Photography)

Of course, white can also be a dominant marking on a cat, as in this kitten who has lots of white, including a big patch on his back. (Photo by Eric Ilasenko Photography)

Calico cats are almost — but not always — female. They are distinguished by the brightness of their markings against a background of white. (Photo by Eric Ilasenko Photography)

The tortoiseshell pattern is another predominantly found among females. In the tortie, the colors of the calico are swirled together. (Photo by Gina Spadafori)

When the red gene comes into play on a male cat, the red tabby is the usual result. The same gene in females can produce a calico, tortoiseshell, or red tabby. (Photo by Eric Ilasenko Photography)

In the interests of nutrition and cost efficiency, we like to recommend a basic diet of dry food with daily rations of canned food to increase your cat's interest in his meals.

When to feed?

Many people like to leave dry rations out for a cat to eat whenever she's hungry, and that's fine, with a couple of exceptions. The most obvious exception is if your cat is overweight — more on that later in this chapter — or is on a diet that's otherwise restricted. Called *free feeding* (also called *ad lib*), leaving dry food out at all times doesn't work if you have two cats who need to eat different foods or if you have a dog who's especially clever about getting into the cat food.

Free feeding also doesn't feel very satisfying to some people, who like the excitement their cats show as they pop open a can of food. If you're one of these people, you can compromise if you like: Offer dry food always and canned food once daily.

Your dog isn't going to like us for telling you this, but the best way to make sure cat food is consumed only by your cat is to put the food dish on something your dog can't reach — like on top of the dryer. Alternatively, you could feed the cat in a room that's off-limits to the dog — and made so by the use of a baby gate. These strategies won't keep your agile cat from chowing down, but they will keep your dog's nose out of the cat-food dish.

What about veterinarian-prescribed foods?

Under certain conditions, your cat's doctor may recommend one of several specially formulated diets that are available only through your veterinarian. If your cat has a health problem that one of these foods may help, your veterinarian may suggest it. These foods come in both dry and canned varieties, so you can choose the kind you and your cat prefer.

In some cases, your cat's time on these foods is temporary; for other conditions, your veterinarian may suggest that your pet stay on the diet for the rest of his life. Any situation that requires your pet to be on a special diet for any length of time also requires you to work with your veterinarian to ensure the management of the disease in other ways, too, and to make sure your questions about the course of the disease are answered.

Although your veterinarian has all the best intentions in recommending these diets, you should be aware that, other than those designed for patients with urinary bladder stones/crystals, obesity, and perhaps kidney disease and some cases of diarrhea, no scientific data is available to support the medicinal claims for these foods. Until such data is available, press your veterinarian for information as to why you are being asked to fork over the extra money for these diets. This will in turn push your veterinarian to pressure the manufacturers to generate and provide the data, or to stop trying to convince veterinarians and pet owners that there is reason to spend the extra money. (If you can't tell, Paul has real concerns about long-term use of "therapeutic" diets.)

A sweet treat for cat lovers

Your cat's nutrition isn't the only thing on our minds — we want to make sure *you* have something special to eat, too. And so Paul has decided to share his recipe for Litter Box Cake, which came to him through his online colleagues at the Veterinary Information Network.

Children love this cake. Adults . . . well, you'd better hope your friends have a sense of humor. The editors at Gina's newspaper didn't. They thought the recipe was "too gross" to put in the newspaper. To them, we say: "Ha! Let them eat Litter Box Cake."

We wouldn't *think* of denying you the pleasure.

Litter Box Cake

1 package spice cake mix

1 package white cake mix

1 package white sandwich cookies

Green food coloring

12 small Tootsie Rolls

1 box vanilla pudding mix (not instant)

1 new, clean litter box

1 new, clean litter-box scoop

Prepare the cake mixes and bake according to their directions. Prepare the pudding mix and chill until ready to assemble. Use a blender on a low setting to crumble the white sandwich cookies in small batches; they tend to stick, so scrape often. Set aside all but about ¼ cup. To the ¼ cup of cookie crumbs, add a few drops of green food coloring and mix by using a fork.

After the cakes cool to room temperature, crumble them into a large bowl. Toss with half the remaining cookie crumbs and the chilled pudding. Gently combine. Line a *new, clean* litter box with plastic wrap. Put the mixture into the box. Put three unwrapped Tootsie Rolls in a microwave-safe dish and heat until they're soft and pliable. Shape the ends so that they're no longer blunt, curving them slightly. Repeat with three more Tootsie Rolls and bury them in the mixture.

Sprinkle the other half of the cookie crumbs over the top of the mixture. Scatter the green cookie crumbs lightly over the top, too — these are supposed to look like the chlorophyll in cat litter. Heat the remaining Toostie Rolls, three at a time, in the microwave until they're almost melted. Taper the ends as before, plop them on top of the cake, and sprinkle with cookie crumbs.

Serve with a *new, clean* cat-box scoop.

Enjoy!

What about a homemade diet?

Although most people don't have the time for or the interest in preparing a homemade diet for their cats, those who do are convinced their pets do better because of the fresh ingredients they get every day. Interest in homemade diets — especially diets comprised almost exclusively of raw meat and bones — has never been higher.

You can create a diet for your pet by using fresh meats or other protein sources, grains, vegetables, and mineral and vitamin supplements, but you can't plan such a diet casually. Several books offer "natural" or "raw-food" diets, and information on these feeding plans — as well as lots of discussion — is prevalent on the Internet.

We don't believe homemade diets are any better for your pet than a high-quality commercial food — and we worry about the possibility that

such a diet won't provide *all* the 60 or so nutrients your cat needs in the right amounts and ratios.

If you're carefully following a good homemade diet plan, though, you aren't likely to cause any harm. A great many cats are on home-prepared diets today, and the proponents of such feeding programs are nearly religious in their belief in the superiority of these diets.

Still, Paul's clinical experience gives him a bad feeling about this practice of preparing homemade meals for your cat. His stand may not be popular with raw-food proponents, but he'd rather wait for solid evidence of benefits than endorse something that may not be best for your cat. In the end, the decision is yours, of course, but you need to make sure you're making a fully informed choice before proceeding.

Treat your cat!

Giving your pet a little something special from time to time isn't going to do him any harm and can be very useful in training situations. Here are a couple things to keep in mind, however:

✔ **All things in moderation.** Treats, whether store-bought or from your dinner plate, don't make a good diet for your pet. Make sure the majority of his food is high quality, complete, and balanced.

✔ **Avoid some foods entirely.** Food that's heavily spiced or has onions can upset your cat's digestion, leading to diarrhea or vomiting. Onion can also lead to severe blood problems in cats. Avoid onion or onion powder in foods you prepare for your cat and in baby foods you may use as an occasional treat or for nursing a sick cat (the latter under the supervision of your veterinarian, of course). (Read the label — not all baby foods have onion or onion powder.)

✔ **Consider your cat.** If you give your cat treats from your plate, you can't complain that he's a pest at mealtime. And if your cat's supposed to be losing weight, you shouldn't give him a treat at all.

We humans tend to confuse food with love, and we extend this idea to our interactions with our companion animals. Your cat doesn't really need treats. Pet your cat, play an interactive game, or just hang out together — these activities are better options in the long run than overdoing the goodies.

Curbing Eating Problems

Although maintaining your pet's nutritional levels may not require much more than choosing good foods and standing back, in the cases of cats who are too fat or too thin, you need to monitor the situation more closely.

A healthy cat generally weighs between 8 and 10 pounds, although some breeds are smaller (such as the Singapura), and others are larger (such as the Ragdoll). You can generally judge your cat's correct weight by his ribs: If they're too prominent, your cat is too thin; if they're too hard to find, your cat is too fat. Your cat's ribs ideally should be covered by a layer of fat, but you should be able to feel his ribs easily if you put your hands on him.

The too-much cat

Obesity is the top nutrition-related problem seen in cats, with up to four out of ten cats showing up at their veterinarian's office carrying too much weight. An overweight cat is prone to a host of related problems, including diabetes; joint, ligament, and tendon problems; breathing problems; and even skin problems in exceptionally fat cats who can't groom themselves correctly.

These cats are also more prone to a very serious and often-fatal liver problem called *hepatic lipidosis*. This condition is most often seen in obese cats that have not eaten for some reason for an extended period of time. Fasting or "starvation diets" should *never* be used as a means of weight loss in a fat cat. Talk with your veterinarian about the correct amount of food for your cat and do what you can through playing to make your cat more active.

The finicky kitty

Although some cats have never met a dish of food they didn't love, others are very picky about what they eat. Feeding a variety of foods from a variety of manufacturers helps to keep cats eating, as does warming the food or feeding them canned rations instead of dry. Be aware, however, that your cat may not be as finicky as you think. If you leave dry food down all the time, he may be nibbling more than a dozen times throughout the day and thus never eating very much in any one observed sitting.

Another possibility occurs if yours is an indoor-outdoor cat: He may be picking up meals at another house besides your own — or maybe at more than one! Or perhaps he's using his natural killer instincts and "cooking" for himself!

Finickiness is not a reason for concern as long as your cat's not losing weight. A half-pound or even a pound up or down is no big deal, but more than that and you need to call your veterinarian. Weight loss is one of the first indications that something's going wrong with your cat. (We talk about some other signs of health problems in Chapter 11.)

Unlike dogs or kids (the human kind), who we insist *will not* starve theselves to death, cats are indeed capable of dying from starvation despite your best efforts.

Some cats simply do not like to eat a variety of foods and will refuse to eat anything but their favorite. Others will simply hold out until they get what they like. Playing "chicken" with your dog or kids is fine with us. They are both great manipulators, so we wish you luck. But playing this game with cats can be serious business — especially when "played" with overweight cats.

Not eating can lead to serious medical problems in cats. This is true for the sick cat who is "off-feed" and losing weight or the cat who refuses to eat. We are not talking about concern over a cat missing one or two meals. That can be normal and healthy (as long as he looks and acts healthy otherwise). We're talking about a cat who simply refuses to eat and is losing weight. Don't take chances. See your veterinarian.

Greens for nibbling

Many cats love to graze, some for the fiber, some because their tummies are upset, and some . . . well, they just like it.

Indulge them by planting safe greens for them to nibble or just enjoy. Here are a few winners:

- **Catnip and valerian:** Most people know about the amazing effect catnip has on some, but not all, cats, but not many people know that valerian *(Valeriana officinalis)* is another plant that tickles a cat's fancy. Plant both of these in catproof areas, or your pet may pull the seedlings out by the root! After

the plant is large enough to stand it, trim some of it and offer it to your pet.

- **Alfalfa, rye, and wheat:** Always keep a batch growing in a sunny area and let your cat graze to her heart's desire.

- **Parsley and thyme:** Another favorite for nibbling, these plants can be grown indoors as well as in your garden.

Not all greens are good for cats, though. Check out our list of the deadly ones in Chapter 22. You can find more information on catnip in Chapter 8.

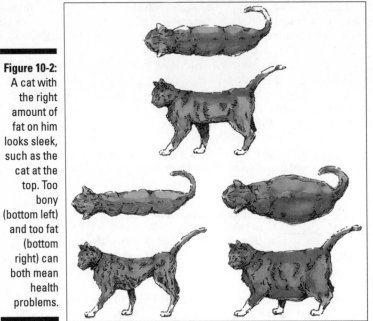

Figure 10-2:
A cat with the right amount of fat on him looks sleek, such as the cat at the top. Too bony (bottom left) and too fat (bottom right) can both mean health problems.

Chapter 11

Preventive Health Care for Your Cat

*W*here your cat's health is concerned, one person makes all the difference in the world as to how long and how well your cat lives. Want to guess who that one person is? Your veterinarian, you say? Great guess — and a very important person, to be sure. Now try again.

You could have — and should have — a top-notch veterinarian, someone who's up-to-date on recent advances in veterinary medicine, someone who is not afraid to say "I don't know, but I'll find out" or to suggest a referral to a specialist. You need someone with whom your cat is relaxed and you are comfortable enough to ask all the questions you need to. But unless you're living with your veterinarian, the most important health-care provider in your cat's life is indisputably *you.*

You are the person who sees your cat every day, who feeds her, and keeps her litter box clean. *You* are the one who knows where she likes to sleep and how much and how well she grooms herself. *You* are the expert on the sound of her voice, which toys are her favorites, and the way she likes to sit on the counter in the bathroom and watch you wash your face in the morning.

More than anyone else, *you* are the person who knows whether anything about your cat isn't "normal." Your powers of observation are the ones that keep her healthy — and maybe save her life. And we want to help you improve those powers.

But this duty involves more than just being a keen observer. Your role in keeping your cat healthy also includes at-home preventive care, such as keeping her teeth clean, as well as the important task of choosing the right veterinarian. The latter is essential, because even though you are the most important element in keeping your cat healthy, you have a partner — and that partner is your veterinarian. Choosing the right one for you and for your cat — and learning how to work with him and his staff efficiently — is essential for your pet's well-being.

Another part of your responsibility to your cat is keeping her well groomed. Grooming is about more than good looks — it's another part of your cat's preventive-care regimen. For the right tools and techniques to keep your cat's coat healthy, see Chapter 9.

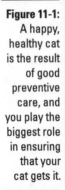

Figure 11-1:
A happy, healthy cat is the result of good preventive care, and you play the biggest role in ensuring that your cat gets it.

Calvin/Photo by Tammy Castleman

Recognizing Signs of Good Health and Bad

Because the signs of illness in cats are often subtle, a cat lover must be a keen observer to spot illness early. The detective work starts before you even suspect that your cat is ill and includes a few of the same kinds of basic diagnostic tools a veterinarian uses.

Make observing your pet a part of your everyday routine. A more thorough going-over should be on your weekly to-do list, but you don't have to make a big production out of it. Just incorporate the health check into a session that begins with petting and ends with your cat's favorite game — or more petting, if that's what your cat prefers. After all, anything that you and your pet find enjoyable you continue to do on a regular basis, and routine health checks need to be regular to be useful.

The physical cat

To identify a potential health problem, you must be able to recognize what is normal for your pet. Hone your instincts and then learn to trust them! You know your cat better than anyone else, and you're the one to decide when to get help. Sometimes your cat's condition may be so serious it leaves no doubt that you'll need a veterinarian, but other times, especially in those cats who do little during the course of a normal day, changes are so subtle you could easily miss them — and recognizing and dealing with these subtle signs of illness promptly is important.

To help you keep on track of changes in your pet, we recommend that you keep a monthly log and record your findings in each of the areas we discuss in this section. Again, it doesn't have to be a big production. A simple notebook and a few jottings are all it takes to spot some little problems before they become big ones. If you find that your readings match our description of what's "abnormal," consult your veterinarian. Some things to watch for include the following:

- **General appearance:** Before starting a hands-on exam, stand back and look at your pet for a few minutes. Consider his posture, activity level, gait, coat, and overall appearance for an impression of good health. *Abnormal:* Exposed skin, thin or dry coat, ribs showing, sluggishness, outright limping or just lack of "spring" in the step, or other subtle signs you can pin down only as being "just not right."

- **Weight:** The hardest thing about weighing your cat is weighing yourself, but you must. Step on the scale with your cat, note the weight, and then step back on alone. Subtract your weight from the total to get your cat's weight. A normal cat weighs about 8 to 10 pounds, but the range is wide, depending on gender and breed. Really big cats such as the Maine Coon can be well over 11 pounds and be perfectly normal.

  Your cat is normal for his body type if a comfortable pad of fat lies over his ribs but you can still feel the ribs if you press your hands gently in, or *palpate.* (You can find more on weight issues in Chapter 10.) After you determine your cat's ideal weight, a difference of a half-pound up or down is normal over the course of a few months; anything more rapid or more weight loss is reason for concern. *Abnormal:* More than a pound of gain or loss — or less if very abrupt — or too little or too much fat overall, even if the weight remains constant; swelling of the belly.

- **Nose:** Moist and clean. *Abnormal:* Dry, cracked, scabbed, or irritated; nasal discharge; or bleeding.

✔ **Eyes:** Bright, moist, and clear, centered between the eyelids, with the pupils of equal size. The whites of the eye should not appear colored and should have only a few visible blood vessels. The pupils should shrink equally as bright light is shined into either eye (test this with a penlight) and enlarge if the cat is excited or scared, if eyes are held closed, or the room is darkened. *Abnormal:* Eyes that are dull or sunken, that appear dry, or have thick discharge. One or both eyes not centered or pupils of unequal size. Yellow, muddy brown, or bloodshot eyes. Pupils that fail to respond or respond differently to changes in the intensity of light.

✔ **Ears:** The skin should be, clean, dry, smooth, and without wounds. The ear canal should be clean and almost odor free. *Abnormal:* Swelling, wounds or scabs, or any sign of a rash. Crust, moisture, discharge, or strong odor in the ear canal. Pain at the touch or an unusual way of holding the head or ears.

✔ **The mouth:** Your cat's teeth should be clean and white, with gums that are uniformly pink. Press on your pet's gum with your finger or thumb and release quickly. The color will become white where you pressed the gum but should return to the same color as the surrounding tissue within one or two seconds. This exercise checks the *capillary refill time,* or *CRT,* and is a crude assessment of how well the heart and circulatory system are working. *Abnormal:* Loose or missing teeth, tartar (discolored, crusty buildup around the base of the teeth) or gums that are red or blue, pale, inflamed, or sore, as well as gums that recede from the tooth. A swollen tongue, lumps and bumps in the mouth, sores in the mouth, big tonsils visible at the back of the mouth. A rapid or slow CRT.

✔ **Breathing:** You should find that hearing your pet breathe is difficult, and his chest wall should move easily to and fro as he does. Most of the act of breathing should be performed by the chest wall. His abdominal (or stomach) wall should barely move. *Abnormal:* Any unusual noise heard while the pet is breathing, such as "crackles" or wheezes, could indicate a problem, especially if you haven't noticed the sound before. Breathing that is labored, rapid, or done with an open mouth, and excessively involves the abdomen. Lumps, bumps, or masses on the chest and neck may also indicate a problem.

✔ **The abdomen:** Start just behind the ribs and gently press your hands into the abdomen. If your pet has just eaten, you may be able to feel an enlargement in the left part of the abdomen just under the ribs. Proceed toward the rear of your pet, passing your hands gently over the abdomen. You should find no lumps, bumps, or masses, and your pet should feel no discomfort as you press gently into him. Some bumps in the abdomen are normal — they're internal organs, such as the kidneys, and they belong there! Starting with a healthy cat is important, as is doing your health checks regularly, because you'll get a sense of what bumps belong there — and what do not. *Abnormal:* Any lump, bump, or mass that you're not used to feeling but that is consistently present when you check. Your cat groans or has difficulty breathing as you palpate. A hard, tense, or swollen abdomen.

✔ **Fluid levels:** Check to ensure that your cat has enough fluids by pulling the skin just behind his shoulder blades into a tent and then releasing quickly. Your pet's skin should snap immediately back into position. Another good sign of proper hydration is that the gums just above the teeth are moist when touched. ***Abnormal:*** The skin returns slowly or remains slightly tented. The gums are dry and tacky when touched, or the eyes have a "sunken" appearance.

Vital signs

Although a hands-on exam is an essential part of determining what's normal for your cat so you can spot problems early, three other diagnostic tools ought to be in every cat lover's bag of tricks: taking your cat's temperature, heart rate, and respiratory rate. This information is useful if you call your veterinarian and can help him determine whether you need to bring your pet in and what he may be facing after you get there.

The time to learn how to take your cat's heart rate, respiratory rate, and temperature is *before* you're faced with a sick cat. Practice at home whenever you and your pet are relaxed. If you're having difficulty, ask your veterinarian to demonstrate the next time you take your cat in for routine preventive care.

Here's how to perform these important tasks:

✔ **Taking your cat's temperature:** Although you can find a special thermometer for pets in any pet-supply catalog or well-equipped pet-supply store, you can also use an ordinary glass mercury or digital-readout "people" device from your pharmacy.

If you use a "people" thermometer, be sure you put a piece of tape around it marked "cat" or something similar so you'll never accidentally use it on yourself. We don't care how clean it is — you won't want that thermometer in your mouth after it has been in your pet's fanny.

Lubricate the thermometer with petroleum jelly or a water-based lubricant, such as K-Y. Gently and slowly insert the thermometer about one or two inches into your cat's rectum. (If the instrument doesn't slide in easily or your cat objects, don't force it.)

Leave the thermometer in place for two minutes and then read and record the temperature. In a normal cat, the temperature should be between 100 degrees and 102.5 degrees (a little higher is fine in a normal cat on hot days), and the thermometer should be almost clean after it's removed. Call your veterinarian if your cat's temperature is below 99 degrees or above 103 degrees, or if you see evidence of mucous, blood, diarrhea, or a black, tarry stool on the thermometer.

✔ **Taking your cat's heart rate:** Feel your cat's heartbeat with one hand over his left side, behind the front leg. Count the number of beats in 15 seconds and multiply by four to get the heart rates in *beats per minute,* or *bpm*. A normal cat is between 140 and 220 bpm, with a relaxed cat on the lower end of the scale. Call your veterinarian if your cat's heart rate is too rapid, is too slow, or is irregular.

✔ **Taking your cat's respiratory rate:** Stand back a bit and watch your cat breathe when he is relaxed and standing. Watch the abdomen and chest wall move. Often it is easier to count the respiratory rate when you watch the abdomen move. Count the number of movements in 60 seconds to get the respiratory rates in *breaths per minute*. A normal cat is between 15 and 25 breaths per minute, with a relaxed cat on the lower end of the scale. Don't try to count the respiratory rate when your cat is hot, or excited and panting. Call your veterinarian if your cat's respiratory rate is too rapid.

You may find taking your cat's temperature and heart rate easier if someone else holds the animal, especially if you're just learning.

If you go to the trouble of measuring temperature, heart rate, and respiratory rate, write it down in a log with the date it was done. Compare future observations to what you measured before. Call your veterinarian if you notice sudden changes or marked and gradual changes over time.

Figure 11-2:
Practice taking your cat's temperature before he's sick so you'll know what to do when you have to.

The emotional cat

You must be aware not only of your cat's body, but also of his personality. Many times, behavioral changes noticed by cat owners are later confirmed as illnesses through the use of such diagnostic tools as blood or urine tests. Again, your instincts are sometimes better than you know! Always be aware of the subtle changes in your pet's behavior, especially regarding the following areas:

- ✔ **Changes in eating habits, especially loss of appetite:** Be aware of how much your cat eats and make a mental note of any changes. More than a day without eating is reason for concern. In a multicat household of free feeders, you may have a hard time figuring who's eating what. Make a conscious effort to see each of your cats at the food dish daily, and if you give them canned rations once a day, feed them separately. Be aware, however, that if your cat is an outdoor cat, his appetite may be influenced by his hunting and by the generosity of your neighbors.

- ✔ **Changes in litter-box habits:** Many times, a "behavior" problem is really a health problem, and avoiding the litter box or using it more often than normal is one of the classic examples. A cat with an undiagnosed urinary-tract infection or diabetes, for example, may break his normal patterns of litter-box use. He's not "bad" — he's sick!

- ✔ **Changes in drinking habits:** Cats drink more in the summer than in the winter, but even taking that into consideration, you should be aware of changes in your cat's drinking habits — too much or too little.

- ✔ **Changes in grooming:** If you notice your cat looking unkempt, he likely has a problem, especially if he's normally fastidious. Grooming is one of the most important parts of a cat's routine, and the cat who isn't taking care of his coat isn't well.

- ✔ **Changes in voice:** You know what's normal for your cat — how often she pipes up and how she sounds when she does. If your cat is noisier than usual or more quiet or the sounds she makes are different, something is going on.

For more on nutrition, see Chapter 10. Tips for figuring out why your cat won't use the litter box are in Chapter 15. Grooming — your part and your cat's — is covered in more depth in Chapter 9. When does your cat need to see a veterinarian immediately? See the sidebar "Emergency!" later in this chapter.

Choosing a Veterinarian

If you're going to have a healthy pet, you need the help of a veterinarian. And although some people believe that these health-care professionals are pretty much interchangeable, distinguished only by convenience and price, perhaps, we feel you're doing your pet a disservice if you don't put a little effort into choosing the *right* veterinarian.

The cost of veterinary care is a legitimate consideration, of course, and pet health insurance may help ease your worries if your cat becomes ill. For more information on health insurance for pets, see Chapter 12.

To work effectively with your veterinarian, you need to develop a relationship over time so she can build a history and become familiar with you and your cat. Group practices are great — two, three, four, or more heads are often better than one when your cat is ill and the diagnosis is not immediately obvious. Even within a group practice, though, working with one veterinarian as your pet's primary caregiver is best.

One of the biggest changes in veterinary medicine in the last decade is that many veterinarians who practice on their own aren't really alone anymore. With a subscription to the Internet's Veterinary Information Network (www.vin.com), a solo practitioner can be part of a group practice of more than 6,000 associates who help each other with difficult cases every day. Paul is one of VIN's founders, and he has worked hard to make this service provide all the help your veterinarian needs so that she can provide the best and most-up-to-date care for your cat.

Your veterinarian should be technically proficient, current on the latest treatments, and willing to seek out more information on your pet's behalf or work with a veterinary specialist. She should be articulate, be able to explain what's going on with your cat in a way you can understand, and be willing to answer your questions so you can make a responsible decision on your pet's behalf. Above all, you must be able to trust your veterinarian. After all, knowing what goes on in a veterinarian's office after you leave your pet behind is impossible.

If you have any concerns, share them with your veterinarian. She will be happy to arrange a hospital tour and show you exactly how and where your cat goes when taken from you for care. Be understanding if the tour needs to be arranged. Like the ER you see on TV, things can get pretty hectic in the back areas of a veterinary hospital. The time when you ask for a tour might not be a good time.

Before you choose a veterinarian, ask friends, coworkers, and neighbors for recommendations. Over the years, animal lovers can tell which veterinarians are knowledgeable, compassionate, and hardworking. Those veterinarians are always talked up by satisfied clients.

Other factors may help you narrow down your list of possibilities:

> ✔ **Is the clinic or hospital conveniently located, with hours you can live with?** If you have a 9-to-5 job, a veterinarian with a 9-to-5 clinic doesn't do your pet much good. Many veterinarians are open late on at least one week night and for at least a half-day on Saturday, or they're willing to make other arrangements to see you and your pet.

✔ **Does the veterinarian consult with a veterinary college staff or independent or in-house specialists, or does he subscribe to an online veterinary service?** A willingness to discuss tough cases with colleagues is the sign of a veterinarian who's putting in effort on your pet's behalf. Online services also assist veterinarians in getting to the bottom of a tough case, as well as offering continuing education and searchable databases of professional journals.

✔ **What kind of emergency care is available, if any?** Although emergency veterinary clinics are prepared for any catastrophe, they're not familiar with your pet. If your veterinarian's practice does *not* offer 24-hour care, does it work with one that does?

✔ **Do you feel a rapport with this person? Are you comfortable asking questions? Discussing fees?** The final call on whether a particular veterinarian is right for you comes down to intangibles. If you don't feel comfortable, you're less likely to deal with your veterinarian, and the lack of productive communication hurts your pet in the long run.

✔ **Will your cat be comfortable here?** You need a practice that runs efficiently enough so that your cat isn't stuck for very long in a waiting room full of dogs. You may also want to consider a feline-only practice, or one with a separate waiting room for cats. The American Association of Feline Practitioners reports that more than 350 cats-only practices are now open in the United States and Canada, nearly triple the amount from a decade ago. Some of them are even staffed by one of the newest veterinary specialists: board-certified feline practitioners. None of which is to say that a general practice can't do well by your cat. We just want you to know all your options.

The Veterinary Information Network offers a free veterinary-referral service at www.vetquest.com. More than 25,000 veterinary practices are in the VetQuest database, and the service even shows you a street map to help you find the hospital or clinic you choose.

Understanding Your Veterinarian's Role in Preventing Illness

Preventive care is easier on you, your cat, and your bank account, which is why you should take advantage of all the measures available today, starting with a thorough annual examination and continuing with vaccines, dental care, and parasite control.

Spaying and neutering are also among the most important preventive-health measures. For more information on these routine surgical procedures, see Chapter 16.

The not-so-routine exam

The cornerstone of your cat's preventive-health regimen is an annual examination by your veterinarian. This important visit is the time for your veterinarian to go over your cat from ear tip to tail tip, slowly and thoroughly, examining every inch for abnormalities, adding to your pet's medical history, and comparing to his past observations. His staff may have already recorded your cat's temperature and pulse rate, but he listens to the sounds of your pet's heart and breathing and gently presses into your pet's body to ensure that internal organs feel normal and that no lumps or masses are present.

Eyes, ears, nose, and mouth all get a good look, too, and your veterinarian asks you questions about your cat's habits. Your cat can't speak for himself, so his body and his owner must speak for him.

Prepare for your cat's annual visit by reviewing your own observations regarding the condition of your cat. Write down any questions you have and make sure that you ask them while you're there.

Vaccinations

Call them "shots" if you want, but vaccinations deserve a lot of respect for cutting the rates of infectious disease in cats. A series of vaccines for kittens and annual vaccines for cats are still believed to be one of the best ways to ensure good health for your cat — even though these preventive-health measures continue to evolve as research expands the body of knowledge in feline medicine.

Be aware that the need for annual boosters beyond the initial kitten series and the first annual booster is being re-evaluated for many of the vaccines given today. The right regimen for each vaccine is not yet known, although the law dictates what must be followed for rabies in each state. Let your veterinarian know that you are interested in discussing the pros and cons of vaccinations and how often they should be repeated. Recommendations for each vaccine will likely change over the next few years.

Vaccines work by putting a tiny amount of a disease-causing virus or other microorganism into your cat, challenging her immune system to create disease-fighting antibodies. Should your pet ever come in contact with the actual disease-causing body, her system will be able to recognize it and will be prepared to fight it. Many vaccines are *killed,* meaning that the disease-causing organism has been rendered lifeless before injection, or *modified-live,* which means it has been altered so it no longer produces the signs of the disease. Although each acts slightly differently in the body, the result, ideally, is the same: an immune system ready to fight the "real" infectious agents should they ever turn up. (We say "ideally" because no vaccine is 100 percent effective and safe.)

Should you pass on vaccines because they're not 100 percent safe or effective? We don't think it's in your cat's best interest. An occasional cat will develop an "allergic" reaction to a vaccine, and these usually become apparent quickly and are managed by your veterinarian. To ensure that this very uncommon complication does not become serious, keep your cat confined and observe her for a few hours after the vaccine is given. If you have any questions or concerns, call or return to your veterinarian.

Another concern regarding vaccines: Some cats will develop a malignant tumor at the site where certain shots are given (generally in the area between the shoulder blades) The incidence of this complication is low — about one cat per 10,000 vaccinated — and is currently thought to be associated with the feline leukemia (FeLV) or rabies vaccines. For help in protecting your cat, see the section "The risk factor," later in this chapter.

Remember the following regarding vaccines:

- ✔ Do not use cancer or allergic reactions as a reason to avoid getting your cat vaccinated. You are much more likely to lose your unvaccinated cat to one of the diseases we vaccinate against, than you are to ever see a tumor in your cat because of vaccination.

- ✔ Pay special attention to your kittens. Young cats are especially fragile — do not even consider skipping the kitten series and first annual booster.

The protection factor

Several vaccines are available to protect your cat from disease; you need to discuss with your veterinarian which are appropriate and at which intervals they need to be administered. (See the following section, "The risk factor," for more information on vaccine concerns.) Here's some information on the vaccinations you're offered for your cat:

- ✔ The common combination vaccine, called *FVRCP,* protects your cat against three diseases: *feline panleukopenia, feline rhinotracheitis,* and *feline calicivirus.* (The initials of the vaccine stand for Feline Viral Rhinotracheitis, Calicivirus, Panleukopenia.) Protection against an additional disease, *feline chlamydiosis,* may be part of this combination vaccine; ask your veterinarian.

- ✔ Vaccination against *rabies* is required by law in many areas but should be part of your cat's regimen even if it's not — for your health as well as your cat's. (See the sidebar "The deadly danger of rabies," later in this chapter.)

- ✔ The vaccine against the *feline leukemia virus,* or FeLV, should not be considered until and unless your cat tests negative for the disease. Experts disagree on whether this vaccine is a good idea for indoor cats; the decision is yours after talking to your veterinarian. For cats likely to come into contact with other felines, the vaccine provides important protection against this deadly contagious disease.

✔ The latest addition to the disease regimen is a vaccine for *feline infectious peritonitis,* or FIP. Cats in multicat households are at the highest risk for FIP, whereas most household pets are considered at low risk. Serious concerns regarding this vaccine have been raised recently. In general, Paul (and more importantly, those colleagues he trusts to guide him in this area) does not recommend widespread use of the FIP vaccine. Discuss with your veterinarian whether your pet needs this vaccine.

We provide information on common cat diseases, including FIP and FeLV, in Chapter 12.

The risk factor

In recent years, cat lovers have been horrified by reports of deadly cancer caused by something that's supposed to save the lives of their cats — routine vaccinations. Unfortunately, this disease, called *vaccine-associated feline sarcoma* or *feline vaccine-site sarcoma,* is more than a rumor, and it has claimed the lives of hundreds of cats. At present, this problem does not seem to be related to the routine upper respiratory vaccines (FVRCP). Rather, researchers now believe that these tumors occur in very low incidence in cats inoculated with feline leukemia (FeLV) or rabies vaccines. Research and controversy continue, so check with your veterinarian for the latest information and recommendations.

Nor is anyone quite sure why this problem occurs, and the risk is low compared to the dangers of not vaccinating your cat — risks not only to your cat's health, but also, in the case of rabies, to your own. To protect your cat, you should take the following precautions:

✔ At your pet's annual examination, discuss with your veterinarian which vaccines your cat really needs. Because of the number of cats infected with rabies — since 1981, more cats than dogs in the United States have been diagnosed with rabies — rabies protection is not only important but is required by law in an increasing number of places. Your cat may not need to be vaccinated against feline leukemia, however, if he's kept indoors and doesn't interact with other cats.

✔ Discuss with your veterinarian the location of the vaccine injections, and ask her to use single-agent vaccines instead of ones that protect against a combination of diseases. Recent recommendations include giving each vaccine in a specific location to help confirm which vaccines are responsible for any problem and to allow for more treatment options should such a problem develop.

✔ Make sure your veterinarian notes the vaccination sites on your pet's health record, as well as information on the vaccines, such as the name of the manufacturer and the serial number.

✔ Be aware of any lumps at the vaccine sites. A small lump immediately after vaccination is normal, but call your veterinarian if the lump grows or persists beyond three weeks.

Kittens and vaccinations

For cats, vaccinations have historically been a part of the yearly checkup recommended for all cats. Kittens, however, need a series of vaccinations to protect them as they grow.

Kittens pick up antibodies from their mothers through the placenta and in the special milk, called *colostrum,* that they drink in the first two days of their lives. These antibodies diminish over time, but until they do, they not only protect the kitten against disease, but they also may block the usefulness of any vaccine.

Although it can be determined exactly when a kitten's maternal antibodies have fallen to the point where a vaccine is necessary, doing so is impractical, so veterinarians give a series of shots to ensure that the kitten is protected.

The first combination vaccine is given after a kitten first visits the veterinarian. If the first shot is given at 6 weeks, others are given at 9, 12, and 16 weeks. If the first shot is given at 8 weeks, the others come at 12 and 16 weeks of age.

Kittens are tested for feline leukemia, and if the owner decides to vaccinate, those shots come at 12 and 16 weeks. *Feline infectious peritonitis* is a controversial vaccine that should be considered only for cats in large multicat households or breeding operations. Talk to your veterinarian about when the vaccine should be given, if at all.

When to vaccinate for rabies is often determined by law; doing so at 12 to 16 weeks is fairly routine, followed by revaccinations one year later and then every two or three years. (The actual frequency likely depends on the law in your area.)

If you are getting multiple vaccinations for your kitten, many veterinarians advise clients to spread the vaccines out and not have more than one or two inoculations given in any one visit. If too many shots are administered at one time, the potential for reactions or interactions may be greater.

Above all, remember that the risk of not vaccinating far outweighs the risk of vaccinating. Much research is ongoing to speed the development of vaccines that are less likely to cause vaccine-associated sarcomas. The first generation of "less reactive" vaccines is on the market now, but it is too early to know if these vaccines will fulfill their promise of being less likely to cause vaccine-associated sarcomas. Consult your veterinarian for the latest information on this important preventive health measure.

Dental care

Ensuring healthy teeth and gums for your pet is one area where you and your veterinarian must work together. Dental scalings and polishings by your veterinarian are an important part of preventive medicine, and keeping teeth clean between veterinary appointments is something that can — and should — be done by cat lovers.

Plaque buildup on teeth causes gums to recede, opening pockets at the root line that are paradise to bacterial infections. Left unchecked, these infections can lead to tooth loss, make eating painful, and put the cat's immune system and internal organs under pressure, causing illness and premature aging. Rotting teeth and gums can become a powerful source of bad breath that some pet owners treat with products that may temporarily fix the smell but do nothing about the real problem.

Although some groomers and cat owners scale plaque themselves, this practice doesn't address the problem at the root line, so regular cleanings under anesthesia by a veterinarian are essential to ensure dental health. In between, brushing two or three times a week with a child's toothbrush or fingertip brush and a toothpaste designed for pets slows the reformation of plaque and extends the time between dental scalings. Brushing your cat's teeth is not always easy to do, but if your cat will allow it, you can make a big difference in his oral health. Doing so also saves you money by increasing the time between dental cleanings at your veterinarian's.

The key to getting a pet used to having his teeth brushed is to do it in small steps over time and to be patient and encouraging. As with nail trims or other procedures your cat may not appreciate, making teeth cleaning part of a session of petting capped by play may make things easier for you both.

The deadly danger of rabies

Although most people associate rabies with dogs, cases of feline rabies are becoming more common. Vaccination is so important for your cat that in many places it's required by law.

Rabies is caused by a viral infection of the nervous system. Most cases of rabies in the United States occur in wild animals. Because many cats share territory with wild animals, they're at risk of being bitten by a rabid wild animal. (Normally timid animals can become aggressive if rabid.) Most cases of rabies in cats can be traced to skunks, foxes, raccoons, and bats.

The risk of contracting rabies from your cat — or any cat — is extremely small, but the disease is so deadly that, if your cat were to contract it, he would need to be humanely killed, and you would need to have a series of inoculations for your own protection.

A cat with rabies may hide, become agitated or nervous, get weak in the hindquarters, or become aggressive. Swallowing difficulties are also common. Whether he's vaccinated or not, if you suspect your cat has tangled with a wild animal, contact your veterinarian and local public health officials immediately. Your life may depend on it! If your cat is current on his vaccination, he'll need to be quarantined, but if not, public health officials may require that he be killed. That's because the only way to tell for certain that an animal is rabid is to test brain tissues.

Need we make our position any clearer? Be sure your pet is vaccinated against this deadly, contagious disease.

Good dental health is especially important in the care of older cats. For more information, see Chapter 13.

Parasite control

Cats pick up all kinds of parasites, both internal pests, such as worms, and external ones, such as fleas and ear mites. Your veterinarian may ask you to bring in a fresh stool sample to check for the presence of worms. If parasites are present, she can prescribe medication to eliminate them.

Heartworms are something that only dog-owners had to worry about previously, but now preventive medication is out there for cats, too. What gives?

Cats are at risk for heartworm disease. The confusing news is that much controversy exists over whether the amount of attention given to this problem is good medicine or good marketing. The good news (driving the marketing) is that there is now effective medication which, given monthly, prevents heartworms from living inside a cat's body.

Does your cat need heartworm prevention medication? Ask your veterinarian. Don't be put off if your veterinarian seems unsure of the response. The answer is not clear to most at this time because the tests for heartworm disease in cats are relatively new and we are not sure how much to trust the results. Therefore we are not sure just how much of a problem heartworm disease is in cats in most regions.

No one likes to give unnecessary medications. However, in this case, the cost of not erring on the side of giving medications might be high. Although heartworm infestation is rare in cats, it is also not easily treated. In most cases where we prove heartworms are present in cats we choose to not treat and simply let the disease take its course because the risks of treating are high.

In areas where heartworm disease is very common in dogs and is being seen in cats, Paul (who is, after all, a board-certified veterinary cardiologist) thinks you should give a monthly prevention. It is safe and effective. In areas where HW disease is not commonly seen in dogs or is not being seen in cats, Paul is neutral on the recommendation. His own cat, PC, does not receive hearthworm prevention because the disease is very rare in dogs and is not seen in cats where he lives in Northern California. If he and PC lived in Florida or parts of Texas, it is likely Paul would give his own cat prevention medication.

Don't bother with worming medications sold at pet-supply stores; they may not treat the kind of parasites your cat has. Better you should have your veterinarian accurately diagnose and treat your cat than subject your pet to medication that doesn't fix the problem. This sort of thing is false economy!

Emergency!

Anything is worth a call to your veterinarian if you're not sure what's wrong with your kitty, but some things require urgent attention. Here are some signs that should have you heading for your veterinarian's — or for the emergency clinic:

- Seizure, fainting, or collapse.

- Eye injury, no matter how mild.

- Vomiting or diarrhea — anything more than two or three times within an hour or so.

- Allergic reactions, such as swelling around the face, or hives, most easily seen on the belly.

- Any suspected poisoning, including antifreeze, rodent or snail bait, or human medication. Cats are also especially sensitive to insecticides (such as flea-control medication for dogs) and any petroleum-based product.

- Snake or venomous spider bite.

- Thermal stress — from being either too cold or too hot — even if the cat seems to have recovered. (The internal story could be quite different.)

- Any wound or laceration that's open and bleeding, or any animal bite.

- Trauma, such as being hit by a car, even if the cat seems fine.

- Any respiratory problem: chronic coughing, trouble breathing, or near drowning.

- Straining to urinate or defecate.

Although some problems don't classify as life threatening, they may be causing your pet irritation and pain and so should be taken care of without delay. Signs of pain include the following: panting, labored breathing, increased body temperature, lethargy, restlessness, crying out, aggression, and loss of appetite.

Note: Some cats may seek you out for reassurance; others may draw within themselves.

Don't take a chance waiting to see whether things "get better" on their own: Call your veterinarian!

The parasite that drives people craziest is the flea. For help in treating this persistent pest, see Chapter 9.

Chapter 12

Common Cat Health Problems

Cats can live long, healthy lives — and many of them do — if they receive the benefits of preventive health care and are protected from accidents and infectious diseases.

If cats get sick, the chances are better than ever before that a veterinarian can help. The growth in the popularity of pet cats has led to an explosion of interest in their health-care needs. Research into feline diseases is ongoing at the world's top schools and colleges of veterinary medicine, and at pharmaceutical companies serving animal health needs. Then, too, the science of veterinary medicine in general has advanced as the diagnostic and treatment tools of human medicine have become widely available to pets as well. Such procedures as CAT scans (appropriately!), MRIs, kidney transplants, and radiation therapy are now routine at veterinary colleges and high-end veterinary practices. The ranks of veterinary specialists have grown as well — Paul (one of the authors of this book) is a board-certified veterinary cardiologist, for example — bringing even more knowledge and options to cat lovers in the area of veterinary care for their pets.

What do all these advances mean for you and your pet? If you're careful to practice preventive health-care measures for your pet, and you're both lucky, you may barely be touched by the revolution in veterinary medicine. But if you need help, it's there — now more than ever before — and getting better all the time.

Despite all the incredible advances in the diagnosis and treatment of feline illness, one of the most important elements in maintaining good health for your pet is still the laying on of hands — yours. For what you need to know to conduct an at-home examination — as well as a full discussion of other important preventive-health measures — see Chapter 11. And don't forget the importance of good nutrition! All you need to know to get your cat eating right is located in Chapter 10.

You can help advance the future of feline health by supporting two charitable organizations that provide grants for companion animal health research: The Winn Feline Foundation and the Morris Animal Foundation. The Winn Feline Foundation is affiliated with the Cat Fanciers' Association. The Morris Animal Foundation was founded in 1948 by the contributions of veterinarian Mark L. Morris, developer of a line of therapeutic diets for pets, and Morris Frank, owner of the first seeing-eye dog in the United States. Information on contacting these groups is in the Additional Resources appendix.

A Cooperative Approach to Cat Health

We named this section "a cooperative approach" because we've come to realize, after years of listening to both pet owners and veterinarians, that what should be a team effort to protect and ensure the health of a pet is sometimes closer to a battle. The relationship between the client (that's you, not your cat) and the veterinarian can become adversarial if neither party respects the contributions of the other and both parties forget the reason that brought them together: to help the *patient* — in other words, your cat.

Sometimes, the task of figuring out what's wrong with an animal is like walking into a movie that began half an hour ago — for one brief moment you have no idea what the story's about and little chance of predicting the outcome. But given the opportunity to see a few more scenes, you start to understand what's going on. For the veterinarian, all too often that one glimpse is all he gets. The client wants an answer, a shot, or a pill to makes things better. He wants the problem fixed — now.

Although the client probably wants an immediate solution to his own health problems, too, he's resigned enough to say "yes" to diagnostic testing to find the right answer — as long as his medical insurance is footing the bill. Can you imagine the malpractice suits that would hit the medical doctor who didn't suggest appropriate tests in trying to diagnose a disease?

Isn't it strange that a physician who won't recommend diagnostic tests and a veterinarian who will are often criticized by their clients? What's the difference? In many cases, money.

Nearly all the time, the client is footing the bill for veterinary procedures. And although veterinary costs are a small fraction of comparable procedures in human medicine, the fact that you're spending hundreds instead of thousands (or hundreds of thousands) of dollars isn't all that reassuring if your budget is stretched as far as many families' are today. We suppose it's natural to wonder if everything you've agreed to on your pet's behalf is necessary.

And what about your veterinarian? What forces are driving him? Your veterinarian wants the best for your cat, but he has bills to pay, too. And he also wants to make his clients happy, which is why many of them fall into the habit of giving the client exactly what he wants — a shot or a pill that takes care of the symptoms, regardless of whether the problem is fixed for the long term.

This practice is not good veterinary medicine, and you should tell your veterinarian that you understand he may not be able to fix what's wrong right now. Let him know you want diagnostic tests (if they're needed, of course) and that you're happy with fewer medicines (if he was considering giving them just to make you think you got something out of the visit). Finally, let your veterinarian know that you value his diagnostic skills and respect his desire to investigate the problem more before acting. Your cat will receive better care as a result of a relationship between you and your veterinarian based on mutual trust and respect. If you have the right veterinarian, he will listen to your concerns about treatments and finances.

You and your veterinarian are on the same team — or you should be — together in the goal of keeping your cat in good health. Your cat deserves the best, and so do you. And so, too, does your veterinarian, who has spent years studying to be able to help your cat. So let him. Take the time to develop a relationship for the good of your cat. You won't feel gouged and your veterinarian won't feel unappreciated if your dealings with each other aren't adversarial.

Choosing the right veterinarian is about more than price-shopping and convenience. The old saying, "You get what you pay for," very much applies when you are selecting a veterinarian; the "lowest-priced" veterinarian is not necessarily the best choice for your cat, or the most truly cost-effective. For a discussion of the factors that should go into choosing a health-care professional with whom you can work for the benefit of your cat, see Chapter 11.

When Does My Cat Need a Specialist?

Although not as many specialists exist in veterinary medicine as in human medicine, you still find a growing presence in your community or within a short drive — and more specialists are likely to turn up in the future. Your veterinarian should be open to referring you to a specialist or consulting one on your behalf, if your pet's condition warrants it.

Although many urban areas can support independent specialists or specialty practices, in less-populated areas you're more likely to find a full complement of specialists at the closest university that has a school or college of veterinary medicine. Current companion animal specialties relevant to cats include the following:

- Anesthesiology
- Behavior
- Cardiology
- Clinical pharmacology
- Dentistry
- Dermatology
- Emergency medicine and critical care
- Internal medicine
- Neurology
- Oncology
- Ophthalmology
- Radiology
- Surgery

What's special about "specialists?" Becoming a veterinary specialist requires additional study in a two- to five-year residency program, as well as a specific examination for each specialty. The result is certification over and above that required to achieve a degree in veterinary medicine.

For veterinarians already in practice, the American Board of Veterinary Practitioners (ABVP) also offers specialty certification. This program does not require a formal residency program prior to examination but is still a very meaningful and rigorous demonstration of a veterinarian's commitment to excellence and lifelong education. Among the subspecialties of ABVP certification are a companion animal (dog and cat), avian practice, and, of special note, feline practice.

If your veterinarian doesn't suggest a referral to a specialist, and you wonder whether seeing one may help your cat, bring the idea up for discussion. Let your veterinarian know that you aren't questioning his care but want to bring more-specialized expertise in to help your pet. If you have a good working relationship with your veterinarian, calling in a specialist is never a problem.

If your veterinarian is reluctant to refer, remember that the final decision in your cat's care is always yours. Keep the lines of communication open, though, and always be sure your regular veterinarian is kept fully informed when you seek specialist care.

The relationship between your regular veterinarian and a specialist is a complementary one, each with respect for the skills of the other. Your veterinarian knows the specialist isn't out to "steal" clients, and the specialist realizes that, to get referrals, she needs to be clear on her limited role. To save time and money, your veterinarian shares your pet's medical history with the specialist and discusses your pet's case. The specialist probably requires additional tests to get the information she needs to make an accurate diagnosis and develop an appropriate course of care. A specialist doesn't practice "shotgun medicine" — if she's brought into the case, her purpose is to figure out exactly what's wrong, if she can, and work to restore your pet to health.

You can help encourage the benefits of a healthy referral system within your community by following a few rules. First, understand you're being referred for help with a special problem to someone your veterinarian believes can help. Do *not* permanently leave your regular veterinarian for this new person unless you, the specialist, and your veterinarian agree doing so is best for your cat. Doing otherwise spoils the relationship between your veterinarian and the specialist. In fact, any specialist who'd agree to taking you on as a permanent client should be looked at as having less-than-ideal ethics and, therefore, perhaps is not the best veterinarian for your cat.

Finally, do not ask that the specialist to perform procedures for which you weren't referred to him — especially routine tests or vaccinations. An ethical specialist would be put in the difficult position of refusing your request out of respect for the referring veterinarian. Are these guidelines necessary? We argue "yes," for without your support and participation, top-notch specialty care for your cat could prove hard to find when your pet needs it.

Two of the greatest challenges that those in veterinary medicine face are the small number of specialists and the lack of a central hospital system where practitioners have "hospital rights" in a facility with advanced diagnostic and treatment capabilities. This reality has created a system with many smaller self-contained hospitals, while limiting the "reach" of specialists and interaction among colleagues. Recent changes in technology have changed the way veterinarians share diagnostic information — and saved time and money as a result.

The online world is changing the way veterinarians consult with colleagues. Members of the Veterinary Information Network, for example, have access to a contingent of colleagues and online specialists, such as cardiologists and surgeons, who, although they may be thousands of miles away, can help diagnose and treat cases. Other services accept and interpret transmitted ultrasound and radiographic images and other data. Laboratories maintain computerized databases of their animal-health records, and should your pet end up somewhere his records are not — such as at an emergency-care clinic on a holiday — the attending veterinarian can, in many cases, access recent test results for comparison and analysis.

Ten Common Health Problems

Although the cat has a reputation for being a pet who doesn't have a lot of health problems, the fact is that a lot of things can go wrong. Despite Paul's desire to tell you about every one of them in such complete detail that you could pass the veterinary boards after reading this book, we're going to stick to ten of the most common problems and give you what you need to know to make the care decisions necessary in working with your veterinarian.

The most important role you play in keeping your cat healthy is preventive. Keep on top of the preventive-care measures your veterinarian recommends, such as vaccines, and get into the habit of noticing changes in your cat's attitude, appearance, or behavior. For more on preventive medicine, see Chapter 11.

A few health problems are more common in older cats, and so we've put them in the older-cat section in Chapter 13. These problems include diabetes and hyperthyroidism, as well as dental problems brought on by neglecting your cat's teeth and gums. Important *preventive* care for your cat's mouth appears in Chapter 11.

Abscesses

Nearly every outdoor cat and even many indoor cats at one time or another develops an *abscess,* or large pocket of pus under the skin. The most common cause of abscesses in cats is puncture wounds, often the result of a bite from another cat during a fight for territory or during mating. (Another good reason for spaying or neutering your pet — see Chapter 16 for even more information.)

A cat's mouth is full of a nasty mix of bacteria, and your cat's body starts trying to fight these bacteria after he's been bitten. At first, you may not even know your cat has been injured. Whether the inciting wound is from a sharp rock or the teeth of a neighbor's cat, the first evidence of a problem may be noticing your cat is limping or just "not doing right." Hints that an abscess is brewing may range from finding nothing but an elevated temperature to finding the abscess itself — either still closed and feeling like fluid in a pocket under the skin or open and draining and smelling disgusting! At the first sign of persistent (more than an hour or so) limping or "not doing right" (being less active, not eating, not drinking, avoiding or seeking out attention), you should get your cat's carrier and make a trip to the veterinarian.

The potent bacteria in a cat's mouth and rabies are two reasons why you need to be careful if you're ever bitten by a cat. Washing the wound thoroughly and seeking medical attention are important for you to do.

If possible, your veterinarian will open the abscess and flush the pus out. He may also insert a *drain* to keep the site from closing up too soon to allow adequate drainage of the pus and give a shot of antibiotics or prescribe some antibiotic pills to be given at home. (For tips on giving pills and other medications, see the section "Giving Your Cat Medication," later in this chapter.)

Believe it or not, finding out that an abscess is the cause of limping or not feeling well is a good thing. An abscess is usually easily diagnosed, treated, and quickly resolved. Repeated abscesses, however, may be a sign of a problem with your cat's immune system — and that may be the first sign of a significant health problem.

The best "treatment" for abscesses is prevention. Indoor, altered cats have the least chance of being bitten by another cat; unneutered roaming males have the greatest.

Figure 12-1:
Outdoor cats are exposed to many more potential health problems than indoor ones, including abscesses and infectious diseases.

Scotty/Photo by Gay Currier

Feline asthma

Gina is a lifelong asthmatic who has ended up in the hospital a few times struggling to breathe. Although she takes medication regularly to help prevent and stave off attacks, sometimes the disease gets the best of her for a while. And she's not alone. Asthma is on the rise in humans, and the experts aren't sure why. Cats frequently get what we call *feline asthma* — and in most cases, veterinary researchers are likewise stumped.

The signs of asthma in cats are very similar to those seen in humans — difficulty breathing, first and foremost. Cats with asthma also "wheeze" and may exhibit a cough that sometimes sounds like gagging. If he's having trouble breathing, a cat sits with his neck extended and inhales and exhales rapidly with his mouth open.

Asthma is not the only disease that can cause difficulty breathing, so neither you nor your veterinarian should immediately assume that asthma must be the cause.

The signs of feline asthma can come on quite suddenly and be very serious — frightening to observe. Like an asthmatic person who feels as if she can't breathe, your cat can panic. You must do all you can to minimize stress while your cat is having difficulty breathing. The best way to do so is by not creating stress: Now is not the time to be chasing your pet and forcing him into a carrier. Let him calm down first.

If this instance is the first time your cat has had a problem breathing, take your cat immediately to your veterinarian or to an emergency clinic (if it happens after normal business hours or on a weekend or holiday). Call ahead so that the clinic can be prepared for your arrival, and be prepared for a stressful wait while the staff finds the cause of your cat's breathing difficulties.

Cats having difficulty breathing are quite fragile, and too much handling can worsen their condition to the point where they may even die. As much as you and your veterinarian want to know the cause of the problem and begin treating immediately, often the best thing for your veterinarian to do is to rule out quickly any obvious problems, such as obstruction of the airway or air or fluid around the lungs, and avoid significant handling while giving medications and time a chance to work. In more serious cases, your cat may need to be given additional oxygen by face mask or oxygen cage until she is more stable and better able to tolerate further treatment or diagnostics.

If your veterinarian has diagnosed asthma in your cat, she probably will have prescribed medications that help ease the symptoms. Whenever your cat is having breathing problems, give him the medication if you can do so without stressing him further; otherwise, wait for him to settle down. Use the time to call your veterinarian and discuss the symptoms and whether your cat needs to come in for treatment. If you're told to bring your cat in, use the carrier he feels so familiar with and, after you get to the office, walk directly to the receptionist for an immediate assessment. Your veterinarian or her staff can determine the severity of the attack, and if warranted, your cat can be immediately seen to get the medications and oxygen that should help relieve his distress.

Although no one knows the cause of feline asthma, minimizing exposure to dust (remember to use low-dust litter and leave off the litter box hood), smoke, aerosol sprays, and other irritants is essential. Keep your ears and eyes open and stay in close contact with your veterinarian so that you can get the newest information relating to the cause, prevention, and treatment of feline asthma.

Three nasty viruses

The three "F" viruses — feline immunodeficiency virus (FIV), feline leukemia virus (FeLV), and feline infectious peritonitis (FIP) deserve their first initials — they are all bad news on your cat's health report card. The viruses also share another attribute: They are all transmitted from cat to cat.

FIV

Feline immunodeficiency virus, or *FIV,* is the feline counterpart to what in human medicine we call human immunodeficiency virus, or HIV, which causes AIDS. Cats infected with FIV may develop opportunistic diseases ranging from cancer to ringworm to bacterial or viral infections. FIV also may make treating other diseases more complicated.

Testing and isolating infected cats is the only way to control this disease; no vaccine or cure currently exists. Testing on kittens is unreliable, so feline health experts recommend testing of all cats more than 6 months old. Only by knowing the FIV status of your cat can you be certain of what you're dealing with and protect the uninfected cats in your household.

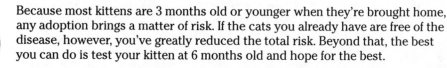

Because most kittens are 3 months old or younger when they're brought home, any adoption brings a matter of risk. If the cats you already have are free of the disease, however, you've greatly reduced the total risk. Beyond that, the best you can do is test your kitten at 6 months old and hope for the best.

A test that is positive for FIV proves only that the cat is or has been infected by the virus and the infection has stimulated production of antibodies to the virus. A positive test performed by your veterinarian doesn't prove your cat is sick from the virus — even if your pet appears sick at the time of the test. Two different tests exist, and you should ask that your cat be retested with the one your veterinarian didn't use to confirm the results before making any decisions regarding your pet.

The good news is that infection with the feline immunodeficiency virus generally carries a better prognosis than does infection with the feline leukemia virus (also covered in this section). A positive FIV test, therefore, should not be considered a reason to change how you treat your cat except that no new cats should be introduced into your home and your cat should stay indoors to protect himself from other diseases and to protect other cats from his infection.

FIV-positive healthy cats may live for months to years — many cats live for six to ten years after diagnosis. To help your pet live longer with FIV, work with your veterinarian to catch health problems early and treat them aggressively. Your cat doesn't have the healthy immune system of a normal cat, so you and your veterinarian must help him out.

Despite what you may have heard, no evidence has been found to suggest that FIV can have ill effects upon humans. FIV may be the feline counterpart to AIDS, but it is a different disease — one that humans cannot catch.

FeLV

Feline leukemia virus, or *FeLV,* is a known killer. FeLV both weakens the immune system and directly contributes to the development of cancers in infected cats. The disease is thought to be the most important infectious contributor to the death and suffering of cats.

Although vaccines are available against this deadly disease (see Chapter 11 for more information on vaccines), they're not foolproof. As with FIV, the best way to protect your cat against feline leukemia is to know the infection status of the cats he associates with and protect him from the infected ones — ideally, that means keeping him inside, alone, or with other FeLV-negative cats.

Test all new kittens or cats before introducing them to the cat or cats you already have and vice versa. (You should test for FeLV before your new pet is vaccinated against the disease anyway.) Your cats should also be retested after exposure to potential FeLV carriers, especially if your pet has been bitten. Because FeLV is associated with many symptoms of illness, your cat should also be tested if he's sick. Outdoor cats or others who are exposed to potential FeLV carriers should be retested annually.

Most veterinarians use a combination FeLV and FIV test that allows them to determine the presence of both of these viral diseases with a single blood sample, and generally for less cost than doing the two tests separately.

FeLV is serious business. Don't let your soft heart convince you to take home a cat or kitten before you know your new pet's FeLV status, especially if you already have a cat or cats at home — you're risking their lives to do so. If you find you have exposed your cat or cats to FeLV, though, do not panic. Isolate your pets from the FeLV-infected cat and have them tested according to your veterinarian's recommendations. Infection with FeLV can require long-time repeated exposure, so don't be too concerned because of one interaction.

What does having your cat test FeLV positive mean? First, realize that having the virus does not equal being sick. Some otherwise healthy FeLV-positive cats live for months or even years with no evidence of disease. If the infected cat is your only pet, you have no known reason to consider changing how you care for him other than not letting him out where he can expose other cats to his disease or be exposed to bad things other cats may be carrying. Take extra care to prevent exposure to diseases and work closely with your veterinarian to diagnose and treat early and aggressively any FeLV-related diseases that may develop.

The good news (yes, we think you deserve some now): Unlike with FIV, many cats can eliminate FeLV infections from their bodies. That's why retesting any cat who tests (and is confirmed) positive within two to three months after the previous test is so important.

FIP

Feline infectious peritonitis, or *FIP,* is a serious concern for those with multiple-cat households or breeding facilities, but the disease is not a common threat to those with single pet cats. Having said that, however, we must note that FIP is a deadly disease whenever and wherever it strikes.

FIP is caused by a virus classified as a *coronavirus.* The confusing part about FIP is that many types of coronaviruses are around, some of which cause disease, and some of which do not. Most disease-causing coronaviruses cause only short-term diarrhea in young kittens. Unfortunately, we have no good way to tell which kind of coronavirus is infecting a cat — the mild kind or the deadly FIP kind. Your veterinarian can tell you your sick cat has been exposed to a coronavirus but can't tell you — until it's too late — whether the disease in your cat is FIP.

As if this situation weren't bad enough, evidence is accumulating that the not-so-bad coronaviruses can rapidly mutate into the very bad FIP virus. The result: You really can't protect your cat from FIP. The virus is pretty tough and can infect a cat after weeks to months of lying around on the floor or floating around in the air. On the plus side, the virus is easily destroyed by common disinfectants and detergents, so basic hygiene helps a lot.

FIP is a "great impersonator" disease, meaning that it can present itself in many ways and is very difficult to definitively diagnose. The disease may look like a spinal or brain disease, a digestive-system disease, an eye disease, or even cancer or heart disease. The most common clues to your veterinarian that FIP is present are found in blood tests, in the results of analysis of fluid from the chest or abdomen, or in the results of a biopsy sample after surgery to find out what's wrong with your cat.

Unfortunately, no known effective treatment exists for FIP, and the outcome is usually fatal. Available treatments are aimed at quieting your cat's immune system and prescribing antibiotics to fight the bacterial infections that may go hand-in-hand with FIP.

Although an FIP vaccine has been produced, many top veterinarians, including Paul's friend Dr. Alice Wolf, of Texas A&M University, believe that little risk of exposure to or of developing FIP in household pets exists. For your cat, then, the current vaccines seem to have little practical application.

Cats in large colonies, catteries, or breeding operations are the greatest risk for developing FIP because of the number of cats in close quarters, but even for those cats, the current vaccine may not be advisable. Studies done at Cornell University raise further questions as to the benefits and maybe even about the safety of vaccinating against FIP.

For now, if yours is a household with one or just a few cats, we recommend that you not vaccinate for FIP. Discuss the situation with your veterinarian, however, because research continues and the situation could change.

Upper respiratory infection

Many cats catch what seem to be "colds" sometime during their lives, and most of these afflictions are caused by viruses. Cats with an upper respiratory infection are lethargic, have fevers and runny eyes and noses, sneeze, and often do not want to eat or drink. These infections are quite contagious, so spreading disease through to other cats is a real concern. Young kittens, and kittens and cats with other diseases that weaken the immune system — such as FIV and FeLV — are most susceptible to these infections.

If your cat develops an upper respiratory infection, call ahead and let your veterinarian know why you are coming in — he may want to take special precautions to help prevent exposing other cats in the waiting room to the virus upon your arrival at the hospital.

As with a cold in humans, so long as the fever is not too high (normal is 100 to 102.5°F) and your cat continues to eat and drink, overnight (or longer) hospitalization can usually be avoided. Keeping your cat's eyes and nostrils free of "crust" by washing gently with a warm, moist cloth helps keep his appetite up. If your cat stops eating and, especially, drinking, dehydration is a danger and hospitalization or home veterinary care is needed. Since upper respiratory infections can be complicated by bacteria, antibiotics are often prescribed as well.

With appropriate care, most cats recover fully in a few days to a week; however, some cases can persist for more than two weeks. If your cat has repeated bouts of upper respiratory infections, or if he is particularly severe or persistent, your veterinarian is likely to be concerned and want to test for diseases that weaken the immune system.

Urologic problems

The *kidneys* are the blood filters of the body. These organs help eliminate excess fluid if a cat drinks more than he needs; retain fluid if the cat drinks

less than he needs; and eliminate waste materials from ing
or medicine, and bodily by-products. The *bladder* stores u
ready to eliminate it from the body (preferably in a litter [
not foolproof, however, and some cats have problems, es[

Cat lovers are often very conscious of their cat's elimination problems,
because a sick cat often stops using the litter box. Making sure a behavior
problem is not a health problem is the first step toward trying to solve it.
After your cat has a clean bill of health, you may need to retrain him in correct litter-box routines. See Chapter 15 for more information.

Kidney diseases

Kidney disease appears mostly in older cats but is possible at any age.
Initially you may notice changes in urination or drinking (more and more
often), but as the disease progresses, you may see weight loss and more-
severe evidence of a buildup of toxins in your cat's body such as vomiting.

A preventable cause of kidney failure in cats is poisoning from the ingestion of
antifreeze. Make sure you protect your pet by cleaning up spills. More information on common household dangers for your pet appears in Chapter 22.

Be concerned if your cat is urinating and drinking excessively. These symptoms can mean any number of problems. Observant owners may also note
reduced appetite, more frequent vomiting, less grooming, and weight loss —
but these symptoms are usually later-stage results of kidney failure.

Some veterinary researchers have proposed that chronic kidney problems
are caused by bacteria entering the blood of cats whose gums are badly
infected. Although the impact of an infected mouth is still under debate,
research does suggest the importance of preventive dental care for your pet.
For more information on preventive dental care, see Chapter 11.

Treatment for kidney failure can include diet changes. Current trends lean
toward low-protein diets, with special attention to low salt if high blood pressure accompanies the problem. Don't be surprised if these recommendations
change — such changes are part of the evolutionary nature of medicine.

You need to work with your veterinarian to monitor the situation of a cat with
kidney disease. Your cat will likely need regular blood tests to spot problems
and changes. Your veterinarian may need to hospitalize your cat to give intravenous fluids and may even ask you to give your cat fluids under the skin at
home. You can help monitor how your cat is coping with the illness by keeping a written daily log of your cat's attitude, appetite, and weight. This record
helps you notice trends that may signal a need for additional attention from
your veterinarian before they become serious.

Unfortunately, no true *cure* for chronic renal failure exists at this time. Treating kidney failure requires long-term effort on your part, and much progress has recently been made in managing this disease. Consult your veterinarian to learn the latest available options, from diet to drugs that stimulate production of red blood cells, to blood pressure control, to kidney transplants.

Feline lower urinary tract disease (FLUTD)

Formerly called *feline urologic syndrome,* or FUS, the term *feline lower urinary tract disease* (FLUTD) encompasses a range of health problems.

In the mildest form, this group of diseases causes irritation to the bladder, which reacts by pushing the cat to urinate more frequently. As anyone who's ever had a bladder infection can attest, irritation of the bladder results in a feeling of always having to "go." If you notice your cat is going to the litter box more often than usual, or suddenly missing the box or using other parts of the house as a litter box, arrange an appointment with your veterinarian. You can provide helpful information by telling the veterinarian if your cat is urinating more frequently with the usual volume or with more volume *and* more frequency.

You can judge volume by the wetness of the litter and how often you need to change the litter.

In its most urgent form, FLUTD causes urinary obstruction. The *urethra* — the tube connected to the bladder that takes urine out of the body — can become blocked by mucus and plugs of crystallized material. Blockage is far more prevalent in male cats because of how they're built — the space through which urine flows is more narrow in male cats. The blockage of the urinary tract is a true veterinary emergency because the situation can result in kidney damage and death if not treated promptly.

In most uncomplicated cases of FLUTD, you see the following symptoms:

- ✓ **Frequent urination.**
- ✓ **Small amount of urine.**
- ✓ **Clear, cloudy, or bloody urine.**
- ✓ **Urine deposits that are not in the litter box.** A cat will often choose to urinate in unusual places such as the sink, bathtub, or shower. A cat with FLUTD often comes to associate the litter box with discomfort and will choose to avoid it.

A cat that is fully obstructed or "blocked" will exhibit frequent straining without successful urination, and will often cry out in pain.

Until the late 1980s, the majority of cats seen with FLUTD were found to have *struvite* crystals or stones forming in the bladder. The theory then was that this condition resulted from too much ash or mineral content in food, especially magnesium. Pet-food companies responded with many diets low in ash. Later, researchers started focusing more on the effects different diets have on the *acid* content of urine. An increase in acidity of the urine helped greatly with struvite stones and crystals but along the way may have caused other health problems.

Struvite crystals and stones have become less common, and cats found to have FLUTD now require more individual investigation to determine what is causing the problem. These conditions include a different kind of crystal or stone (including calcium oxalate and urate), infections of the bladder, and a condition called *interstitial cystitis*.

Your cat's inability to urinate normally is an urgent health problem that needs to be addressed immediately. Your veterinarian will take action to relieve the buildup of urine and then suggest tests to help figure out the source of the problem.

Heart disease

Heart disease is relatively common in cats. Your veterinarian generally first detects heart disease in your cat in one of the following two ways:

- **Hearing an abnormal sound** (a murmur, a gallop sound, or an irregular beat) with her stethoscope during a routine physical examination
- **Examining your cat** after you first notice your cat is breathing rapidly or having trouble breathing

In the case of a breathing problem, heart disease can appear to come on very suddenly. You may think your cat is fine and then a few hours later notice her gasping for breath.

What many cat owners see as "sudden" usually has been building to a noticeable state over time. This is why we give you the information you need to take your cat's heart rate and respiratory rate in Chapter 11 so you know what's normal and what's not before you're faced with an emergency situation.

Other signs of heart disease you may notice include

- **Changes in weight.** More than a half pound or pound weight loss or gain that occurs within a couple of weeks.
- **Coughing.** Sometimes, determining whether your cat is coughing, as opposed to vomiting and gagging, is difficult. If your cat demonstrates either frequently, consult your veterinarian.

✔ **Weakness or paralysis of one or more legs — most commonly a hind limb(s).** Some cats with heart disease develop blood clots in the heart that can then suddenly leave the heart and block the arteries that "feed" the body. These most commonly affect the hind limbs but can affect any area of the body, including the forelimbs, kidneys, brain, and so on.

✔ **Not feeling well.** This last one fits into the category of what Paul calls the Ain't Doing Right (ADR) cat.

Congenital heart disease is not as common in cats as in dogs but is seen from time to time. A murmur heard in a kitten should be evaluated by a specialist. Many cats with congenital heart disease appear normal until they reach several years of age.

If serious heart disease is found or suspected in your cat, the primary concern is to stabilize any life-threatening situations. Your veterinarian may suggest the removal of fluid from in or around the lungs by using medication or a needle and syringe.

If the situation is not as acute and you suspect heart disease — or if your cat was having trouble breathing and is now feeling better — your veterinarian is still going to want to know what's wrong with your cat. Diagnosis in such cases usually requires a chest radiograph (X-ray) and an echocardiogram (cardiac ultrasound). Electrocardiograms (ECG) may also be helpful.

If you have limited funds, the most valuable money you can spend in this situation is often for the echocardiogram and an experienced veterinarian or specialist who knows how to read it.

After an accurate diagnosis is made, your veterinarian or the veterinary specialist works with you to determine the best combination of medications, diet, and monitoring that gives your cat the best chance at a long, healthy life. Nothing is guaranteed, however, and a cat with heart problems is always a candidate for sudden death. As difficult as this fact is to deal with, you need to be prepared.

Don't despair! The area of cardiology is one of the bright spots in feline health in the last 20 years. There was a time when tens of thousands of cats died from a heart condition called *dilated cardiomyopathy,* but thanks to research breakthrough, such deaths don't happen much anymore. As more becomes known about feline diseases, other research breakthroughs will make a difference in the lives of cats.

Tumors

Tumors are, unfortunately, common in cats. Many can be traced back to feline leukemia virus, but others . . . well, no one knows why they occur. Some tumors can be ultimately fatal; others are of little concern at all.

TIP

Health insurance for cats?

Money looms over every suggestion a veterinarian makes and every decision a client considers. One way to tame the beast a little is to purchase health insurance for your cat.

Pet-lovers in the United States have been slow in warming to the concept, which is well established in Europe: In Sweden, 17 percent of all pets are insured, as are 5 percent of the cats and dogs in Great Britain. Still, it's worth investigating.

Ask your veterinarian about health insurance plans that may help you cope with the cost of veterinary care. Some veterinary hospitals are even experimenting with their own HMOs!

The most important things to remember about tumors is that you should carefully monitor your cat for lumps and bumps — he enjoys your loving rubbing, poking, and prodding, and the more you do this sort of thing, the more you get to know what's normal for your cat and what's a new "growth." You should also be constantly aware of weight loss or other signs of your cat not feeling well. At the first sign of a problem, consult your veterinarian. She will want to examine your cat and probably perform some diagnostic tests, including blood tests and perhaps a fine needle aspirate of any suspicious masses. If cancer is suspected, the most important test to pursue is a biopsy.

Your veterinarian may recommend a consultation with a veterinary oncologist to assess the seriousness of the tumor and the options for care. Commonly available treatments include surgery, chemotherapy, and radiation — often a combination of treatments is used. Your veterinarian, perhaps with the help of a veterinary oncologist, can help you understand what to expect from the tumor type diagnosed.

Remember that what veterinarians tell you is their best guess based on what happens to most patients, and that your cat could do much better or worse than average. Your veterinarian will help you make decisions regarding treatment options based on what they believe is best for your cat.

The very vaccinations that have saved so many feline lives have ended up killing a few, who end up with malignant tumors at the injection sites. The risk is low, however, and you're putting your cat at much greater risk if you avoid vaccinations because of your worries. For more information on the risks of vaccinations — and the benefits, of course — see Chapter 11.

Giving Your Cat Medication

No matter how much you and your cat hate the idea, at some point in your pet's life, you're going to come home from the veterinary office with medication, and you're going to need to give that medication to your cat. Is it easy? Not really, but we can help make the process easier. Is it necessary? You bet. Seeing your veterinarian and then not following through on care instructions is worse than a waste of money: It may be dangerous for your pet.

Your veterinarian depends on you to report whether the medication given is helping or hurting. Do not hesitate to call your veterinarian and let her know if you think the medications are making a difference — positive or negative. Sometimes, the only way to know is to stop the medication. Just don't do so without talking to your veterinarian so that she knows and agrees. And don't adjust the dose — up or down — without your veterinarian's knowledge and approval. Doing so is like playing with fire. Only in this case, your pet is the one who may get burned!

Pilling your pet

Gina once asked her readers for their best tips on getting pills down their pets, and her phone was ringing off the hook for days. Most people try the sneak method, attempting to disguise a pill in a bit of something yummy in hopes that their pet doesn't notice the pill inside. You can try this approach, but honestly, it works a lot better for dogs, who are "wolfers," than it does for cats, who eat carefully, considering every mouthful.

Better still is the straightforward approach: Take a firm but gentle grip on your pet's head from above, pry open his jaw with the index finger of your other hand, and press the pill far enough back on the tongue to trigger swallowing. Some people have good luck with "pill guns" (available in pet-supply outlets). These plastic devices enable you to put the pill on the tip and then press it to the top of your cat's throat.

Although experienced cat lovers — and, of course, veterinarians and veterinary-health technicians — can make pill-popping look like an easy, one-person job, you're likely to find the task easier at first if you have someone else hold your cat while you pill her.

One of the best suggestions to come out of Gina's poll came from the fellow who "screened" his cat to pill her. He "hung" her by her claws on the screen door and then gave her the pill. Tough on the screen door but easier on the owner — and in some cases, the cat!

Figure 12-2:
A firm, swift, and gentle approach is best when giving your cat medication in pill form.

Liquid medication

For liquid medications, ask your veterinarian for some large syringes with the needles removed. These syringes have measurements marked on the sides, and they are very handy at getting liquid medicine in the right place. An eye-dropper works well, too.

Raise your cat's muzzle with a firm but gentle hold on the top of her head and lift her lip on one side. Ease the tip between the teeth and toward the back of the mouth and then release the liquid in a slow, steady motion. Your cat will swallow naturally. Pause if she needs more time to swallow.

Ear medication

Lay a large towel across your lap and draw your pet up, relaxing her with stroking and soothing words. After she's relaxed, apply the ear drops, massaging the base of the ear gently. Be prepared to have her shake her head, throwing some of the medication in every direction! The dosage takes this shaking into account, though, so don't double-dose your pet.

Figure 12-3:
Release
liquid
medication
into the
back of the
throat with a
slow, steady
motion.

Eye medication

To use eye medication, restrain your pet and gently apply a line of ointment from the tube across the length of the eye, being careful not to touch the surface of the eye. Try to land drops squarely in the center. Close the lid for a couple of seconds to let the medication distribute evenly.

As with anything your pet would rather avoid, be patient, gentle, and firm when giving medication — and follow with praise and petting. If you're having trouble medicating your pet, have your veterinarian walk you through the process — or discuss alternatives.

Chapter 13

Caring for an Older Cat

● ●

In This Chapter

▶ Understanding the normal signs of aging

▶ Caring for your cat's teeth

▶ Coping with three common health problems

▶ Knowing when to let go

▶ Providing for your cat in your will

● ●

*U*ntil recently, many people had cats who came and went — mostly went — with sad regularity. The common wisdom: You didn't "own" cats. You fed them, admired their beauty, and enjoyed their company. You let them in and out of your house with a degree of good humor and grieved for them after they disappeared, after a year or two or maybe five, but generally not much more.

The reality can be so much different now. The popularity of cats has led to an explosion in knowledge of how to care for them at all stages of their lives, and geriatric care is no exception. Barring accidents, cats can live healthier, happier lives years longer than they ever have before — 10, 12, 14 years. Protected from the outside world, some cats can live even longer, with 16, 18, and even 20 years a possibility.

The difference in life span is not in the cats themselves but in the relationship we humans have with them — the expansion of both knowledge and responsibility. The secret to a cat's long and comfortable life rests as much in your care as in the genes she inherited from her mother and father — and we help you make the most of both in this chapter.

We focus in this chapter on preventive-care measures that are especially important to older cats and diseases that are more common in felines that are middle-aged or older (more on age stages later in this chapter). You should also check out our more-general preventive-care guidelines in Chapter 11, especially the section on spotting health problems early.

To live with an older cat is to share a lifetime of love in a look, a pat, a purr. The bond you've spent years building is a thing of wonder now. You know each other. You're comfortable and relaxed with each other. You love each other effortlessly. These years are special, and you should enjoy them.

Of course, these are also the years when you realize your cat isn't going to be with you forever, and these thoughts can dampen your enjoyment of this special stage. Don't feel sorry for your cat or yourself. Take a lesson from her and enjoy each day wholly. Your cat lives in the now and has no concept that the changes in her life are part of a natural process. She doesn't know where the years lead. She lives day to day, spending her time purring in your lap or sleeping in the sun, demanding her dinner or chasing a toy across the carpet. If she feels good and is with you, she is happy. And so, too, should you be.

You're the one who has the biggest influence over your cat's life span. Protection, prevention, and early detection are the words to remember as your cat ages. We're not going to sugarcoat this advice for you: The two most important things you can do to ensure your cat a long, healthy life is keep your pet inside and take care of spaying and neutering. An indoor cat is protected from the hazards of the outdoor world, especially cars and contagious viruses. And an altered cat is protected from health problems, such as reproductive-related cancers and infections and, especially in males, the constant pressure to roam in search of mates and to fight in defense of territory.

For more information on the indoor versus outdoor controversy, see Chapter 1. For more information on spaying and neutering, see Chapter 16.

How Old Is "Old"?

A widely held belief for determining whether a cat is middle-aged or old is that one year in a cat's life equals four in a human's. In truth, the situation is not that neat, and if you think about it, you can easily see why. Under a "one equals four" rule, a 1-year-old cat would be the equivalent in terms of mental and physical maturity to a human 4-year-old, and that's clearly off.

A better equation is to count the first year of a cat's life as being comparable to the time a human reaches the early stages of adulthood — the age of 15 or so. Like a human adolescent, a 1-year-old cat looks fairly grown up and is physically capable of becoming a parent but lacks emotional maturity.

The second year of a cat's life picks up some of that maturity and takes a cat to the first stages of full adulthood in humans — a 2-year-old cat is roughly equivalent to a person in the mid-20s.

From there, the "four equals one" rule works pretty well. A cat of 3 is still young, comparable to a person of 29. A 6-year-old cat, similar to a 41-year-old person, is in the throes of middle age; a 12-year-old cat, similar to a 65-year-old person, has earned the right to slow down a little. A cat who lives to be 20 is the feline equivalent of nearly 100 in terms of human life span!

Figure 13-1:
Sammy was 19 when he posed for his formal portrait, a good example of the difference a lifetime of proper care can make.

Sammy/Photo by Hope Harris

As with humans, age is relative. An unloved and uncared-for cat is not going to enjoy life at 6, whereas one twice that age, given proper care and nutrition, may be nearly as playful as a kitten.

Normal Signs of Aging

Aging comes in a mostly predictable way to cats, so subtle that you may not notice the signs at first until suddenly you look at your pet and think: "How long has she been losing weight?" or "When did she stop trying to jump up to her favorite spot?" The thought right after that is often even more upsetting: "Is this serious? Should I be worried?"

Although anything that worries you warrants checking in with your veterinarian, if for nothing more than your peace of mind, knowing what's normal for your cat goes a long way toward easing the years for you both. (A keen observer of body language and emotion, your cat knows if you're upset, after all.)

Normal signs of aging are gradual. Sudden problems may be indicative of a serious health problem. If your cat changes quickly in appearance or behavior, have her seen by your veterinarian right away.

Decline of the senses

As your cat ages, her senses of hearing, vision, and smell may worsen, although different cats age in different ways. Some of these changes may be barely noticeable to you as your cat adapts to them, and others may be more obvious, such as foul breath due to dental disease that requires more-frequent attention to control with advancing age.

Other changes can be very hard to notice. Some people aren't even aware that their pets are deaf, although imagining how that can happen isn't that hard. After all, even in the best of circumstances, your cat pays attention only when she wants to!

You may suspect that your cat has a hearing loss when you notice that your cat isn't reacting to the sounds that always used to get a response, such as the whirring of the electric can opener near dinner time. To test your hunch, check by snapping your fingers behind her head. Her ears should swivel back to the sound.

Although your cat can get along just fine indoors if her hearing isn't as keen as it was, deafness really does put her at risk outdoors. Even the cat who has survived into old age by being street savvy can't dodge a car if she can't hear it coming.

Your cat's sense of taste may have an important effect on her appetite, resulting in a problem in some older cats. Smell is extremely important when your cat is determining what's enticing enough to try, and if this sense has declined, nothing may seem worth tasting.

Heat makes smell more intense. If your cat isn't eating, call your veterinarian. If everything checks out okay there, try enticing your cat by serving canned food at room temperature or a bit warmer.

Changes in appearance

Because your cat's body is undergoing changes internally, you may notice changes externally. Cats lose muscle mass as they age, so your pet may seem bonier than when he was young. Other cats may become obese, eating the same amount of calories despite a reduced level of activity. (For more information on obesity, see Chapter 10.)

Change may show up in your pet's coat, leaving it feeling drier and more sparse and the skin less supple. Your cat may not be as efficient at grooming himself as he ages — or, as he becomes more fragile, he may not be able to do the chore so diligently or have the interest in grooming that he once did.

Your cat looks better and feels better if you assist him with his grooming. For more information on how to help, see Chapter 9.

Behavior changes

The temperament of healthy older cats is really something to anticipate with pleasure in many cases. Your cat may mellow over time, becoming more interested in lapsitting and less in crawling up your drapes and performing death-defying leaps from atop tall pieces of furniture. This softening of attitude may be what you notice most as you consider your older cat, but other behavior changes may appear that you should also think about.

Your cat may sleep more, but you need to watch that, too. Extreme disinterest in the world around him can also be a sign of disease, as can an increased energy level. Be aware, too, of changes in appetite or thirst — although your cat needs fewer calories and more fluids as he ages, extreme changes need to be checked out.

A new kitten?

Because older cats do so poorly when stressed, think very seriously before introducing a kitten to your household.

A kitten's playful ways just aren't appreciated by a geriatric cat and may prompt behavior problems such as litter box avoidance or a loss of appetite — the latter a serious health concern in all cats, but especially in older ones.

Keep your older cat healthy by playing with him by using a cat fishing pole or toy on a string.

He's going to appreciate the time you spend with him, especially because you're happy to play on his terms, leave him alone after he's had enough, and not keep pestering him like you do with a kitten.

You have plenty of time in your life for a new kitten. If you have an older cat, postpone adding a youngster and let your cat enjoy his senior years as he sees fit.

Figure 13-2:
Many older
cats tend
to sleep
more —
and they
deserve
their naps!
Watch out,
however, for
signs of
extreme
disinterest
in life.

Omar/Photo by Michael Brewton

Because behavior changes in older cats are often the result of health problems, be aware of these changes and be sensitive to how quickly they occur. The formerly sweet-natured cat who's now cranky or defensive, for example, may act that way because of chronic pain. Or the cat who suddenly neglects his litter box routines may have an infection or even diabetes. Because your cat can't talk about what's bothering him, you need to listen to his body and be aware.

Special Care for Kitty Teeth

Some cats, like some people, can go a lifetime without rigorous dental care without ill effects (other than disgusting everyone who smells their breath). However, this is the exception and not the rule. A little care can go a long way toward making your cat more appealing to be near as well as preventing significant dental problems. If you've paid attention to his teeth his entire life, you've done your pet a wonderful service. If you haven't, you have some catching up to do to ensure that dental problems don't make your cat unhappy. Bad teeth can lead to pain while eating. In addition, some people believe periodontal disease can lead to other ill effects when bacteria (causing disease in the mouth) enters the bloodstream and causes infection in the kidneys and other organs. Don't ignore these problems!

The older-cat physical

Annual physicals are even more important as your cat ages and need to be more extensive than when she was younger. Your veterinarian may suggest blood and urine tests, for example, to determine what's normal for your cat so that subsequent changes in the test values are more apparent.

This *well-cat appointment* is a good time to address your concerns about your cat's aging and get all your questions answered. Encourage your veterinarian to discuss your cat's condition thoroughly and all the care options that are available to you.

Although feeling comfortable with your veterinarian and confident in her abilities is always important, such considerations are especially important if your cat is older. You're working together as a team to ensure your cat's health: Make sure your veterinarian is someone you trust so you can make the best decisions on your cat's behalf. (Information on choosing a veterinarian is in Chapter 11.)

When your cat is comfortable and relaxed, gently raise his lip and take a look. You're sure to see the yellowing and wear that's a normal part of the aging process of his teeth, and that's okay. You're looking for signs of developing periodontal disease, which is a relentless chronic process that inevitably leads to oral discomfort, tooth loss, and poor general health. These signs include plaque; a brown, brittle substance called *calculus* that builds up on the tooth surfaces, especially near the gumline; and gingivitis, which is the inflammation of gum tissue. In severely affected mouths, tooth root abscesses are not uncommon and require prompt veterinary attention.

You can keep your pet's teeth healthy by brushing them at least three times a week — see Chapter 11 for how to make the task easy on you both. Before you can start such preventive care, however, your veterinarian must treat the problems that have already developed. This care likely involves a cleaning and polishing under anesthesia, along with the treatment or removal of any diseased teeth and diagnosis and management of any further dental problems

If your cat had nothing more than plaque buildup and mild inflammation, he's likely to go home with clean teeth and dental care instructions. From there, the task of keeping those teeth in good shape with regular brushing and an eye toward the need for further veterinary care is in your hands.

Common Problems

Most health problems older cats get are also seen in younger cats, with the notable exception of hyperthyroidism, which we discuss in this section. Some diseases pop up frequently in older cats, however, and we want to make sure that you're aware of them.

Because many health problems can occur at any age, please don't neglect the more-general chapters on veterinary care, especially Chapters 11 and 12, which include sections on preventive-care measures that can keep some worries from ever surfacing at all.

An excellent book-length source of information on older cats is *Your Aging Cat: How to Keep Your Cat Physically and Mentally Healthy into Old Age*, by Kim Campbell Thornton and Dr. John Hamil (IDG Books Worldwide).

Diabetes

Diabetes is a loss of control of the amount of sugar in the blood — a cat with diabetes has a very high concentration of sugar in the blood and urine. There are two types of diabetes: The first is called *insulin-dependent diabetes,* in which the pancreas fails to produce enough of the hormone *insulin* to regulate blood-sugar levels; the other form of the disease occurs when the body does not respond properly to the insulin that the pancreas produces.

Fat cats are more susceptible to diabetes, which is another reason that preventing obesity is so important.

Cats with diabetes may appear to be losing weight while eating actively. They will also drink and urinate more frequently in large volumes. You may notice your cat's urine is "sticky," like sugar water, as a result of the high sugar content.

Don't take these symptoms lightly! In more advanced cases, cats can become acutely ill, even comatose. Any markedly depressed cat should be considered potentially very ill, and you should seek veterinary care immediately.

If your cat is diagnosed with diabetes, your veterinarian will suggest dietary changes that may include controlled weight loss and high-fiber diets. Sometimes, medications can help to control the blood sugar level. In most cases, though, you will need to give insulin injections to your cat. Your veterinarian will demonstrate giving injections and discuss how you will together monitor your cat's progress and medication needs. Be sure to keep a diary of all changes to your cat's medication needs and responses; this diary will help you and your veterinarian better control your cat's diabetes.

Some cases of diabetes can be cured by finding and treating other diseases that are making the cat's system more resistant to insulin. Some cats will spontaneously recover permanently or temporarily from diabetes. We are not trying to raise false hopes that your cat will have a miracle cure, but rather trying to increase your awareness that healthy or ill, you need to remain always aware of changes in your cat's behavior.

Hyperthyroidism

What got into that cat? It's a question people with older cats often wonder, as their pets seem to lose weight, even though they're eating more, and perhaps get even more energetic as they age, instead of less.

Although having an oldster with the energy of a kitten may seem wonderful, that zooming cat may be sick with a disease that can kill if left unchecked. *Hyperthyroidism,* the overproduction of thyroid hormone, is among the most common maladies in older cats. Hyperthyroidism is certainly the great impersonator within older cats. Paul has a very focused approach to medicine and is largely not in favor of "shotgun" testing, but he does believe that every older cat should have thyroid hormone levels monitored or at least tested at the first sign of any change in health. Hyperthyroidism can be present in many ways — ranging from the overactive thin cat who eats all the time to the "just ain't doing right cat" that befuddles veterinarian after veterinarian.

When a cat produces too much thyroid hormone, his metabolic rate can soar to the point where it can burn off a third of his body weight. Left unchecked, kidney, heart, liver, and other problems can develop, sometimes leading to death. However, remember that none of these symptoms *must* be present, and even overweight cats may be suffering from hyperthyroidism.

The treatment of hyperthyroidism is one of the bright spots of feline geriatric medicine. Although the disease is common, several good care options can, in many cases, cure the problem.

Veterinary medicine offers three methods for treating hyperthyroidism. The one chosen often depends on location and the overall health and disposition of the pet. Here are your options:

- ✔ **Radioactive iodine therapy:** This option is the preferred method of treatment, and you can easily see why: cure rates of 90 to 95 percent, with no further treatment. The cat gets one dose of a radioactive substance that kills the overproducing cells without directly harming other body functions. It's a one-day matter, but what follows presents a dilemma for many owners: The treatment creates a radioactive cat that must be kept on site at the clinic or college for 7 to 14 days, after which the animal is considered safe to go home. Another problem is that this treatment is not available in all areas, adding travel time to the equation for those who want to pursue it. Veterinary colleges are one source of this treatment, as are specialty practices in many urban areas.

- ✔ **Surgery:** Another option is a *thyroidectomy,* the surgical removal of the offending thyroid gland or glands, which can be done by a pet's regular veterinarian or colleague nearby. The problem: The surgery is delicate, with a chance that other problems may result. Surgery is a good option if radioactive iodine treatment is not available, or if the cat hasn't the temperament to endure confinement.

✔ **Medication:** Hyperthyroidism can be treated with drugs. Tapazole is most commonly prescribed but other options are available. Some cats don't tolerate Tapazole well, and some owners aren't up to the task of administering multiple daily pills for the duration of a pet's life. Because of these problems, drug therapy is often used to stabilize a cat prior to the other treatments in order to address the immediate health problems caused by hyperthyroidism until a long-term solution can be put into place.

Anesthesia and the older cat

As common as anesthesia is in veterinary medicine, many misconceptions exist about its use where older animals are concerned. The idea that the risk of anesthesia outweighs the importance of preventive veterinary care (such as dentistry) is no longer valid. Yes, it is true that no anesthetic procedure is without risk. However, in the hands of a good veterinarian and his staff, anesthesia, even in the elderly patient, has become a routine and very safe procedure.

The risks can be greatly minimized by a history, physical examination, and a few basic tests beforehand, including a laboratory evaluation of blood and urine, and possibly a chest X ray. Although these tests admittedly add to the cost of a procedure, they enable your veterinarian to understand fully the health status of your cat before anesthetizing him. During the procedure, placement of an intravenous catheter and administration of fluids can further add to the safety of the procedure. In the case of dental work, your veterinarian may prescribe antibiotics before, during, and after the procedure.

If finances are a big concern and you have to choose where to save in order to be able to afford the needed procedure, money spent on appropriate anesthetic monitoring and IV fluids during the anesthetic procedure likely provides the greatest return in ensuring that your cat's anesthetic procedure is as eventless as possible.

No discussion of anesthetic danger can be complete without a few words on your responsibilities where anesthesia is concerned:

✔ Follow your veterinarian's instructions on preparing your pet for surgery. If no food is specified, make sure you deliver your pet with an empty stomach. Following this one piece of advice is one of the easiest and most basic ways to reduce risk. During anesthesia, the contents of a full stomach can be regurgitated with the unfortunate potential complication of being inhaled into the lungs. In general, you should completely withhold food the night before but continue to allow free access to water until the morning of the procedure.

✔ Be prepared to provide special home care for your pet after surgery. Releasing animals before sedation wears off fully may be common practice for some veterinarians. Such animals must be kept safe from hot or cold environments because their reflexes are reduced. If you do not feel comfortable caring for a sedated pet, arrange for your veterinarian to extend the care. If your veterinarian does not run a 24-hour hospital, be sure to have the number of your local emergency clinic handy in case complications develop following your cat's anesthesia.

✔ Make sure that you understand what the procedures are and what to expect. Pets commonly have a cough after anesthesia, for example, because the tube used to deliver the gas may cause some irritation. If the cough does not clear in a couple days, call your veterinarian.

No matter what the age of the pet, the chances are very high that the anesthetic will present no problem if both you and your veterinarian work to minimize the risk. And the payoffs, especially those involving dental care, can be significant.

Recent evidence suggests a small percentage of cats treated for hyperthyroidism develop kidney problems. This slight risk should not dissuade you from treating your cat. It may be a reason to try drug therapy first to "test" the response of the kidneys to treatment. We expect that more information will be available on this in the near future and recommend that you discuss this issue with your veterinarian before making a final therapy decision.

Obstipation

Obstipation is the complete inability to defecate, resulting in a very painful and serious condition for your cat that needs veterinary attention. The causes of this backup are not well understood. The intestines become dilated and unable to push stool out of the body normally.

Be alert to your cat's litter box habits. If your indoor cat is straining or crying out while trying to defecate or if you notice an absence of feces, your cat has a problem. Oddly, this blockage may initially appear as diarrhea, because your cat's body, so irritated by the retained feces, may generate lots of watery fluid or mucus to try to cope. This discharge may seem like "ordinary" loose stools when passed.

Any change in your cat's litter box habits is potentially a sign of disease and must be checked out by your veterinarian to ensure that problems are caught while they can still be treated.

Your veterinarian is likely to suggest taking an X ray to determine what's behind the problem. Enemas are the short-term solution; drugs or surgical methods may eventually be required. Long-term care may require the use of drugs or laxatives to keep stools soft, as well as an increased attention to your cat's grooming to cut down the volume of hair he swallows. Drug treatments have met with mixed results. Surgery to remove part of the colon is rather extensive and can lead to problems with diarrhea; however, in many cats the surgery can be rewarding.

We touch on just a few of the most common health problems in older cats, but many other health conditions afflict cats young and old. Check out our more general health care information in Chapter 12, and learn the importance of good preventive care by reading Chapter 11. Above all, consult your veterinarian.

Knowing When It's "Time"

Euthanasia, the technical term for "putting a pet to sleep," is one of the hardest decisions you must ever make, and it doesn't get any easier, no matter how many times over the years you face it. Your veterinarian can offer you advice, and your friends can offer you support, but no one can make the decision for you. If you live with an elderly or terminally ill pet, you look in her eyes every morning and ask yourself: Is this the day?

To know for sure is impossible. But take solace in knowing that in almost 20 years of practice, Paul has only four times had to look at an owner and say, "Hey, it is time." Although we say to know for sure is impossible, Paul firmly believes that owners *do* know when it is time and respects their decisions without question. Asking guidance from your friends, family, and veterinarian is very appropriate, but only you can make the final decision. Good friends, family, and veterinarians will offer good "if it were my pet" advice, but they should also respect your decision without question.

Some owners don't wait until their pet's discomfort becomes pain, and they choose euthanasia much sooner than many other people would. Some owners use an animal's appetite as the guide — if an old or ill animal is no longer interested in eating, they reason, he's not interested in anything at all. Other owners wait until no doubt remains that the time is at hand. Each guideline is the right one for some cat and some owner at some time. You do the best you can, and then you try to put the decision behind you and deal with the grief.

The incredible advances in veterinary medicine in the past couple of decades have made the decisions even more difficult for many people. Not too long ago, the best you could do for a seriously ill pet was to make her comfortable until that wasn't possible anymore. Nowadays, nearly every advantage of human medicine — from chemotherapy to pacemakers — is available to our pets.

If you can afford such care and have a realistic expectation that it can improve your pet's life — instead of simply prolonging it — then it's an option that you should pursue. But let nothing push you into making a decision based on guilt or wishful thinking.

Euthanasia options

Should you be with your pet at the end? What should you do with the remains? The questions are all difficult, but no answers are wrong.

Euthanasia is a quick and peaceful process as performed by a veterinarian. The animal is unconscious within seconds and dead within less than a minute; the euphemism "put to sleep" is a perfect description. Those who attend the procedure come away reassured that their pets felt no fear or pain.

Some people say that staying with a pet at his death is the final gift of love, but no decision you make regarding the last few minutes of an animal's life changes the love you shared for the years that preceded those final moments. If you want to be there, by all means stay. We believe you may later find it comforting, and staying until the end will help you with closure. But leaving is no less a humane and loving gesture. You know in your heart what's best for you and your cat.

Call ahead to set the appointment and make clear to the receptionist what you're coming for. That way, the practice can ensure you don't need to sit in the waiting room but instead are immediately ushered into an exam room if you choose to remain with your cat.

Your veterinarian is going to do his best to make sure that all your questions are answered and that you're comfortable with everything before proceeding. He may clip the fur on your cat's foreleg for easier and quicker access to the vein for the injection of the euthanizing agent; he may also choose to insert a catheter or sedate your pet.

Crying is normal, and your veterinarian understands. So, too, we believe, does your pet.

You may want to spend a few minutes with your pet afterward, and your veterinarian understands that, as well, and will give you all the time you need alone to begin the process of dealing with your loss. (If your pet dies while in the veterinarian's care, you may also choose to view the body to give yourself closure and let the healing begin. Discuss this decision with your veterinarian.)

You may be more comfortable with having your pet euthanized at home. If so, discuss the matter with your veterinarian directly. Many vets extend this special service to long-time clients. If yours doesn't, you may consider making arrangements with a veterinarian who does house calls.

Dealing with loss

Many people are surprised at the powerful emotions that erupt after a pet's death, and they're embarrassed by their grief. Remembering that pets have meaning in our lives beyond the love we feel for the animal may help. Often, we don't realize that we're grieving not only for the pet we loved but also for the special time the animal represented and the ties to other people in our lives. The death of a cat who was a gift as a kitten from a friend who has died, for example, may trigger bittersweet memories of another love lost.

Taking care of yourself is important at this difficult time. Some people — the "it's just a cat" crowd — don't understand your feelings and may shrug off your grief as foolish. The company of other animal lovers is very important. Seek them out to share your feelings. You may be able to find a pet-loss support group in your community, or you can go to the Internet, where sites for sharing the loss are plentiful. The outpouring of support in these virtual communities is heartfelt.

A difficult time, no doubt, but remember: In time, the memories become a source of pleasure, not pain. You're not on any set timetable, but it happens. We promise.

A handful of books and one really fine video may help you to help your child with the loss of a pet. From Fred Rogers (yes, "Mr. Rogers," of the Neighborhood) comes the book *When a Pet Dies* (Putnam) and the video *Death of a Goldfish*. Rachel Biale's *My Pet Died* (Tricycle Press) not only helps children cope better by giving them pages to fill in, but also offers parents advice in special pages that can be torn out. Finally, Judith Viorst's *The Tenth Good Thing About Barney* (Aladdin) is a book that experts in pet loss have been recommending for years.

A great book for adults is Dr. Wallace Sife's *The Loss of a Pet* (Howell Book House).

What about the remains?

You can handle your pet's remains in many ways, and doing so is easier if you make your decisions beforehand. The choices include having your municipal animal-control department pick up the body, burying the pet in your backyard or at another site (where it's legal and with the land owner's permission, of course), arranging for cremation, or contracting with a pet cemetery for full services and burial. Again, no choice is "wrong." Whatever feels right to you and comforts you best is what you should do.

The next topic is a difficult one but one that Paul insisted we add to this second edition. The issue is postmortem examination. If your pet dies unexpectedly or while under the care of your veterinarian, and there is any question as to the cause of death or your veterinarian believes there are lessons to be learned by performing a postmortem examination, we encourage you to agree. This may not help your cat but it may very well help hundreds or thousands of other cats. What better way to demonstrate your love of your cat than to assist in the advancement of care for other cats with similar health problems?

Finally, several manufacturers offer tasteful and attractive markers for your yard to memorialize your pet; these items are often advertised in the back of such magazines as *Cat Fancy*. Other marker choices include large rocks or slabs of stone or a tree or rose bush. Even if you choose not to have your pet's body or ashes returned, placing a memorial in a special spot may soothe you.

One great way to celebrate the memory of your cat is to make a donation to your local humane society, regional school of veterinary medicine, or other favorite animal charity. A donation in a beloved pet's name is a wonderful thing to do for a friend who's lost a pet as well.

You're not alone

You may find talking to others about your pet's death helpful. Ask your veterinarian about pet-loss support groups. Almost unheard of a couple decades ago, such groups are available in many communities today. An excellent resource online is The Association for Pet Loss and Bereavement www.aplb.org.

Veterinary schools and colleges have been among the leaders in creating programs to help pet lovers deal with loss. A handful now operate pet-loss hot lines staffed by veterinary students trained to answer questions, offer materials that may help you (including guidelines for helping children with loss), and just plain listen. These are wonderful programs, and they're free for the cost of the call. (If you call during off hours, they call you back, collect.)

Locations, operating hours, and phone numbers of pet-loss hot lines are as follows:

University of California at Davis
School of Veterinary Medicine
Hours of operation: 6:30 to 9:30 p.m., Mondays through Fridays; Tuesdays through Thursdays during summer
530-752-4200

Cornell University
College of Veterinary Medicine
Hours of operation: 6 to 9 p.m., Tuesdays through Thursdays
607-253-3932

Washington State University
College of Veterinary Medicine
Hours of operation: 6:30 to 9 p.m., Mondays through Thursdays; 1 to 3 p.m. Saturdays
509-335-5704

University of Florida
College of Veterinary Medicine
Hours of operation: 7 to 9 p.m., Mondays through Fridays
352-392-4700, Ext. 4080

Michigan State University
College of Veterinary Medicine
Hours of operation: 6:30 to 9:30 p.m. Tuesday, Wednesday, and Thursday
517-432-2696

Ohio State University
College of Veterinary Medicine
Hours of operation: 6:30 to 9:30 p.m., Monday, Wednesday, and Friday
614-292-1823

Tufts University
School of Veterinary Medicine
Hours of operation: 6 to 9 p.m., Monday though Friday
508-839-7966

Virginia-Maryland Regional College of Veterinary Medicine
Hours of operation: 6 to 9 p.m., Tuesday and Thursday
540-231-8038

University of Illinois at Champaign Urbana
College of Veterinary Medicine
Hours of operation: 7 to 9 p.m., Tuesday, Thursday and Sunday
217-244-2273

Iowa State University
College of Veterinary Medicine
Hours of operation: 6 to 9 p.m., Monday through Friday
888-478-7574

What If You Go First?

First things first: You can't leave your estate to your cat, because in the eyes of the law, an animal is an "it," with little more legal status than a chair. Nor can you set up a trust for your pet for the same reason. The beneficiary of a trust must be a bona fide human being, and the fact that you think of your cat as a person doesn't really matter, because the courts don't.

Although you should discuss this matter with your attorney, talking it over with your friends and family is even more important, because finding one of them whom you trust to care for your pet after you're gone is what you must do. You must leave your feline "property" to that person, along with enough money to provide for the animal's care for life. You have no real control over the outcome, which is why you need to choose someone you trust and then hope for your cat's sake that things turn out okay.

No one likes to think about dying. But you have a responsibility to those you leave behind, and that includes your pets. Talk to your friends, family, and even your veterinarian. Call an attorney. Just don't rely on the kindness of strangers to care for your pet if something happens to you. Your cat deserves better than that.

The Association of the Bar of New York City offers a low-cost pamphlet on providing for your pet if you can't. To order "Providing for Your Pets in the Event of Your Death or Hospitalization," send a $2 money order or check made out to the Association of the Bar and a self-addressed, stamped, legal-sized envelope to the association's Office of Communications, 42 W. 44th St., New York, NY 10036.

Part IV
Living Happily with Your Cat

The 5th Wave   By Rich Tennant

18 MONTHS OFF THE AFRICAN COAST

"'Let me bring him on board', you said. 'He's so cute and cuddly, he'll make a nice mascot for the trip home'. Well, bloody nice mascot he's turned out to be!!"

In this part . . .

This part explains how to understand your cat better, and work through the challenges that come up in your life together. We've included a chapter on the subtle body language of the cat, as well as tried-and-true strategies for resolving behavior problems such as clawing furniture, chewing houseplants, or avoiding the litter box. Have you taken in a homeless cat who's pregnant? We tell you what you need to know to help her, and raise and place her babies in loving homes. Finally, we show you how to travel with your cat, or how to find the best care when you leave your pet behind.

Chapter 14

Solving Behavior Problems

● ●

In This Chapter

▶ Realizing why cats do what they do

▶ Figuring out possible causes of "bad" behavior

▶ Working to correct the problems

▶ The controversy over declawing

● ●

Cats are among the easiest of animals to live with as pets, which in part accounts for their massive and ever-growing appeal. Cats are naturally quiet, clean, affectionate, and largely self-sufficient, capable of adapting to any kind of dwelling, any definition of family.

But when things go wrong . . . they go very, very wrong from the human point of view. A cat with a behavior problem such as aggression can be a source of strife and even heartbreak in your family, with the cat the eventual loser. Cats also can ruin your belongings — covering them with the hard-to-remove stench of urine, clawing them into tatters, or chewing them into bits. Your furniture isn't safe, nor are your houseplants, nor are your own hands, for some cats seem quite deranged at times, purring one minute and biting the next.

To some cat lovers, these behaviors can seem unpredictable, unfathomable, and even spiteful, when, in fact, they're nothing of the sort. What cat lovers call "bad" behavior often makes complete sense to a cat, who's just doing what comes naturally to him, coping with boredom, illness, stress, or change in the way cats have always done. What cat lovers call "problems" are natural behaviors to cats, as much a part of their genetic makeup as super-keen hearing or whisper-soft paws.

To *solve* problem behavior, you must *understand* problem behavior.

Unfortunately, too many cat lovers don't even try to understand, reacting instead in the way that makes sense to the *human* animal — in anger that can start with physical punishment (which never works on a cat) and can end with a one-way trip to the shelter.

For your cat's sake and for your own, we offer alternatives to spare you both the confusion, anger, and resentment that feline behavior problems cause and to restore contentment and trust in your home — to help you reclaim the loving relationship you both deserve.

In this chapter, we help you understand what's causing your cat's unwanted behavior and show you how to set up a program to turn the situation into something you both can live with. Your cat's not perfect, and neither are you, and that's something to keep in mind as you work with behavior problems. Problems often take time to develop, and they also take time to fix.

The process takes patience and a certain degree of accommodation on your part. But most cat-behavior problems can be worked out to both your satisfactions. Don't give up. Read on.

The first step in solving any behavior problem is to make sure it's not a medical problem. We can't stress this fact enough. The signs of illness in cats can be very subtle — see Chapter 11 for more information — and are often disguised as behavior problems. Talk to your veterinarian before attempting to change your pet's behavior, because your efforts will likely fail if you're working with a sick cat. This advice is doubly true if your cat's behavior change is sudden. In that case, he's likely sick, especially if you can't pinpoint any other environmental changes, such as a new person or pet in the home, as a reason for the behavior change.

Your veterinarian can also guide you with your plans for changing a healthy cat's errant behavior — or refer you to a behavior specialist who can. Behavior is one of the fastest-growing areas of knowledge in veterinary medicine, a result of the profession's realization that behavior problems end up killing more animals than do diseases. This new emphasis has increased the use of drug therapy to help with behavior problems, including use of some of the same antidepressant and antianxiety medications used in human medicine. These medications aren't miracles, but they can give your cat a fresh start as you work to cure behavior problems.

Because litter box problems are the top behavior complaint, we offer help in solving them in a new and expanded chapter. We encourage you to read this chapter first to understand what goes into solving any behavior problem. Then read Chapter 15 for specific strategies to get your cat hitting the litter box again.

Understanding "Bad" Behavior

Here's an enjoyable way to spend an afternoon and learn a lot about your cat at the same time: Go to your video store or library and check out a documentary on tigers.

You're certain to be astonished at how much the cat purring in your lap reminds you of this stunning wild cat. The way the tiger walks, with understated elegance and always the promise of power. The way the tiger hunts, still and focused except for the tiniest twitch at the end of the tail.

Now, pay attention to the part of the film about "territory," how tigers need one of their own and how tigers let each other know where one animal's hunting turf ends and another begins. They rub against things, they spray, and they claw.

Admittedly, seeing a tiger do these things is much more dramatic than watching an eight-pound domesticated cat do them. A scent-marking head bump from a tiger may knock a person over. And as for the other two behaviors, you wouldn't even want to be around. If a tiger wants to leave a message (or refresh an old one), he stands up on his hind legs and digs his claws into a tree, putting deep slashes (along with his scent) on the hapless plant. And then, just to make the point a little more emphatic, he turns, faces away from the tree, raises his tail, and squirts a great blast of urine at it. And then he turns again and sniffs, with a gaping expression (called a *Flehmen response*) that looks like a sneer but is really enabling him to "taste" the smell through a sensory organ in the roof of his mouth.

With no one to yell at him for doing these things (as you would if your cat behaved similarly in the corner of a couch or a pile of dirty laundry), he ambles happily off. His world smells the way he thinks it ought to, and he's content.

Now maybe you're beginning to see the problem. The very same things the tiger does to mark territory are natural behaviors for your cat, too. And yet you want your pet to abandon them entirely? We have news for you: It's just not possible. Nor is asking fair.

Fixing feline behavior problems is like taming a tiger: You must work slowly to reshape your pet's natural behaviors in ways that you both can live with.

Looking at the Root of Unwanted Behavior

You're asking a lot of a cat whenever you bring her into your home, and the fact that, in most cases, the situation works as well as it does says a great deal about the bond between cats and people. You ask your cat to relieve herself where you want her to instead of anywhere in her territory. You ask her to scratch in one place instead of marking every surface in her life. You ask her to ignore her ability to jump gracefully onto tables and countertops and adjust her naturally nocturnal schedule to your daytime one.

Most cats make the compromises. For those who don't, you need to figure out why before any problem solving can begin. Here are some things to consider:

- **Medical problems:** As we mention at the beginning of this chapter, behavior problems are often really signs of illness. A cat with untreated diabetes, for example, drinks and urinates frequently, may overwhelm your efforts at keeping the box clean, and starts choosing other sites to relieve himself. A cat who suddenly starts biting may be in pain and is only lashing out to protect himself. A cat with a urinary tract infection may find urinating painful and come to associate the pain with his litter box. Are you really surprised he's going to stop using it? All the behavior techniques in the world aren't going to cure a medical problem. You need your veterinarian's help for that.

- **Stress:** Cats find change stressful and can react by altering their behavior in an attempt to cope. Maybe a cat marks territory in a home that's just been "invaded" by a new pet or person. In a cat's mind, this behavior makes sense and is calming: Making the world smell like himself is comforting to him, if not to you. You need to calm your cat's stress in other ways, by limiting his territory for a while, for example, or by putting him on medication.

- **Unreasonable demands:** You need to look at your own role in any behavior problem. Are you asking something of your cat that's not possible for him to give? Your cat may not want to use the litter box you give him if it's rarely clean, for example, and asking him to leave the couch alone is really not fair if he has nothing else in the house to scratch. You need to provide him with some alternatives before you can hope for good behavior.

- **Boredom:** You've asked your cat to give up the whole world, and all you're offering in return is a few hours of your presence a day and maybe a catnip mouse? *Boring!* Indoor cats need lots of things to keep themselves amused — lots of toys and lots of games, and lots of attention from you. You needn't spend loads of money on cat toys — we've got a section on freebies in Chapter 8 — but you need to make an effort to help your cat play with them. If you're gone from home a great deal, another cat (or even a dog) may provide your pet with exercise, companionship, and amusement. We've also put some tips on keeping indoor cats amused in Chapter 23.

- **Never trained correctly in the first place:** If all you're ever doing is screaming or hitting at your cat, you're probably not teaching him anything except that you're someone best avoided. Physical correction has no place in changing a cat's behavior — cats just don't understand it. And using such correction just stresses them out, leading to even *more* problems.

Look at what has been going on in your life. How has your cat reacted to the situation, and how have you? Keep a journal of problems to help you spot and understand trends and to remove some of the emotion involved in living with a problem pet. Realizing that your cat's behavior isn't spiteful or capricious can make the problem easier for you to live with while you work on turning the situation around.

Figure 14-1:
Whether this kitten's story will have a happy ending or not will depend on how well his new owner copes with behavior challenges.

Photo by Richard D. Schmidt

Strategies for Changing Behavior

Unlike dogs, cats don't have a built-in mechanism for working with a family. Dogs take naturally to the idea of a family, because their ancestors lived and hunted in cooperative teams called *packs,* which have a highly developed social structure. With the exception of lions, cats large and small are solitary hunters, and they're used to taking care of themselves. You can't make cats do what they don't want to do, so to change any behavior, you must offer an alternative you both can accept, even while you work to make the "bad" behavior less appealing.

Your cat loves you and enjoys your company, but if you want to convince him to do things your way, you must answer the quintessential cat question: What's in it for me?

The good news is that cats are creatures of habit. After yours learns where scratching, chewing, or relieving himself is okay, you can put away all the gadgets you've used to convince him.

Yes, kitty!

Reward your cat for good behavior with praise, with treats, with petting, and with games. If your cat uses the scratching post instead of the couch, make sure she knows you approve by playing with her with a cat fishing pole or a toy on a string. Tell her that she's good for using the litter box, for eating *her* plants instead of yours, and for attacking her toys instead of your slippers. Your cat isn't born knowing the rules of living among humans, and if you make following the rules pleasant, you have much better luck getting her to follow them.

No, kitty!

Never hit your cat, and never let her think any discipline is coming from *you.* Physical discipline is worse than meaningless to cats — and it can make a situation even worse by making your cat stressed out and afraid of you.

What works in cats is to make them believe that whatever they're doing wrong triggers an automatic response they don't like — and that you have nothing to do with it as far as they can tell. The couch they used to enjoy clawing is now covered with something they don't like to touch. Every time they get on the counter a tingle of static electricity tingles under their paws or a stream of water hits them in the fanny.

Following is a list of booby traps that work well to discourage cats and help you and your kitty live together in harmony:

- ✔ **Use water and loud noises:** Try slyly squirting your cat with a squirt bottle or setting off compressed air in a can (with or without a horn). You can also loudly shake pennies in an empty soda can or squeeze a squeaky dog toy (cats don't like the sound, but you can't use this device if you also have a dog, because they do!). All these techniques stop your cat in the middle of a bad act and convince her that maybe a repeat isn't in her best interest.

- ✔ **Take cover:** Covering areas you don't want your cat to touch with double-sided tape, foil or plastic, or plastic carpet runners with the points up is also a good plan. An electric mat called a Scat Mat (available in pet-supply stores and catalogs) that gives off a slight shock is great for furniture and countertops.

- ✔ **Set wooden mousetraps:** Wooden mousetraps are another device to give your cat the message about being where he ought not. Get a few of the kind that aren't prebaited and set them *upside down* on countertops or in wastebaskets, with a sheet of newspaper over them. The devices aren't meant to hurt or trap your cat but just to startle him. After he bumps a trap, it jumps and closes with an eye-opening *crack,* helping to convince your pet that the area you've booby-trapped is better left alone.

✔ **Coat with something icky:** Coating something you don't want your cat near with a substance that tastes horrible — such as Bitter Apple or Tabasco sauce — is another form of booby-trapping that works in some cases. You don't need much: Your cat's smell and taste are very keen!

Figure 14-2: Squirt bottles are one tool for curing behavior problems, but they work best when the water comes "out of nowhere" as far as your cat's concerned.

Calm kitty

Sometimes you need to go back to the beginning and reduce your cat's stress by giving her a smaller area for a while, the same behavior modification technique we recommend when you first bring your cat or kitten home. (See Chapter 6 for more information on introductions.) This *safe room* is not a punishment for your cat; on the contrary, it's a relief from whatever's bothering her in a new environment and a chance to refocus her on the behaviors you want — using a scratching post or a litter box, for example. The safe room is excellent therapy for marking, because your cat doesn't have a large territory to defend.

We want you to play with her and pet her and tell her she's loved. But for short periods — a week, maybe two, followed by a gradual reintroduction to the house, room by room — a safe room can ease both your minds and get her retraining off to a good start.

Veterinarians are increasingly able to offer medications to help during the retraining of your cat, drugs that are also used in human medicine to relieve anxiety. These medications can really help, but they're usually a short-term solution. You still need to deal with the underlying problems in order to achieve long-term success. Discuss the use of these medications — or a possible referral to a veterinary behaviorist — with your veterinarian.

Fairness

Make sure that what you expect from your cat is fair in two ways: Are you being reasonable? Are you being consistent?

Being *reasonable* involves offering your cat alternatives: a litter box and a location he likes, for example, or a scratching post in a choice location. You also need to consider whether you're fulfilling your cat's needs — is he getting enough exercise and play?

If your cat's constantly in need of something to do and you're not there to play with him constantly — and few of us are — consider getting another cat for a playmate. Be aware, however, that not all cats will take to a newcomer. Some are such loners that the addition of another cat may cause more problems than it cures. Unfortunately, there's no way to predict which way your cat will go.

Living with more than one cat brings both joys and challenges. Find out about both in our new Chapter 17.

Consistency is about always expecting the same standards of behavior. Letting your pet on the counter while you're both home alone but expecting him to stay off after guests arrive simply isn't fair.

Attacking Behavior Problems

We gave you the keys to solving most cat behavior problems earlier in this chapter: Make sure that your cat has no health problems and then make sure that what you want your cat to do is more attractive than what you don't want him to do. The same rules apply for other cat problems, but we include a few more tips in the following sections to help you cope with some specifics.

Where to find help with behavior problems

Many people are reluctant to seek help if faced with a pet-behavior problem, either because they think the idea of a "pet shrink" is crazy or because they don't think the money would be well spent.

If you're one of these people, think again. Consulting a behaviorist can save you time, money, and aggravation. You save time, because someone with experience in animal behavior can quickly determine the root of the problem, without the emotional baggage that a pet owner may bring to the situation. ("He's doing it for spite!") You save money, because a consultation or two is a great deal cheaper than a new sofa. And aggravation? We don't need to explain that one if you're living with a cat who's driving you nuts.

More importantly, getting help can save your cat's life! Behavior problems are among the top reasons why cat owners "divorce" their feline companions. Here, divorce means giving your pet to another person or animal shelter, requesting they be humanely killed (often the ultimate result for a cat with behavior problems who ends up at a shelter), or abandoning your pet to the streets.

Be aware, however, that animal behavior is an unregulated field — anyone can call himself a behaviorist.

You're best off choosing a veterinarian who's board-certified by the American College of Veterinary Behaviorists. These professionals have gone through years of study in animal health and behavior and have done a residency in the field as well. Your best bet at finding one of these veterinarians is to contact your closest school or college of veterinary medicine's teaching hospital.

People with other academic degrees (such as psychology), general-practice veterinarians, and people who've picked up their cat knowledge completely in the field also make themselves available for advising on behavior. You find good and not-so-good people in all three areas, which makes getting recommendations and checking references important.

In addition to checking with your closest school or college of veterinary medicine, check with your own veterinarian or local humane society, any of which may be able to refer you to someone who can help. Some humane societies also offer behavior classes or consulting.

Aggression

You need to do a little detective work and figure out what's causing your cat to bite or claw you. Aggression takes many forms, and the solution depends on the cause, some of which may be as follows:

> ✔ **Fear or pain:** If your cat is striking out because he's afraid or hurting, your best bet is to leave him alone and work on the underlying problem. A cat in pain or fear has his ears flat back against his head and his body rolled into a defensive posture low against the ground with claws up and ready. This cat is saying, "Don't come near me!" You need to let your cat

calm down — hide if need be — before you can get your veterinarian to check her out. Often under these circumstances that carrier your cat seems to hate will seem like a haven. Place the carrier with the door wide open in the room with your cat. Your cat may choose to go in there, saving you the "fight" of forcing him in the carrier for the trip to the veterinarian. ***Remember:*** Don't fight with your cat. *You will lose.*

✔ **Overstimulation:** You're petting your cat when suddenly he grabs you with his claws and teeth. Not a full-powered attack, but you've still got those sharp tips around your hand. What to do? In the short run, freeze. Don't fight your cat, or you may trigger a real bite. Sometimes smacking your other hand against a hard surface — a table top, for example — may startle your cat into breaking off the attack. If you stay still, however, he usually calms down and releases you.

That's the solution if you've gotten to the attack stage. The better option is to be familiar with your cat and his body language and stop petting before he becomes overstimulated. Cat lovers often think such attacks come without warning, but the fact is that they missed the warning signs of a cat who's simply had enough. The tail is the key: If your cat starts twitching his tail in a jerky fashion, time to call off the petting has arrived. If you watch your cat's body language — more on that subject in Chapter 7 — you can slowly build up your petting time. Three pats, then four, then five. Push up to, but never over, your cat's level of tolerance and build slowly on your successes.

Often these "I've had enough" attacks come if you've been petting your cat's belly. This is a very sensitive area for cats, and even if yours offers it to you, you're better off petting somewhere else. One reason is sexual in nature: Your male cat becomes aroused when his belly is rubbed, and reacts with a bite because that's what feline mating behavior involves. (For more on cat sex — it hurts! — see Chapter 16.)

✔ **Play aggression:** Sure, it hurts all the same, but the cat who pounces on your feet and then careens off the wall isn't trying to hurt you — he's playing. You need to increase your play sessions with your cat with an appropriate toy, such as a cat fishing pole or toy on a string — not one of your body parts — to help your cat burn off his excess energy before you try for a quiet pet session. Let him know that attacks on you are not permitted by letting him have it with a blast from an air horn or a spray bottle. A little Bitter Apple on your hand can help, too.

✔ **Redirected aggression:** Your cat sees another cat, an intruder, outside your living room window. He becomes enraged. You walk by, and he nails you. What gives? You were just the victim of redirected aggression. This one's tough to fix. Try to discourage strange cats in your yard: Thump on the window or put the air horn out the door and give them a blast.

Nick/Photo by Angie Hunckler

Counter-cruising

Use your squirt bottle, air horn, or other deterrent to discipline your cat if you see him on countertops and tables. As much as possible, try to stay out of sight so that your cat associates the annoyance with the table or counter. A Scat Mat (a plastic mat that gives off a tingle if touched) is great for this: It disciplines your cat when you're not around, and from the floor, your cat can't tell whether it's still there or not.

Clawing

Start on this project by getting your cat a good scratching post or cat tree. (See Chapter 8 for information on these items.) A cat tree or post must be stable enough for your cat to climb and pull on, covered with material your cat can dig her claws into, and put in a prominent area so that your cat uses it.

After you have the post or tree in place, encourage your cat to use it by teasing her with a cat toy and praising her for digging in her claws. If your cat enjoys catnip, rub some on the post to encourage her to spend more time there and give her treats for being on the tree as well. Make sure that she knows in no uncertain terms that climbing and clawing on her scratching post or cat tree are perfectly fine and encouraged. Don't put her paws on the post, however — cats don't like to be "forced" to do anything!

Don't choose a scratching post covered in the same texture of carpet as that in your house, or your cat may have a hard time making the distinction between why clawing carpet on the post is okay but not on the floor. Better yet: Choose a post or tree covered with *sisal,* a rough-textured rope material that cats love to dig into.

Make the areas you don't want your pet to touch less appealing during the retraining process by covering them with foil, plastic sheeting, or plastic carpet runners with the pointy side out. Use double-sided tape generously as well — cats hate the feel of sticky stuff under their paws. You can still use the furniture yourself by applying the foil, plastic, or what-have-you to pieces of cardboard that you can lift off if you want to sit down.

When aggression can't be fixed

You must *never* forget that the combination of agility, climbing acumen, sharp claws and teeth, and a stubborn streak larger than any one person could ever possess makes almost any cat a creature you don't want to get on the wrong side of. We don't wish to instill fear or shy you away from the joys of living with a cat, but we do want to emphasize a couple bits of advice.

Unless you feel *very* competent at restraining cats, never attempt to force your cat to do anything by using any but the most gentle of physical means. The best way to deal with a cat who has gone "over the edge" is to leave him alone. Don't try to restrain or punish him. Leave the room or let him leave the area and find a quiet place to calm down.

If you *ever* find yourself facing a vicious cat, call for help. Occasionally a cat will seem to go nuts, sometimes for no reason at all, and Paul has experienced this first-hand. The following experience is fortunately quite rare. We hesitated to even include it — but felt it our responsibility to do so.

Paul once found himself rushing to rescue his sister from her beloved cat, who had suddenly turned aggressive and imprisoned her within a single bedroom (with a phone, luckily) in her New York City apartment. Thinking this situation was humorous, Paul entered the apartment to find a cat who had gone crazy and quickly convinced Paul that his only safe haven was on the terrace.

Paul will never forget watching this once-friendly cat lunge at the plate-glass window trying to reach him. Talking with his sister through the bedroom window, Paul convinced her to call animal control, which finally came and captured the cat with appropriate equipment. Unfortunately, this cat never calmed down and had to be euthanized. Although a post-mortem examination did not reveal any explanation for the sudden rage behavior, Paul believes this must have been a medical problem with an unfortunate outcome.

Now that we have scared you, let us reassure you that you are unlikely to ever face such a situation. It has certainly not caused Paul to abandon cat ownership, nor has it ever caused him to dissuade anyone from cat ownership — quite the contrary!

Because clawing is also a territory marker, move the cat tree into a prominent place, near that clawed corner of the couch in the center of the room, now covered with deterrents. Praise your cat for using the post instead. Move the post slowly — a few inches a day — to a place more to your taste.

If you catch your cat clawing, squirt with a spray bottle or use another distracting device. Try to stay out of sight whenever you do so and don't lose your temper. The idea is to get the cat to believe that the furniture itself is doing the disciplining. ("Wow, I put my claws in there and got water on me!")

Yes, your house is going to look pretty ugly for a while, with cat deterrents all over the furniture and a cat tree in the middle of the room. You must live with these unsightly accessories until your cat's new pattern of clawing only where acceptable is established. If you're patient and consistent, that new pattern will eventually take root.

Figure 14-4:
Kittens and cats love to dig their claws into things. Putting items out of reach is one way to redirect behavior.

Lightning/Photo by Lisa Wolff

For some cats, nail tips help with clawing problems. Glued onto the nails every six weeks or so, these Soft Paws tips even come in a variety of colors.

Keeping your cat's nails trimmed is another way to reduce his destructive capabilities. For instructions on how to do this task safely, see Chapter 9.

The plant terminator

Plants and cats are natural together, at least from the cat's point of view. The leaves are good for nibbling, and if the pot has enough room — and it doesn't take much — the soil looks like a suitable alternative to the litter box. Pity that people don't see things the same way.

The key to peaceful coexistence between cats and houseplants is to give your kitty a garden of her own and make the rest of the plants as undesirable or as hard to get to as possible. We put a list of cat-friendly plants in Chapter 10;

keeping fresh greens growing takes care of your cat's need to nibble. As for your other plants, here are some tips on keeping them safe from kitty:

- ✔ **Make the pots unattractive.** Use foil or plastic carpet runners with the pointed-side up under the pots to discourage your cat from approaching, and put decorative rock over the soil to discourage digging.

- ✔ **Make the plants taste bad.** Putting Bitter Apple or Tabasco sauce on the leaves makes your cat think twice about munching.

- ✔ **Convert them all to hanging plants.** If all else fails, this strategy is by far the most successful for keeping plants untouched around a determined leaf chewer.

Don't count on any deterrent to keep your cats from plants that are toxic — don't have them in your house, period. We include a list of toxic plants from the National Animal Poison Control Center in Chapter 22.

Figure 14-5:
Putting rocks in pots and foil around them will help teach cats to leave plants alone.

The cloth chewer

Some cats like to chew and suck on clothes, especially wool sweaters — a problem behaviorists call "wool chewing." This destructive habit was originally thought to be associated with a cat who'd been weaned too young, but now behaviorists believe that the tendency is genetic and more common in some breeds or mixes — such as the Siamese or other Orientals — than in others.

Increasing fiber in the diet (such as adding a teaspoon of canned pumpkin daily) may help, as may offering substitute chew articles such as sheepskin-covered dog toys. Regular, active play sessions also may help your cat shed some of his excess energy.

Wool chewing is a case where the most effective way to change your cat's behavior is to change your own. Keep the objects of your cat's obsession out of reach in closed hampers or drawers!

The trash cruiser

Should you consider declawing?

If any one topic is sure to produce a discussion among cat lovers, it's declawing. The procedure is widely performed to end scratching and is just as widely vilified. Some breeders and humane societies refuse to place a cat or kitten with any adopter who doesn't promise not to declaw. Even Paul and Gina don't agree on the subject.

Declawing is the surgical amputation under general anesthesia of the last part of the toe — comparable to the removal of your fingertip at the first joint. The skin is glued or stitched over the exposed joint, the feet bandaged, and the cat sent home to heal for the next couple weeks. In most cases, only the front claws are removed.

Although the procedure is a successful way to curb destructive behavior, Gina feels that, too often, declawing is performed at the first sign of clawing or — worse — is considered as automatic a part of owning a cat as vaccinations. Paul believes that declawing is perhaps not what your cat would choose, but when done properly, the procedure — which results in some short-lived and very controllable discomfort — is easily justified. Declawing may be especially necessary in those cat-owning families in which everyone doesn't agree on the value of the cat to the household. To those who are not the cat lovers in the house, the cat will lose when it comes down to a choice between the leather couch or the cat.

Scratching is natural and satisfying for cats, and you owe your pet the effort to teach him to scratch in appropriate places before you opt to declaw him. Gina feels that declawing should be reserved for those cats who can't be reformed and are facing euthanasia because of their behavioral problems. Paul argues that many cat owners know their tolerance for destruction and don't want to even risk damaging their furniture, so they opt for declawing as a preventive measure.

Paul adds that frequent attention to trimming your cat's nails — keeping the points off — can accomplish the task nearly as well, but most people just aren't religious enough about this task to stay ahead of the risk to the furniture.

By the way, Paul's cat, PC, is not declawed. She and Paul have an understanding that she abides by, so the issue has not needed to be addressed.

One thing that Gina and Paul agree on concerning declawing: If you *do* choose to declaw your cat, you *must* keep him inside — without his claws, he's less able to defend himself against dogs and other dangers; he can't swat and has a harder time climbing to safety if attacked. (Although don't ever think for a moment that declawing diminishes the threat posed by a good sharp set of cat teeth!)

You can foil the cat who gets into wastebaskets by using a single, marvelous innovation — a can with a lid. Why struggle with your cat if a pop-up lid fixes the problem? Another alternative: Put the basket behind a cupboard door.

Having mousetraps in the top of the trash startles your cat, and double-sided tape along the rim discourages him. These deterrents also make using the basket a little harder for you, which is why we prefer the lid-it-or-hide-it approach.

Noisiness

Some cats are chattier than others; indeed, "talkativeness" is an adored breed trait in the Siamese and other Orientals. If you've got a noisy Siamese, to a certain extent you're just going to have to live with the problem — in other words, you can't change the stripes on a tiger!

Some noisiness is inborn: Kittens call to their moms when they want something. Some noisiness is actually *trained* into cats by humans. If you hop up and accommodate her every time your cat demands something — to be fed or let out or in — you've taught her that the squeaky wheel gets the grease, even in the middle of the night or at the crack of dawn.

To retrain your cat, resolve not to give in to her demands. If you start out by ignoring her yowling and then give in anyway, you've taught her that all she needs to do to get her way is to make *more* noise, not less. Correct her for the noise — with a shot of air or water — and then go about your business. She gets the point soon enough that her demanding gets her nowhere. Realize that in the short run your cat will be even more insistent. If you give in, you're sunk. So don't. This, too, shall pass.

Can your cat learn a trick or two?

Some people point to the dog's ability to learn obedience commands and tricks as proof that the dog is smarter than the cat. Others point to the same as proof that the cat is smarter than the dog.

We're not getting into that argument. The important thing to remember is that cats and dogs are *different* in how they relate to us. Dogs have an ingrained need to be part of a family structure — to have a job to do within that family. Dogs are that way because wolves are that way — survival depends on the family, or pack.

The cat came from a different place — from solitary hunters who didn't need teamwork to survive. If you want to put a good spin on it as a cat lover, you could say that dogs *need* to be with us, but cats *choose* to.

Because of this distinction, you absolutely cannot get a cat to do something he doesn't want to. Something must be in it for him. With training tricks, that something is usually food (although some cats will work for a toy, or

petting). Teach the cat an association between a word — such as "sit" — and an action by using treats and praise.

According to animal trainer Anne Gordon, in her book *Show Biz Tricks for Cats* (Adams), you start teaching the "sit" command with a hungry cat, a table, and a quiet room. Get your cat to stand up by touching her in front of her tail and then hold the treat a little over her head, saying her name and the command "sit." Slowly move the treat between your cat's ears, but not high enough for her to pick her front paws off the ground and grab the tidbit. Instead, she'll sit. After she does, praise her and give her the treat. Work in short sessions and be patient. Your cat eventually gets the idea!

Sound crazy? Gordon has trained dozens of animals — including many cats — for commercials, TV shows, and movies. Her book offers precise instructions for teaching 30 tricks, including jumping through a hoop, climbing a ladder, and rolling over. Great fun!

Chapter 15

Getting Good Litter Box Behavior

- -

- -

*F*ew behavior problems strain the relationship between cats and humans more than that of the cat who refuses to use the litter box. Even the most tolerant cat lovers, capable of overlooking couch shredding, plant chewing, or overexuberant claws-out playfulness, have a hard time maintaining their good nature when faced with a cat who urinates on the beds, in the bathtub, or on clean laundry.

The cat who won't use the litter box can strain human relations as well: It's not uncommon for one partner to be willing to work on the problem, while the other one wants an immediate solution — the cat must go. While we know of no one who has divorced over the cat, we know of many angry arguments caused by a cat with a litter box problem.

Sometimes a cat who has a litter box problem becomes an outdoor cat; other times he ends up in need of a new home. Neither prospect is necessarily a good one: Exposed to dangers ranging from foraging coyotes to speeding cars, an outdoor cat's life span is considerably shorter than an indoor one's.

For a discussion of the pros and cons of keeping cats inside or letting them roam, see Chapter 1.

Despite the risks, some formerly indoor cats do well enough outside. But you can't say the same thing about a cat given up to a shelter. That cat may have the shortest life span of all, especially if he has a behavior problem. Almost nobody wants to adopt a cat who avoids the litter box — especially when so many problem-free cats and kittens are out there. Putting your pet outdoors is not a good option, and giving him up is even worse, which is why you need to commit to working on the problem.

When we decided to revise this book, we knew we needed to expand the information on how to deal with litter box problems. The need is great: House-training problems — called *inappropriate elimination* — are the number one behavior-related complaint from cat lovers. That's the bad news. The good news is that by approaching the problem in a systematic, thorough, and unemotional way, you'll be doing your best to get your cat on the right track. And chances are good that you'll be able to live happily with your cat once again.

You must understand *why* your cat isn't using the litter box if you want to have a chance at figuring out *how* to get your cat to use the litter box again. No one-size-fits-all cure exists for litter box problems. Getting your cat to use a litter box is a matter of figuring out what kind of inappropriate elimination is involved (and remember that there may be more than one) and applying the right strategy (or strategies) to get your cat comfortable with going where you want him to.

You use some of the same strategies for addressing litter box and marking problems that you use for other behavior problems. We strongly advise you to read our more general behavior chapter, Chapter 14, in tandem with this chapter. That way you'll have a good overview of the feline psyche, including an understanding of why punishment doesn't work well with cats. And you do need to understand that advice, because nothing seems to make some people feel like spanking a cat more than inappropriate elimination — even though corporal punishment is counterproductive!

Defining the Problem

Many times people see inappropriate elimination as one problem, when in fact it's potentially several problems, some of which may be related — or not. The most basic behaviors are those intended to mark territory and those that express dissatisfaction or discomfort with using a litter box. You must first observe what, exactly, your cat is doing — marking territory or avoiding the box — before you can figure out what to do about it.

Start a journal of your cat's errant deposits. A simple steno notebook works well. In it, write down the date and time, what you found (urine or feces), where you found it (on a horizontal surface or, in the case of urine, on a vertical one, such as the side of a couch), and the location in the house of the mess (in the bathtub, on a throw rug, next to the litter box). Note taking not only helps you to figure out what kind of behavior the problem is and how you should approach it, but also helps you spot even small signs of progress. And perhaps most importantly, having a written record provides you with the information your veterinarian needs to help diagnose any medical problems.

What's being done, and where?

With many animals, urine and feces are almost as much about marking territory as they are about eliminating waste products from the body. A dog who lifts his leg on every piece of furniture and wall corner in the house, for example, is making a far different statement than the one who hikes his leg once and lets flow all the urine stored in his bladder. The first is marking territory; the second doesn't understand where he's allowed to relieve himself, or has been cut off from that spot, or both.

The same scenario can be true with cats, especially male ones. Sometimes a cat's relieving himself, and sometimes he's sending a message. The difference is often one of location and context. Where is the mess? And what's going on in the cat's environment?

Recognizing "I gotta go" behavior

A cat who's not relieving himself where he should deposits urine on a horizontal surface. If you see him releasing urine, you'll notice that he squats. Squatting is a very different behavior from the one used to mark territory, as you see in the next section.

If you have a cat who's leaving urine on a flat surface — even an elevated one such as the bottom of a sink — you have a cat who's relieving himself in an inappropriate way, as opposed to a cat who's marking territory.

Distinguishing "I'm sending a message" behavior

The cat who's marking territory — *spraying* is the term behaviorists use — takes an entirely different approach to the release of urine. He sniffs the object of his interest and then turns and backs up to it. With his tail held high and quivering, he releases a small spray of urine straight back onto the surface. Sometimes he shifts his weight from one back leg to another as he sprays.

All cats have the potential to become sprayers, male and female both. That being said, the worst offenders, hands down, are unneutered males.

Okay, but what about feces?

It's not too hard to figure out what's going on with urine — wet spots on flat surfaces and squatting are the signs of a cat relieving himself, while wet spots on vertical surfaces from a standing position are the signs of a cat marking territory. But what about those little gift piles? What do they mean?

Although some cats use uncovered feces to mark territory — the word for the behavior is *middening* — it's more likely that gift piles are signs of a cat who is avoiding the litter box.

Which cat is the culprit?

Because many people share their lives with more than one cat, when they're faced with a wet spot or a gift pile, the question immediately arises: "Okay, which one of you did this?" Unfortunately, it's not so easy to tell.

Some behaviorists suggest isolating each cat, one after the other, in a safe room (more on that in "Retraining through isolation," later in this chapter). But that approach may not work if a territory dispute is at the heart of the problem. The culprit cat may react positively to the separation and quit his inappropriate behavior, but when you put the cats back together, the problem reappears. And you still don't know which cat is responsible.

One solution veterinarians use to help identify a problem cat in a multicat household is to give a fluorescent dye to one cat at a time. The dye will pass in the urine and can be detected through the use of what's called a Wood's Lamp. To figure out which cat is leaving gift piles, ordinary food coloring will do. Place a few drops of green or blue in the cat's mouth before he eats. The stool of the marked cat should come out darker than the other's.

Is Your Cat Sick?

After you know which cat is responsible for the messes, you can start to work on solving the problem. *The absolute first step you must take is to make an appointment with your veterinarian.*

Why? Inappropriate elimination problems are often caused by, or were started by, a physical problem — commonly a bladder infection. If you don't have the health problem correctly diagnosed and treated, you have almost no possibility of fixing the behavior problem. Further, you're not being fair to your cat.

If you have a sick cat, all the behavioral strategies in the world will not do you much good. Your cat must be healthy to have a shot at changing behavior you don't like.

So what are the possibilities that a medical condition is causing your cat to avoid the litter box or spray? Pretty good really, and numerous, besides. Your veterinarian may recommend urine and blood tests and an ultrasound or X-ray of the abdomen to rule out many medical possibilities before giving your cat a clean bill of health.

Your cat can't speak, so his body must speak for him. Your veterinarian has been trained to listen and look for the clues to what may be a pretty difficult puzzle. You own observations are extremely important, too, so bring along your notes. And realize, finally, that diagnostic tools such as blood and urine tests are not "padding the bill" — they're essential to making an accurate diagnosis.

We put a more thorough discussion of how best to work with your veterinarian to get the best health care for your cat in Chapter 11. For more information on common diagnostic tests used in veterinary medicine, see Chapter 12.

Urinary tract problems are a common reason why cats don't use the litter box, but certainly that's not the only one. Here are a few things your veterinarian looks for (but this list by no means includes all the possibilities):

- ✔ **Urinary tract or bladder problems:** A cat with urinary tract or bladder problems finds it painful to urinate — it burns! Because cats can't think to themselves, "Oh, I bet I'm sick," they think, "Oh, when I go in the box, it hurts!" So they stop using the box. These kinds of problems may even encourage spraying.

- ✔ **Medications:** Your cat may be on a medication — such as a steroid or diuretic — that may cause her to drink more and to urinate more volume and more frequently, or have looser stools. Either of these conditions may cause a cat to need to go before she has time to get to the litter box.

- ✔ **Infectious disease:** The feline leukemia virus (FeLV), feline immunodeficiency virus (FIV), or feline infection peritonitis (FIP) may make a cat sick enough so that bothering with a litter box isn't a high priority. (You can find out more about all these nasty "F" words in Chapter 12.)

- ✔ **Noninfectious disease:** Untreated diabetes can increase the amount of urine a cat produces — in fact, more frequent urination is a symptom that veterinarians ask about when they suspect the disease. Hyperthyroidism, primarily a disease of older cats caused by an overactive thyroid gland, also increases urine production. (We discuss more about both of these diseases in Chapter 13.)

- ✔ **Old-age-related causes:** Some cats may become a little senile as they age, so they're not as particular about where they go. Other cats may have arthritis, making it difficult to climb in and out of a box or to access a box on a different floor of your house.

- ✔ **Constipation or obstipation:** Stools that are difficult to pass or cannot be passed cause a cat a great deal of discomfort, which she tries to relieve by straining to pass the stool. The results can be something that looks like diarrhea — a soft substance produced by frequent efforts to pass the stool. As with a urinary tract infection, a cat may come to associate the box with pain and start avoiding it. (You can find more about *obstipation,* a complete blockage more commonly seen in older cats, in Chapter 13.)

✔ **Diarrhea:** Loose stools can be a problem, too, making it difficult for a cat to "hold it" until she gets to the litter box. Diarrhea is a symptom; the causes can vary, especially in long-term cases.

✔ **Parasites:** Some parasites reproduce by sending their eggs or larvae out with the stools, where another animal can come in contact and get infected. Grown worms, too, end up in stools. Having a load of worms can make it very difficult for a cat to "hold it" long enough to find the litter box.

Correct diagnosis and proper treatment alone may take care of a problem with inappropriate eliminations, but not always. The cat who learned to associate the box with discomfort, for example, or the cat who learned it's just as easy to go on the rug will need retraining — *after* the medical problem has been resolved. In other words, getting your cat a clean bill of health is an essential step — we cannot stress this enough — but it's often just the first step.

When we say "a clean bill of health," we're talking about *making sure* your cat is healthy. For that, you need your veterinarian to do some follow-ups. Too often, people make one trip for an exam, refuse any testing, and leave the veterinarian with little more to offer than her best guess and a course of antibiotics. Even if the veterinarian guesses correctly and the problem *is* a urinary infection, for example, your cat may need more than one course or more than one kind of antibiotic to eliminate the problem. More importantly, they may miss discovering another problem that underlies the urinary tract infection, such as bladder stones or a tumor. Until the underlying problem is addressed, the infection and signs will recur. If you just assume your cat is fine because she has been on antibiotics, you may still have a sick cat. And that means three things: She's still suffering; in the end it will cost you more money than if you had dealt with the issues earlier; and any behavioral strategies you try will not be effective.

Use the Box, Kitty!

At the beginning of this chapter, we warn you that you need patience and thoroughness to help your cat to use a litter box again. You've likely used some of these qualities in making sure your cat has no health problems that would contribute to his not using the litter box. Now you need to draw on these resources again, in addition to taking a nonemotional approach.

Although you may get lucky and fix the problem with the first strategy you try, chances are, you won't be so fortunate. Getting a cat to use the litter box is a matter not only of trial and error but also of getting the combination of factors just right to encourage proper behavior.

Figure 15-1: Illness is the trigger for many kinds of misbehavior, including failure to use the litter box. You must have your cat thoroughly checked out by your veterinarian before attempting any retraining.

The same notebook we suggest earlier in this chapter to track problems can now be used to note progress. And we very much encourage you to keep up the notes. Progress can be slow when dealing with inappropriate elimination, and it may well help you to keep your sanity if you can, indeed, see that your cat has improved.

Cleanliness is next to catliness

Cats are fastidious animals, and if the litter box is dirty, they look elsewhere for a place to go. Think of how you felt the last time you were faced with a dirty public restroom, and you can probably empathize!

So how clean is the litter box? Is it something you "get around to" every few days, or maybe just on the weekend? Do you wait until you can't stand the smell of it, or the lumpy-clumpy sight of it, before you clean it? And even then, do you really clean it, or do you simply half-heartedly fish out a few stools or clumps and add more litter?

If you don't keep the litter box clean, you can't expect your cat to use it. You need to start with a clean box and keep it clean.

Starting out clean

Even if the box you bought is brand-new, give it a good scrubbing with hot water and soap, rinse well, and let it air-dry. Cats have a much better sense of smell than we do, and they may be put off by the odor a new box has picked up through its manufacturing, shipping, and storage before you bought it.

If the box has been used before, follow the soap-and-water scrub with a bleach soak — one-half cup to a gallon of water will do — and then rinse, rinse, rinse, and allow to air-dry.

Diluted bleach is a safe disinfectant, but other types of disinfectant shouldn't be used — their lingering scent may cause more harm than good. Ammonia, for example, shares some chemical properties with urine and can make a clean box smell dirty to a cat.

Keeping it clean

All the scrubbing in the world isn't going to help you if you offer your cat a clean box and then don't bother to keep it that way. Some cats are so fussy that a box that has been used even once may be unsuitable. If you can't scoop immediately — and honestly, not many of us can — try to scoop twice a day, or daily at least.

You can almost always offer your cat a clean bathroom if you provide two litter boxes, placed side by side. Some cats even prefer the two-box system: They urinate in one and defecate in the other. (More about multiple litter boxes later in this section.)

Don't forget that even if you're very good about scooping frequently, you'll still have to scrub out and disinfect your litter box completely on a regular basis. When in doubt, clean it out!

Some people use plastic liners to make cleaning easier. Problem is, some cats don't like them — they find the odor offensive or they don't like the feel of the plastic underfoot when their claws catch on them.

The Litter Maid self-cleaning box has caused a lot of discussion since its release, but it is a pretty promising piece of equipment. The machine uses an electric eye to note a cat's entry and exit, and then runs a rake through the litter to sift out the clumps, putting them into a holding area for later disposal. Reviews are mixed for the product, however. Some cats are put off by the noise and motion, while some owners complain that the mechanism clogs too easily, especially in multicat households. That said, many cats and owners are quite happy using the Litter Maid; for them, the cleanliness and convenience are worth every penny.

Offering alternatives

Here's where it gets interesting. After you've worked with your veterinarian to establish your cat's good health and are dedicated to the ideals of feline cleanliness, you can embark on the excitement of finding out exactly what litter box arrangements your cat finds suitable.

Many choices people make to suit their own tastes don't match with what their cat wants, but when you're talking litter boxes (filler and location) your cat's opinion is the only one that really counts.

Remember that notebook we keep mentioning? This is where it comes in. A notebook will help you keep track of what works and what doesn't as you try to figure out what combination of factors will keep your cat happy.

Changing the box and filler

Many times the litter box or filler is one chosen in an attempt to reduce the odor that people find offensive. Covered boxes and litters with deodorants may fool *our* pathetic sense of smell, but they aren't going to fool your cat. And often people let cleaning chores wait because the box isn't making *them* crazy. Sorry, but you still have to clean it even if you can't smell it.

Try various boxes, various fillers, and even various depths of litter in the box. Some cats like the privacy of a covered box, for example, while others don't. Another problem with covered boxes is that they often don't get cleaned as regularly, because the humans in the house follow the out-of-sight, out-of-mind approach. You may not notice a problem in there, but we'll guarantee you that your cat does!

If your cat's an asthmatic, skip the covered litter box. A covered box traps the dust kicked up from the litter, and that dust can trigger an attack. For more on feline asthma, see Chapter 12.

Other health problems may dictate the kind of box that works best for your cat. An arthritic cat may have difficulty getting in and out of the box. A box with low sides or a box that you've customized by cutting down a side may help with this problem.

A high-sided box, on the other hand, may be just the ticket if your cat doesn't squat all the way, either from stiffness or just plain personal preference. Some cats nearly stand while using the litter box and shoot their waste over the side. (Cut one side down, though, to make it easier for an older cat to get into the box.)

Also experiment with filler — try clumping and nonclumping, scented and unscented, and so on. Studies suggest, however, that a high-quality, unscented, clumping litter is favored by more cats, so that's probably the best kind to start with.

Changing location

Is the location of your cat's box convenient for you — or for your cat? Does your cat feel safe using the box, or does he feel as if he's going to be ambushed? Pick a location that's quiet and out of the way of traffic, and where your cat can keep an eye on things so he won't be surprised.

Your cat's box should be away from his food and water dishes. You don't eat near the toilet, so why should your cat?

Also, consider how easy it is for your cat to get to the box. Maybe you like the box in the farthest corner of the garage or basement, but does your cat? And finally, is the location always accessible? A spare bathroom is a good place to keep the litter box, but only if everyone in the house remembers to leave the door open. (If you have a dog, the accessibility of the litter box can cause a problem. Check out our sidebar on "Litter-munching dogs" in this chapter for help with this disgusting problem.)

Using multiple boxes

Two boxes side by side may help with the cat who simply must have the cleanest box around — or the cat who uses one for urinating and the other for defecating. You should also try increasing the number of boxes and locations where your cat can find a litter box.

In a multilevel home, it often helps to have a litter box on each floor. You've got a cat who, for whatever reason, isn't that interested in using a litter box. Make it as convenient for him as possible!

In multicat households, a good general guideline is one litter box per cat. Some cats gladly share, but many won't. Extra boxes are the only way to give every cat what she wants.

Discouraging misbehavior

At the same time you're making your cat's litter boxes more inviting, you should be gently suggesting that he shouldn't revisit the sites he used instead of the box. The trick to keeping your cat away from inappropriate elimination spots is to make those areas unappealing and even revolting. How do you do that? Through the use of smell, touch, and even some basic cat knowledge.

The first step is to thoroughly clean the area where an accident occurred, using a enzymatic cleaner designed for use on pet messes. Any lingering odor invites reuse. After the area is clean, try some of the following methods to discourage reuse or to change the way your cat uses the area:

- ✔ Put food bowls on the spot. Cats don't like to relieve themselves where they eat. You can gradually move the bowls to another location when your cat is using the litter box reliably again.

  ✔ Put a deterrent on the area. You can cover the area with material that a
     cat doesn't like to set foot on, such as double-sided tape, aluminum foil,
     or plastic carpet runners with the pointed side up. Scat Mats — plastic
     mats that give off a slight static shock when stepped on — are another
     option. Also try to spray the area with a scent that cats hate, such as
     citrus. If your cat uses houseplants for litter boxes, cover the top of the
     soil with sharp rocks or small pinecones.

  ✔ Put a litter box on the spot. This is the "if you can't beat 'em, join 'em"
     technique. After your cat is using the litter box, you can gradually
     change its location.

One form of discouragement we don't recommend is physical punishment.
For one thing, it doesn't work. For another, punishing the cat who's already
avoiding the litter box because he's stressed out won't do anything to make
him more relaxed. The old nose-in-it-and-swat method of training isn't even
recommended for dogs anymore. Don't use anything like it on your cat.

Don't forget the value of praise! If you see your cat using the litter box,
reward him with a tasty treat.

Stopping Sprayers in Their Tracks

Although both male and female cats spray, unneutered males are the biggest
offenders, followed by unspayed females in season. The first rule of dealing
with this stinky problem is to make sure that your pet is neutered — this procedure takes care of the problem in 90 percent of the cases if done before
sexual maturity is attained at about 6 months.

For those cats who don't respond to neutering, environmental stresses —
such as a new person in the house, a move to a new house, or another major
change in routine — may trigger the spraying. Antianxiety drugs may help
(see our sidebar, "What about behavioral medications?"); so can cleaning
sprayed areas thoroughly and covering them with foil and citrus odor to discourage fresh marking. (Cats dislike anything involving foil, and the sound of
urine hitting the stuff really annoys them.) One product that may help is
called Feliway, which helps to remove the odor that triggers a repeat performance. (Check with your veterinarian or a veterinary behaviorist for advice
on buying and using this product.)

One common trigger for marking behavior is the sight of outdoor cats.
Because cats are so territorial, seeing cats on the other side of the window
can annoy an indoor cat to the point of spraying. If you can't discourage the
traipsing of other cats across your property, restrict your own cat's access to
any area where he can see the intruders.

Litter-munching dogs

Gina gets calls all the time from readers who are astonished that their dogs consider the contents of a litter box as some kind of special treat.

When faced with a constant supply of litter "munchies" and ready access to them, no dog can resist for long, which is why efforts to train a dog to leave the litter box alone are rarely successful. The better plan is to restrict access, which you can accomplish in many ways. Here are a few suggestions:

✔ Purchase covered litter boxes. Some cats don't like them, and cats with asthma can't use them. (See Chapter 12 for more on feline asthma.) If your cat falls into either category, this solution isn't going to work for you.

✔ Change the litter box's location. You must be careful not to upset your cats. But experimenting with such ploys as gradually moving the litter box to a location above the dog's reach usually doesn't hurt.

✔ Provide barriers. One way is to rig the door to the room containing the litter box so that it stays open wide enough for the cat but not for the dog. Another possibility is to put a cat-sized door through the door to the litter box room if your dog is medium-sized or larger. For small dogs, try a baby gate — the cat can jump it, but the dog can't.

✔ Keep it clean. Don't forget to keep the box scooped: A dog can't eat what a dog can't find.

Figure 15-2: Cats often need to be restricted to a small area of the house so they can "chill out" during retraining.

Kiko/photo by Lisa Wolff

Retraining through isolation

If your cat is marking or avoiding the litter box after you've tried to change the environment to discourage errant behavior, it's time to try keeping him in a small area for a few days. By offering no other options for a cat to relieve himself, this technique helps to calm an anxious cat and helps to retrain one who has learned to avoid the litter box.

A spare bathroom is an ideal spot, but any quiet, small area with a door will do. The room should contain food and water, a litter box, a scratching post, and a toy or two. Make sure that the room has no good options besides the litter box for elimination — no carpet, no pile of dirty laundry. Block off the bathtub — keep an inch of water in it to discourage its use as a place to go.

Visit your cat in his safe room and indulge him with loving sessions of petting and some energy-burning play. This attention helps him settle down into his new routine.

After your cat is reliably using the litter box in his safe room, let him slowly expand his territory again. As long as you keep up your end of the bargain and keep the litter box appealing, he should keep up his end and use it, too.

The *safe room* is also good for introducing new cats to the household and for moving cats from one home to another. For information on introductions, see Chapter 6. Chapter 18 has tips on helping your cat through a moving day.

What about behavioral medications?

In recent years, veterinary behaviorists have started using medications to help with behavioral problems. For most cats, these medications are of short-term benefit, a way to ease a cat's anxiety while you work on making it easier and more appealing for him to use the litter box, or to help him ignore triggers that prompt spraying.

Their availability, however, is another reason to work with your veterinarian or get a referral to a veterinary behaviorist for more specific, long-term help with difficult cases. Your cat's health-care professional can help manage the overall attack on inappropriate elimination, ensuring that your cat is healthy, reviewing your plans for adjusting his environment, and prescribing antianxiety medications as necessary to help with the transition.

Chapter 16

Littering: Should Your Cat Become a Parent?

*I*f you take a kitten or cat into your life, you take on the responsibility for caring for your new pet. You ensure your pet's good health by taking her to your veterinarian, by feeding her well, and by grooming her. You keep both of you entertained through play, and you give her love and receive her love in return.

Truly, the bond between people and cats is remarkable, a pact of companionship that lasts for years, but it brings with it responsibility for making the right decisions for the good of your cat and for all cats.

Your kitten will be barely settled into your house when you must make one of the most important decisions for a cat owner: Do I allow my cat to breed?

For most people, the answer is a decisive "no." And because of that answer, your cat is a better pet, remains in better health, and doesn't contribute to the tragic surplus of cats and kittens, millions of whom die without ever knowing what your cat knows: what being a loving and well-cared-for pet is like.

Still, the decision is yours to make. And sometimes it's really not your decision at all, because your young cat could end up pregnant before you expected, or a pregnant cat could end up on your doorstep. After the deed is done, you have another set of responsibilities: helping your cat through the pregnancy and birth, helping her raise her kittens, and finding them responsible homes.

The Case Against Breeding

According to a 1995 survey by the American Animal Hospital Association, nearly 80 percent of the cats and dogs in the United States and Canada are spayed or neutered. What do these people know that you don't? Consider these facts:

✔ A neutered male is less likely to roam, less likely to fight (and thus less likely to cost you money to patch him up), and less likely to spray urine everywhere to mark his territory. He's likely to live longer, because the cat who's looking for a mate is really looking for trouble. If a car doesn't get him, infectious disease (spread by fighting or mating) or cancer may.

✔ A spayed female is a more attentive and loving pet, because her energy isn't constantly directed toward finding a mate. (Cats are in heat nearly all the time until they become pregnant.) If you spay your cat, you protect her from some cancers and infections and from sexually transmitted infectious diseases.

✔ A cat of either sex who isn't altered can be obnoxious to live with. Reproduction is their reason for living, and if you don't let them follow their instincts, they drive you crazy trying to get out and crying endlessly. If you want to live with such annoyances, that's your business, but if you truly love cats, you want to consider another reason why spaying and neutering is so important: Millions of unwanted cats and kittens are euthanized every year because not enough homes are out there for them.

✔ If kittens are plentiful, overwhelmed shelters can't even give them all a chance at adoption: They pull the one or two cutest or healthiest babies out and send the rest back to be euthanized. Millions and millions of kittens end up this way.

Spay or neuter your cat, we implore you. It's the right thing to do. If you love kittens and can't do without them in your life, volunteer at your local humane society or SPCA. You don't actually need to work at the shelter, which some people find "depressing." Many volunteers foster orphaned or sick kittens until they can be placed in responsible homes.

If you have children, please don't feel they need to experience "the miracle of birth" and, therefore, allow your cat to breed. Instead of contributing more kittens to the world — when watching a video can teach your children about birth just as well — let your children learn the lessons of caring and responsibility that living with a pet brings.

Figure 16-1:
Too much
breeding
means too
many kittens
needing
homes. This
little one
was
adopted, but
many aren't
so lucky.

Photo by Richard D. Schmidt

Spaying and Neutering: What's Involved?

Spaying and *neutering* are the everyday terms for the surgical sterilization of a pet — spaying for the female, neutering for the male. Neutering — or *altering* — is also used to describe both procedures. The clinical terms for the two operations are *ovariohysterectomy* for the female and *castration* for the male.

Both spaying and neutering must be done only by a veterinarian, and both procedures require general anesthesia.

Spaying involves the removal of the female's entire reproduction system: The uterus, fallopian tubes, and ovaries are taken out through an incision in the abdomen. In *neutering,* the cat's testicles are removed through incisions in the *scrotum,* the pouch holding the testicles. These incisions are generally left unsutured in this relatively minor procedure.

Your veterinarian may require you to return to have your female cat's stitches removed in about ten days, or he may use stitches that are absorbed into the body. Recovery is fast, taking just a few days, during which you should limit your cat's activities — no jumping or boisterous play. You may not notice much difference in your female's personality, unless you've lived with her through her nearly constant heat cycles and endured her noisy efforts at attracting a mate — along with the fighting, yowling, urine-spraying toms who answered her call. Those days are thankfully behind you both.

Stitches that are absorbed into the body are essential when it comes to altering feral cats. These wild cats often cannot be caught twice — once to get altered, and again to remove stitches. For more on feral cats, see Chapter 4.

Postoperative care for male cats normally involves monitoring and keeping the incisions clean and dry. Many veterinarians recommend keeping the cat inside (if he's not already an indoor pet) and using shredded newspaper in place of litter until the incisions close, which usually occurs within three to five days.

Behavioral changes can be dramatic in neutered males. Fighting, urine spraying, and roaming can be almost completely prevented in cats neutered before sexual maturity — the age of 6 months or so. These behaviors are also dramatically reduced in older neutered males as well, although some retraining for behavior problems such as urine spraying may prove necessary (see Chapter 15).

Spaying and neutering are among the most common medical procedures in the United States and Canada and carry very little risk for your pet. However don't for a minute think that *common* — meaning that your veterinarian is good and fast at it because he does it often — means *trivial*. Cat alterings can and do result in rapid death if done wrong. This procedure is major surgery. Don't let the common name (spay) or the low cost (a losing proposition for most veterinarians) fool you.

Given the choice, pay more for what looks like more-complete attention to details. Ask about and discuss the following:

- ✔ **Anesthesia:** What combination of inhalants or injectables is used?

- ✔ **Sterility:** Are fresh sterile instruments used for every animal?

- ✔ **Monitoring:** Is someone besides the surgeon there to monitor anesthesia? And what about afterward? Will someone check on your pet? If overnight care is not part of the plan, who will take your call if you suspect a problem? Will your veterinarian explain what you should be looking out for?

- ✔ **Emergency provisions:** Is a "crash cart" kept in the surgery room? Are there trained personnel who can respond as astutely as your favorite doctors do on TV?

- ✔ **Suture material:** What type is used and why?

Do you really need to take so many precautions? Consider this true story: In 1987, one of Paul's cats almost died after a complication from her spaying done at one of the best animal hospitals in the world — the University of California, Davis, Veterinary Medical Teaching Hospital. She survived because Paul was there to notice the problem and the excellent staff and facilities were there to provide life-saving care, without which she would have certainly died.

Spaying and neutering are *not* the areas to save a few dollars.

The Birds and the Bees, Kitty-Style

The more you know about feline reproduction, the more you're amazed that so many cats are in this world. Think about it some more, and you're even more amazed at the sheer power of instinct in the life of a cat.

Why all the amazement? Because mating doesn't seem like much fun for cats; in fact, it's *painful*. He bites the nape of her neck to start, and then he mounts her; she slashes him after the ordeal's over. They both scream to raise the dead. She rolls around ignoring him afterward, and yet he sticks around to keep another male from having her, even though doing so means that he must fight and get bitten and clawed by her other suitors. Before long, she wants him again — desperately. More biting, more screaming, more slashing. (One study counted up to 36 matings in 36 hours.)

She may mate with some other tomcat if she can; she doesn't care who. After the boys are done with her, they're after the scent of someone new; they don't care who either.

Two months later, give or take a few days, she has her kittens. The father (or fathers) is nowhere to be found. Makes the sex scandals that rock the media seem kind of tame by comparison, doesn't it?

Choosing a mate

If you plan to breed your cat, make sure she's at least a year old. She should also be free of viral diseases, such as feline leukemia, and current on her vaccinations. Don't wait until after she's pregnant to vaccinate her, as this practice can lead to serious problems for the developing kittens. Schedule a visit to your veterinarian and discuss your plans for your cat; he can advise you on necessary preventive-care measures.

You want a healthy mate as well, and to start finding him, talk to your cat's breeder. Don't just search for a cat of the same breed "with papers," or you could be setting yourself up for a genetic catastrophe. Reputable breeders breed "nonfolded" Scottish fold cats to "folded" Scottish folds, for example, and Manx cats with tails to Manxes without. That's because breeding "tail to tail" or "folded ear to folded ear" often produces kittens with serious congenital defects — babies that suffer and die or must be humanely killed. Understanding the genetics behind your cat before choosing her mate is essential, and the best person to help with that is an experienced and knowledgeable breeder.

If you plan to breed your mixed-breed cat — or allow her to breed on her own — we strongly encourage you to reconsider. We're not being elitists: Pedigreed cats must be carefully bred, or their breeds may disappear. Mixed-breed cats are in such oversupply that millions of them are killed as "surplus" every year. Supply and demand is the name of the game, and no one is clamoring for more mixed-breed kittens, no matter how adorable.

Still, if you're going to choose a mate for her, insist on his getting an exam as well to establish that he's in good health and free of contagious diseases.

Figure 16-2:
When in season, the female cat may cry, pace, rub and roll to attract males. Males fight with each other to protect their chance to mate.

The "oops" pairing

The truth is that many people never see their free-roaming cat being bred. Many of them meant to have her spayed but just didn't get around to it. Then, one day, they notice that she's pregnant. Some people are so unaware of the signs that their cats are in season — rolling, crying, pacing — that they bring them to their veterinarians, convinced they're in pain.

If you suspect your cat is pregnant — she's putting on weight, for example — and you don't want her to be, talk to your veterinarian about your options. You can have her spayed, even when she's pregnant. Otherwise, congratulations! You're going to be a grandparent.

Caring for a Pregnant Cat

About two weeks after a successful mating, a cat's nipples darken from light pink to a rosier hue, but the casual owner of a free-roaming cat may not notice a pregnancy until it's patently obvious — until the cat is nearly ready to deliver, in other words.

To ensure a safe pregnancy and a healthy birth, your veterinarian may suggest basic blood work to establish baseline readings and spot any potential problems. An ultrasound can be useful early on to diagnose pregnancy and later to assess fetal age, viability, and development. X rays after the 45th day can be helpful in determining the number of kittens and their relative size so you know what to expect and when, and can therefore better evaluate the situation when your cat is actually giving birth.

Follow your veterinarian's suggestions for prenatal care and don't give your pet vitamins, medications, or other supplements without discussing them with your veterinarian first.

Your cat becomes restless about two weeks before giving birth, searching for a safe place to have her babies. She should be confined at this time to the house — if she's not an indoor cat already — and provided with a box in which to give birth. Even better, confine her to a single room — your bedroom, ideally.

This *queening* box can be a cardboard box with one side cut down or the bottom half of a medium-sized plastic carrier. Place the box in a spot where she feels safe — a dim corner of a room that you can keep warm and dry — and line the box with newspapers. Put her food and water dishes and the litter box nearby but not right next to the queening box.

Some breeders dislike using newspapers in the queening box because of the ink. You can buy blank newsprint instead: Many newspapers sell the ends of newsprint rolls at a low cost. Check with your local newspaper to see whether this clean paper is available.

Keep your cat sequestered in her room. If you let her out into the house, she may have her kittens in a laundry basket or opened dresser drawer; if you let her out of the house entirely, she may have them under the front porch. The more socialization kittens get, the better, so do your best to make sure she delivers her babies where you have easy access to them.

Older cats need good homes, too!

Kittens aren't the only ones who need responsible, loving homes. A lot of older cats do, too. If a stray turns up on your back porch and you can't find an owner, if you inherit an older cat from a sick relative, or if you end up with an extra cat for any other reason, you want to find the best home you can. Adult cats can be very, very hard to place — they have the lowest rates of adoption for all animals at the shelter. If you're patient and persistent, however, you may find a home. Here are some tips to follow:

✔ Do everything you can to make the animal more adoptable. The pet has a better chance for adoption if her vaccinations are current, she uses her litter box reliably, and she's altered. (If you're trying to place your own pet because of a behavioral problem, please see whether our tips for solving them in Chapters 14 and 15 can help you keep your pet instead.)

✔ Ask a price. People show more respect for something they've paid for. In addition, a price tag dampens the interest of profiteers, such as those who collect "free to good home" pets for sale to research labs or to people who train dogs for fighting. (Dog fighting is illegal in most places, but still remarkably common.) A good general rule: Charge an amount to cover the cost of the spaying/neutering and vaccinations.

✔ Don't lie about the pet's problems or why she's being placed. Although finding a new home for a pet with behavioral problems takes longer, you can usually still do so. But the person who gets such a pet without warning is likely to bring her back, take her to the shelter, or give her away — maybe to a horrible situation.

✔ Spread the news. Make up flyers and take out an ad in your local newspaper. Post the flyers everywhere you can: on bulletin boards at work, at pet-supply stores, and at your veterinarian's. Give some to your friends and family to post where they work, too. Talk the cat up with everyone you know, at least briefly: Even people who don't like cats (or who don't want one) know people who may be looking for a pet. The more exposure you can get, the better. If a thousand people hear or read about the animal, you'll probably get no interest from 999, but you need only one person to provide a good home for the cat, and that's the one you need to reach.

✔ Ask lots of questions and verify that the answers are true. Don't forget to ask prospective adopters whether they've had pets before and what happened to them. Make sure you're dealing with people who realize that owning a pet is a long-term commitment.

✔ Take your cat to a shelter if time runs out. Sad to say, better a small chance at adoption and a painless death than a short life of suffering and fear. Do not take a cat "to the country" or otherwise turn him loose to fend for himself — people who live in the country can't always care for the pets who are dumped. The kinder ones take them to the shelter; others shoot them, poison them, or drown them. Even in "the wilderness," the lives of feral cats are full of suffering, shortened by disease or accident. Don't put a cat through this horror: Take him to the shelter if you can't find him a home.

Happy Birth Day, Babies

The usual length of a pregnancy is 66 days from ovulation, but because ovulation occurs after mating — and you may not know when your cat mated — you may have a hard time figuring out her due date. Let her physical symptoms and "nesting" behavior be your guide as to when to confine her.

Your cat's temperature — normally between 100.4°F. and 102.5°F. — falls two to three degrees in the first stage of labor, but most pet owners are probably better off not bothering with temperature-taking at this stage. Instead, watch for enlarged nipples and the secretion of a tiny amount of milk. Your cat may accept some food if offered, or she may just be content to rest in her box, purring and waiting.

Your cat is usually best left to her own devices, but take the time to collect a few "just-in-case" items, including some clean towels, Betadine antiseptic, scissors, a spool of thread, and a baby syringe. If your cat is a longhair, trim the fur under her tail, at the back of her legs, and around her nipples. Finally, have your veterinarian's number at hand and check to make sure she's available for after-hours calls; if not, ask her to recommend the number of an emergency clinic. Keep that number on hand, too, and know where the clinic is located in case you need to take your cat and her kittens in.

Special delivery!

The best thing you can do for your cat at the time of delivery is to ensure her maternity suite doesn't turn into a circus. Respect her privacy during this quiet time: If your children want to watch, that's fine, but have them keep a few feet away and quiet. (They may remain speechless anyway, because the birth process is so riveting!)

The active stage of labor is characterized by straining and a discharge that begins as watery but then becomes darker. The first kitten usually appears within an hour, wrapped in a translucent membrane known as the *amniotic sac,* which the mother bites to release the kitten, licking the baby's face to start his breathing.

Although you're usually best off leaving the mother alone, if she doesn't attend to her kitten within a minute or so, you can peel away the membrane and rub the kitten with a towel to start his breathing. Tie the umbilical cord off with a piece of thread about 1 inch out and cut the cord with scissors just outside the tie; then dab the tip with Betadine and place the baby at the mother's side. If the kitten isn't breathing, remove the fluid from his mouth with the baby syringe; then hold the kitten carefully in your hand — supporting his head carefully and securely — and swing him downward abruptly two or three times. Clear the fluid again if the kitten still isn't breathing and then swing him again. You may not be able to save the kitten, but at least you'll know you tried.

Subsequent kittens are born at intervals of 30 minutes to an hour, with the *placenta,* the tissue that attaches the kitten to the womb, coming within 15 to 30 minutes after each kitten — or sometimes all the placentas at once, if the delivery was rapid.

You need to discuss the situation with your veterinarian if your cat hasn't delivered her kittens by the 70th day after her first breeding. You need to call your veterinarian *immediately* if any of the following occur:

- ✔ Your cat has had strong, persistent contractions for more than 30 minutes or has been actively straining for an hour without the expulsion of a baby.

- ✔ Your cat rests (with no straining) for more than four hours after the first kitten is born.

- ✔ Your cat's contractions are weak or irregular beyond two or three hours.

- ✔ Your cat starts vomiting, appearing weak, panting or breathing rapidly, or crying or showing any other signs of undue pain.

- ✔ Your cat discharges material that is yellow or white or seems exceptionally bloody.

- ✔ Your cat doesn't deliver a placenta for each kitten.

When in doubt about anything, call your veterinarian! It doesn't take much in the way of time or money to do so, and it will get you the help you need.

After the birth

A normal cat eats the placentas and tears the umbilical cord; if left to her own devices, she probably eats any stillborn kittens as well. As distasteful as this act seems to us, it's perfectly normal behavior. You probably want to wrap up any dead kittens in newspaper and dispose of them properly — call your veterinarian or animal-control department for guidance.

Some breeders remove the placentas as well, and that's fine, too, but make sure you have one for each kitten.

Kittens are born blind and deaf, but they have their sense of smell and use it to find their mother's nipples. The first milk they take in is very important. Called *colostrum,* this milk contains antibodies from the mother and other important substances that give the kittens initial protection against diseases at a time when their own immune systems are not yet functioning well.

If the family appears healthy and content, check on them but leave them pretty much alone for the first two weeks. Call your veterinarian if the mother or kittens appear agitated or listless.

If the kittens are not thriving, or the mother becomes ill, you must step in to care for them, tube-feeding and, later, bottle-feeding them. This task is an around-the-clock job, and you need to discuss with your veterinarian what and when to feed the kittens. If you're lucky, your veterinarian may know of another cat with kittens who can care for yours as well; if not, your kittens' survival is up to you!

It's common for veterinary students or the staff at veterinary hospitals or shelter volunteers to take over the bottle-raising of orphan kittens. If you are not able to care for kittens who need help, call your veterinarian, nearby veterinary college, or shelter. They may be able to match you up with experienced kitten-raisers.

Kitten Development

Cats have been raising kittens without much assistance from humans for thousands of years, and things usually go along just fine if you let your cat handle her babies on her own. Watching kittens develop is a rare opportunity, however, so take plenty of time to enjoy the experience.

Figure 16-3: If the mama cat and her babies appear healthy and content, leave them alone as much as possible in the first two weeks.

Photo by Linda Stark

Birth to two weeks

Growth is the priority these first couple of weeks, as the kittens nurse constantly and double their weight in the first week. Their mother is constantly in attendance, providing them with milk and licking them to stimulate them to release their waste, which she eats. Umbilical cords fall off in two to three days, and eyes start opening after about a week to ten days.

Leave the litter alone as much as possible, checking only to ensure that everyone is comfortable and eating well.

If you were planning to let your cat have "just one litter," don't wait long to get her spayed. The kittens are barely weaned before your cat can get pregnant again. When you take your cat and her kittens in to be checked out by your veterinarian, discuss when to have her spayed — and make an appointment!

Sometimes gender is hard to determine in kittens. Lift up the tails and compare. Your veterinarian can help if you just can't make heads or tails of it.

Your role as a "grandparent"

Cats are generally wonderful mothers, caring for their kittens diligently and lovingly and moving them to safety at the first sign of trouble. They teach them to use the litter box and play nicely with their siblings, and they often teach them the hunting skills they need should they fall on hard times.

With such a capable mother, do you really need to do anything to ensure that your cat's kittens grow up to be loving pets? Yes, you do.

A mother cat can teach her babies to be a cat, but she can't teach them everything they need to know about living in the world of humans. For kittens to become confident, outgoing adults, they need to be exposed early to the realities of life among the two-legged.

Handle the kittens after the first couple of weeks, and have other people over to handle them, too: men and women, children and adults — the more the merrier! Make sure all the interactions are positive and gentle. Kittens who miss out on human contact before the age of 12 weeks or so may always be nervous or even aggressive around people.

Supervised exposure to other pets, especially dogs, is important, too, so that your kittens can easily handle being placed in homes with other pets.

The best thing about your role as "grandparent"? It's fun! Play with the kittens all you want — it's good for you all.

Two weeks to eight weeks

The kittens' hearing and vision mature between two and five weeks, and by the fourth week, the babies begin to walk, run, and even jump, becoming agile and fast-moving surprisingly quickly. Still, their mother looks after them, reacting to their cries and bringing them home in her mouth if they stray too far. The first kitten teeth appear about the same time their eyes open.

After about three weeks, the mother starts to tire of nursing; this period is when you can begin to wean the kittens and step up your gentle handling of them. The mother is still involved with her babies, however: This period is when she begins to teach them to hunt.

Make solid food available to the kittens from three weeks on; softening dry food with warm water and placing a dab on a kitten's nose makes the transition easier. The mother helps by becoming increasingly unavailable for nursing, and the kittens should be completely weaned by the age of seven weeks or so.

Give the kittens access to a litter box from the age of three weeks on, and they'll learn from their mother how to use it.

Don't allow your kittens to think human fingers and feet are for pouncing, or you could be setting yourself up — or setting up your kittens' future owners — for problems later on. Stop the game if kittens attack, even in play. Better yet: Use interactive toys, such as a cat fishing pole or toy on a string, to play with your babies.

Figure 16-4: It can be hard to tell the boys from the girls when kittens are young. The male is on the left; the female on the right. Ask your veterinarian if you're in doubt.

Eight weeks to fourteen weeks

By the age of two months, kittens have teeth and all their senses, and they're nimble and playful. This stage is a great deal of fun for the owner, and you hardly need to be convinced to play with your kittens, getting them used to a lot of handling.

Although some people start giving away kittens as soon as they're weaned, they're best off staying with their mother and littermates for the first 12 to 14 weeks. Kittens who're removed from their littermates and mother may have a difficult time as adults in accepting other cats.

Still, this time is good to start lining up homes for your babies. (See the section "Saying Goodbye to the Babies," later in this chapter.) Now's the time, too, to take them to your veterinarian for health checks and any vaccinations, wormings, or other preventive-health measures your vet recommends.

The adolescent kitten

If you keep any kittens, you get to continue to enjoy their development. Kittenhood ends at sexual maturity — which may come as early as five months of age — although your young one may continue to act kittenish at times for the first year.

Kittens grow up very fast and can have kittens of their own before you think possible. Discuss spaying and neutering with your veterinarian at the earliest opportunity, or you may end up dealing with a new crop of babies soon.

Saying Good-bye to the Babies

If you've done your job right, you have something truly remarkable to offer: fat, friendly, well-socialized kittens who promise a lifetime of good health and companionship. You want to make sure that the people who take them are worthy of such wonderful babies.

Kittens are so cute that you can "get rid of" them in minutes by giving them away in front of the closest grocery store, but we hope you don't want your babies to go to just anyone you aren't reasonably sure plans to take good care of them. The problem with casually acquired pets is that people are all too often casual about them — they've picked them up on impulse and may dump them just as fast.

Please take the time to place your kittens in good homes. Take out an ad in the newspaper and put up flyers, but make sure you carefully screen those people who're interested. If your cat is pedigreed and you've been working with a reputable breeder, ask for her help in placing the kittens. She may have a waiting list!

Pedigreed or just simply adorable, every kitten deserves a responsible home. Here are some questions you can ask of potential adopters to ensure your babies find one:

- ✔ **Have you had cats before? What happened to them?** Wrong answers include "lots" and "they ran away," "we moved," or "he got hit." Accidents happen to even the most conscientious of pet lovers, but a pattern of mishaps says a great deal about the way the prospective buyer treats cats — and it's not good.

- ✔ **What's your living arrangement?** Cats can handle nearly any kind of household: big families and singles, city apartments and rural acreage, stay-at-home seniors, and busy career people. Look for a person who has given a great deal of thought to the responsibility of keeping an animal and who's prepared to ensure your kitten's needs will be met. Some breeders refuse to place kittens with people who aren't willing to keep them exclusively inside, and if you feel strongly about the issue, you can do so, too.

- ✔ **Do you have children? What ages?** If you sense you're dealing with a person who doesn't care what her children do, you could be putting a fragile kitten in a very dangerous environment. Listen for the person who realizes an animal is a part of the family, not a toy for the kids.

- ✔ **Do you intend to breed your cat? Declaw her?** Again, the "right" answers depend on your own views. If you're against declawing (or against "automatic" declawing before even a sign of behavioral problems), you can use this time as a chance to educate. If you're offering pedigreed kittens who aren't breeding quality, sell them with "nonbreeding" registration or hold the papers until the buyer gives you proof of spaying or neutering. Some breeders also offer rebates on the purchase price for proof of altering. Better yet: Spay or neuter the kittens before they go to new homes. (See the sidebar "Spaying and neutering kittens," later in this chapter.)

Be cordial and informative with buyers, but be persistent. Ask to see a driver's license. Check references, including calling the person's veterinarian. A person who has owned numerous pets and *doesn't* have a veterinary reference is another to cross off your list. Don't be afraid to turn people down. Although doing so may not be pleasant, you must do what's best for your kittens! You've put a lot of effort into them, and you want them to live with someone who will continue to love and care for them as you have.

Remember, always, that you want your kittens to go to good homes, and the *only one* who has a chance at making that happen is you.

Look, we don't want to scare you — well, maybe a little — but we do want you to be careful. The world's full of scary people. Here's a story about one of them: A serial killer went to the same high school that Gina did, and after he was caught, the police discovered that, before he killed people, he'd "practiced" on free-to-good-home animals, including *lots* of kittens. *Please* don't make "he wanted one and came right over" the only criterion for someone adopting one of your babies!

Spaying and neutering kittens

One surefire way to make sure you're not adding to the problem of pet overpopulation is to spay and neuter your kittens before they go to their new homes.

Ask your veterinarian whether early altering is appropriate for your kittens. The procedures have traditionally been performed starting at the age of five months, but in recent years early spay-neuters on kittens as young as eight weeks old have been widely approved by veterinary and humane groups and breed registries. Many shelters now alter kittens before they're adopted in an effort to stop the revolving door of "kitten out, kittens in" that so many struggle with. An increasing number of reputable breeders also spay or neuter kittens they don't intend to show before they go to their new homes.

Yes, this procedure involves an added expense, but some adopters may appreciate the convenience and the sign that they're dealing with someone who has the best interests of the cats in mind. Adjust your price to cover the cost of the surgery — or ask for the cost of the surgery if you were planning to give the kittens away.

Chapter 17

One Is Never Enough: The Multicat Household

Cats have an instinct for locating humans with the kindest of hearts, which is likely why so many cat lovers have more than one cat. Once you know the special companionship of a cat and appreciate the special beauty of a cat, wanting another seems only natural — especially with so many cats in need of a home. Whose heart wouldn't be moved?

The jump to owning more than one cat — even many more than one cat — can seem quite effortless. In researching this chapter, Gina ran across one cat lover who had gone from one cat to more than a dozen in just a few years. Yes, caring for that many is a lot of work, the woman admitted, but she didn't regret her decision to adopt . . . and adopt . . . and adopt.

The difference between this woman and those who can't successfully handle a household with more than one cat is knowing what's involved in owning two cats, four cats, or even sixteen. Before you become the caretaker to more than one cat, figure out what you can afford, what you can tolerate, and what you can't. Love at first sight may be a wonderful thing, but hard work, patience, and understanding are what make a relationship last. That's true with people, and it's true with pets, too. The difference is that your pet isn't capable of providing for himself after the break-up!

We're not trying to discourage you from having more than one cat. We're in favor of multicat households, which are good for both cats and cat lovers. But as with every other aspect of cat care we discuss throughout this book, you need to know what you're getting into before you leap. Use your head, and follow your heart.

In this chapter, we talk about the challenge of living with more than one fully domesticated cat. Some people spend their time taking care of another kind of cat family — a colony of wild, or *feral,* cats. If you've started feeding wild cats, see our suggestions for helping them in Chapter 4.

You're in Good Company

Here's a quiz for you: How is it that cats are the No. 1 pet in the United States when more households own dogs? You're probably ahead of us. Dogs tend to be a one-to-a-household kind of pet — although you couldn't prove that by either Gina or Paul — while cats tend to be owned in multiples.

By how much do cats outnumber dogs as pets in the United States? The American Veterinary Medical Association estimates that 65 million cats are kept as pets, as opposed to 50 million dogs. Cats took over the top spot in the mid-'80s and have never looked back.

The changing demographics of our lives have made the cat a more suitable pet in many households, and those same factors are among the reasons why it's so good to have more than one cat. For you, and for your cat, the extra company can be very important.

Another cat, for your cat

For many households, the *Leave It to Beaver* family is an historical artifact. The stay-at-home mom so identified with post-World War II America isn't all that common anymore. Today, households can be made up of a single person, a single parent with one child or more, two working adults without children, two working adults with children — any way you slice it, a lot of homes are empty during the day.

Longer work hours, longer commutes, and organized activities outside the home also are factors in today's lifestyle, leaving those homes empty even longer. This situation is especially bad for dogs, who as pack animals need companionship, as well as the exercise and training many people don't have time for. Cats are far more adaptable, thriving in all manner of living situations. They don't need to be walked, and they can handle time alone without as much risk of behavior problems.

But are they lonely? The answer to that question is key to understanding why your cat may well benefit from the company of another of her kind.

The loneliness of the indoor cat

In addition to the change in human lifestyles, many cats live a life unimagined even a few decades ago: They spend their entire lives inside. Although this change has resulted in cats who live longer, healthier lives on average than their free-roaming relatives, it also leaves some cats unhappy. And the stress of being unhappy can show up in different ways, including illness and behavior problems.

You can't keep a cat indoors without offering her an environment that has been enriched to compensate for some of what she lost when you closed the door to the outside. One of the best gifts you can give your indoor cat is the companionship of another cat. Although not all cats seem interested in sharing, and the introductory period may be rocky, if your cat is alone for long stretches of time, chances are that she'll benefit from having another cat around.

Another cat isn't the only thing we suggest to make your indoor cat happy. We include a whole slate of suggestions in Chapter 23. From plants for nibbling to perches for enjoying the view, your cat will benefit from our suggestions.

The free-roaming cat

The cat who comes and goes as he pleases may already have cat companions, or at least a hard-won treaty outlining what territory belongs to which neighborhood cat. An indoor-outdoor cat probably doesn't need to share you with another cat as much as the indoor-only cat might. The decision about whether to get another cat in such a case depends more on what you want and how easygoing your cat is toward other cats. Some cats are very aggressive toward other cats on their turf, while some could hardly care less.

If you're going to have more than one cat, you may want to consider making them all inside cats, for reasons of health and economy. Cats in the "closed" environment of your home aren't exposed to the contagious problems of other cats in your neighborhood, such as parasites or viruses. Tips on how to convert an outdoor cat to an indoor one can be found in Chapter 6.

Another cat, for you

Face it: You really can't be sure what your cat will or won't like if you decide to add to your feline family. Although you may think of your cat's needs first and foremost — especially if he's an indoor cat with some boredom issues — chances are, you're considering primarily your own needs.

In short: You want another cat.

Before you trip on over to the shelter, call a reputable breeder, or say "yes" to the coworker who's trying to give away an "oops litter," take some time to consider what you're getting into.

Knowing your limits

Love may be without limits, but you can't say the same about time and money. Nobody has an endless amount of both. Have you the time to scoop litter boxes more frequently? What about grooming your cats, or taking them to the veterinarian? Time is a valuable commodity these days, so don't underestimate the amount of it you'll need to care for additional cats.

And what about money? Taking proper care of any pet can be an expensive proposition, and it's not much reduced by the economies of scale. Sure, if you have a houseful of cats, you can buy food and litter in bulk and not be short-changing your pets one bit. But when taking care of their health, make sure every cat has the same level of care you would provide if you had only one cat.

Consider flea control as an example of pet care that you can't neglect just because you have more than one cat. Today's spot-on remedies available from your veterinarian have virtually eliminated fleas in many households. But the monthly cost of application that may seem quite reasonable for one cat can seem like a big hit for a half-dozen. So what do you do? Live with fleas (and tapeworms, which are transmitted by fleas) and let your cats be miserable? When we put it that bluntly, we're sure you'll agree that those health hazards are not an appealing option.

We queried the veterinarians of the Veterinary Information Network (www.vin.com) on what problems they saw in their practices with multicat households. We were surprised to see the cost issue pop up among all those that were strictly medical in nature. But it underscores a very real problem.

Never have more cats than you have time and money to care for. If you can't honestly say each of your cats is being cared for as well as he would be if he were your only cat, you're not doing the best you can for your cats.

Full speed ahead

We discuss some factors that may make you realize you shouldn't get an additional cat, but this book doesn't have enough space to list all the reasons why you should add to your feline family. We'll just sum it up this way: Do you love cats? Can you care for additional cats? Then you're all set. It's time to start looking for an additional cat — or two, or more.

Short hair, long hair, active, or sedate? Because you'll want to consider these questions, we have the answers in Chapter 2, with lots of suggestions for finding the right cat to fit your lifestyle.

Adding to the Family

Life doesn't always work so neatly that you can plan every aspect of it, and that's certainly true when it comes to adding a cat. Sometimes a stray adopts you, or you meet a cat or kitten you just can't live without — and for whom you may be the cat's very last chance.

It's still a good idea to be prepared as much as you can be. And that means discovering how cats work together and what combinations may be perfect for your living situation.

Understanding territoriality

Dogs have a built-in ability to live with one another, based on the ancestral needs of wild dogs and wolves to cooperate in finding food. That doesn't mean, of course, that all dogs get along well with other dogs or other people, but it does mean that the basic wiring for group living is in every dog to some extent.

You don't find that packlike tendency in cats, at least not in the same way. Cats don't hunt cooperatively, as dogs do — with the notable exceptions of African lions, most cats are solitary hunters. When they're not hunting, they're protecting their hunting space — their territory — from other cats. There's only so much game to go around, you see, and they don't want another cat cutting in on their action.

And yet the domestic cat is perfectly capable of forming strong bonds with other cats. When the need to compete for food is removed, cats can live in harmony and even happiness with one another, as many cat lovers will attest.

Issues of territoriality still pop up, however. Although you may not notice it, your cats will be constantly negotiating and renegotiating territory. When there's enough to go around, you'll never notice the bargaining. When there isn't, you'll know the signs — fighting, marking, and avoiding litter boxes.

If you want your cats to live happily together, be patient in introducing them and make sure they're not competing for space, for food, or for litter boxes.

Choosing compatible cats

Most cats learn to live together well enough if you set up your house so each cat has what he or she needs to feel safe and secure. Still, some combinations seem to work out more easily than others, or at least more quickly.

- ✔ **A pair of kittens:** Starting with two kittens is probably the easiest of all. They can be littermates or unrelated; it doesn't matter. They come to your home at an age where they're more interested in playing than in fighting over turf, and they usually grow up to be the best of friends.

- ✔ **A pair of cats:** If you haven't any cats at all, adopting two adults cats at once isn't that difficult. They're not going to be so thrilled with one another at first as a pair of kittens are, but because neither is invading the previously claimed turf of the other, they should settle in soon enough.

- ✔ **Established cat, new kitten:** Unless your cat is too old and cranky to handle the high energy of a kitten, picking an immature cat as your second cat shouldn't be too hard a transition. Most adult cats are fairly tolerant of immature cats — they may not like them, but they're more inclined to leave the scene than attack. Give your older cat a break by wearing out your kitten with interactive games such as chasing a toy on a string.

- ✔ **Established cat, new cat:** Most pairings work out in time, but this combination is one of the more difficult. Bringing a mature challenger onto another mature cat's home turf is guaranteed to make the fur fly until everyone can settle in with a corner of the world to call his own.

Cats are very much creatures of habit, and they become easily upset about changes in their environment. A move to a new home, a new baby, and certainly a new cat can trigger behavior problems. The best way to introduce change to a cat is *slowly*. For help with introductions, see Chapter 6. For strategies for working with behavior problems, see Chapters 14 and 15.

Best tip? Get 'em fixed

Although some territory squabbles will always be going on among your cats — negotiations are constant, even if you don't notice them — the best way to ensure domestic tranquility is to have all your cats altered.

Cats who haven't been spayed or neutered — what veterinarians and breeders call *intact* — are under increased pressure to establish territory, driven by hormones that never give them a break. Intact males are inclined toward spraying to mark territory, and in a multicat household, one or more intact males will make you believe you're living in a war zone, with urine marking as the weapon of choice.

Intact females are in a near-constant state of heat, yowling and rolling in their desire to attract a mate. Take our word for this: You do not want to be living in a household of intact cats! With sexually mature, sexually driven cats, it's not the more the merrier — it's the more the messier and the more the noisier, at best!

Camden and Cleo/Photo by Michelle Vukas

Caring for More than One Cat

You can help prevent some conflicts that naturally arise between cats by
making sure they feel comfortable in their environment, and seeing they're
not denied something they need by another cat. Each cat needs to have a
place where he feels comfortable and safe enough to relieve himself, to get
away from others, and to eat.

Litter box strategies

Cat territorial issues become big problems in the eyes of the human members
of the family when they take the form of litter box avoidance. Setting up litter
boxes in the multicat family involves some trial and error, to be sure, but the
bottom line is that if your cats aren't happy, they're going to make you
unhappy. Fortunately, cats don't need much to make them happy when it
comes to litter boxes.

The first rule of litter boxes in the multicat household: Don't expect cats to
share. The depositing of urine and feces isn't just about eliminating waste; it's
also about marking territory. The litter box that one cat uses likely won't be
one that another cat will want to step into.

The basic guideline is to have one litter box for every cat, arranged in different locations throughout the house so every cat can have his own sandy piece of heaven.

Your placement of litter boxes can also help to encourage your cats to use them. Cats do *not* want to be ambushed when relieving themselves — really, who does? — so position the litter box so your cat can keep an eye on what may be ready to jump him. For some cats, the perfect box set-up is a location away from the wall with a 360-degree field of vision. For others, having two sides of the box against the wall gives them a feeling of security. Try placing different litter boxes in different ways, and let your cat sort out which appeals the most.

Here's the final rule of litter boxes in the multicat household — or in the single-cat household for that matter: Scoop often. Daily at a minimum, but even two or three times a day wouldn't be too often. Especially if you're lucky enough to have cats who actually share a litter box, don't push your luck by letting the mess pile up. Your cats will find someplace else to go if you do.

Everything you need to know about litter boxes, including how to choose one and what to put in it, can be found in Chapters 8 and 15.

Cat trees, cubbies, and hiding places

Space is another factor in keeping a colony of cats happy. The good news is that you don't have to move into a mansion — unless you want to, of course — to provide your cats with room to maneuver.

Cats love to make the most of high spaces, and by giving your cats plenty of room up above to move about, you're giving each cat a room of her own. Tall furniture with flat tops — such as bookcases or entertainment centers — are ideal, as long as you leave room enough for a cat or two among the decorations. A more obvious solution is to invest in a couple extra cat trees, especially those with platforms at the top and cubbyholes for hiding. Your cats will love them!

One of Gina's friends has five cats, and when Gina stays in that house, she loves to observe how each animal has carved out a bit of turf for himself or herself. Her favorite cat in that family, a longhaired old calico named Darlene, had claimed the top of a bookshelf in an upstairs bedroom for "her" space. She was pretty easygoing with her feline housemates — as long as each of them remembered that the only cat allowed to sleep on top of that bookcase was Queen Darlene.

Who's doing what?

Even in the most harmonious of households, a cat can stop using the litter box. Remember that it's not always about territory: Sometimes a cat is sick. But which cat? In a multicat household, tracking down the culprit can be very difficult.

You can try to isolate the cat with problems by mixing food coloring — blue or green — with canned food and offering it to one cat at a time. You can tell which feces came from the "marked" cat, because the food coloring will pass right through.

Urine is a little harder to figure out, but your veterinarian should be able to help — or refer you to a veterinary behaviorist who can. You'll end up with fluorescent dye and and a black light. The dye shows up in the urine, and the black light reveals it.

After you know which cat is spraying or not using the litter box, review Chapter 15 to come up with a strategy for solving this messy problem.

Feeding time at the cat ranch

Cats are generally not as protective about their food as dogs are. Most cats actually share pretty well, eating cheek by jowl quite happily as long as they feel secure in knowing that plenty of food exists for all.

Figure 17-2: Getting all your cats comfortable with being together will take planning and time on your part.

Even given the easygoing nature of the cat at feeding time, you may want to consider which way of feeding a multicat household works best for your cats.

✔ **Strategy No. 1 — all food, all the time:** Keeping a bowl of dry food available at all times is probably the easiest way to keep your cats fed. And if your cats do well on this plan, that's fine. But a lot of cats don't. Some cats are bullies and keep others away from the food. And some cats are just pigs, eating themselves into obesity.

If you have a bully, maintain two bowls of dry food at all times, in different parts of the house. Your bully cat can't be in two places at once, so your other cat or cats can eat. As long as everyone maintains a healthy weight — neither too fat nor too thin — you're all set.

If you have one cat who isn't capable of maintaining a normal weight with food constantly available, you must change the way you feed your cats.

✔ **Strategy No. 2 — individual meals:** If you have cats with different dietary needs — a cat who's on a prescription diet, for example, or one who's overweight — you may have to feed each cat individually. If your cats get fussy with one another — if one is afraid to eat in another's presence, for example — feed them away from one another.

You may not have to feed your cats in different rooms. Different levels may be fine. Some cats feel most comfortable eating on a countertop or table — it gives them a feeling of security knowing they won't be ambushed. (If you can't stand the thought of cats on a kitchen counter or table, try the washing machine or dryer.)

✔ **Strategy No. 3 — kitty buffet, with special service:** Some people like to keep dry food constantly available and also treat their cats to a couple tablespoons of more palatable canned food once a day. The cats love the wet stuff! The advantage to this feeding strategy is that you know your cats always have food — and you also see that each of them eats every day. Because loss of appetite can be a sign of illness, this information can be of value in spotting a health problem early.

One of Gina's reader's once pointed out another benefit of feeding a couple tablespoons of canned food every night: It brings in the wanderers for the evening. Nighttime is arguably the riskiest time for a free-roaming cat, and if you can keep yours inside at night, you're making his life safer. Once cats know they'll be treated to a delicious meal just before dusk, they'll show up at the appointed hour no matter where they've been playing.

Multicat Medical Concerns

Cats in a multicat setting get sick with the same kinds of things a single cat does. The difference is that many health problems never seem to go away unless you're really dedicated to getting them settled — they just seem to pass from one cat to another and back again.

The best way to keep cats healthy is to keep them inside, and that's doubly true in a multicat household. After you establish a "closed" colony of healthy cats, you have little to fear from parasites or infectious diseases. When cats come and go, however, they often return with health problems that can be easily passed along to other cats in the household.

As mentioned earlier, shared but separate food bowls and litter boxes are some of the real challenges of the multicat household. This concern multiplies with respect to medical issues. Be sure to remind your veterinarian that yours is a multicat household, and he will help you with tricks and strategies for maintaining optimal health for all your pets.

Parasite problems

Some of the most difficult health challenges to get a handle on in a multicat household involve parasites. By their very nature, parasites are extremely good at jumping from one host to another. Too often, if one cat is infested with a parasite, they all are.

Fleas and ticks

Fleas are a bigger problem for cats than ticks are, generally. Cats are so diligent about grooming that they usually keep themselves free of ticks (unless the pests lodge somewhere they cannot reach easily). Fleas are quite another issue, however. Flea control is relatively easy these days with spot-on medications available from veterinarians, but some people find the monthly costs for these medications a little steep if they have more than a couple of cats. (We address the issue of cost earlier in this chapter.) If all your cats are inside, you may be able to control fleas by removing the cats from the premises and treating your home with a pesticide — or having a pest-control company do it for you. If you introduce flea-free cats to a flea-free environment, you shouldn't have any further problems. That's a mighty big "if," though, and if you can't get a handle on fleas — or if your cats come and go — you'll likely have to pony up the money for preventive medications.

Ear mites

These small pests feed off the inside lining of the ears. They can be highly contagious, and many cat lovers have a hard time getting rid of them. If one cat in the household has ear mites, chances are they all do. Discuss treatment options with your veterinarian.

The biggest problem with treating ear mites is follow-through. Medicating cats is no picnic. And because it's so difficult — especially in a multicat household — many people stop treatment when they first notice the ear mites seem to be disappearing. However, the problem is, they're not gone; they're just regrouping. If you don't continue the medication for as long as your veterinarian recommends, a new generation of pests will hatch, and you'll be right back where you started.

Intestinal worms

Other parasites that can be passed from cat to cat include worms such as the tapeworm, which is a pest that gets help from fleas. As with any other pest, if you have one cat with fleas, you probably have more than one cat with them. See your veterinarian for proper diagnosis and treatment.

One "worm" that isn't is ringworm, which is really a fungus — and which can be transmitted from cat to human as well as from cat to cat. Although only your veterinarian can make a certain diagnosis of this condition, some signs to look out for on your cat include circular areas of hair loss and sometimes scaly or crusty skin. After you talk to your veterinarian, you may need to talk to your own doctor as well because the problem can be passed on to human family members.

Infectious viral diseases

Although parasites can give you and your cats fits, contagious viral diseases such as feline leukemia (FeLV) or feline immunodeficiency virus (FIV) can pose grave health risks to your cats. So, too, can feline infectious peritonitis, which is a disease the owners of a single cat don't need to be concerned with as much as those people who share their homes with many cats.

We discuss these serious infectious diseases — and what steps you can take to protect your cats — in Chapters 11 and 12. The most important advice we can give is to work with your veterinarian on the most appropriate preventive health program for your cats.

Chapter 18

Out and About with Your Cat

● ●

In This Chapter

▶ Determining whether your cat should travel

▶ Choosing a pet-sitter or kennel

▶ Traveling by air or car

▶ Easing your cat through a change of address

▶ Figuring out whether your cat is showable

● ●

*I*f you left the decision to your cat, the chances are good that neither of you would ever go anywhere. Not to work. Not to a lovely getaway week-end with the two-legged love of your life. And certainly not to the veterinarian. Cats love routine, they love territory, and they *especially* love routine *in* their territory. If they had their choice, you'd be home all the time, catering to their every whim for food, play, and petting, admiring their beauty as they settle into that warm sunlit patch on the livingroom armchair for the first, fourth, or tenth of the day's oh-so-essential catnaps.

A well-run home, meals on time, warm places to sleep, and the attentions of a loving human — to a cat, these pleasures are heaven.

To humans, however, such an existence is boring. We're a considerably more nomadic lot than our cats are, and most of us love an occasional change of scenery every bit as much as we appreciate the comforts of our homes. Then, too, sometimes the choice to travel is not ours, with family, friends, and work keeping us moving — to that business conference a half-day's flight away, to a friend's wedding, or to a relative's funeral.

No matter where you're going and why, carefully plan for your cat's care so that she'll be as happy as possible under the circumstances. Most of the times you go away, you're leaving your cat behind, but if you're taking her with you, make the journey as safe and comfortable as possible for her. And if you can't have her with you, see that her needs are provided for by pet-sitters or boarding facilities so that you don't need to worry.

Figure 18-1:
Most cats
would
rather
snooze at
home than
travel,
and this
old-timer is
definitely
one of them.

Noodles/Photo by Richard D. Schmidt

We certainly don't want you to worry, whether you take your cat or leave her behind. This is why we tell you everything you need to know to make the right choices for your pet, whether you're going away for the weekend or picking up stakes and moving your household — cat included, of course — cross-country. You want your cat to be happy. And so do we.

Although most cats prefer to avoid a life on the road, a few handle the challenges well. Put in this category not only top show cats, but also show-*biz* cats, who travel with their trainers for work in television, movies, and advertising. For the ultimate cat-travel story, however, check out the experiences of Peter Gether's Scottish Fold, Norton, in his books, *The Cat Who Went to Paris* and *A Cat Abroad: The Further Adventures of Norton, the Cat Who Went to Paris, and His Human* (both in paperback from Fawcett). Norton has passed away, but in his time, he was quite a cat!

Is Your Cat Up to Travel?

Not that many cats take to travel the way dogs do, and if you want yours to have a chance at enjoying a life on the road, you probably need to start when your pet is a kitten. An adult can be more difficult to introduce to new places and people and may never adjust enough to enjoy the experience.

Some trips aren't avoidable, especially if you're moving. (See the section "Moving Your Cat to a New Home," later in this chapter.) How much discretionary travel you attempt with your cat is basically up to your cat and comes down to two questions: Is your pet healthy enough to travel? Does your pet have the personality to adapt to travel?

You must answer those questions for yourself with input from your veterinarian and, of course, your cat. And maybe experiment a little with some short pleasure trips to make sure that they're enjoyable for you both. Like Norton, the "Cat Who Went to Paris," some cats are made for a life lapping cream in French cafés; others are delighted to be traveling comfortably in a well-equipped motor home. Maybe your pet is one of these vagabonds!

The trip almost no cat likes is the one to the veterinary hospital. We put tips on making that particular journey easier — for you, your cat, and your veterinarian — in Chapter 11.

Health considerations

Before undertaking anything more than a cross-town trip with your cat, take her to the veterinarian to make sure she's in good health and current on all the preventive-care measures your veterinarian recommends. A cat who's in poor health is not well suited to be a traveling companion.

Talk to your veterinarian about your travel and your concerns for your cat. If you're traveling by air, you need a health certificate. (You can find more information on air travel in the section "Taking Your Pet with You," later in this chapter.) If you're traveling by car or by air, ask for a copy of your cat's vaccination record, especially rabies. The thought that your cat may bite someone or tangle with a wild creature is horrible, but in case she does, you want proof of her rabies vaccination with you.

If you think your cat may be better off traveling sedated, discuss this option with your veterinarian.

If your cat is a Persian or Exotic Shorthair — or any mix that has these breeds' trademark short muzzles — traveling may be a real hazard. That's because breathing is more difficult for these short-faced pets. Air travel in a cargo hold should probably be ruled out. Ask your veterinarian what can ensure your pet's safety any time that you must travel with her.

Temperament considerations

You know your cat better than anyone else. Is she shy and nervous or relaxed and outgoing? Does she adjust well to change? To noise? To changes in feed time or location? If your cat takes two days to "chill out" after a short car trip, you may decide that only essential trips are in her future.

If your cat is borderline, however, give her a chance. You may both enjoy the extra time together, wherever you are.

Leaving Your Pet Behind

You need to know what to do if you can't take your cat with you, which is probably most of the time you're away from home. Your cat may not be one of those rare ones who enjoys the challenge of travel, and even if he is, you can't always take him along. Business travel is necessary, after all, and so, too, is that emergency trip cross-country to handle the estate of a relative. Another place you may need to go where your cat can't is the hospital.

Ask your friends, neighbors, and coworkers what they do with their cats when they're gone. Ask your veterinarian, too, for referrals to pet-sitters or boarding facilities, if he doesn't have his own boarding facilities.

If you have a service in mind, whether a boarding facility or sitter, call and ask for references and then check it out — a step few people take. Ask about professional affiliations, such as the American Boarding Kennel Association or Pet Sitters International, both of which offer materials and training to U.S. and Canadian members to encourage a higher degree of performance from their members.

No matter what kind of care you choose for your pet while you're gone, make your arrangements early, if you can. Pet-sitters and boarding facilities are booked weeks and sometimes months in advance for peak travel times, such as summer or the winter holidays.

Prepare for emergencies

One of the easiest things to overlook in leaving your pet behind — whether with a friend, a pet-sitter, or a boarding facility — is how you want him cared for should he become ill. Discuss care options with your veterinarian in advance and then clue in the person who's caring for your cat.

Setting up emergency care arrangements works best if you have a good relationship with your veterinarian — but then, so does everything else concerning your pet's health. Gina's veterinarian knows the kind of health care she expects, and she trusts his judgment if he can't get in touch with her. In her pets' records is a note from him saying that, no matter who shows up with her animals, the hospital is to provide care, and her credit card number is on file to handle the charges.

You're well advised to set up a similar relationship to the one Gina has with her veterinarian so that your cat's care is something you don't need to worry about while you're away. Touch base with your veterinarian on this point at your cat's annual exam or before you leave him to go on a trip to make sure that no misunderstandings come up.

For the ultimate in preparing for a trip where you can't take your pet, see the information in Chapter 13 on providing for your cat in your will. We don't mean to be flippant about something so serious, but we do want you to be sure your pet is covered in any eventuality.

Pet-sitters

A wide range of services is lumped under the general title of *pet-sitter,* covering everything from a reciprocal agreement between friends to care for each other's pets, to paying a neighbor kid to look in on your cat, to hiring a professional pet-sitting service to care for your pet in your own home.

The benefit of having your pet stay in your own home is that she's familiar with the surroundings — which is a very important consideration where cats are concerned. And pet-sitters can do more than just look in on your pet: They can take in your mail and newspaper, water your houseplants, and turn lights on and off.

Discuss services and prices with pet-sitters beforehand, and if you're dealing with a service, make sure that their employees are bonded and insured.

The biggest drawback to pet-sitters is that your pet is left alone a great deal of the time, because most pet-sitters probably can't spend much time giving your pet individual attention. (An arrangement with a young person — or a house-sitter to stay in your home while you're gone — may give your pet more opportunities to be petted or played with.) If your pet becomes ill or manages to escape, a pet-sitter may not come back to notice before some time has passed. And, finally, some people just aren't comfortable having people in their home while they're gone.

Informal arrangements for house-sitting — actually having the person move in while you're gone — or pet-sitting — having the person just drop in once or twice a day to check on your cat — can be even trickier than hiring a professional service. Just ask the friend of Gina's who left her house and pets in the care of a friend's college-aged daughter, only to find out that the young woman had been anything but a quiet resident. She'd had guests and even parties. The house was a bit worse for wear, but at least the pets were fine! If you're going to go with a young person — and many people do, with no regrets — confirm that parental oversight is part of the agreement.

One of the best solutions is to *trade* pet-sitting services. Most animal lovers have friends who also have pets, and making a deal with a friend to cover each other whenever you're gone can work out very well. Trading care is a solution that's both reassuring — if you have friends who love animals as much as you do, that is — and inexpensive. All the arrangement requires is your own time in return.

Boarding facilities

Boarding facilities are another option, ideal for friendly, well-adjusted cats. Despite all the recommendations in the world, however, don't leave your pet at a business you haven't inspected yourself. You should see clean, comfortable, and well-maintained facilities, and if you don't, go elsewhere.

Ask where your pet would stay and ask to see the premises. Make sure your cat will be housed completely away from dogs and separated from other cats — although your own cats can be housed together, unacquainted cats should *never* be mixed.

The facility operators should seem sincerely interested in tailoring their facility to make your cat's stay more comfortable. They should be prepared to feed your cat as you do, especially if he's on a special diet, and they should be willing to allow you to leave behind toys or articles containing your smell — a dirty sock, for example — to reassure your pet.

Figure 18-2:
Many cats are most comfortable staying home while you're gone and having a pet-sitting friend drop in.

Showing off: Is your cat star material?

People who are involved in the sport of breeding and showing cats — known as the *cat fancy* — come from all backgrounds and every corner of the world, sharing only their firm belief that the cat is the most beautiful of all beings. For some, the sport is both an obsession and a love.

If your cat is in good health and can handle the stress of travel and of being looked at and handled by strangers, you're welcome to enter him in the next cat show that comes up in your area. Before you do, however, read the cat magazines to see what kinds of shows are common in your region. Also write to the registry (such as the Cat Fanciers' Association) for show rules to make sure that your cat is eligible. In some registries, for example, declawed cats are not allowed, whereas in others, your cat's breed may not be recognized to compete at all.

After you read the rules, attend a show as a spectator and pick up all the information you can find. Look for fliers on upcoming shows and

pamphlets on how to exhibit, and buttonhole every friendly exhibitor you can to get all your questions answered.

Your cat doesn't need to be a registered, pedigreed animal to compete at most cat shows. Many people happily show in the household pet competition, but for others, household pet is just the beginning. They eventually choose a breed (or more than one) to compete for other awards and to develop a breeding program.

One way to determine whether your cat may be show material is to consider how she behaves on her trips to the veterinarian. If she's relatively easy to handle and friendly, she's probably okay for showing. If she's terrified, spitting and slashing, you probably need to resign yourself to attending cat shows as a spectator, at least until you add a more amenable cat to your family. We've put more on how to enjoy a show as a spectator in Chapter 2.

Photo courtesy of Michael Brim/Cat Fanciers' Association

Boarding your cat has a few advantages over hiring a pet-sitting service. Boarding facilities are usually very secure, and the best ones always have someone on-site to check in on your cat. Some businesses make up for the fact that they're out in the sticks by picking up and delivering your pet.

If you don't have a home yet in a city you're moving to, a reputable boarding facility may meet your pet at the airport in advance of your arrival and care for her until you get there. Alternatively, you can often leave your pet while you're house-hunting and arrange for the facility to ship her after you find suitable lodgings. (See the section "Air travel," later in this chapter.) In general, we prefer to recommend accompanied air travel, but your circumstances may not permit it. If that's the case, a reputable boarding facility can help.

Many veterinarians have boarding facilities, too, and if yours is among them, this option may well be the best boarding choice for your pet. The biggest advantage is that the staff is already familiar with your pet and her medical background — a real plus if your cat is elderly or has a chronic health condition.

Do not patronize a boarding facility that does not ask you for proof of up-to-date vaccinations. If they do not insist that *your* pet is healthy and well-protected from disease, they're not asking these questions of other boarders, either, and not doing so puts your pet at risk. No matter what, we don't recommend boarding a kitten who hasn't had all his vaccinations. The increased possibility for disease isn't worth the risk.

Taking Your Pet with You

No matter whether by car or air, traveling with your cat is easier if you plan ahead and bring gear to make the trip easier. You need to travel a bit more lightly if going by air, but if you're heading out by car, load up!

We cover only air and automobile travel because for most people those are the only options if you want your cat to accompany you. Most cruise ships usually don't allow animals, nor do many bus or rail lines, including Amtrak.

The following list describes some travel essentials for your cat. Check out Chapter 8 for more information on choosing pet supplies and the Additional Resources appendix at the end of this book for contact information on pet-supply catalogs.

> ✔ **Carrier:** An airline-approved travel carrier — also called a *crate* — can get you through any situation with your cat. Shop around for value, but don't skimp on quality: Get a sturdy crate made of high-impact plastic, large enough for your cat to stand up and turn around in and not much more. This carrier can safely take your cat to the veterinarian and around the world, if need be, and is the most essential piece of travel gear for any cat.

If you travel cross-country in a car, you may want to get a larger carrier, sized for a medium-sized dog, so that you have room for a litter box inside the crate on a long drive. Another carrier option is a soft-sided bag (we like the ones made by Sherpa), which may be more comfortable for you and your pet if you're traveling by air — but *only* if he's with you in the passenger compartment. You need a hard-plastic, airline-approved carrier for use in the cargo hold.

✔ **Harness, ID, and leash:** A frightened or startled cat is harder to hold onto than a hot frying pan. Make sure that, if yours wriggles out of your grasp, he's going no farther than the end of a leash. Keep a cat harness with an ID tag on him and attach a leash to the harness anytime he's out of the crate. One nice leash for travel is a reel-type Flexi; the smallest size is lightweight enough for cats and gives your pet 10 feet of freedom. We like IDs that offer 24-hour tracking and assistance, such as those from 1-800-HELP4PETS.

✔ **Litter box and filler:** Although we generally recommend sticking with your cat's regular brand, you're likely to find that clumping litter is easiest to deal with on the road. Don't forget to pack a litter scoop and airtight, sealable plastic bags for keeping clumps smell-free until you can put them in a trash bin. You may find disposable cardboard litter boxes easiest to deal with, especially if you're not using clumping litter — just toss litter and box as needed, even daily. Another possibility is buying a plastic storage bin with a snap-on lid. Although it doesn't fit in a crate, such a bin holds a trip's worth of clumping litter without spilling — just keep the lid on except when you're offering your pet a potty break in the bin. And keep the clumps removed.

✔ **Food, water, and bowls:** Pack your pet's regular rations and, if you're using moist food, don't forget a fork and a can opener (or choose pop tops). Keep a bottle of water in the car so your cat can always have a fresh drink, and offer refreshment often. Another possibility is to use a hanging bottle on the crate. These bottles come in sizes appropriate for animals from mice to Great Danes; cat-sized ones may be marked for rabbits. Finally, don't forget some treats.

✔ **First-aid and grooming supplies:** Keep a basic first-aid kit at hand and pack in a comb and a brush as well. Don't forget to bring along any regular medication your cat needs, too. For more information on the contents of a first-aid kit, see the Cheat Sheet at the front of this book or buy a ready-made kit. We list a contact number for one such manufacturer, PET-PAK, Inc., in the Additional Resources appendix.

✔ **Paper towels and a spray bottle of a general-purpose cleaner:** You're going to need these, we promise. Throw in a few old towels, too. They're good for beds, restraints in an emergency — see Chapter 12 for more information on emergencies — and any kind of cleanup. Aerosol air freshener is another good thing to bring.

  ✔ **A couple of your cat's favorite toys, including an interactive one such as a cat fishing pole or a toy on a string:** Hey, what else are you going to do in a motel room besides keep your cat amused?

  ✔ **Travel guides:** Although cats are a lot easier to get into hotels, motels, and inns than are dogs (and a hundred times easier to sneak in, in a pinch, but we didn't say so), you still need a reference to find out which places welcome pets. AAA and Mobil travel guides note where pets are welcome, and many books deal exclusively with traveling with your pet.

Now, obviously, you're going to tailor what you bring to the kind of trip you're taking. You aren't going to pack everything for a short air trip, but you need the lot if you're traveling hundreds of miles by car.

Air travel

Although horror stories make the news, the truth is that airline travel is relatively safe for most pets. Your pet will do fine, too, if you play by the rules, plan carefully, and are prepared to be a little pushy on your cat's behalf.

Animals move through the airline system in two ways: as cargo or as accompanied baggage. Your cat is better off if you're traveling with him so that you can make sure he's well cared for.

Some airlines allow animals in the passenger cabin if their carriers can fit in the space beneath the seat, which is true in the case of most cats. *Cabin seating is by far the best way your cat can fly, because he never leaves your care during the course of the trip.* Not all airlines allow animals to travel in the cabin, however, and others put a limit on the number of pets in the cabin, so making your arrangements far in advance pays. *Check and double-check.*

If your cat isn't allowed in the cabin, he flies below, in a pressurized cargo hold. This situation isn't ideal, but many cats do fine with it. The Air Transport Association estimates that more than half a million dogs and cats are transported on commercial airlines each year, and the industry group insists that 99 percent reach their destination without incident.

To make sure your pet is one of them, pay careful attention to the following tips:

  ✔ **Talk to the airline.** Some carriers, especially the new, no-frills companies, don't take animals at all. Even those that do have limits on the number of animals on a flight, both in the passenger cabin and the cargo hold. You also need to know where and when your pet must be presented and what papers, such as the health certificate and so on, you need to bring.

✔ **Make sure your pet is in good health and isn't a short-nosed breed.**
These cats find breathing a little difficult under the best of circumstances, and the stress of airline travel may be more than they can
handle. Talk to your veterinarian in advance about any concerns.

✔ **Use an approved carrier that bears tags with contact phone numbers
where you can be reached at both ends of the journey.** (Your home
number doesn't help if you're not at home.) Whether you carry your pet
on board into the passenger cabin or must check him as cargo, include
identification on your carrier. By law, the carrier should be just big
enough for your cat to stand up and turn around in.

Make sure all the bolts securing the halves of the carriers are in place
and tightened before checking in your pet. Don't forget to put a safe harness and ID on your pet. In addition, you may want to consider inserting
a microchip ID in your cat before you travel. (See Chapter 8 for more
information on microchipping.)

✔ **Don't ship your pet if the weather is bad or when air traffic is heavi-
est.** Avoid peak travel days such as around the Christmas holidays.
Choose flights that are on the ground when the temperature is neither
too hot nor too cold, not only at the departure airport, but also at the
connecting and arriving airports. Although temperature doesn't make a
difference if your pet's up top with you, it makes a big difference below:
Cargo holds aren't heated or cooled. In summer, a night flight is likely
better, while the reverse is true in the winter. Be aware that there are
regulations regarding the range of temperatures when a pet may be
shipped. If the temperature on the ground in your departing, connecting,
or arriving city falls outside these limits, you may run into unexpected
delays or cancellations of your pet's travel plans. Plan ahead.

✔ **Choose a direct flight; if that's not possible, try for a route with a
short layover.** Most pet fatalities occur on the ground, when animals are
left in their crates on the hot tarmac or in stifling cargo holds. Direct
flights eliminate layovers, and short layovers reduce the time on the
ground.

✔ **Remember that your cat's life depends on the attentiveness of airline
personnel if he's not in your care in the passenger cabin.** Most of
these employees are excellent and caring, but mistakes do happen. You
should be prepared to pester airline personnel to confirm that your pet
has been loaded and has made the same connections you have. If your
pet is flying unaccompanied, talk to freight-handling personnel at every
airport your cat visits. Be polite but persistent; don't take "I'm sure he's
fine; have some delicious honey-roasted peanuts" as an answer from a
flight attendant. Make the staff *check* and report back.

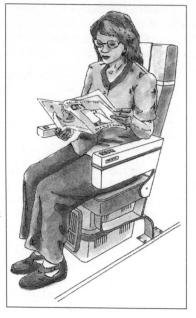

Figure 18-3:
The best way for your cat to fly is in the passenger compartment with you. If his carrier fits under the seat, many airlines allow him aboard.

Contrary to popular belief, you're generally better off *not* having your cat tranquilized before flying. The combination of high altitude and limited oxygen is a challenge that your pet's body is better prepared to meet if she's not sedated. Still, your pet may be an exception. In the end, you and your veterinarian should decide on this issue.

The Air Transport Association has a free booklet, *Air Travel for Your Dog or Cat.* The booklet is available by sending a self-addressed, stamped, business-sized envelope to: ATA, 1301 Pennsylvania Blvd. N.W., Suite 1100, Washington, DC 20004.

Car travel

We know you love your cat's company. We know that you love his purrfect puss. We also know that, for safety's sake, your pet should be out of sight whenever the car is moving, appropriately confined in his carrier. A loose cat in a car is a danger that shouldn't be risked — even if he doesn't get under your feet, he could get up so far under the seat that you have a very hard time getting him out after you stop.

Your cat may be more comfortable — and certainly more quiet — if you cover his crate with a towel while the car is in motion. Experiment to see which method your cat likes best. If your cat doesn't stop crying no matter what, bring along a squirt bottle and give him a shot of water whenever he pipes up. Either that or bring plenty of headache remedy, because after a few minutes of listening, you're going to need it.

Your cat can go for as long as you can without stretching his legs. After you stop, put on his leash for safety before you let him out into the car and offer him water and a litter break — unless both are already available in his crate. Food is probably best left for morning and night in your motel room.

Never leave your cat unattended in a car. If the heat doesn't get him, a thief may. If you're traveling with your cat, your meals are mostly going to be of the drive-through variety. If you absolutely must leave your cat in the car — for your bathroom break, for example — park in the shade, roll the windows down a little, and be *quick* — and we mean like five minutes. Even better, take your cat and his carrier inside the stall with you. He has seen you in there before; he's not going to be shocked.

If you want to kick around for a while, shopping and sightseeing, and still make sure your cat is safe, look up a local veterinarian in the phone book and see whether you can make arrangements for a few hours' boarding. Gina has done so for years and found most veterinarians very amenable to helping out — usually at a very reasonable cost. You can also leave your pet in your motel room — but always in a crate for safety.

Moving Your Cat to a New Home

For many cats, one of the most stressful events of their lives is a distracting time for their owners as well — changing addresses. Combine traveling with suddenly being in unfamiliar surroundings — which may even smell like former animal occupants — and you can easily understand why more than a few cats spend a very long time freaked out and hiding under a bed after a move.

Your cat thinks his current home is just perfect, but because he really doesn't get to vote, try to make the move as easy on him as possible. The key to success is to keep your cat secure before, during, and after the move. Anticipate possible problems and make your cat as comfortable as possible at every stage of the game.

One way to up the security factor is to order an ID tag with your new address and phone number as soon as you know them, and add it to your cat's collar along with the old ID. That way, you can make sure that the new information is securely on your cat's collar before any packing begins. If you're traveling a long distance to your new home, use paper-key tags (available very cheaply from your local hardware or variety store) for temporary ID. Just jot your daily information, such as your name, phone number, and hotel room number, on the tag and put it on your cat's collar. (More information on collars and IDs is in Chapter 8.)

Using a safe room for moving

The best way to move your cat is to confine him to a *safe room* before and after the move. The ideal setting is a room where your cat isn't going to be disturbed — a spare bathroom is perfect — and outfit it with food and water, a litter box, a scratching post, a bed, and toys. (Don't feel bad about confining your pet: He's more comfortable in a small space, and he isn't subjected to the stress of seeing people — perhaps *strangers* — tromping out of the house with his belongings. And don't forget that his belongings, after all, include everything in your — um . . . we mean *his* — house.)

A safe room is also good for bringing a new cat into your home and for retraining any cat with furniture-destroying or litter-box-avoiding habits. For more information on how to use a safe room while introducing a new cat to your home, see Chapter 6. For help with feline behavior problems, see Chapters 14 and 15.

Confining your cat also prevents his slipping out, which is a danger at both the old home and the new. Your cat could easily become scared, take off, and get lost, even in his familiar neighborhood. If your cat turns up back at your old place, a reunion can be hard to arrange, especially if you've moved to another city.

Your cat should be confined in his safe room the day before packing begins, moved to his new home in a carrier, and then confined again in his new safe room until the moving is over, the furniture arranged, and most of the dust settled.

A carrier is one of the best investments you can make in your cat's safety. For more information on choosing one, see Chapter 8. A carrier plays a crucial role in disaster preparedness for pets; more information on planning for an emergency is in Chapter 20.

After everything's settled, open the door to the safe room and let your cat explore at will, on his terms — but just within the limits of the house. He still needs to be kept completely inside for a couple weeks even if he's not a completely indoor cat. This period of home detention helps him to start forming a bond with his new surroundings.

Trying to force a scared and stressed-out cat to do anything he doesn't want to is hazardous to your health. After you arrive at your new home, don't pull your cat out of his carrier. Instead, put the carrier in his safe room, open the carrier door, and let him come out into the room when he wants to — even if it's not for an hour or more. After he's a little calmer, you can coax him out with some fresh food or treats if you want, but don't rush him, and don't drag him out — or you may be bitten or scratched.

Figure 18-4:
Keeping
your cat
confined
before and
after you
move makes
the transi-
tion easier
and safer.

Leave the carrier, with the door open, in the safe room. It is the most familiar place in your new home in your cat's mind and will likely be his chosen spot for a while until this new house becomes his new home.

Moving to a new home is a great time to convert your cat to an indoor-only pet. In your old home, he'd complain to the skies if you denied him access to his outside territory (until he got used to the fact that you're not letting him out, that is). But in a new home, his new territory is what you let him have and no more. The transition to his being an indoor-only cat isn't very hard on either of you and is certainly better for your cat in the long run.

Anticipating problems

Starting your cat off in a safe room after a move offers another benefit. It gives you a chance to refresh his training about your house rules, especially regarding destructive clawing, urine spraying, and litter box avoidance — all behavioral problems that can spring up if your cat is stressed and disoriented.

By limiting your cat's options to the litter box and scratching post in his safe room, he quickly redevelops the good habits he had in your old home. After you start letting him out of the safe room to explore the rest of the house, add another litter box or two throughout the house to make the transition easier. You can gradually reduce the number of litter boxes later, after you're sure your pet's going where you want him to go.

Although your cat's likely to settle back into his old, good habits in a couple weeks if you keep him confined and allow him to relax, talk to your veterinarian about any problems that continue. Your cat may be ill, or he may need antianxiety medication to help him settle in. And don't forget to check out our advice on behavior problems in Chapters 14 and 15.

Allowing time for readjustment

Your cat probably needs a couple weeks to settle into his new routine — to come out of the safe room, become familiar with the house, and use his scratching post and litter box normally again. Don't rush him. Be observant of the signs that your cat is becoming less tentative and more confident in his explorations and, above all, don't allow him outside until he's comfortable with the inside of your house.

Cat body language can be very subtle. Learn how to tell when your cat's relaxed, playful, or unhappy by reading Chapter 7.

Lost . . . and found, we hope

Although any cat can turn up missing at any time, moving is a time to be especially vigilant in protecting your cat.

Preventing a missing cat is a lot easier than trying to find one, which is why confinement indoors — permanent, ideally — is the number one way to keep your cat from getting lost.

Even indoor cats can slip out, though, which is why all pets should carry a current ID tag on their collar and even an imbedded microchip for permanent ID. (See Chapter 8 for more information on both.) Another just-in-case measure: Keep good-quality pictures of your cat on hand in case you need to throw together a "lost cat" flier.

If your cat doesn't show up for dinner one night, don't just assume he's going to turn up in a day or so — take action! Place an ad in your local newspaper and create and distribute fliers that include the cat's picture, a description, and a reward, if you're offering one (and we recommend that you do).

Post the fliers around the neighborhood and take some to area shelters and veterinarians and especially to emergency clinics. Scan "found" ads in the paper and check the shelters every other day, in person.

Don't give up too soon: Pets have turned up weeks after their disappearance, so keep checking — and keep hoping.

If you plan to let your cat outside, take him out on a harness and leash and follow him around as he becomes familiar with the new area. Coax him back in by using praise and treats — let him walk in, if you can, instead of carrying him. Follow each outing with special play or petting time so that he develops a positive association with your new house and is therefore more likely to recognize it as home.

When is the right time to just let him loose? To be honest, it's always a gamble. Do your best to give your cat all the time he needs to settle in and then let him explore the outside for another week or more under your supervision. In the end, however, if you insist on letting your cat outdoors, you just must chance it and hope for the best. If you take the time your cat needs to adjust, he's probably going to stick around.

The home-again cat

Because cats bond to places as well as to people, some cat lovers find that their free-roaming pets keep showing up at their old home after a move, especially if the new home isn't more than a couple miles from the old one.

If your pet is one of these home-again cats, the best suggestion we have for you is to convert your cat to an indoor pet, because crossing streets to go "home" considerably ups his risk factor, which is already much higher than an indoor cat's. (See Chapters 8 and 23 for the gear you need to keep your cat happy indoors.)

If permanent confinement is not possible, bring your cat inside for another couple weeks — you may have let him outdoors too soon. Dedicate extra time to playing with him, especially interactive games such as a cat fishing pole or toy on a string. This extra time helps to relieve him of some of his stress or excess anxiety and helps him form new attachments to his new home and you in it. Because unneutered males roam the most, having your cat altered if you haven't already done so is also a good idea.

After you let your cat outdoors again, make sure the new people at your old home aren't encouraging your cat to stay. Ask them not to feed him or pet him and to use a squirt bottle or other deterrent if they see him around.

Gina has an interesting case of a "home-again cat" who believes that her home is still his. Fortunately, his new home is right next door. George, a marmalade tabby, was once owned by the former owners of Gina's house, who left him with the next-door neighbor after they moved. Although George and Gina's dog, Andy, are sworn enemies, the cat always knows when the dogs aren't home and Gina is — and he often pops in the pet door to say hello. Finding George's scent in the house later drives Andy crazy, which no doubt delights the gregarious tabby.

Part V
The Part of Tens

The 5th Wave   By Rich Tennant

"Well, she now claims she's a descendant of the royal Egyptian line of cats, but I'm not buying that just yet."

In this part . . .

This part has a little bit of everything, and is truly what is meant by the saying "last, but not least." In these chapters we debunk some old myths about cats, tell you how to protect your cat should a disaster strike your community, and clue you in to common dangers your pet may face in your own home. Then, just for fun, we take you on a tour of some of the best cat-related Web sites on the Internet and offer you some of the best things ever said about cats.

Chapter 19

Ten Cat Myths Debunked

*T*he cat was worshipped as a god in ancient Egypt, was vilified as a demon in medieval Europe, and is treasured as a companion around the world today. Despite the changes in our attitudes over the centuries, the cat herself is not much altered in form or temperament. She is much the same creature she was when first she chose to associate herself with our kind.

We now know more than ever before about our cats, but a surprising amount of information that's just plain *wrong* still hangs about in our culture. Worse, incorrect and oftentimes harmful old information keeps popping up in strange new places — such as on the Internet, or in movies.

Researching old ideas about cats is an interesting way to discover how our feline companions have been viewed throughout the ages, but in no way should these myths and legends take the place of modern knowledge in caring for your cat.

From the earliest mousers through the mysterious origins of the Manx and Maine Coon to the legends developing about cats today, Virginia C. Holmgren investigates them all in her fascinating book *Cats in Fact and Folklore* (IDG Books Worldwide, Inc.). Did the medieval church's hatred for cats — who were tortured and killed by the thousands — bring about the Great Plague after mouse and rat populations swelled without cats to keep them in check? Did cats live in the New World before the Europeans arrived? Holmgren answers "yes" to these questions and argues a myriad of other points in a most entertaining way.

Enjoy the old stories — they make fine reading with your cat on your lap on some wintry evening. But remember always to keep fact and fiction separate for the good of your cat.

Cats Have Nine Lives

Cats are survivors, no doubt of that. More so than any other domesticated animal, they keep their wildness about them, often approaching the line that separates the feral from the tame. On city streets and in country barns alike, cats live as they did thousands of years ago, dispatching rodents with efficiency, breeding prodigiously, and accepting whatever handouts come their way without giving up one ounce of their independence.

Many people work to make the lives of feral cats easier — and to bring those that can be tamed back into the loving companionship we humans can offer. Check out our information on feral cats — including how to tame and maintain them — in Chapter 4.

The efforts of humankind have changed cats' bodies hardly at all, except in the cases of the more extreme breeds of purebreds, such as the heavy-coated Persian and near-naked Sphynx, which are poorly equipped for a rough-and-tumble life. (Even these breeds show minor meddling compared to the changes we've put in place with purebred dogs!) The cat known commonly as an ordinary "alley cat" in the U.S. or "moggie" in the United Kingdom — and more formally as the *domestic shorthair* or *domestic longhair* — is seemingly well equipped to handle the challenges of outdoor life. Finely tuned to the slightest hint of danger, the not-so-ordinary "ordinary" cat can run fast, climb faster, and, if cornered by an adversary, defend himself with a formidable array of claws and teeth. The slender, lithe bodies of cats — celebrated in word and art throughout the centuries — can fit through the tiniest hole or balance on the most slender plank. And if his high-wire act isn't quite up to snuff, the cat can miraculously right himself on the way earthward, often landing unhurt and on his feet from a surprising height.

With so much going for them, is it any wonder people came to believe that cats had not one chance at life but nine?

The truth of the matter is that cats are more fragile than we think. Cats as a species have proven resilient, but as individuals, they are every bit as mortal as we ourselves are — and they are very vulnerable in the world. Although a well-cared-for indoor cat can live into his late teens, a cat exposed to the outdoor life is lucky to live a fraction as long. The dangers of modern life — cars, predators, ill-intentioned neighbors, communicable diseases — are just too many, and they claim the lives of even the more-street-smart cats by the thousands.

Cats have but one life, and they need our love and protection to make that life a long, healthy, and happy one.

For more on the controversy over indoor versus outdoor cats, see Chapter 1. For tips on how to make your home happier for your indoor cat, see Chapter 23, and for information on the best cat gear around, see Chapter 8. Some household hazards to avoid appear in Chapter 22.

Cats Need to Drink Milk

Gina's mother has a soft spot in her heart for a wandering cat, offering the wild ones who come up from the creek near her home a safe place to eat and drink and to watch the birds and squirrels that she also feeds. Her yard is a spa for wayward kitties, and one item on the menu is always milk. "Cats love milk," she says. "It must be good for them."

Cats *do* love milk, as anyone knows who's ever been around an old-fashioned cow barn at milking time — or seen one on TV, in the case of us city-folk. Cats young and old line up for a squirt of the real thing: warm, tasty, and oh-so-fresh. Mmmmm!

But is cow's milk the perfect food for cats? Not at all! Milk can prove a very messy proposition for you and your pet, producing an uncomfortable gastric disturbance and even diarrhea. Although that possibility may not bother Gina's mom, with her collection of half-wild wayfarers for whom the great outdoors is a litter box, it may bother you plenty if your kitty is an indoor cat and you must clean out the litter box (or a toilet location of which you don't approve).

Which is not to say milk is an absolute no-no for all cats. Mother's milk — from their own cat mama — is the perfect food for kittens, and while they're little, they get everything they need from it, including important antibodies. After the age of 12 weeks or so, however, some cats (like some people) lose the ability to digest the lactose in the milk; for those cats, milk isn't recommended. (If your cat's one of these, you'll most likely see signs in the litter box.) For cats who aren't lactose intolerant, though, milk can be a source of protein, minerals, and vitamins — although they'll also find those nutrients in a well-balanced commercial diet.

In the wild, kittens never drink milk after they're weaned, and yours have no reason to either. If your cat likes and can tolerate milk, however, feel free to offer it as an occasional treat — but remember that it's never a substitute for a proper diet or for fresh water. If you never, ever set a saucer of milk down for your pet, you may rest assured that he does just fine without.

Liquid nutrition is very important to orphaned kittens; in fact, getting handfed through a bottle is their only chance at survival! For more on what and how to feed a kitten in need, see Chapter 16.

Cats Purr Whenever They're Happy

Purring is one of the most special elements of a cat, as far as most humans are concerned. Caressing a purring pet has proven to relax the one doing the stroking and lower the blood pressure, too. A purring cat or kitten is sure to bring a smile to the face of any human, young or old, and cats have made a real difference in the lives of those in nursing homes or other institutional settings, just by the simple act of being a cat.

But careful observers of the cat know that purring isn't just a sound of contentment. Cats also purr if they're injured, while giving birth — even when dying. British zoologist Desmond Morris has observed that purring is "a sign of friendship — either when [the cat] is contented with a friend or when it is in need of friendship — as with a cat in trouble."

Our friend Dr. Margie Scherk, a board-certified specialist in feline health, likens a purr to the human smile. You smile when you're happy, to be sure, but you can also smile when nervous, or even when faced with a threat. In the latter two situations, it's kind of a "Hi, I'm a nice person, don't hurt me" sign. And the same is true with purring.

Kittens start purring even before they open their eyes, rumbling while nursing in what must be a reassuring sound to their mother — who's likely purring herself.

Our cats have one thing to lord over the "King of Beasts" and other more formidable felines. A cat can purr, but the lion can't, nor can any of the other big felines. The tiger can rumble a friendly greeting but only on the exhale. No big cat can get his motor running the way our household kitties can, purring constantly as effortlessly as breathing, both in and out. To even things out, however, big cats possess the ability to roar. On the whole, the little cat got the better part of that deal, at least where humans are concerned.

Although the experts are pretty clear on *why* cats purr, they're not yet certain as to *how*. The most common explanation has the sweet sound originating in the voicebox, with what are called the *vestibular folds,* or false vocal cords. The passing of air across these structures is thought to produce the purr all cat lovers adore.

Cats Eat Plants if They're Sick

Cats are so fond of chewing on greenery that many cat owners have widely assumed plants to be an important part of the feline diet. And the idea makes sense, too, if you look at all the undigested plant matter in the "gift" your cat leaves on your carpet (why never on the tile or hardwoods?) after a kitty barf-fest. You probably figure that your cat eats plants to help bring up what-ever's upsetting her tummy.

Although the experts debate how much plant matter is necessary in a cat's diet, one thing is obvious to anyone who's ever tried to maintain both house-plants and a house cat — kitties nibble on greens simply because *they love to*. For a cat, "just because" is usually reason enough.

For a discussion of what your cat needs to eat and why, check out Chapter 10. We also tell you which plants are cat-friendly in Chapter 10 and what you need to know about catnip in Chapter 8. Plants can be deadly, too; to avoid any cat-astrophes in your home, check out the list of toxic plants in Chapter 22.

Cats Are Dangerous around Babies

So many cats find themselves looking for new homes when a baby is expected that you could say babies are dangerous to cats!

You *don't* need to find a new home for your pet if you become pregnant, no matter what well-meaning relatives and friends may say to the contrary. Cats do *not* maliciously smother or suck the breath out of babies, as the myths hold. Still, to best protect your baby, you do need to be aware of the facts and exercise a little caution.

Cats don't suck the breath of infants, but the myth that they do probably came from their natural curiosity to investigate a new addition to the family, coupled with the tragedy of Sudden Infant Death Syndrome, or SIDS. We can easily understand how, hundreds of years ago, people may have seen a cat in the crib — perhaps sniffing at a baby's milk-scented breath — and later found a dead child and then tried to find an explanation for the loss by linking the two events.

Common sense dictates that no animal be left unattended with a small child. This advice is for your baby's protection *and* for your cat's. The Humane Society of the United States, which keeps statistics on injuries inflicted by ani-mals on people, knows of no documented case of a cat smothering an infant by resting on the child's face. Other experts, however, point out that such a sce-nario, although unlikely, is *not impossible* and suggest taking precautions — which makes perfect sense: You don't want your baby to be the first to be harmed in such a way.

After your child is older, you still want to remain on the lookout for problems. Toddlers don't understand that pets need gentle handling, and although most cats catch on very quickly to the notion that small children are best avoided, a possibility always exists that your pet, if cornered, could scratch or bite your child or even be hurt himself.

Cats are wonderful family pets, and don't let anyone tell you otherwise. A cat is the perfect pet for many families — a little more flexible and self-sufficient than a dog but still an affectionate and nonjudgmental companion. Just be aware that small children and cats have the potential to hurt each other; keep an eye on them while they're together.

Pregnancy and your cat

One reason that pregnant women are often advised to find a new home for their cats has to do with the transmission of the protozoan parasite *Toxoplasma gondii,* which causes the disease called *toxoplasmosis.*

The disease presents little danger to healthy human adults, but if a fetus contracts it through the placenta from a newly infected mother, he or she faces a risk of death or spontaneous abortion, as well as birth defects in those fetuses that survive. That's serious stuff, to be sure.

Cats are a cause for concern because they're an important part of the life cycle of this microscopic entity, shedding the creature in their feces at its infectious stage. Cats aren't the only way you may come in contact with the disease, however: Raw or poorly cooked meat is another.

About half the human population of the United States is already carrying the parasite. In any event, transmission of the parasites is oral — you become infected by eating the creatures by accident.

If you're already a carrier — your doctor can test you to see — you can't pass the parasite on to the child you're carrying. The danger is in becoming infected for the first time *while* you're pregnant.

The risk is great enough that pregnant women *must take precautions* to protect the child they carry. Ideally, someone else should take over the maintenance of the litter box for the duration of the pregnancy, and even before the pregnancy in the case of couples who are attempting to conceive.

If no one except you can maintain the litter box, wear gloves and a mask, dispose of the contents in sealed plastic, and then wash your hands thoroughly. Experts also recommend wearing gloves while gardening (to avoid cat feces in soil), keeping children's sandboxes covered when not in use, and keeping cats out of sandboxes.

These same precautions apply to people who have impaired immune systems, such as those who are HIV-positive or are receiving cancer treatments. Although healthy adults usually have no problems should they become infected, those with immune-system problems can be at grave risk. In some urban areas, well-organized volunteers take over the tasks of pet care, so the important social benefits of keeping a cat aren't overshadowed by the potentially dangerous physical ones.

If you have questions about your cat and toxoplasmosis, consult your physician, veterinarian, or local public health officials.

Cats Can Be Kept from Using Their Claws

Oh, don't you wish! Despite all efforts to keep cats from clawing up the furniture — and you can read about all of them in Chapter 14 — the best you can do for your cat and your possessions is redirect your pet's scratching effort, because he needs to scratch.

Scratching is an important part of feline behavior, as much a part of being a cat as purring. Scratching stretches your cat's muscles in ways that are both important and satisfying to him. Cats live in a world of smells, and marking things — including you — for their own is also very natural, important behavior. Digging claws into the corner of your sofa is one way your pet makes himself feel at home, leaving his own reassuring scent behind from scent glands in his feet.

Some have said that to live with a cat is to caress a tiger, and scratching is one trait your pet shares with all his wild kin. It's healthy and it's natural, and you *can* deal with it in a way that satisfies you both, likely *without* declawing, which is also discussed in Chapter 14, by the way.

A Well-Fed Cat Doesn't Hunt

The ability to hunt is hard-wired into all cats, but the level of desire varies by an individual's genetics and early experiences, not by the rumbling in his belly. The play of kittens is really hunting behavior. Pouncing and leaping on any little thing that moves, from your finger to a leaf, is an early sign of the prowess that has kept the welcome mat out for cats throughout human existence.

Although the desire to hunt may be undeniable, whether your cat *kills* may have more to do with hunger than anything else, argues zoologist Desmond Morris. He says that the cat's much-observed tendency to play with its prey is really a matter of the animal's not being hungry enough to eat it but still being instinctively driven to hunt. And so the cat pounces again and again. In mother cats, the desire to keep prey half-alive is based on her duties to her babies: She uses the little creature to teach them hunting skills.

And here's something really interesting: Morris argues that your cat is seeing you as a kitten if she brings freshly killed prey back to you. She recognizes that you're a hopeless hunter, and she's trying to help you out. What a sweetie!

The fact that you find such love offerings appalling are rather beside the point, and no amount of yelling can change your cat's behavior. (Punishment *never* works with cats, anyway, so don't bother.) Just do your very best to accept the gift as civilly and graciously as you can. Then dispose of the poor creature with all proper precautions — use a newspaper to pick it up, and wash your hands thoroughly afterward.

Hunting behavior in cats is very controversial, especially if the prey is songbirds or endangered rodent species. Fitting your cat's collar with a small bell or other noise-making device has little effect on his ability to hunt — cats learn to stalk without jostling the bell! Turning your cat into an indoor dweller is the only way to protect wildlife from him — and you from his thoughtful "gifts." An indoor cat is also protected from the harm that wildlife can do to *him* — transmit parasites and injure him with bites.

In Lancaster, England, a male tabby is touted as one of history's greatest mousers, catching more than 22,000 mice in 23 years. Another claim is made on behalf of a female tabby, also in England. She was said to have killed more than 12,000 rats in six years, or five or six rats a day. Both are amazing accomplishments, certainly, but we'd like to know one thing: Who on earth counted all those dead rodents?

Cat Fur Causes Allergies

If people are allergic to animals, their bodies are reacting not to fur but to proteins in skin secretions and saliva, commonly known as *dander*. These particles are applied generously to a cat's fur by the act of grooming and are liberally applied to every surface she rubs against. Every shake puts the particles airborne, where they're easily inhaled into the sensitive tissues of the lungs or sinuses.

More people are allergic to cats than to dogs, and the allergies to cats are often more severe. Some allergy experts have even gone so far as to theorize that the popularity of cats is one reason that asthma has become more prevalent — and dangerous — in recent years.

Myths persist about "hypoallergenic" breeds of cats, such as the nearly naked Sphynx or the lightly coated Devon or Cornish Rex. Many of these breeds are actively promoted by their fanciers as being good for allergy sufferers, but allergists argue otherwise. All warm-blooded pets have saliva and skin secretions; all warm-blooded pets, therefore, are potential problems for allergy sufferers. Believe us, we wish we could say otherwise. We'd love to get more cats into the homes of people who'll love them!

One the other side of the issue is this fascinating little tidbit: A study by Long Island College Hospital in Brooklyn, N.Y., suggests that darker cats are worse for allergy sufferers than their lighter-colored relatives. Don't take it too seriously yet, though: The study was with a small group of people, and the researchers themselves said more work was needed to show more definitively the connection between feline coat color and allergies.

Although it's probably not a great idea for people with the worst allergies, many cat lovers juggle allergies and cats pretty well. For some medical and housekeeping strategies that may make cat owning possible if you have allergies, see Chapter 1.

Black Cats Are Bad Luck

Black may be an unlucky color all right — for a cat. Black cats have been associated with the forces of evil for hundreds of years, and humane societies warn that this myth has cost many of them their lives. Black cats are often the targets of those who want to practice Satanic-like rituals that include the torture and killing of animals. Such horrors are especially clustered around Halloween, humane groups say, adding that the perpetrators aren't especially picky; if a black cat isn't available, any cat may serve their purposes in a pinch. So even if your cat usually chooses whether he's in or out, keep him inside until this particular holiday has passed.

Black may be an unfortunate color for another reason: visibility. Thousands of cats are killed by cars every year, and the difference between a hit or a near miss may be the driver's ability to see the cat darting across the road before him. At night, patches of light-colored fur are a distinct advantage to a kitty.

If a black cat crosses your path, are you likely to see this event as a sign of good or bad luck? Depends on where you live. In the United States, a black cat is typically thought to bring bad luck, but in England, the opposite is true. Although Americans tend to think that a black cat is a bad omen, the Brits believe that seeing "the devil" in person is a sign they've been spared any bad luck.

Either way, the claims that black cats have special powers for good or evil are nothing more than superstitions.

Figure 19-1:
How can anyone feel unlucky to have such a wonderful pet?

All Calicoes Are Female

Almost all calico (and tortoiseshell — often called *torties*) cats are female, but not quite all. According to a study by the College of Veterinary Medicine at the University of Missouri, about 1 in 3,000 so-marked cats are male . . . well, sort of.

The gene that governs how the red/orange color in cats displays is on the X, or female, chromosome. Any cat, male or female, can be orange, but in males, that color is usually expressed in one way: the tabby pattern, often called a "ginger tom" or marmalade tabby. Females, however, can be red tabbies, torties, or calicoes. (The last two are genetically similar, except that the calico has patches of color and white spotting, while the colors of the tortie are swirled together.)

Because red females are divided among calicoes, torties, and tabbies, people often think that most red tabbies are males, and statistically, males do make up the majority of red tabbies. But for females to be red tabbies is a lot more common than for males to be either calicoes or torties.

That's because, for a cat to be a calico or tortoiseshell, it must have two X chromosomes, which means that, in the overwhelming majority of cases, the animal is female. If the calico or tortoiseshell pattern exists in males, the reason is that the cat actually has an extra chromosome — two X and one Y — a genetic rarity that occasionally pops up in cats (and in people, too). These so-called *Klinefelter* males are usually — but not always — sterile.

Chapter 20

Ten Things to Know in Case of Disaster

In This Chapter

▶ Planning for the worst

▶ Working with your veterinarian

▶ Putting together a disaster kit

▶ Preparing to help others

*H*urricanes, earthquakes, floods, twisters, fires, and even volcanoes have brought home to us all in recent years that a disaster can happen at any time, to any community. In the aftermath of such natural calamities has come a new awareness of the need for disaster planning for our pets, both on a community level and in our own homes.

Although animals aren't allowed in most disaster-relief shelters, an increasing number of animal shelters and veterinarians are better prepared now than ever before to take in animals during an emergency.

Some regional veterinary associations work to appoint a volunteer veterinarian in each community to help coordinate animal-relief efforts. And veterinarians certainly aren't alone in the effort to help animals when a disaster strikes. Probably the most influential group in the field of animal disaster relief is the Emergency Animal Rescue Service, a group based in Sacramento, California, that is prepared to do for animals what the Red Cross does for people. EARS-trained volunteers have worked on behalf of animals all over the world.

Terri Crisp, founder of the Emergency Animal Rescue Service, has done more than any other person to change how animals are dealt with in times of disaster. Her story is a compelling read for any animal lover, and she shares it in her book *Out of Harm's Way: The Extraordinary True Story of One Woman's Lifelong Devotion to Animal Rescue* (Pocket Books).

Behind the big changes of recent years is a growing realization that animals need help, too, and that some people choose to put their lives in danger rather than abandon their pets.

Just as you can't leave preparing for your human family members to chance, you need a plan to ensure the safety of your cats (and other animals!). Living in California, we've seen plenty of disasters — fires, floods, earthquakes, and more. We're believers in disaster preparation, and we want you to be, too.

Have a Plan

Prepare for all possibilities, including that you may be away from home when disaster strikes. Make sure that everyone in your family — children included — is prepared in the event of an emergency. Make a plan and go over it until everyone knows what to do.

People need to rely on each other during emergencies, and this fact is just as true for your pets. Get to know your neighbors, and put a plan in place to help each other out. Find out from local shelters and veterinary organizations what their emergency response plans are and how you fit into those plans in case of a disaster.

Ask your veterinarian whether he has a disaster plan and how he plans to work with other veterinarians in an emergency. If he's never thought about the situation, pushing him a little on the subject doesn't hurt.

Corral Your Cat

Obviously, you're not going to get advance warning of some disasters, such as earthquakes. But if you know that a worrisome tropical storm is just off the coast or that the rivers are starting to rise, find your cat, *now!*

Even if your cat is a "combo kitty" — coming and going as she pleases — make her an indoor one while trouble is in the air. If you leave your cat outside to fend for herself during a disaster, she's going to run and hide as best she can; in the aftermath, she may not be able to find her way home through the mess — and you may not be there even if she *can* find her way home.

You can't evacuate a cat you can't find, so know where yours is so that you can put her in a carrier whenever you think you may need to leave in a hurry.

Maintain Your Cat's ID

Most animals survive a disaster, but too many never see their families again. That's because many pets aren't equipped with a way to determine which pet belongs to which family. Pets should always wear a collar and identification tags. Better still is a permanent identification that can't slip off, such as an imbedded microchip.

Keep temporary ID tags at hand, too, to put on your pet if you're forced to evacuate. (Your pet's permanent ID isn't much use if you aren't home to answer the phone, if you even still have a phone or a home.) One of the best tips we can offer on temporary ID is to keep cheap key tags around the house. You can jot your temporary number on the tag, slip it into a plastic housing, and then attach it to your pet's collar.

A lot of people refuse to put a collar on their cats, worried that the kitty may get caught on some branch while jumping and then strangle. Others find that their cats give so many collars the slip that these owners give up trying to keep collars on their pets.

Figure 20-1:
You have a much better chance of being reunited with your cat if he's wearing a collar with ID tags.

Dante/Photo by Heather Dinsmore

A collar can save your pet's life. Remember these words from an animal-control officer: "Every day, I put to death a dozen lost kitties who obviously belong to someone — animals we can't match up with the families who're missing them. I wish they had collars and tags, so I could locate their owners. I've put to death more lost pets than I can count, but I've never, ever been called out to remove the body of a cat hanging by his collar in a tree."

Equipping your cat with a collar, tags, and a microchip are among the most important safety measures you can take on your cat's behalf. Find out more about these items in Chapter 8.

Keep Preventive Care Measures and Health Records Current

Infectious diseases can spread from cat to cat in the high-stress environment of an emergency shelter, which is why keeping pets' immunity against disease up-to-date with vaccinations as your veterinarian recommends is essential.

Prepare a file with up-to-date medical and vaccination records, your pets' microchip numbers, your veterinarian's phone number and address, feeding and medication instructions, and recent pictures of your animals. Trade copies of emergency files with another pet-loving friend; having someone else who knows about your pet is a good idea should *anything* happen to you.

The routine vaccination of cats against all potential diseases is a matter of much discussion in the veterinary and cat-owning community today. Find out what you need to know about vaccines, the diseases they prevent, and those they may cause in Chapter 11.

Have Restraints Ready

Even normally laid-back cats can freak if they're stressed. If you don't want to get bitten or clawed, be prepared to restrain your pet — for your pet's safety as well as your own.

Keep carriers and other forms of restraint ready for emergencies. *Ready* means *at hand* — the means to transport your pet shouldn't be something you need to find in an out-of-the-way storage area.

Cat carriers are probably the least-thought-of pieces of emergency equipment for pet owners — but are among the most important. Sturdy carriers keep pets safe and give rescuers more options in housing pets. They give *you* more options, too, in the homes of friends or relatives or in shelters outside of the area. Depending on weather conditions, you may also safely leave pets in their carriers overnight in vehicles in an emergency.

Sturdy, cat-sized carriers belong on the list of "must-haves," and even a top-quality one made of high-impact plastic — which we recommend over cardboard — doesn't even cost you as much as a fancy meal out: around $25, tops. And the carrier lasts forever. If you are hesitant to use a carrier because it's always a fight to get your cat in it, don't be. Cats who resist getting in the carrier at home often find it the most comforting retreat during times of stress or when away from home. To them it represents the "way home." For more on choosing the right carrier for your cat, see Chapter 8.

A terrified cat is a danger to anyone who tries to handle her — a whirling menace of flying claws and slashing teeth. Make sure that restraints and a muzzle are part of your emergency-care kit. Cat muzzles are made to fit comfortably over the entire face, including the eyes. A soft restraint designed for cats is a comfortable way to secure an unhappy cat: These cloth accessories enclose the body but provide select access through a handful of well-positioned openings in case your cat needs emergency treatment (or even just a nail trim). Many a pillow case has served as an emergency cat carrier, as well. If nothing else, throw a large old bath towel in with your emergency supplies. In a pinch, you can wrap up a panicky cat in that with no harm to either one of you.

If you need to hold onto a cat in an emergency, grasp him firmly behind the neck in a hold that veterinarians call *scruffing*. You can find out more about proper handling techniques for your cat in Chapter 6.

Figure 20-2:
In an emergency, you can restrain your cat by "scruffing" him. A muzzle is another item that's a must-have for your emergency kit.

Rotate the Supplies Your Cat Needs

Keep several days' worth of food and safe drinking water as well as any necessary medicines packed and ready to go in the event of a disaster. Rotate your supplies so they don't get stale. If your pet eats canned food, keep an extra can opener and spoon tucked in among the emergency supplies — or use cans with flip-top lids.

Your emergency kit should also include disposable litter boxes and at least a week's supply of litter, as well as a litter scoop and sealable plastic bags for disposing of the waste.

Keep First-Aid Supplies on Hand — with Directions

Pet-supply stores sell ready-made first-aid kits, or you can put your own together fairly easily. Remember to keep the kit stocked and keep it handy.

Keep a first-aid book with your supplies, but give the book a quick read before you store it so you have a passing familiarity with what to do in case of a feline health emergency. Most of these books include a list of the supplies you need to have on hand.

PET-PAK, Inc., manufactures animal first-aid kits in five sizes, all neatly packed in a plastic container. (The four largest have handles.) The kit contains the basics for emergency care, along with a pamphlet on using the supplies. For more information, see the Additional Resources appendix.

Know the Locations of Nearby Veterinary Hospitals and Other Animal Services

Your veterinary hospital may become damaged in the disaster, which is why having some backup plans for boarding and care is a good idea. Know where to find other veterinary hospitals in your area, as well as animal shelters and animal-control facilities. Boarding facilities should also be noted, as well as groomers — all these places may be able to help out in a pinch. Photocopy the appropriate pages from your local yellow pages, or compile and print a list on your home computer. Then tuck the list in with your emergency supplies.

If you lose your pet, you can also check with these facilities in hope that she turns up at one of them.

Keep a "Lost Kitty" Kit Ready

In case of a disaster, you may not be able to get flyers made, so prepare some generic ones and keep them with your emergency supplies. In the biggest type size you can, center the words "LOST CAT," along with a good-quality picture of your pet. Below the picture include a description of your pet, along with any identifying marks, and leave a space to add the phone number where you can be reached, as well as any backup contacts, friends, relatives, neighbors, or your veterinarian. Print up 100 copies and keep them in a safe, dry, and accessible place.

A staple gun allows you to post your notices; keep one loaded and with your supplies, along with thumbtacks and electrical tape.

If your cat becomes lost, post flyers in your neighborhood and beyond, and distribute them at veterinary hospitals and shelters. Although relying on the kindness of strangers is nice, offering a reward makes many strangers just a little bit kinder.

Be Prepared to Help Others

You may be lucky to survive a disaster nearly untouched, but others in your community may not be so fortunate. Contact your local humane society and veterinary organization now to train as a volunteer so that you can help out in a pinch. Disaster-relief workers do everything from distributing food to stranded animals to helping reunite pets with their families — and finding new homes for those who need them.

Volunteering in a pinch is not only a good thing to do — it feels good, and it's the *right thing* for anyone who cares about animals and people.

Chapter 21

Ten Cat-Related Attractions on the Information Superhighway

In This Chapter

▶ Web browser's delights

▶ Cat pictures by the millions

▶ Pampered cats — and needy ones

▶ Goodies galore

▶ A place for remembering

*F*irst, a confession: We're serious online geeks. Paul has spent more than a decade building and running the Veterinary Information Network, Inc. (`www.vin.com`), the world's largest online service for veterinary professionals and the content provider for VIN-sponsored Pet Care Forum (`www.vin.com/ petcare`). And Gina uses the Internet to do research and to stay in touch with animal-loving friends and fellow writers around the world. And a lot of what she writes ends up online, on the Pet Care Forum and on the Pets.com website.

Still, the worldwide network of computers we all know now as the Internet is an incredible resource for any cat lover, not just longtime computer geeks like we are. With a computer and a modem to hook into your phone line, you can shop for your cat, research breeds and health topics, enjoy some kitty humor, or just plain look at cat pictures, of which the Internet seems to have millions — and the numbers climb every minute. *Internet for Cats* (No Starch Press) author Judy Heim observes: "There's a popular saying on the Internet: No one knows you're a dog, but everyone knows what your cat looks like."

One of the easiest ways for beginners to poke around is to use the graphical part of the Net, called the World Wide Web. We also think you might enjoy joining an e-mail list, which is an online discussion group dealing with a specific topic — a breed of cat, for example, or holistic cat care. Arguably the largest collection of e-mail lists can be found at the Onelist Web site (`www.onelist.com`). Just enter "cat" in the site's search engine and join the groups that interest you.

A list of ten sites can't begin to hit all the best cat sites on the Web. A hundred wouldn't do the job, nor would a thousand. If you feed the word *cat* into any search engine, a site that searches the Web, you'll find that the subject triggers millions of suggested places to look on the Web. And that's just when *we* did it. By the time you read this book, you're likely to find millions more such references, such is the Internet's speed of growth. If sex-related topics are the No. 1 draw on the Internet, we think that you can make a good case that cats are No. 2.

Try out our humble offerings and don't be shy about exploring on your own. Many pages offer connections, called *links,* that take you to other cat sites if you click them with your mouse; in fact, some pages are nothing *but* links. Curiosity may have killed the cat, but it never hurt a Web browser. Following some of these links can turn up some real gems.

Don't forget to make sure your cat is comfortably settled in your lap as you begin. And please forgive us if some of the Web sites we offer are missing. The Internet is a very fast-changing place, remember. You should be able to locate sites that have moved by using any search engine.

A Link for Everyone

The Cat Fanciers site (at www.fanciers.com) is the best starting place on the Web for cat lovers. This site is page after page after page of links to breed descriptions, general information, cat clubs, cat shows and registries, veterinary medical resources, breeders, rescuers and shelters, and every other cat-related site the creators of the page could find.

Cat Fanciers is a real treasure trove, no doubt about it, assembled by people who love and respect cats and want the very best information on them made available to us all. Bravo!

You could spend weeks exploring all the links — and the links' links — from the Cat Fanciers site, including one to the Federazione Italiana Associazioni Feline (which Gina uses her college Italian to translate as "Italian Cat Page" . . . or something like that).

In any case, set up your unlimited-time Internet account before heading to the Fanciers site, because time surely does fly when you're having the kind of fun we had reading it.

When exploring the Fanciers site, be sure to click on the collection of cat FAQs (that's Internet-speak for Frequently Asked Questions). The FAQs here are a repository of knowledge and fun information that has been building since before most people had even heard of the Internet. You can access the FAQs directly at www.fanciers.com/cat-faqs/.

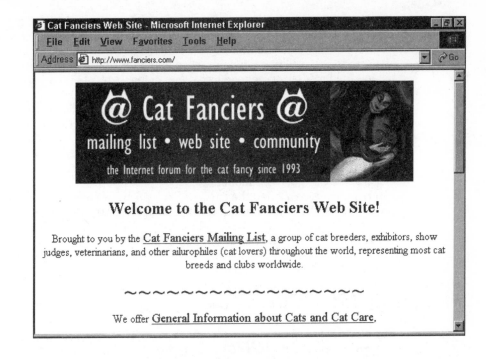

Pictures! Get Your Cat Pictures Here!

"The Web was originally designed to make it easier for scientists to send information to each other," explains humorist John Scalzi, "but the minute they figured how to send pictures through the pipe, you just know that some scientist posted the Very First Cat Picture on the Web." And your point, John?

Because so many cat pictures are on the Web, we're guessing you could spend the rest of your life looking at them and not see them all. Fat cats. Skinny cats. Young and old, of every imaginable color and pose and background. Cats on couches; cats on cars; cats in laundry hampers. *Meow!*

Almost any cat-related site has cat pictures, and even those that don't have pictures link to other sites that do. We decided that our favorite was Cat Delight (at www.dell.homestead.com/cat/home.html). And we're not alone: Thousands of people dropped in before us, and many of them left pictures of their own cats behind. You can, too.

You don't need an excuse to enjoy this site. Or to put your own cat out there for everyone to see, because, be honest, doesn't the world deserve to see your cat? How can you deny people such joy? Your cat is likely to get tired of looking at other cats long before you do. If that happens, check out, with your cat, Lil' Fishies Cam (at www.riebesell.net/cam/), a constantly changing view of aquariums full of real, plump — and probably yummy — fish.

Little Cat Laughs — and Big Ones, Too

Living with cats will fine-tune any sense of humor, and we can tell the folks behind the ErotiCat Homepage have been living with cats for a very, very long time.

The site, `home.ican.net/~otiss/menu/menu.html`, is a G-rated send-up of the Internet's oh-so ubiquitous sex sites, with a kitty twist. ErotiCat breathlessly exposes such "scandals" as people who sleep with their cats (er . . . on the bed, we mean) and offers lots of pictures of naked cats — yes, with no clothes at all! — getting affectionate.

A very clever site in all, and full of lots of beautiful cats. But what would you expect for a site dedicated to "celebrat[ing] the eternal and sensuous beauty of the feline form"? A higher calling, we've never heard of.

A Place for Pedigrees

The world is full of cat registries, and you can link to many of them from the Fanciers directory, mentioned in the section "A Link for Everyone," earlier in this chapter. The Cat Fanciers' Association — no relation to the Fanciers Web site — is the world's largest registry of pedigreed cats, and its Web site (at `www.cfainc.org/cfa`) deserves a visit.

Everything you want to know about pedigreed cats you can find there: official CFA breed standards, pictures of top-winning cats, cat-care guidelines, and a tour of the organization and what it stands for. A pretty basic site, to be sure, but if you're interested in pedigreed cats, this one is a great place to visit.

You can jump from the CFA site to the related Winn Feline Foundation, or you can go there directly by pointing your browser to `www.winnfelinehealth.org`. The foundation is an important source of funding for research into cat health. We encourage you to check out this worthwhile organization.

Help for the Homeless

Feral cats are everywhere, from the alleyways of big cities such as London, Rome, and New York to the edges of rural encampments everywhere. Ferals are domestic cats gone wild — former pets and the offspring of former pets: animals abandoned in the mistaken belief that cats can fend for themselves.

They can't. Ferals survive by scavenging, by hunting, and by handouts, but no individual cat can live this life for very long. They die miserably, and they die young.

Alley Cat Allies is a group that's trying to deal with the problem by stabilizing feral populations through its catch, neuter, and release program. As do many feral cat advocates, they argue that maintaining stable, nonbreeding colonies of cats is a more humane and cost-effective way of dealing with the problem than the constant effort people expend to exterminate wild cats.

The coalition's Web site (at www.alleycat.org) is a resource for those who feel the same way, with information on why the trap, neuter, and release program is a viable solution, along with articles on how to set up such a program in your community. The site also contains fact sheets for veterinarians on how to treat ferals and information on rabies, trapping, and relocation. The site's a must-see for the compassionate cat lover. Another great resource on feral cats can be found at the Web site of San Diego's Feral Cat Coalition (www.feralcat.com).

These sites are marvelous, but don't forget that we've put lots of information on helping feral cats in our own Chapter 4. Attitudes toward homeless pets of all kinds have been undergoing a dramatic change with the spread of the no-kill shelter movement.

In the forefront of all these changes is Maddies Fund, a foundation that seeks to help communities with no-kill solutions. Maddies Fund also has a Web site that's jam-packed with excellent information on reducing the number of homeless animals. It's a must-see Web site, at www.maddiesfund.org.

Where Tradition Lives On

You don't need to be much more than a casual observer to have noticed that fashions change in cats as well as in clothing. And in no case is this change more apparent than with the Siamese.

A few decades ago, the Siamese was a robust creature, with a solid body and an "apple head," as its fanciers described it. That cat is a far cry from the Siamese shown today, a slender creature with a wedge-shaped head. The only apparent similarities between the two styles is the cats' "chattiness" and the characteristic Siamese markings: light-colored body with darker "points" on the face, ears, legs, and tail.

The change was not popular with some people, and one of them, Diana Fineran, decided to do something about the situation. In 1987, she started working for the preservation of the "traditional" Siamese, which she believed was not only more attractive but also healthier. She found some breeders with "apple head" Siamese and put together an organization, the Traditional Cat Association, to support them. The association now also includes "traditional" Burmese, Colorpoint Shorthairs, Persians (which have gone from the older, "doll-faced" variety toward extremely short-faced cats with health problems), Himalayans, Bengals, Nebelungs, and Chantilly/Tiffanys.

The TCA Web site (at www.tcainc.org) offers standards for the older types of these breeds, as well as pictures, breeder referrals, and membership information.

For Serious Lovers of Cats and Books

Annette K. Gaskins is a book hound, if you'll pardon the description, and a very dedicated cat lover. She has combined her two loves in her "Cat Lover's Bibliography" site (at www.fanciers.com/other-faqs/gaskins-bib.html).

The page is the perfect spot to visit if you're planning a trip to the library or attempting to expand your home reference collection on cats. Her lists are fairly extensive and include both fiction and nonfiction, as well as magazines, videotapes, and cat organizations. It's not complete, to be sure (this book isn't in it, for example!), but it's a great start to finding out what's available to cat lovers.

Because Gina loves reading fiction about animals, she especially appreciated the list of cat-related mystery writers (although she'd add the *Midnight Louie* series from Carol Nelson Douglas to the page, as well as the works of Shirley Rousseau Murphy). The listings of cat books with poems, biographies, pictures, essays, and humor are commendable, as is Gaskins's research into basic care and training books.

The willingness to share information in the online community is one of the best things about the Internet, and to find such a generous effort on behalf of cats and those who love them is really inspiring. Good job!

Veterinary Resources

As mentioned early in this chapter, Paul runs the Veterinary Information Network, Inc., an online service that offers its subscribing veterinary professionals access to continuing education, top-quality specialty consultants, bulletin boards for discussing cases with colleagues, and searchable databases of dozens of professional journals. Through the Pet Care Forum (www.vin.com/petcare), these professionals share their veterinary expertise with pet lovers, especially in The Veterinary Hospital, where veterinarians respond to questions on the many bulletin boards.

Probably the best-known veterinary site on the Web is NetVet (at netvet .wustl.edu/vet.htm), put together by Dr. Ken Boschert, a veterinarian in Washington University's division of comparative medicine, in St. Louis, Missouri. His cat section offers a lot of solid information and many good links.

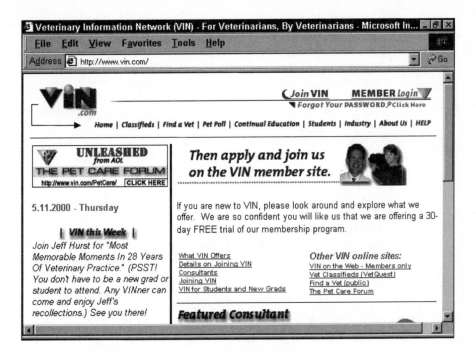

Two other sites are worth exploring. The first is the U.S. Food and Drug Administration's Center for Veterinary Medicine (at `www.fda.gov/cvm`), which keeps its visitors up-to-date on the latest approved drugs for veterinary uses. The site also offers links to other animal-related government resources, as well as U.S. colleges of veterinary medicine. (The colleges themselves often offer links to veterinary schools worldwide.)

Shopping for Kitty

Enough of this serious stuff! Time to go shopping. You can find almost as many cat-toy vendors on the Web as you can cat pictures, and you can get a list of these sites from the Cat Fanciers site or find links to them from practically every other cat site on the Web. You can also put the words *cat* and *toy* into a search engine and let it rip.

Since we wrote our first edition of this book, the online retail world has gone mad with huge and well-funded Web sites such as `pets.com` and `petsmart.com`. (Gina's an essayist for `pets.com`.) These sites are hotly competitive, to say the least, and we're glad to see them in the mix.

With their multi-gazillion-dollar advertising budgets, they don't need our help in promoting them. So we also want to draw your attention to a couple small niche players we've enjoyed buying from over the years.

Cat Faeries (at www.catfaeries.com) was one of the first shopping sites on the Internet for cat lovers, dating back to the dark ages of 1993. We like the site not only because it's cool (which it is) and because it offers cool toys (which it does) but also because we like Gail Colombo, the person who makes it all go. Gina met Gail at the Cat Fanciers' Association International show and knew in a second that Gail was a cat-loving woman — and not just because she was wearing a fuzzy cat-shaped backpack. Cats adore her, and the feeling is clearly mutual, as her well-chosen collection of fabulous cat toys and accessories attests. Cat Faeries stocks organic catnip, and each order comes with a note from the boss, Betty the Rushin' Blue cybercat (pictures of whom appear on the site, of course!).

Fat Cat, Inc., (at www.kittyhoots.com), has a motto you just gotta love: "We're a company dedicated to making the cats of the world happy — oh, and we make cat toys too!" This sleek site has a great collection of cool cat toys, including those in the shape of prey, politicians, or dogs. Would your kitty like Toss Perot or Revenge Rover? You may need to get them both to find out.

A Memorial Space

One of the saddest places to find cat pictures on the Web is on sites dedicated to the memory of beloved pets who've passed on. We found such places sad, true, but we also found them beautiful and inspiring. One such site is the Rainbow Bridge Tribute Pages (at /rainbow-bridge.org/bridge.htm).

The Rainbow Bridge refers to a lovely story that has given many pet lovers comfort over the years. After our animal companions die, the story goes, they're restored to health and vigor and are well cared for in a special place. They're happy, except for the fact that they miss us. After we die, we see them again and cross the Rainbow Bridge together.

A wonderful story, and we hope it's true, for we'd like to see many, many animals again.

The site offers stories, poems, and pictures, each and every one guaranteed to tug at your heartstrings. The last page notes that this site was "made with love," and we have no doubt about that. Creators Meggie O'Brien and Kathie Maffit are providing a much-needed service to us all.

Cats 'n' computers

Two products are custom-made for cat-loving computer jockeys. The first is Catz, a software package that produces an interactive pet to live in your computer. You choose a kitten to adopt from a handful of contenders and give him a name. You can pet him, feed him, play fetch, or take his picture. It's all great fun! To order, visit the company's Web site at www.pfmagic.com or check with your local computer store.

A good deal and a good deed are the outcome if you order the second product, the Computa-Cat poster from the San Francisco Society for the Prevention of Cruelty to Animals. Originally designed to promote adoptions, the work — designed and written by Paul Glassner — is a clever homage to computer advertising. A handsome tabby is in the middle of the poster, surrounded by a "product description," such as the following description for the cat brain: "Semi-programmable. Central Control Unit functions independently." The Computa-Cat poster is $17 from the SFSPCA, 2500 16th Street, San Francisco, CA 94103. Proceeds go to the society's programs for helping animals and people. You can see the poster on the group's Web site, at www.sfspca.org.

Chapter 22

Ten Common Household Dangers to Your Cat

In This Chapter

▶ Protecting against poisons

▶ Ties that bind — up

▶ Avoiding two-ton hazards

▶ Looking out for two-legged trouble

*O*ur friends who work as critical care veterinarians have seen every imaginable problem a cat can get into.

They see people who bring in healthy pets with minor health problems — such as worms — that could wait for morning or even next week. They see people who bring in their ancient or terminally ill pets late at night to be put to sleep, because after they finally make this heart-breaking decision, they want to act on it. They see cats mauled by dogs, by wild animals such as coyotes, or by other cats. They see cats sick with feline leukemia. They even see animals deliberately injured by people — shot with BB guns, set afire, kicked in the ribs. A lot of what they see, incidentally, is as good an argument as you could possibly find for keeping your cat indoors.

Although every animal lost is a tragedy, some of those are a little harder to take than others. Into this class falls those pets whose deaths were the results of something an owner could have done to protect them but didn't know about.

We want you to know about them, so we've assembled in this chapter the most common household dangers your cat may face. Forewarned is forearmed, we believe. So read this chapter, and do your best to protect your cat from these avoidable dangers.

What constitutes a veterinary emergency? Chapter 11 offers the information you need to make the decision that may save your cat's life. Find out when your cat needs a veterinarian's help now — and what can safely wait until morning.

Strings and Similar Things

What would you call a kitten with a ball of yarn? A perfect time to reach for your camera? How about an accident waiting to happen?

Kittens and cats love playing with yarn, as well as string, ribbon, and anything that twists and dances. They like to stalk, to pounce, to flip their slender prey in the air, and to start stalking again. That's all good, clean fun, but there's always a chance that your cat won't stop with play and will decide to eat his plaything. And that's where the fun stops, because any sort of yarn, ribbon, Christmas tinsel, or string can cause havoc in your cat's intestines, causing a problem that may need to be surgically treated.

If you knit or sew, put your supplies securely away after you're done with them, and if you're opening or wrapping packages, clean up after you're done. Packing material such as foam peanuts can be a health hazard for your pet, too.

Even if your pet's not really the playful type, she may find one kind of string irresistible: juice-soaked string from a roast or turkey. Dispose of these tempting dangers carefully, putting them in a container your cat can't get into.

Everything you need to know about safe playthings for your pet is in Chapter 8. We even include suggestions for cat-friendly freebies!

Figure 22-1:
Cats love to play with strings and ribbons, but you shouldn't let them do so unsupervised.

Nick/Photo by Angie Hunckler

A Shocking Experience

Chewing on electrical cords is more of a risk for inquisitive kittens, but protecting your grown-up cat against them wouldn't hurt either. Tuck cords out of the way, and if you notice any you can't hide and that are attracting kitty teeth, coat them in something nasty, such as Bitter Apple (available at pet-supply stores) to convince your cat or kitten to chomp elsewhere.

Cords aren't the only things cats love to chew on — some are especially drawn to wool fabrics. For help with getting your pet to leave your sweaters (and other cloth objects) alone, see Chapter 14. More on kitten-proofing your home is in Chapter 6.

The Warm and Deadly Dryer

Cats love warm, dark hiding places, and a dryer full of freshly dried clothes is a favorite spot of many. So what's the worry? Some cats have been killed after their owners have accidentally closed and turned on a dryer with a sleeping cat inside.

Sounds implausible, you say? You'd be surprised how often cats are killed this way, and surprised, too, at how easily you can throw a few extra clothes in, close the door, and turn on the dryer without noticing your cat is inside. One of Gina's friends lost his cat in just such a way.

Prevention is simple, but must be practiced by your whole family to be effective. Keep the dryer door closed and make sure whoever's doing the laundry knows to always check for your cat — just in case. Keep an eye out, too, in the washer, dishwasher, or oven. This situation is one case in which the saying "curiosity killed the cat" can prove to be tragically true.

If you find your cat in the dryer, oven, washing machine, or dishwasher, take a deep breath and do something that seems cruel but has your cat's best interest at heart: Scare the fur off him. Close the door with him inside, and then pound on the appliance for a few seconds, making a racket that could wake the dead. Then open the door and let him make his escape. You can't always be sure everyone in your house remembers to keep appliance doors closed or checks for a cat before hitting the "on" switch. Convincing your cat to avoid such sleeping places provides another kind of insurance against tragedy. We wouldn't suggest such drastic measures if it weren't such a horrible way to die.

Figure 22-2: Cats are drawn to the warmth of the dryer, but this is one hiding place that can be deadly. Keep the dryer door closed at all times, and always check for your cat before turning on the appliance.

Bitsy Bob/Photo by Johanna Bader

Pain Medicines That Kill

Here's an easy rule to remember: Never give your cat *any* medication without clearing it with your veterinarian first.

That's a good rule to remember in general, but in particular, it applies to painkillers. Although you can safely give aspirin to arthritic dogs, the smaller size and different metabolism of cats make aspirin a dangerous proposition for them. Acetaminophen, the active ingredient in Tylenol, can kill your cat, as can some of the newer, longer-lasting painkillers available in nonprescription form for human use.

If your cat is in pain, call your veterinarian immediately. Cats are very stoic, and if you're noticing your pet's discomfort, he's really suffering and needs immediate care. As for chronic pain, your veterinarian can prescribe something that's effective and cat-safe.

Attack of the Killer Plants

Cats love to nosh greenery. Some experts suggest that cats crave the half-digested plant matter that they'd find in the bellies of their vegetarian prey, but just as good an explanation is that cats eat plants simply because they *want* to.

Indulge your cat with plants he can nibble on — the elements of a cat-friendly garden appear in Chapter 10 — but make sure he isn't munching on anything that can make him sick. You can discourage cats from chewing on house-plants — you find some tips in Chapter 14 — but you can't guarantee they'll leave them alone. Your best bet is to make sure that anything your cat can get into isn't going to hurt him.

Although you obviously can't control what your outside cat is eating on his rambles, you should be aware of signs of illness. Check them out in Chapter 11.

The poinsettia has long been considered a poisonous plant, but that's no longer thought to be the case. No less an authority than the National Animal Poison Control Center says that the holiday plant is no longer considered deadly, although ingesting a considerable amount of it may still give your cat a tummy ache.

Garage Dangers

Most people just aren't very neat in their garages. In addition to ignoring the drips and puddles coming from their cars — which can include deadly antifreeze, of course — folks can be careless about storing insecticides, paints, cleaning supplies, and fertilizers, all of which can be toxic.

Although cats are considerably more discriminating in what they eat than dogs are, making sure you safely store household chemicals and clean up all spills promptly is still a good idea.

Another garage danger: the door. A garage door in the open position makes a nifty high hiding place for a cat, but that secure perch can injure your pet if you set the door in motion while he's there.

And while you're at it, don't forget to check out other places cats get into — and sometimes shut up in — such as basements and closets.

Toxic plants

Cats can be deadly to plants, but more than a few plants are quite capable of getting revenge. The ASPCA/National Animal Poison Control Center, a resource for veterinarians, says this list contains some of the bad seeds. Most "just" make your pet sick, but a few of them can kill. If your pet has tangled with any of these, call your veterinarian. And don't forget: Even "good" plants can cause problems if they've been sprayed with insecticide.

Aloe Vera (Medicine Plant)
Amaryllis
Andromeda Japonica
Apple (seeds)
Apricot (pit)
Asparagus Fern
Autumn Crocus
Avocado (fruit and pit)
Azalea
Baby Doll Ti
Baby's Breath
Bird of Paradise
Bittersweet
Branching Ivy
Buckeye
Buddhist Pine
Caladium
Calla Lily
Castor Bean
Ceriman
Cherry (wilting leaves and seeds)
China Doll
Chinese Evergreen
Christmas Cactus
Christmas Rose
Chrysanthemum
Cineraria
Clematis
Cordatum
Corn Plant (all Dracaena species)
Crown Vetch
Cyclamen
Daffodil
Daisy
Day Lily
Devil's Ivy

Dieffenbachia (all varieties; commonly called Dumb Cane)
Dracaena Palm
Dragon Tree
Elephant Ears
Emerald Feather
English Ivy
Fiddle-Leaf Fig
Flamingo Plant
Foxglove
Fruit Salad Plant
Geranium
German Ivy
Glacier Ivy
Gladiola
Glory Lily
Hawaiian Ti
Heavenly Bamboo
Hibiscus
Holly
Hurricane Plant
Hyacinth
Hydrangea
Impatiens
Indian Laurel
Indian Rubber Plant
Iris
Japanese Yew
Jerusalem Cherry
Kalanchoe
Lilium species (includes Easter lily, Japanese Show Lily, Oriental Lily, Tiger Lily, and so on)
Lily of the Valley
Marble Queen
Marijuana

Mexican Breadfruit
Miniature Croton (and other varieties)
Mistletoe
Morning Glory
Mother-in-Law's Tongue
Narcissus
Needlepoint Ivy
Nephthytis
Nightshade (Solanum species)
Norfolk Pine
Oleander
Onion
Peace Lily
Peach (wilting leaves and pit)
Pencil Cactus
Philodendron (all varieties)
Plum (wilting leaves and pit)
Plumosa Fern
Pothos (all varieties)
Precatory Bean
Primula
Privet
Rhododendron
Ribbon Plant
Sago Palm (Cycas)
Schefflera
String of Pearls/Beads
Sweet Pea
Taro Vine
Tomato Plant (green fruit, stem, and leaves)
Tulip
Weeping Fig
Yesterday, Today, Tomorrow Plant
Yucca

Antifreeze? Anti-Cat

If you're a shade-tree mechanic, be extra careful when changing your car's coolant. That's because most antifreeze poses a severe risk to animals — and to children, as well. Every year, nearly 120,000 pets in the United States are poisoned by antifreeze, and more than 90,000 of them die.

It doesn't take much of this deadly substance to kill a cat. Less than a teaspoon is all it takes. Antifreeze has a sweet taste that may appeal to your cat, or your pet may ingest a lethal dose merely by licking her paws clean after walking through a spill.

Clean up carefully with a rag after changing coolant, and always be alert for puddles on your garage floor. If you think your cat got any antifreeze into her system, get her to a veterinarian right away. Doing so may be her only chance at survival.

Less toxic kinds of antifreeze are now available. They're made from propylene glycol instead of the ethylene glycol of conventional coolants. These new products are available at most auto-supplies outlets. Make the change!

Four-Wheeled Menace

Probably the biggest danger cars present to cats is when the vehicles are in motion. The meeting of a two-ton car with a ten-pound kitty never comes out in favor of the feline. But even a stationary vehicle can become a deadly temptation for a cat.

Cats are heat seekers, and many of them discover that engines are warm for a long time after they're turned off. These cats slip into the engine compartment from underneath, snuggle against the warm metal, and settle in for a catnap. On a cold night, such a protected place must seem a godsend to an outdoor cat.

A running engine is no place for a kitty to be, however, and the cat that's still inside after the car's started can get badly injured or killed.

Even if your own cat's an indoor one who never has access to the engine compartment of your car, you can save another cat's life by getting into one simple habit: Before you get into your car — especially on a cold morning — pound on the hood for a couple seconds. If a cat's in your engine compartment, she's sure to wake up and take off at the sound.

Towering Danger

Paul's a city kid, and he did his cardiology residency at New York City's Animal Medical Center, the largest hospital in the world for companion animals. While he was there, he saw a lot of cats who'd fallen — or maybe jumped — from high-rise apartments. Some cats survive a fall like that. Many others don't.

Did they fall or did they jump? No one knows for sure, although most speculate these falls are accidental. And although cats are very good at landing on their feet, the impact from several stories up can be deadly.

Prevention is the key to avoiding such accidents: Keep screens on your windows, and never let your cat out on your terrace.

Paul has seen some kitties survive from pretty far up, as high as 15 stories or more. And, in fact, studies of "high-rise syndrome" in cats reveals that the cats most likely to survive a tumble are the ones who started at the intermediate floors. From the lower floors, a cat hasn't time to prepare himself for impact by righting himself. From the highest, the fall's too great to survive. In between, however, is a margin of survivability — although few cats walk away unscathed.

Don't Do Doggie Dips

You may think a flea product designed to be safe for dogs and puppies is likewise safe for your cat. As solid as that reasoning may seem, however, it's wrong — dead wrong.

Never use a flea-control product designed for dogs on your cat. Many people tend to take these products lightly, but insecticides are designed to walk a very fine line: enough toxins to kill the parasites but not enough to endanger the pet. A product engineered to meet these challenges for dogs may not do so for cats. Check the label. Ask your veterinarian. Call the manufacturer *before* using any product. Your cat's life is at stake.

For safe, effective flea control in cats — including the latest new products available from your veterinarian — see Chapter 9.

Chapter 23

Ten Ways to Make Your Indoor Cat Happier

*W*hen we first became interested in a career involving animals, the idea of keeping a cat inside at all times was considered unusual at best, and cruel at worst. Cats are free spirits, people argued, and should be allowed to roam at will. About the only people who kept their cats inside were those in high-rise apartments or those who had pedigreed show cats. As for the rest of the cats, they came and went as they pleased, and few people saw any reason to change how they cared for their pets.

In the last couple of decades, the trend toward keeping cats indoors has gone mainstream. If you want a pedigreed cat, most reputable breeders won't sell you a pet unless you promise to keep the animal inside. Shelters, too, have started to push the idea of keeping cats indoors — and even insisting on it, in some cases. Some of the largest animal-advocacy groups are likewise spreading the word: Indoor cats live longer lives, they say.

The real change came from cat lovers themselves. Instead of just accepting the belief that to own a cat was to lose them young to the hazards of the outdoor world, cat lovers decided to protect them by keeping them inside. The idea has been catching on ever since, and many cats are living longer and healthier lives as a result. But are they happier lives? The debate still rages among cat lovers.

Indoor cats are so common these days that you can even buy books dedicated to the care of indoor cats. One book we particularly like is Christine Church's *Housecat: How to Keep Your Indoor Cat Sane and Sound* (IDG Books Worldwide, Inc.).

If you're still on the fence when it comes to bringing your cat indoors for good, read up on our reasons why it's a good idea in Chapter 1. You'll find our tips on the best way to convert your free-roaming cat to the indoor life in Chapter 6.

You can't just bring a cat or kitten inside, close the door, and expect instant contentment. Cats who have access to the outdoors claim a considerable amount of turf — an acre or more, some experts say — and spend their days exploring their territory. Cats can find plenty to interest them outdoors, with a constantly changing array of sights, smells, and sounds.

If you ask your cat to give up all that, you have to make some adjustments. You need to provide your pet with what zookeepers call *environmental enrichment* to keep your pet happy. What's in it for you? Plenty! Boredom is stressful for a pet, and stress can be a factor in illness. Further, if you don't provide your cat with things to do, he'll make up activities on his own. You may not like his choices quite so well, especially if they involve clawing your best piece of furniture to bits.

We're not trying to scare you off the idea of keeping your cat indoors. We're in favor of it! With some effort and creativity on your part, your cat can be blissfully happy with the indoor life — and you'll see the benefits, too.

A Cat Can't Have Enough Toys

You don't have to spend a lot of money on cat toys. Some of the most amazingly cat-appealing toys are even free, so go nuts. (We put a list of our favorite freebies in Chapter 8.) Surprise your cat with a constantly changing variety of cat toys — toys to stalk, toys to bat, toys to bunny-kick, and toys to snuggle with.

Toys do more than keep a cat from being bored; they also speak to her basic need to hunt. Toys are prey substitutes, and if you watch your cat in play, you'll see her as the hunter — the stalking on her unsuspecting "victim," the leap, the bite, it's all there. No matter that her prey is a little ball with a bell inside or a piece of rabbit fur shaped like a mouse. The challenge of a toy hunt is pleasing to your cat and quite a lot nicer for us humans than having to deal with the results of a real hunt!

Cat toys come in two basic varieties — those meant for play between cat and human, and those meant for play by cat alone. Your indoor cat should have both, because when you're home you should be putting aside some quality time for your cat.

Cat toys is one area of the pet industry where the entrepreneurial spirit has flourished. You can find basic, mass-produced toys at any pet-supply store, catalog, or Web site, and it's a good idea to lay in a supply. But keep an eye out for toys offered in smaller quantities. You can find these handmade items (a labor of love from people with home-based toy businesses) in booths at any cat show. Some of these toys are among the most adorable and whimsical you'll ever find, and they're well worth seeking out.

You can also find handmade cat toys on the Internet; in fact, we feature one of these "catrepreneurs," Cat Faeries, in Chapter 21.

Make sure you're thinking of safety when choosing toys, especially those toys your cat will have constant access to. Stay clear of anything with sharp edges, or strings or fringes that a cat can chew off and swallow. (The "fishing pole" toys are wonderful for interactive play with your cat, but you should put them away when you're not supervising.) And while kittens love to play with a ball of yarn, don't indulge your pet in this whim — unless you're looking forward to taking your pet to the veterinarian to have the yarn removed from his intestine!

Scratch, Climb, Stretch . . . Ahhhhh

Every cat needs a cat tree. Scratching is natural behavior for cats, and doing it feels good to them, besides. Cats use scratching to keep their claws sharp, to mark territory with their scent, and to get a really, really good stretch. These are all important activities to a cat, and even more so to a pet who's not going to get the chance to do the heavy-duty scratching that's available on a variety of outdoor surfaces, from trees to fence posts.

A cat tree or post should be

- ✔ Stable enough for your cat to climb and to pull on.
- ✔ Covered with material your cat can dig her claws into.
- ✔ Placed in a prominent area so your cat uses it.

You can make your own cat tree or post pretty easily, but you can also find them in the usual pet-supply outlets, and in more unusual places like flea markets.

While it's a good idea to offer several varieties of smaller scratching posts or pads, make sure your cat has at least one tall tree with platforms and cubbyholes. That way, your cat can do some recreational climbing and, once at the top, find a quiet and utterly hidden place to take a nap. It's the perfect place to stay as far as your cat's concerned until . . . dinner!

If you find someone locally who makes cat trees, ask if you can choose colors to match your décor. Cat trees may not be the most attractive piece of furniture you'll ever own, but yours will surely look better if covered in a complementary color.

A Constant Supply of Nibblies

Cats with access to the outdoors like to nibble on plants. Cats who are kept indoors like to nibble on plants. The difference? Outdoors, cats are chewing on fresh shoots of grass. Indoors, they're chewing on your houseplants.

Even if you put aside the issue that some plants are toxic — we include a list of those in Chapter 22 — you didn't fill your house with greenery only to have your cat destroy it. So give your cats some plants of his own, perfect for chewing.

We talk about how to keep cats out of the houseplants in Chapter 14.

Have a constantly growing supply of chewable plants on hand to help keep your housecat happy. One of the most popular treats is simple rye grass planted in small flats. The tender shoots are what cats adore, so always keep one pot of young plants available to your cat and another pot growing.

Figure 23-1: Providing your indoor cat with fresh grass seedlings will keep him happy — and help keep him away from your houseplants.

You can also use your cat's own food to keep him entertained. Some clever manufacturers have come up with products that release kibble in small amounts over time. With one such product, you fill small balls with a little kibble, and the machine releases the balls one by one at preset intervals. The cat can bat the food around, and when she's done, she has some food to munch on. Clever idea!

Hide and Go Seek

Cats are hunters, and the nature of a hunter is to seek out prey. Your cat doesn't need to seek out prey to eat — you've covered that need — but he'll enjoy the hunt anyway if you give him a reason to go looking.

What should you hide? Small toys and bits of kibble are naturals for this game, and so, too, are sprigs of fresh catnip. If your cat is on a diet, hold a few kibbles back from his daily ration for hiding. For cats who aren't on portion controls or special diets, you can use any of a variety of treats made for cats.

Your cat may not be among those who get a thrill out of catnip — the ability to enjoy the herb is genetic. For information on catnip, including how to grow a fresh supply for your pet, see Chapter 8.

Use your imagination when hiding items for your cat to find. Tuck a toy into the cubbyhole atop the cat tree, or hide a cat treat on a windowsill or on top of the cushions at the back of the couch. Let your cat watch you while you hide the treats so she can get the idea, and then hide a couple unobserved.

Maybe you'll feel a little crazy hiding treats for your cat. Remember that everything you do to make your cat's time alone more interesting will reduce his stress, and that pays off in good health and a relaxed attitude.

Cat TV? Why Not?

If you've balked at hiding goodies for your cat, heaven knows what you'll do with our next suggestion: Find a television show for your cat to watch. This idea is not as crazy as it sounds: Many owners report that their cats are fascinated by some TV shows, usually those with animals and animal sounds. Some manufacturers have taken this idea a step further and produced videos designed to amuse cats, with clips of colorful chirping birds and lively rodents to catch and hold feline attention.

You can use such a video, or you can just put your TV on a timer set to come on during a block of nature programming. Track down a simple lamp timer at any hardware store and set it up to turn on the TV, if yours is a kind that can be left in an "on" position. If that won't work, you can just tune in a nature channel and leave the set on.

A TV or radio has a use beyond the entertainment factor. If noise is a problem at your home — if you live in a big city or near a major roadway — you can use TV or radio to mask outdoor sound, making it easier for your cat to snooze away a large part of the day. You can do the same thing with music by setting an easy-listening CD to loop continuously throughout the day.

A Room with a View

Even if they're not allowed out in the world, cats still like to see what's going on outside. Cats also like to sleep in the warmth of a sunny window. You can help your cat achieve both goals by giving your cat her own "window seat."

If you don't have an existing window seat, you can easily create one by placing a chest of drawers under a window to give your cat a place to sit and watch. You can also buy a ready-made "cat perch" that you can mount on a windowsill.

Consider the view when choosing which window to turn into a cat perch. Gina has one window that overlooks a cherry tree. When the cherries are ripe, the tree attracts dozens of hungry birds — and a few human passersby, since the tree is on the street. Gina never seems to get more than a couple bowlfuls of cherries, but the tree itself is guaranteed entertainment for cats.

You can even set up a birdfeeder outside a favorite window, a move that would both entertain your cat and keep the neighborhood birds happy. Make sure that you mount the feeders in such a way to keep the birds safe from roaming cats.

Roaming cats could be a problem for your indoor cat, too. Some cats get so bothered by the sight of cats in "their territory" that they spray, or clobber the nearest living thing — perhaps you — in a burst of what the experts call *redirected aggression.* We cover how to work with this problem in Chapter 14.

Figure 23-2: Window perches give a cat a chance to enjoy the world from the safety of the indoors.

Miti/Photo by Shannon Ross

Higher and Higher, Baby

We love Bob Walker, whom we feature in a sidebar at the end of this chapter. This creative man has set the standard for making a home cat-friendly, and he has provided all kinds of cat lovers with ideas to try on their own.

Perhaps the most innovative device Bob dreamed up is the catwalk. While you don't have to install a catwalk in every room in vibrant colors as Bob did, you might think about installing a couple of them in the family room or other places where you and your cat spend a lot of time. Unless you're especially handy, you'll need the help of a contractor to keep the lumber for the catwalks properly positioned and anchored. You can find detailed instructions in Bob's book *The Cat's House,* or just come up with your own plans and wing it.

If you don't want to be so bold — or if you're renting or thinking of resale value — some tall bookcases may give your cat a place to be superior. If you're inclined to cover the top of the shelves with bric-a-brac, reconsider. We think a cat bed might be a better choice.

What about those shelves you don't want your cat to visit? We offer some tips on protecting your breakables in Chapter 6.

A Whiff of Fresh Air

If you're fortunate enough to have a screened-in porch, it shouldn't be difficult to allow your cat access to it. Consider cutting a cat door through the wall to give your cat a way to come and go into this safe piece of the (almost) outdoors.

After you allow your cat access to the porch, add some interest to the room. Chewable greens are a natural, and so, too, is another cat tree. For a more natural effect, keep an eye out for a sizable tree limb — you should be able to get one for free from a local tree service or even a neighbor. Strip the limb of leaves and anchor it in such a way to give your cat both scratching and climbing fun.

If your home doesn't have a screened porch, your cat can still get some fresh air. You can make or purchase a small cat enclosure — like a dog run, but with a top — and allow your pet access through a cat door cut through a wall.

Simply leaving a window open with a screen in place can provide your cat with fresh air, too, but be aware of the security risks of leaving a window open while you're away.

Another way to get your cat some fresh air is to walk her on a leash. Any reputable pet-supply outlet will have comfortable harnesses and light leashes for cats. Allow your cat to become slowly accustomed to the feel of the restraints, and then you'll be set for your walk.

Never leave a leashed or tethered cat unsupervised. She's a sitting duck for a cat-hating dog or hungry coyote, among other dangers.

Someone to Play With

The ultimate cat toy for your pet while you're away is another cat. If your job keeps you away for long hours, and especially if you're often away overnight or on weekends, getting a second cat is a particularly good idea. There's only so much your cat can do to keep himself occupied — at some point he's still going to get lonely.

The good news is that two cats aren't quite twice the work as one. Sure, you'll have to scoop twice as often and fill extra bowls. The costs are double, of course, when you're buying for two, and taking two cats to the veterinarian instead of one. But beyond that, having a pair of cats can actually make your life somewhat easier, since they have each other for company and for playing. And knowing that they have each other for company will definitely ease your burden of guilt when you have to leave your pets alone.

For tips on introducing cats, see Chapter 6. We also include a whole chapter on the joys and challenges of living with more than one cat — sometimes a lot more, for many cat lovers. You'll find all that information in Chapter 17.

The You Factor

Even if you've done everything possible to make your home more interesting from your cat's point of view, perhaps the most important piece of the puzzle will always be missing when you're gone — because it's *you*.

Make time for your cat. Combing and brushing your cat is a great way to bond with your pet while taking care of a basic responsibility. But don't forget in all that feeding, grooming, and taking-to-the-vet regimen to leave time just for the pleasure of being together.

Spend time with your cat. Make your evenings the time for petting and for play. Get out that cat-fishing toy and get him all worked up. Watch TV or read with your cat in your lap. Companionship is the best part of having a cat. Be your cat's best friend, and you'll find that devotion and attention returned many times over.

Chapter 24

Ten of the Best Things Ever Said about Cats

. . . .

In This Chapter
▶ The feline muse
▶ Quotations from cat lovers

. . . .

*W*ith their beauty and their mysterious ways, cats have inspired creative souls of all kinds for centuries — poets and essayists, novelists and playwrights, painters and sculptors, photographers, and even advertising copywriters. The legacy of these cat-loving people has been passed down through the generations. And although the media have changed — witness, for example, the feline explosion on the Internet — the cat has not.

The words of writers such as Geoffrey Chaucer ("And if the cattes skyn be slyk and gay;/she wol nat dwelle in house half a day"), Edgar Allen Poe ("This [cat] was a remarkably large and beautiful animal, entirely black, and sagacious to an astonishing degree"), and Oscar Wilde ("Come forth my lovely languorous Sphinx! and put your head upon my knee! /And let me stroke your throat and see your body spotted like the Lynx!") strike a chord of recognition in cat lovers today.

Those who celebrate the cat's special — some would say "superior" — qualities have always been around and always will be. Today, writers such as Desmond Morris, Roger Caras, the late Alf Wright (better known as James Herriott), and mystery writers Lilian Jackson Braun, Rita Mae Brown, and Carole Nelson Douglas provide cat-loving readers with plenty from which to choose in libraries and bookstores. Brown even credits her cat, Sneaky Pie, as coauthor!

Yes, we know we promised you only ten quotes about cats. But you'll forgive us if we offer you a couple more, won't you?

Maybe *you're* the next great cat writer! If that's so, consider joining the non-profit Cat Writers' Association, an organization founded in 1992 to promote and support those writers, editors, artists, and photographers who look to cats for their inspiration. The CWA offers two e-mail lists for cat-loving writers, an annual writing conference, as well as a yearly writing competition, with more than $5,000 given out to the winners. For information on the CWA, visit the group's Web site at www.catwriters.org or write to Cheryl S. Smith, CWA Secretary, 496 Gasman Road, Port Angeles, WA 98362.

The cat as inspiration

I look on the cat as a poem waiting to happen, its pause mere prologue to prankish delight, its purr a sweet river of song. A cat touches the soul. Whispy whisker-kisses, moist nosebumps — these are gifts beyond measure. To artists, a loving cat is an eternal muse.

— Amy Shojai

The cat as cybernaut

Most Internet flame wars are started by cats who did not get what they wanted for supper.

— Judy Heim

The cat as an individual

Cats must have three names — an everyday name, such as Peter; a more particular, dignified name, such as Quaxo, Bombalurina, or Jellyorum; and, thirdly, the name the cat thinks up for himself, his deep and inscrutable singular Name.

— T. S. Eliot

Managing senior programmers is like herding cats.

— Dave Platt

Cats are smarter than dogs. You can't get eight cats to pull a sled through the snow.

— Jeff Valdez

The cat as the Boss

There is no snooze button on a cat who wants breakfast.

— unknown

As every cat owner knows, nobody owns a cat.

— Ellen Perry Berkeley

Dogs have owners; cats have staff.

— unknown

The cat as companion

There is something about the presence of a cat . . . that seems to take the bite out of being alone.

— Louis J. Camuti

One cat just leads to another.

— Ernest Hemingway

The cat as wild

As dogs of shy neighbourhoods usually betray a slinking consciousness of being in poor circumstances — for the most part manifested in an aspect of anxiety, an awkwardness in their play, and a misgiving that someone is going to harness them to something, to pick up a living — so the cats of shy neighbourhoods exhibit a strong tendency to relapse into barbarism.

— Charles Dickens

The cat as superior

It is easy to see why the rabble dislike cats. A cat is beautiful; it suggests ideas of luxury, cleanliness, voluptuous pleasures.

— Charles Baudelaire

Thousands of years ago cats were worshipped as gods. Cats have never forgotten this.

— unknown

The cat mourned

Pet was never mourned as you,/Purrer of the spotless hue,/Plumy tail, and wistful gaze,/While you humoured our queer ways . . . Never another pet for me!/Let your place all vacant be . . .

— Thomas Hardy

No heaven will not ever heaven be, unless my cats are there to welcome me.

— unknown

The cat as honest

A cat has emotional honesty: Human beings, for one reason or another, may hide their feelings, but the cat does not.

— Ernest Hemingway

The cat as perfection

The smallest feline is a masterpiece.

— Leonardo da Vinci

Additional Resources

· ·

Breed registries and show-governing organizations

American Association of Cat Enthusiasts (AACE)
P.O. Box 213
Pine Brook, NJ 07058
201-335-6717
info@aaceinc.org
www.aaceinc.org

American Cat Association (ACA)
8101 Katherine Avenue
Panorama City, CA 91402
818-781-5656

American Cat Fanciers Association (ACFA)
P.O. Box 203
Point Lookout, MO 65726
417-334-5430
www.acfacat.com

Australian Cat Federation Inc.
Post Office Box 3305
Port Adelaide SA 5015
08-8449-5880
acf@catlover.com
www.acf.asn.au

Canadian Cat Association/Association Feline Canadienne (CCA/AFC)
289 Rutherford Rd. South, Unit 18
Brampton, Ontario L6W 3R9
Canada
905-459-1481
office@cca-afc.com
www.cca-afc.com

Cat Fanciers' Association, Inc. (CFA)
P.O. Box 1005
Manasquan, NJ 08736-0805
908-528-9797
cfa@cfainc.org
www.cfainc.org

Cat Fanciers Federation (CFF)
P.O. Box 661
Gratis, OH 45330
513-787-9009
www.cffinc.org

Federation International Feline (FIFe)
Little Dene
Lenham Heath
Maidstone, Kent ME17 2BS
England
www.fife.org

Federazione Italiana Associazioni Feline
c/o Rag. Cesare Ghisi
Via Carlo Poma n.20
46100 - Mantova
0376-224600
Italy
www.zero.it/fiaf/fiafe.htm

The Governing Council of the Cat Fancy
4-6, Penel Orlieu
Bridgewater, Somerset TA6 3PG
England
127-842-7575
gccf_cats@compuserve.com
ourworld.compuserve.com/homepages/gccf_cats/

Happy Household Pet Cat Club
Lauretta Nawojski, Secretary
6364 Montcalm Avenue
Newark, CA 94560
510-791-2646
www.best.com/~slewis/HHPCC/

The International Cat Association (TICA)
P.O. Box 2684
Harlingen, TX 78551
210-428-8046
ticaeo@xanadu2.net
www.tica.org

Traditional Cat Association (TCA)
10340 Live Oak Lane
Penn Valley, CA 95946
lgil@cts.com
asenec@asenec.com
www.tcainc.org

Veterinary groups

American Association of Feline Practitioners
530 Church Street, Suite 700
Nashville, TN 37219
615-254-3687
800-204-3514
nvaccaro@wmgt.org
www.avma.org/aafp/

American Animal Hospital Association
P.O. Box 150899
Denver, CO 80215-0899
800-883-6301
aahapr@aol.com
www.healthypet.com

American Veterinary Medical Association
Public Information Division
1931 North Meacham Road, Suite 100
Schaumburg, IL 60173-4360
847-925-8070
avmainfo@avma.org
www.avma.org

British Veterinary Association
Mr. James Baird
7 Mansfield Street
London, WIM OAT
England
0170-636-6541
bvahq@bva.co.uk
www.bva.co.uk

Canadian Veterinary Medical Association
339 Booth Street
5 Camwood Crescent
Ottowa, Ontario K1R 7K1
Canada
613-236-1162
www.cvma-acmv.org

VetQuest (a veterinary referral service)
Veterinary Information Network, Inc.
Pet Care Forum
PMB 106-131
1411 W. Covell Boulevard
Davis, CA 95616
800-700-4636
530-756-4881
vingram@vin.com
www.vetquest.com
www.vin.com

World Veterinary Association
Lars Holsaae, Executive Secretary
Rosenlunds Alle' 8
DK-2720 Vanlose
Denmark
45-38-71-01-56
wva@ddd.dk
www.worldvet.org

Magazines and newsletters

All About Cats
21 C Heathman's Road
London SW6 4TJ
England

Cat Fancy
Fancy Publications
P.O. Box 6050
Mission Viejo, CA 92690
www.animalnetwork.com

Cat Fanciers' Almanac
Official Journal of the Cat Fanciers' Association
P.O. Box 1005
Manasquan, NJ 08736-1005
908-528-9797
cfa@cfainc.org
www.cfainc.org

CatNip: A Newsletter for Caring Cat Owners
Tufts University School of Veterinary Medicine
P.O. Box 420014
Palm Coast, FL 32142-0014
catnip@polk.com
www.vec.tufts.edu/vetgeneral/newsletters/catnip.html

Cats: Official Journal of the Governing Council of the Cat Fancy
5 James Leigh Street
Manchester M16 6EX
England
127-842-7575
gccf_cats@compuserve.com
ourworld.compuserve.com/homepages/gccf_cats

Cats Magazine
Primedia Special Interests
260 Madison Avenue, 8th Floor
New York, NY 10016
info@catsmag.com
www.catsmag.com

Cats U.S.A.
Fancy Publications
P.O. Box 6050
Mission Viejo, CA 92690
www.animalnetwork.com

CatWatch: The Newsletter for Cat People
Cornell University College of Veterinary Medicine
P.O. Box 420235
Palm Coast, FL 32142
800-829-8893
www.vet.cornell.edu/publicresources/cat.htm

Cat World
Avalon Court, Star Road
Partridge Green, West Sussex RH13 8RY
England
44-0-1403-711511
info@catworld.co.uk
www.catworld.co.uk/

I Love Cats
450 Seventh Avenue, No. 1701
New York, NY 10123
net.puzz@ix.netcom.com
www.iluvcats.com

Kittens U.S.A.
Fancy Publications
P.O. Box 6050
Mission Viejo, CA 92690
www.animalnetwork.com

TICA Trend: Official Journal of The International Cat Association
P.O. Box 2684
Harlington, TX 78551
210-428-8046
ticaeo@xanadu2.net
www.tica.org

Pet-supply sources

1-800-HELP4PETS (pet locator service)
8721 Santa Monica Boulevard, Suite 710
Los Angeles, CA 90069
www.help4pets.com

Adams Pet Supplies
7052 103rd Street, Suite 305
Jacksonville, FL 32210
877-322-7387 (PETS)
info@adamspetsupplies.com
adamspetsupplies.com

Drs. Foster and Smith
P.O. Box 100
2253 Air Park Road
Rhinelander, WI 54501
800-381-7179
www.drsfostersmith.com

Fins N Fur Pet Supplies
7480 Inga Drive
Prince George, B.C. Canada
V2N 5W4
250-963-8714
debra@finsnfurpetsupplies.com
www.finsnfurpetsupplies.com

J-B Wholesale Pet Supplies
5 Raritan Rd.
Oakland, NJ 07436
800-526-0388
www.jbpet.com
jbpet@intac.com

Noah's Pet Supplies
5376 Highland Road
Baton Rouge, LA 70808
800-318-2412
customerservice@noahspets.com
noahspets.com/

Pet Expo
11600 Manchaca Road, Suite 101
Austin, Texas 78748
888-738-3976
512-282-0624
pet-expo@pet-expo.com
www.pet-expo.com/frame3.htm

Pet Market.Com
P.O. Box 523
Laurel, DE 19956
888-738-6758
info@PETmarket.com
www.petmarket.com

Pet Warehouse
P.O. Box 752138
Dayton, OH 45475
800-443-1160
service@petwhse.com
www.petwhse.com

PETCO Animal Supplies, Inc.
9125 Rehco Road
San Diego, CA 92121
858-453-7845
www.petco.com

PET-PAK, Inc. (pet first-aid kits)
P.O. Box 982
Edison, NJ 08818-0982
732-906-9200
sjcinc61@aol.com
www.petpak.com

Pets.com
435 Brannan St., Suite 100
San Francisco, CA 94107
888-321-PETS (7387)
service@pets.com

PETsMART, Inc.
19601 N. 27th Avenue
Phoenix, AZ 85027
623-580-6100
cs@petsmart.com
www.petsmart.com

San Francisco SPCA
(Kate Gamble feline behavior videos, Computa-Cat poster)
2500 16th Street
San Francisco, CA 94103
publicinfo@sfspca.org
www.sfspca.org

Animal charities

Alley Cat Allies
1801 Belmont Road NW, Suite 201
Washington, DC 20009-5164
www.alleycat.org

United Animal Nations
Emergency Animal Rescue Service
5829A South Land Drive
P.O. Box 188890
Sacramento, CA 95818
www.uan.org

Morris Animal Foundation
45 Inverness Drive East.
Englewood, CO 80112-5480
www.morrisanimalfoundation.org

Winn Feline Foundation
P.O. Box 1005
Manasquan, NJ 08736-0805
www.winnfelinehealth.org/

Cat Fanciers' Association Foundation, Inc.
P.O. Box 1005
Manasquan, NJ 08736-0805
www.cfainc.org/

(*Authors' Note:* As you consider charitable giving, please don't forget your
local humane society, SPCA, or other shelter or rescue group. These local
organizations are on the front lines of helping cats, and they deserve your
support.)

Index

• *M* •

• *T* •